# Training for a Rapidly Changing Workplace

# Training for a Rapidly Changing Workplace

## APPLICATIONS OF PSYCHOLOGICAL RESEARCH

*Edited by*

Miguel A. Quiñones and Addie Ehrenstein

American Psychological Association
*Washington, DC*

Published by
American Psychological Association
750 First Street, NE
Washington, DC 20002

Copies may be ordered from
APA Order Department
P.O. Box 92984
Washington, DC 20090-2984

In the UK and Europe, copies may be ordered from
American Psychological Association
3 Henrietta Street
Covent Garden, London
WC2E 8LU England

Typeset in Futura and New Baskerville by EPS Group Inc., Easton, MD

Printer: Data Reproductions Corp., Rochester Hills, MI
Cover Designer: Debra Naylor, Upper Marlboro, MD
Project Manager: Debbie K. Hardin, Reston, VA

**Library of Congress Cataloging-in-Publication Data**
Training for a rapidly changing workplace : applications of psychological
    research / Miguel A. Quiñones and Addie Ehrenstein, editors.
        p.   cm.
    Includes bibliographical references and index.
    ISBN 1-55798-386-0 (alk. paper)
    1. Employees—Training of—Psychological aspects.   2. Educational
psychology.   3. Psychology, Industrial.   4. Psychology, Applied.
I. Quiñones, Miguel A.   II. Ehrenstein, Addie
HF5549.5.T7T667      1996
658.3′12404—dc21                                                    96-29550
                                                                        CIP

**British Cataloguing-in-Publication Data**
A CIP record is available from the British Library.

*Printed in the United States of America*
*First Edition*

# Contents

Contributors     ix

Preface: Toward a Synthesis of Psychological
Research on Training     xi

Introduction: Psychological Perspectives on
Training in Organizations     1
*Miguel A. Quiñones and Addie Ehrenstein*

**Part One: Challenges for Training Design and Implementation**     11

Chapter 1     A Rapidly Changing World: Some Implications
for Training Systems in the Year 2001 and
Beyond     15
*Paul W. Thayer*

Chapter 2     Organizational Barriers to Implementing a
Rational Model of Training     31
*Robert L. Dipboye*

**Part Two: Optimizing Learning by Structuring Training**     61

Chapter 3     Evaluating Training *During* Training: Obstacles
and Opportunities     63
*Dina Ghodsian, Robert A. Bjork,
and Aaron S. Benjamin*

Chapter 4    Building Adaptive Expertise: Implications for
             Training Design Strategies                               89
             *Eleanor M. Smith, J. Kevin Ford,*
             *and Steve W. J. Kozlowski*

Chapter 5    Some Fundamentals of Training and Transfer:
             Practice Benefits Are Not Automatic                     119
             *Addie Ehrenstein, Bruce N. Walker,*
             *Mary Czerwinski, and Evan M. Feldman*

**Part Three: Designing Effective Training Systems**                 149

Chapter 6    Linking Training Objectives to Evaluation
             Criteria                                                151
             *Kurt Kraiger and Katharine M. Jung*

Chapter 7    Contextual Influences on Training
             Effectiveness                                           177
             *Miguel A. Quiñones*

Chapter 8    Training Design and Pedagogy: Implications
             for Skill Acquisition, Maintenance,
             and Generalization                                      201
             *Marilyn E. Gist*

**Part Four: Integrating Training Methodologies and Workplace
Technologies**                                                       223

Chapter 9    Advanced Technologies in Training:
             Intelligent Tutoring Systems and Virtual
             Reality                                                 225
             *Debra Steele-Johnson and Belinda Gaye Hyde*

Chapter 10   Methods, Tools, and Strategies for Team
             Training                                                249
             *Eduardo Salas and Janis A. Cannon-Bowers*

Chapter 11    The Use of Animation in Software Training:
              Pitfalls and Benefits                                281
              *Robert Atlas, Larry Cornett, David M. Lane,*
              *and H. Albert Napier*

Chapter 12    Toward Minimalist Training: Supporting the
              Sense-Making Activities of Computer Users           303
              *John M. Carroll*

              Index                                               329
              About the Editors                                   345

# Contributors

**Robert Atlas,** IBM, Charlotte, North Carolina
**Aaron S. Benjamin,** University of California, Los Angeles
**Robert A. Bjork,** University of California, Los Angeles
**Janis A. Cannon-Bowers,** Naval Air Warfare Center
**John M. Carroll,** Virginia Tech
**Larry Cornett,** Apple Computer, Inc.
**Mary Czerwinski,** Microsoft Corporation
**Robert L. Dipboye,** Rice University
**Evan M. Feldman,** Microsoft Corporation
**J. Kevin Ford,** Michigan State University
**Marilyn E. Gist,** University of Washington
**Dina Ghodsian,** University of California, Los Angeles
**Belinda Gaye Hyde,** University of Houston
**Debra Steele Johnson,** Wright State University
**Katharine M. Jung,** University of California at Berkeley
**Kurt Kraiger,** University of Colorado at Denver
**Steve W. J. Kozlowski,** Michigan State University
**David M. Lane,** Rice University
**H. Albert Napier,** Rice University
**Eduardo Salas,** Naval Air Warfare Center
**Eleanor M. Smith,** Aon Consulting
**Paul W. Thayer,** North Carolina State University
**Bruce N. Walker,** Rice University

# Preface: Toward a Synthesis of Psychological Research on Training

n a recent issue of the *American Psychologist* (1995, Vol. 50), Wayne Cascio identified training and development as one of the six key areas in the context of changes in work technology in which industrial and organizational psychologists can contribute to the "betterment of human welfare" (p. 928). Cascio emphasized the need for research-based answers to questions of adaptation to changing technologies. At about the same time that Cascio published his article, the first issue of the *Training Research Journal* was published. Commenting on the mission of this new journal, Kurt Kraiger wrote about the need to "loosen existing paradigms of training and instruction which are rooted within singular disciplines and to encourage the development of more inclusive paradigms that cut across multiple disciples" (p. 5). Thus, at the same time the need for research in the area of training was increasing, Kraiger was lamenting the fractionalization of this research and calling for an open dialogue between areas. Our own experiences are a case in point.

When we first arrived at the Department of Psychology at Rice University in 1993, we were both convinced that each of our research programs dealt with the issue of training. However, as we began to learn about each other's research, we quickly realized that our conceptualizations of the critical issues and methods of research in this area were vastly different. To those of us trained as industrial–organizational psychologists, training was inherently an applied enterprise in which organizations attempt to change individuals in a way that is consistent with the job requirements. Because training occurs in organizations, technological, social, and individual factors were the primary issues to consider. However, to those of us trained as human factors psychologists or cognitive psychologists, training was a way of applying principles of human learning and skill acquisition. Because the focus is on individual capability, information processing demands and task characteristics are the focus of most study.

We were struck by the differences in approach and, more important, how little we knew about the approaches taken in the other's area. After hosting a small conference in which we invited researchers from areas within and outside of our own, we were convinced that it was necessary to bring together these diverse approaches to training. This volume is the vehicle we chose for accomplishing our objective.

The book brings together researchers from the areas of industrial–organizational psychology, human factors psychology, cognitive psychology, human–computer interaction, and computer science. Our hope is that the diverse perspectives presented in this volume will stimulate cross-fertilization and enhance our understanding of human learning and its applications to training. The book is organized around four general themes. The first two chapters address the broad societal and institutional issues driving the need for training. The chapters outline the challenge faced by organizations and training researchers in the coming century and beyond. The second examines basic research in learning and skill acquisition as it applies to training. The third section addresses issues involved in designing and implementing an operational training system. Issues of training system design, evaluation, and implementation are addressed in this section. The fourth and final section examines the impact of future technologies and ways of organizing work on the training enterprise.

There are a number of individuals whose work, inspiration, and encouragement have made this volume possible. Jim Pomerantz and David Schneider encouraged us to pursue our common interests while Robert Dipboye and David Lane helped organize and shape our efforts. Bill Howell encouraged us to present the product of our efforts as an edited volume. Other individuals who provided helpful comments include Irv Goldstein, Mark Teachout, Roy Lachman, and John Brelsford. Finally, to all our colleagues and students at Rice University for their support and encouragement, we extend our sincerest thanks.

Miguel A. Quiñones
Addie Ehrenstein

# Introduction: Psychological Perspectives on Training in Organizations

## Miguel A. Quiñones and Addie Ehrenstein

**T**raining, or passing knowledge and skills to those who need them, is a necessary part of the human endeavor. Throughout the history of civilization, humans have devised ways of cataloging the knowledge of one generation and communicating it to the next. Direct instruction by experts in the field and apprenticeships for many years were the primary means of communicating knowledge of skills and crafts (Steinmetz, 1976). However, with the advent of the industrial revolution came drastic changes in the amount and diversity of knowledge and in the structure of the workplace. The explosion of new techniques and required skills—as well as the number of people employing these skills —necessitated the development of formal industrial training programs. Such programs began to be developed in the early 1800s, and have been with us ever since.

A second revolution is underway that is again changing the way we work and, as a consequence, the way knowledge and skills might best be trained. This has been dubbed the information revolution. One of the most talked about trends in the workplace is that manual labor has largely been replaced by more cognitive skills. For example, Drucker (1994) described our era as one in which the industrial worker is being replaced by the knowledge worker. Because of changes in the nature of the tasks to be performed and the diversity of jobs to be faced by any one individual, this new type of worker will require much more formal education than the industrial worker. Moreover, continuous learning will be necessary for workers to keep pace with technological advances.

Changes in the nature of work and the requirements for workers have been accompanied, or in some cases motivated, by changes in the way that organizations are structured. The dominant trends in organizations have been restructuring and downsizing. In a recent survey by *The New York Times* ("The Downsizing of America," 1996), 72% of respondents indicated that they, or someone they knew well, had been laid off within the past 15 years. Approximately 43 million jobs have vanished from the United States since 1979, and layoffs and restructurings continue even during periods of record profits. Perhaps more dramatic are the announced layoffs of 40,000 workers by AT&T. Other companies like IBM and General Motors have eliminated, or have announced the elimination of, nearly a third of their workforce. The only thing that is certain in the world of work is that things will continue to change.

Against this background of uncertainty and change, training and development programs often have been designated as the means of adapting to the turbulent environment in organizations. As training becomes more important, so does the need for solid empirical research and the means to apply it (Quiñones, 1996). The field of training is replete with stories of false promises and fancy training gadgets with no proven value (Goldstein, 1993). There is, however, a large body of research and theory within the various subfields of psychology that addresses issues in training. There traditionally has been little cross-fertilization between the various approaches to the study of training. However, there are encouraging signs that point to a more integrated view of the training process, and we believe that there is reason for optimism in training program development. Our goal in this book is to communicate recent research from the various fields of psychology that provide theoretical support for training and to present views on how such research can inform the development of training programs in organizations.

## State of the Discipline

Before describing the state of psychological research related to training it is perhaps necessary to define what we mean by *training*. Goldstein defined training as "the systematic acquisition of skills, rules, concepts, or attitudes that result in improved performance in another environment" (1993, p. 3). Two things should be noted in this definition. First, training is different from learning in the sense that it is a planned set of activities that has cognitive, behavioral, or affective change (i.e., learning) as one of its goals (Kraiger, Ford, & Salas, 1993). It is clear that learning can occur in other contexts outside of what might be called training. The second notable aspect of this definition makes clear that training seeks to create changes that last beyond the immediate training environment.

To some extent, different subdisciplines within psychology each have taken a different perspective on training. For example, cognitive psychologists have tended to focus on more basic psychological principles underlying learning and skill acquisition. Anderson's ACT-R theory of the acquisition of cognitive skills (cf. Anderson, 1993) provides an illustration of the depth and rigor that some of this research can take. Human factors psychologists have tended to focus on the design of training technology such as simulators and computer software programs to maximize learning. Industrial–organizational psychologists have focused on individual differences and organizational factors associated with both training and transfer performance.

Of course these are generalizations. However, they serve to illustrate how different research psychologists studying training can do very different things. Moreover, even when perspectives taken within the subdisciplines of psychology overlap, the theoretical frameworks and methodologies used often differ enough so that little communication is possible between researchers. This phenomenon is exacerbated by the fact that scientists tend to publish their research findings in journals that are read only by others within their subdiscipline.

Kraiger (1995) noted how psychologists from different subdisciplines working on essentially the same problem—transfer of training —employ different definitions of transfer and, as a consequence, conduct vastly different types of research. We believe strongly that different perspectives on the same problem contribute positively to scientific discovery. However, the benefits of these various perspectives can be reaped only when these various findings are integrated into a coherent and comprehensive view of the problem.

In the industrial–organizational literature, Kraiger (1995) noted, transfer research tends to focus on the application of knowledge, skills, and abilities from training to the work setting (see Baldwin & Ford, 1988, for a review). By contrast, cognitive psychologists tend to define transfer as the change in performance in Task B as a result of having learned to perform Task A (Gick & Holyoak, 1987; Royer, 1979). It is not surprising that these two definitions of the same phenomenon, transfer of training, have resulted in different research paradigms and the investigation of different variables.

Perhaps the most salient difference between these two approaches concerns the type of tasks examined. Industrial–organizational psychologists studying transfer of training tend to focus on real-world complex tasks that individuals perform on the job—such as the use of computer software or mechanical troubleshooting and repair (cf., Ford, Quiñones, Sego, & Sorra, 1992). In contrast, the cognitive approach tends to focus on simpler tasks that have a number of known properties believed to be related to transfer. Thus, a researcher may examine the extent to which learning verbal analogies results in higher performance in a transfer task containing verbal analogies when compared to a group trained to solve conditional syllogisms (Phye, 1990).

In addition to using different tasks, researchers in different sub-disciplines tend to focus on different sets of variables. Because the industrial–organizational psychologist is interested in the extent to which an individual can perform the same task in a new setting, work environment or contextual factors are often examined. For example, Rouiller and Goldstein (1993) identified and measured a "climate for transfer" within organizations that facilitated or hindered a trainee's ability and willingness to transfer the learned skills to the workplace. Rather than examining global attributes of the transfer situation, cognitive and human factors psychologists are more likely to focus on the characteristics that the training and transfer tasks share and the extent to which specific subskills can be trained effectively (e.g., Fredericksen & White, 1989).

There are, of course, researchers conducting transfer of training research that takes a slightly different approach—falling somewhere between these two general approaches (e.g., see Schmidt & Bjork, 1992). However, this example serves to illustrate the point that separate groups of researchers can conduct research on the same topic (transfer of training), which can appear to be very different. Perhaps the most important point to note is that one approach is not better than the other because they share the goal of optimizing transfer to the work environment. Findings from both areas form pieces of a larger puzzle. It is our hope that this book will be the first of many attempts to bring the separate pieces together.

There have been recent calls to integrate some areas of psychological research that address similar problems. For example, the most recent annual meeting of the Human Factors and Ergonomics Society featured a symposium devoted to whether human factors and industrial–organizational psychology should be reintegrated in graduate training programs (Smolensky, 1995). Although views on the subject were mixed, the consensus was that integration of the two areas would provide specialists in either area with better problem-solving skills and a greater understanding of the organization of work. In addition to providing researchers and practitioners with a greater variety of possible solutions to problems, awareness and knowledge of both fields should go a long way toward improving communication in the training field. Human–machine and human–environment interactions become more important to industrial–organizational psychologists as new training methodologies that depend heavily on such interactions become more common, and it is futile to develop efficient training methodologies if they are not accepted by organizations and individuals within them.

## Toward a Systems Perspective

The military, because of its need to train a large number of recruits for a variety of jobs, was perhaps the first to recognize the need for an integrated *systems* view of training (see Goldstein, 1993). Within this perspective, the training function is seen as a subsystem of the larger organizational entity. Thus, aspects of the organization such as overall goals and strategy as well as financial resources can affect the design, delivery, and effectiveness of a training program. In the same way, training can have an influence on other organizational systems such as compensation, career progression, and recruitment. Therefore, an important outcome of a systems perspective is the need to consider multiple sources of information as well as the potential for cross-level effects on training effectiveness.

For example, Ostroff and Ford (1989) identified several key pieces of information and the critical levels of analysis that must be considered when assessing training needs. Consider the typical process of conducting a task analysis to determine the knowledge, skills, and abilities necessary for an individual to perform the various duties of any given position. This process focuses on the demands placed on the individual by the technology, as well as on the cognitive processes involved in performing individual tasks. However, a consideration of the workgroup or subunit level may reveal that the task also involves exchanging information between several coworkers and, therefore, issues such as group norms become important. At the organizational level, one may find that a strategy calls for a change in the technology that will be used for carrying out the task. It is clear that focusing on only the smallest task level may result in the design of a training program that is inadequate for meeting the real needs of the organization and may actually miss critical knowledges, skills, and abilities. In the same way, ignoring task-level characteristics related to learning and transfer also will result in a deficient training program.

In addition, there is a real need to integrate research on training and learning with training systems in organizations. As other researchers (e.g., Gramopadhye, 1995) have lamented, the application of research on training and learning in organizations is the exception rather than the rule. Gramopadhye also noted that traditional on-the-job training has largely given way to classroom training and now even to computer-based multimedia training as advances are made in training technology.

However, in order to develop efficient and effective training activities, we need a better understanding of fundamental psychological principles such as skill acquisition. Traditional task analysis methods often fail to address the structure of skilled performance with the level of detail required to develop specific skills (Proctor & Dutta, 1995). Mumaw and Roth (1995) emphasized the need to tie factual knowledge and theory to the specific task context. A failure to do this during training requires relearning or retraining to integrate factual knowledge with procedural skills.

A broad systems perspective that takes into account factors from several levels of analysis can serve as an organizing scheme for incorporating various approaches to training research. Recognizing that variables occurring at the task, workgroup, and organizational level can have various effects on training program effectiveness is perhaps the first step in understanding the way in which the various pieces of the training puzzle fit together.

## General Scope and Organization of the Book

The chapters contained in this book reflect the depth and breadth of current psychological research in training. Perspectives range from broad societal and organizational issues to task-specific issues such as stimulus–response compatibility and skill automaticity. Furthermore, the chapters cover the full range of issues facing training researchers and practitioners, such as fundamental learning principles, training design, training delivery systems and technology, as well as training evaluation.

The book is divided into four parts: challenges for training design and implementation, optimizing learning by structuring training, designing effective training systems, and integrating training methodologies and workplace technologies. A general introduction and brief description of each chapter is presented at the beginning of each part. Part One describes both societal as well as organizational factors that are likely to influence the need for, and implementation of, training systems in the future. Changes in the demographic characteristics of the workforce, as well as the technological aspects of work and their implications for training, are discussed. The role of organizational culture, norms, and politics in the implementation of training are linked to training design. This type of analysis represents a unique perspective on training issues by bridging the traditional training design literature with work examining training from a sociological and institutional perspective.

Part Two presents innovative perspectives and some challenges to existing theories of human learning. The common assumption that training systems that lead to the most learning during training will also lead to the most transfer is brought into question by reviewing cutting-edge research examining this issue. Path-breaking theories from the cognitive domains are used to develop new models of training design that include training skills such as metacognition and adaptive expertise. Research examining the role of practice with significant implications for the design and evaluation of training systems is reviewed. Overall, the research presented in Part Two represents much of the foundation on which a sound training program must be built.

Part Three takes a step back from the fundamental learning principles discussed in the previous section to consider more practical concerns that arise when designing a training system in an existing organization. A major issue that has concerned training developers in the past is the link between training objectives (what is to be learned) and the measurement techniques used to assess the effectiveness of the training intervention. Until now, little guidance existed in making this critical linkage. The rapidly expanding body of research demonstrating the need to consider organizational factors such as support, climate, and assignment of trainees is also reviewed in this section. More important, a conceptual model linking these contextual factors with training and transfer outcomes is developed. The model advances current theory by hypothesizing a central role for individual differences in trainee attitudes and motivation. This section also considers the role of training design factors on important training outcomes such as acquisition, maintenance, and generalization of skill.

Part Four reviews current research related to the use of emerging technologies such as computers and virtual reality for delivering training. New technologies have invaded every aspect of work, including training. However, designers and developers have often incorporated technology into training because of its flashy appearance rather than its proven efficacy. The chapters in this section summarize both past research and previously unpublished research related to the use and effectiveness of these new technologies. In addition to incorporating new technologies into their processes, organizations have restructured their hierarchies and adopted a team concept. However, we know very little about how to design, implement, and deliver effective training for teams. Current theories and research related to team training are also presented in this section.

## Purpose and Audience

It is our hope that this book will provide a starting place for researchers and practitioners who would like a quick update on the state of the art in training and training program implementation or for people in the field who are seeking to diversify their perspective. We believe that researchers working on problems in training within the fields of cognitive, human factors, or industrial–organizational psychology will find chapters in this book that challenge them to look beyond their current approaches to broaden their understanding of the problems facing the training enterprise. We also hope that training practitioners will find the information contained in this book invaluable for making decisions about training content, design, delivery, and evaluation.

In addition to researchers working in this area, we think this book will be useful for individuals wishing to get a broad overview of the types of questions being addressed by training researchers. The broad perspectives presented make it ideal for a graduate or undergraduate course in training and development, skill acquisition, learning, and human resource management. Each chapter can stand on its own, so it is not necessary to assign the entire book or to read the chapters in the order of presentation.

## References

Anderson, J. (1993). Problem solving and learning. *American Psychologist, 48,* 35–44.

Baldwin, T., & Ford, J. K. (1988). Transfer of training: A review and directions for future research. *Personnel Psychology, 41,* 63–105.

Downsizing of America, The. (1996, March 3). *New York Times,* p. 1.

Drucker, P. F. (1994). The age of social transformation. *Atlantic Monthly, 274*(5), 53–80.

Ford, J. K., Quiñones, M. A., Sego, D., & Sorra, J. (1992). Factors affecting the opportunity to perform trained tasks on the job. *Personnel Psychology, 45,* 511–527.

Frederiksen, J. R., & White, B. Y. (1989). An approach to training based upon principled task decomposition. *Acta Psychologica, 71,* 89–146.

Gick, M. L., & Holyoak, K. J. (1987). The cognitive basis of knowledge transfer. In S. M. Cormier & J. D. Hagman (Eds.), *Transfer of learning* (pp. 9–46). New York: Academic Press.

Goldstein, I. L. (1993). *Training in organizations* (3rd ed). Pacific Grove, CA: Brooks/Cole.

Gramopadhye, A. K. (1995). Training effectiveness in industry. *Proceedings of the Human Factors Society 39th Annual Meeting* (p. 1283). Santa Monica, CA: Human Factors Society.

Kraiger, K. (1995). Integrating training research. *Training Research Journal, 1,* 5–16.

Kraiger, K., Ford, J. K., & Salas, E. (1993). Application of cognitive, skill-based, and affective theories of learning outcomes to new methods of training evaluation. *Journal of Applied Psychology, 78,* 311–328.

Mumaw, R. J., & Roth, E. M. (1995). Training complex tasks in a functional context. *Proceedings of the Human Factors Society 39th Annual Meeting* (pp. 1253–1257). Santa Monica, CA: Human Factors Society.

Ostroff, C., & Ford, J. K. (1989). Assessing training needs: Critical levels of analysis. In I. L. Goldstein (Ed.), *Training and development in organizations* (pp. 25–62). San Francisco: Jossey-Bass.

Phye, G. D. (1990). Inductive problem solving: Schema inducement and memory-based transfer. *Journal of Educational Psychology, 82,* 826–831.

Proctor, R. W., & Dutta, A. (1995). *Skill acquisition and human performance.* Thousand Oaks, CA: Sage.

Quiñones, M. A. (1996). Training and development in organizations: Now more than ever. *Psychological Science Agenda, 9*(2), 8–9.

Royer, J. M. (1979). Theories of the transfer of learning. *Educational Psychologist, 14,* 53–69.

Rouiller, J. Z., & Goldstein, I. L. (1993). The relationship between organizational transfer climate and positive transfer of training. *Human Resource Development Quarterly, 4,* 377–390.

Schmidt, R. A., & Bjork, R. A. (1992). New conceptualizations of practice: Common principles in three paradigms suggest new concepts for training. *Psychological Science, 3,* 207–217.

Smolensky, M. W. (1995). Should human factors psychology and industrial/organizational psychology be re-integrated for graduate training? *Proceedings of the Human Factors Society 39th Annual Meeting* (pp. 775–777). Santa Monica, CA: Human Factors Society.

Steinmetz, C. S. (1976). The history of training. In R. L. Craig (Ed.), *Training and development handbook* (pp. 3–14). New York: McGraw-Hill.

# Part One

# Challenges for Training Design and Implementation

**A**ll demographic, economic, and social trends point toward an uncertain future in which organizations will have to adapt continuously to an ever changing and increasingly volatile job market. Companies are downsizing as a consequence of the implementation of new technological processes or the obsolescence of existing processes; jobs are eliminated as a result of new technology, improved processes, or new ways of organizing work. Organizations that wish to remain profitable will have to find ways to adapt to the changes in the workforce and workplace that are occurring, and individuals will need to adapt to technological changes in order to keep or replace their jobs. A pivotal role in adapting to change will be played by training programs. More sophisticated and advanced equipment requires better trained employees, and such training in turn requires a higher level of investment in the individual by the company.

At the same time, however, organizations are becoming more cost conscious. Therefore, training expenditures are more likely to come under increased scrutiny. In addition, tangible outcomes from training are likely to become more important. The increased need for training and the scrutiny placed on results point to the need for advanced knowledge of learning principles, design and delivery systems, as well as evaluation techniques. It is interesting to note that organizations have tended to rely on high technology to improve their training programs. However, the mere use of the latest training gadget will not ensure an adequate return on the training investment dollar. It is clear that the future holds many challenges for the development and implementation of effective training systems.

The chapters in this section describe these challenges and identify ways of keeping training programs up to date and focusing on the factors that are likely to influence the nature of training in organizations at the turn of the century. It also describes the challenges facing organizations when they attempt to use training as a way of adapting to change.

In chapter 1, Thayer documents four critical trends taking place in the world of work, as well as society as a whole, and describes their implications for training. These are changes in the workforce, changes in jobs, organizational downsizing, and changes in the political climate. Although these forces will increase the overall need for training, they should also motivate innovation and creativity on the part of training developers. Furthermore, Thayer argues that there is a serious need for research addressing relatively unexplored, yet potentially critical, areas such as training a diverse workforce for jobs that may not even exist now.

In chapter 2, Dipboye addresses a number of critical challenges facing organizations as they attempt to implement training using the traditional instructional systems design model. He argues that organizations often fail to properly implement training programs because of factors such as pressures to achieve the personal needs of users, a lack of a good person–organization fit, social justice concerns, issues of power, and the need for approval from important constituencies. Although these factors can lead organizations to stray from the instructional systems design model, Dipboye argues that such deviations are legitimate in light of the fact that these concerns should be considered in the design, implementation, and evaluation of training. He advocates a broader conception of the training process in which the role of training is expanded beyond providing a good fit to the knowledge, skill, and ability requirements of the job to include these other functions.

Both chapters in this section point toward a need for cross-fertilization by training researchers from various areas of psychology and beyond. They present areas that are in need of research attention and should serve to guide the research agenda into the upcoming century. It is clear that a number of new skills such as problem solving, statistics, monitoring, and synthesizing information, to name but a few, are likely to become more important in the future. Research needs to address the most effective way to train the workforce on these skills.

Technology will also affect the way training is delivered. The extent to which these new technologies enhance training effectiveness depends to a great degree on the quality of the research conducted in this area. Finally, as organizations change their internal structures and processes to adapt to their environment, training system designers will need to consider these factors during all phases of training development.

# A Rapidly Changing World: Some Implications for Training Systems in the Year 2001 and Beyond

## Paul W. Thayer

**A** number of significant events and forces will have major effects on training in the next decade. Demographic, political, economic, social, organizational, and technological forces all will alter the training enterprise. Although it is impossible to specify the exact effects of these forces, it is possible to recognize that they are affecting us already, and their cumulative impact over time will be substantial.

Most of this book deals with specific changes in the training enterprise: optimizing learning, designing effective training systems, and using advances in technology. This chapter differs from others because in it I explore broader trends and their implications; I will describe some of the changes in the workforce, including downsizing, organizational attachment, job and technology changes, and the changing political climate.

I will begin by examining the effects of increases in the proportion of older workers. Age-related changes in learning, cognitive, sensory, and motor abilities will require adaptations in training and job design. Next, I will discuss changes in age, gender, ethnic, and national diversity and consequent modification of training and training procedures, and I will emphasize the need for more research on such training.

Then I will discuss increasing job complexity as a function of increased use of computers and robotics, and follow this with a look at the impact of a growing service sector. I then will cover downsizing and out-sourcing and their effects on the training process and the organizational structures that provide training, as well as their impact on employee loyalty and training motivation. In addition to these topics, I will explore some political and social trends, and their implications for training and training delivery.

## Changes in the Workforce

The workforce is aging and becoming increasingly diverse. In this section, I describe these changes and the implications on training.

### The Workforce Grows Older

> The workforce in the United States will grow more slowly than it has in the past, and the number of young entrants will decrease even more sharply. (Goldstein & Gilliam, 1990)

In 1990, 23% of the population was 20 to 29 years old, but that age group will decrease to 18% of the population in the year 2000: The proportion in the 50- to 59-year-old age group is expected to jump from 13% to 17% in 2000 and to 21% in 2010 (Warr, 1994). Thus, the portion of the population from which new employees are typically recruited will decline, and at the same time the number of older workers will increase.

As that population shift occurs, there is also a trend toward increased longevity and vitality of older people. Older people are more active physically and mentally, and life-span projections are increasing. As more baby boomers born after World War II reach age 60, the Social Security fund is being stretched beyond its limits, and many proposals are being made in the U.S. Congress and elsewhere to revise eligibility standards for receipts of benefits. Some proposals include a postponement of initiation of full benefits from the current age 65 to ages 67, 68, or even 70. Further, Social Security benefits and pensions may not support the 20 to 30 years of retirement that may come with increased longevity, and many older people will prefer to work during what are considered "normal" retirement years. Whereas the traditional age bracket for "older workers" has been 45 to 64 (Charness & Bosman, 1992), these trends forecast an ever-increasing number of active employees in their late 60s and 70s, thus necessitating the definition of "older worker" to encompass those aged 50 to 70+.

### Training Implications of an Aging Workforce

Considerable progress has been made in understanding the nature of cognitive and performance changes that occur with age. In an excellent summary of research in this area, Horn and Hofer (1992) pointed out that not all intellectual abilities decline with age. Reasoning, short-term memory, and processing speed decline with age starting in the early 20s, but acculturation knowledge (i.e., depth and breadth of knowledge of one's culture), long-term memory, and quantitative knowledge appear to increase through most of adulthood. This is consistent with research on cognitive processing, which shows that age-related slowing in basic processes account for much of the variance in the decline of intellectual functioning (Birren & Fisher, 1995).

Birren and Fisher (1995) pointed to the work of Salthouse (e.g., 1993) that demonstrates that tasks depending on speed will show marked age-related differences, whereas those that depend on knowledge will show only minor age effects. Birren and Fisher argued that this fundamental distinction will permit one to estimate the effects of age through a careful analysis of the task to be learned or performed.

With regard to the older worker, one might expect little decline in performance even in complex jobs, if the job requires knowledge already incorporated in complex schema for the worker. Chess players, for example, continue to demonstrate their skills into middle-age (45 to 64 years old) and early old age (65 to 74; Charness, 1981). In the same way, one would expect managerial decision making, which depends on recognizing various complex schema, to show little deficit with age. However, older workers may suffer more from rapidly changing and unfamiliar job requirements than younger workers. Acquiring skills demanding new, elaborate schema would be much more difficult for the older worker and would take more time (Park, 1992).

The trainer also should be aware of the decline in the senses with age. Acuity, motion detection, color, contrast, and sensitivity to glare all become visual problems for the older worker (Charness & Bosman, 1992). Auditory thresholds increase, and the ability to hear speech or warning signals is adversely affected by noise and reverberation. Charness and Bosman (1992) made a number of recommendations to mitigate these negative sensory changes. Jobs may have to be redesigned and training environments modified to offset these declines. Increasing illuminations levels, increasing the size of critical visual details, and increasing contrast may offset visual decline. Because older people are more susceptible to glare, that will have to be reduced also. To accommodate hearing loss, noise and reverberation must be reduced if older workers are to understand speech and hear warning signals. Charness and Bosman (1992) have additional recommendations for other sensory and motor losses.

However, there is a decided tendency for organizations to retire or transfer older workers rather than retrain them. With seemingly few productive years left for the older worker, organizations sometimes argue that there would be minimal (or no) return on the training investment. Given the expected increase in the proportion of older workers, and the increase in the retirement age, this tendency may lessen. Further, Hall and Mirvis (1995) argued that future organizations will have made a continuing investment in employee development over an individual's career, so that it will be more expensive to replace an older worker with a less developed younger one. Such workers may become coaches or mentors for younger workers or be used to develop better relations with suppliers or customers by farming them out to those organizations. In brief, Hall and Mirvis have envisioned job assignments as a means of challenging and developing employees and imagine that such assignments will continue over a "protean career" (1995) in which the individual takes advantage of old experiences and training to modify and manage his or her career.

Older workers can acquire new skills, of course. Knowing what the older worker already knows will be crucial in the design of a training system. Given the slower processing speed of older workers, extra time should be provided relative to younger workers. Self-pacing in the acquisition of new skills may be more appropriate for older workers. Not much is known about the effects of such differential treatment in training, so trainers should be alert to the possibility of adverse reactions. Younger employees may resent special treatment for older employees, whereas the latter may resent being singled out.

It also may be essential to either simplify the task or to provide the older worker with environmental supports—checklists, lists of steps, or other job aids—to both acquire and maintain skills and knowledge (Park, 1992). Task simplification and job aids may benefit both older and younger workers, just as the redesign of jobs and equipment for women also aided men working on AT&T outside craft jobs (e.g., telephone installers) (Sheridan, 1975). Given the projected growth in the proportion of older workers, it is clear that trainers should keep up with this rapidly developing field of research.

## Increased Diversity

As the age mix changes, the workforce will become more diverse through an increase in the proportion of minorities and women. The proportions of minorities will increase substantially (Goldstein & Gilliam, 1990) over the next several years. The Bureau of Labor Statistics predicts that 57% of the growth in the workforce by the year 2000 will be accounted for by minorities. More than 20% of these new workers will be immigrants (Jackson & Schuler, 1990). In addition, the proportion of women will increase somewhat, from 45% in 1988 to a projected 47% in 2000 (Fullerton, 1989).

## Training Implications of Diversity

Many see a more diverse workforce to be a substantial advantage to organizations using teams and to those marketing products to a more diverse population. They argue that diversity adds to the team's mix of viewpoints regarding problem solving and that therefore the overall output will be superior to that of more homogeneous teams. Indeed, as we are able to produce more and more tailored products to different segments of the population, such diversity within the organization appears to be a real asset (Hage, 1995).

Francis (1995) raised an interesting point regarding the increasing proportion of workers who will be immigrants. Francis noted that forecasts predict nearly 10% of the U.S. workforce in 2000 will be immigrants, and she speculated that trainers will have to be sensitive to cultural differences in *uncertainty avoidance* and *power distance*. Uncertainty avoidance refers to feelings of threat from unstructured, unpredictable situations; power distance describes the degree to which people are self-directed or trainer-directed. She referred to research suggesting that Latin and Asian cultures would be less tolerant of ambiguity and more dependent on trainer authority, whereas American and northern European cultures would be more tolerant of ambiguity and more self-directed in their learning. These differences, in turn, might have an impact on the effectiveness of different training techniques, suggesting lectures would work better with the former and simulations and exercises with the latter. These comprise an interesting set of hypotheses that merits exploration. My experience in training managers in Japan (where students are very instructor-focused) versus managers in the United States and Canada is consistent with Francis's ideas.

It is interesting to note that the very definition of diversity is changing (Filipczak, 1994; Ghiselin, 1995). Many students of human resources are beginning to add to race, gender, age, and nationality differences in values, abilities, organizational function, tenure, and personality

(Wheeler, 1994). The need to include such differences becomes apparent when one considers the increasing use of teams in the workplace. Much research must be done to understand various forms of diversity and the effect of these differences on work teams and the training of teams.

Wheeler (1994) reported that a survey by the Conference Board (a nonprofit research and educational group supported by hundreds of companies across the country) revealed that more than 60% of companies surveyed reported some sort of diversity training. Companies typically reported reasons for training as business need and a desire to remain competitive. Training ranged from creating awareness in all employees of racial, ethnic, gender, and other differences, to supervisory and interpersonal skills training offered primarily to managers and supervisors.

Although such training is widespread, there has been little effort to perform rigorous evaluations (Noe & Ford, 1992). Only questionnaire follow-ups, focus groups, and discussions with participants are common (Wheeler, 1994). A survey of 785 human resource professionals showed that companies adopting diversity training programs were larger, had visible top management support, specialized human resources staffs, and a number of other diversity-related policies and programs (Rynes & Rosen, 1995). Only 33% of the respondents believed their programs were successful, however, a figure almost identical to that reported by the Conference Board (Wheeler, 1994).

Along similar lines, Goldstein and Gilliam (1990) pointed out despite the overwhelming evidence that there are barriers to women entering nontraditional fields, there is no evidence that the knowledge, skills, and abilities required for successful performance are different from those required of men. Despite that, there are ". . . thousands of . . . specialized programs for women, even though data supporting accomplishments of these programs is virtually nonexistent" (Goldstein & Gilliam, 1990, p. 140). It is still often true that lack of evaluation of any training programs "lies in management's reluctance to 'waste time' in testing something it has convinced itself is good" (Wallace & Twichell, 1953, p. 25). Failure to do the proper needs analyses continues to haunt trainers and organizations, with the result that millions of dollars and person hours are wasted. Goldstein and Gilliam (1990) concluded that although diversification programs may not be necessary, it is clear that an organizational analysis might reveal that people within the organization may need training in providing a supportive climate for representatives of diverse populations.

There are many ways to enhance diversity within organizations, and diversity training is only one of them. Our lack of knowledge concerning such training is distressing. Programs appear to be instituted without adequate needs assessment, without even a person analysis to determine existing attitudes. Given the rapidly changing diversity of the workforce, there is a real need to evaluate such training not only to determine whether such interventions achieve objectives but also to determine what kinds of interventions are effective. Failure to do so may result in their being abandoned as capriciously as they have been adopted.

## Changes in Jobs

Although some jobs are becoming more complex, the increasing service sector has many low-paying jobs. Downsizing has changed jobs, abruptly altered careers, and changed the nature of employer–employee relationships.

### Increasing Complexity

The increasing impact of computers, robotics and other high tech innovations will make many jobs more complex and increase demands for highly educated employees who will undergo frequent retraining (see Turnage, 1990). Howell and Cooke (1989) noted that smart machines such as robots increase the complexity of the jobs of human beings. The cognitive demands of the job increase sharply as the human is required to trouble-shoot such devices, so that the individual is required to make inferences, diagnoses, and judgments, instead of following routine procedures. Advanced manufacturing techniques (AMT) involving computer-driven manufacturing machinery also can provide for tailoring products to the specific needs of a customer through easy and rapid changes in the computer's software (Wall & Jackson, 1995). Making such modifications will also increase cognitive demands on workers.

In the same way, Just in Time Inventory Systems (JIT) and Total Quality Management (TQM) systems can make increased cognitive demands on workers (Wall & Jackson, 1995). These, along with AMT, place a good deal more responsibility on the individual worker and often have the effect of enlarging and enhancing the job.

Such systems and technological advances do not necessarily increase cognitive demands, however; they instead may make the job one of machine monitoring. There is considerable debate in progress as to whether "smart machines" will turn workers into low-level monitors or skilled trouble-shooters (Howard, 1995b; Wall & Jackson, 1995). Wall and Jackson (1995) have contended that whether or not cognitive demands will increase depends on the extent to which greater decision making on the job is required. If machines continue to "learn," there may be an increasing separation between high-technology, highly paid jobs and low-level, poorly paid jobs (Howard, 1995b).

However, the increasing use of teams in manufacturing will probably result in increasing cognitive demands. Workers will be required not only to know how to perform many or all the tasks required of the team, but they also will have to develop the knowledge and skills demanded by coordinated effort (Cannon-Bowers, Tannenbaum, Salas, & Volpe, 1995; Stevens & Campion, 1994). And as we have discussed already, an increase in diversity may increase the demand for interpersonal skills among workers.

At least as important as the aforementioned changes has been the shift from an industrial to a knowledge society (Drucker, 1994). Drucker pointed out that in the industrial society, the workers could not own the tools that made production possible. In a knowledge society, knowledge is the tool, and it is in the workers' heads and in the computers they take from job to job. The workers own the tools that make productivity possible. This change will have a great impact on our society as well as on the training enterprise.

## Training Implications of Complexity

If smart machines increase the cognitive complexity of tasks performed by workers, making them do more than follow a set of procedures, requiring inferences, judgments, diagnoses leading to decisions, 4 years of college or graduate work may be required to master the training material and manuals required to operate such equipment. Community colleges may have to place more emphasis on advanced technical training to supply needed personnel to industry.

There is a good possibility that the remedial training in mathematics, reading, and writing being provided by some organizations (Bureau of Labor Statistics, 1995) will not be of much assistance for complex jobs. Drucker (1994) and Howard (1995a) have argued that the

U.S. educational system is failing us and that remediation is not enough. As Howard pointed out, a novice typist could not attain the required speed and accuracy with language skills at less than the seventh-grade level (1995b, p. 526). Trainers may have to rely on careful screening for complex job training to ensure that prospective trainees have the appropriate educational background.

Trainers need to be alert, however, to the possibility that AMT, JIT, and TQM may not always lead to increased cognitive demands (Wall & Jackson, 1995). Thorough task analyses should guide the trainer in any decision regarding training. Trainers should also be aware that JIT training, rather than general skill development, may become increasingly important as individual jobs dissolve into more flexible clusters of activities (Howard, 1995b).

Another change in jobs comes about from increasing international competition. Transfers of employees and their families are common. Training employees in language, customs, and business practices is important for both transferees and those who work with foreign nationals transferred to the United States. Families of international transferees also will have to be trained in order to avoid adverse effects of culture change. Ronen (1989) has many valuable suggestions in this area, including job previews, language training, cultural training, and pre-assignment visits to the new country.

## An Increase in the Service Sector

As these changes discussed previously are occurring, there is a decline in manufacturing jobs and a growth of service jobs. Three fourths of the workforce is currently employed in the service sector, and projections indicate further growth (Howard, 1995b). Service jobs, especially at the entry level, are most often paid at a low rate (Goldstein & Gilliam, 1990).

It is not clear the extent or direction in which technology will affect service jobs. For some, there may be no effect (e.g., hair stylists). For others, they may be "dumbed-down," eliminated, or the complexity may be increased. Many teller jobs are being eliminated in banks, for example, and automatic teller machines are replacing them. Other service jobs will be eliminated also, and some workers will be turned into equipment monitors, as with manufacturing. But other jobs will become more complex as workers use high technology equipment to deliver services tailored to individual customers.

## Training Implications of an Increase in the Service Sector

It is clear that remedial education may be helpful for many service jobs, and in fact it probably will become essential and widespread. The increasing growth of the service sector also will have a direct effect on training and training research. Most service jobs involve direct contact with the customer. Indeed, the employee is responsible for delivering service efficiently and effectively to ensure customer satisfaction. Not much is known about training people-to-people skills, nor are companies willing to face the fact that service delivery skills resemble, but differ from, normal human interactions. Many managers seem to assume that interpersonal skills training is no more necessary than is interviewer training. As with interviewer training, the assumption seems to be that normal conversational skills are all that is needed to be a good interviewer. That belief is no longer as widely held as it used to be. Unfortunately, it appears that managers must accept the fact that day-to-day interactive skills are not enough to ensure effective service delivery. People need to be trained in such skills. The fact that they resemble day-to-day behaviors and that those behaviors are based on strong habits makes them difficult to modify. Training is more difficult and it takes more practice than is required to acquire new knowledge or skill. Research on people-to-people skills needed for service delivery and how to train people in those skills is essential to improve performance in the service sector.

---

## Downsizing and Related Phenomena

Downsizing in the public and private sectors has affected almost every community. More than 5 million private-sector jobs were lost to downsizing in the 1980s, with more losses projected for the 1990s, and the military is being reduced by more than 30% (Kozlowski, Chao, Smith, & Hedlund, 1993). Many older workers (aged 50 and older) have been offered severance packages, thereby reducing the numbers of high-salaried employees with considerable experience.

Although many reasons are given for downsizing, including overstaffing and excess expenses, a substantial force behind the move has been the need to provide more flexible, responsive organizations that can compete in a high technology world. Globalization, sophisticated information technology, and rapid growth in knowledge require many organizations to respond quickly to opportunities worldwide (Davis, 1995).

Downsizing by organizations has greatly altered the nature of the social contract between employer and employee. In the typical bureaucratic structure that characterized the industrial age, people joined a company at an early age, developed organization-specific skills, assimilated the organization's culture, and expected development, promotion, and long-term employment in return (Rousseau & Wade-Benzoni, 1995). In the postbureaucratic or high-technology phase of organizations, some (Davis, 1995; Rousseau & Wade-Benzoni, 1995) see vastly different relationships between employees and the organization.

Rousseau and Wade-Benzoni (1995) have envisioned a differentiated workforce with a core of experienced workers supplemented by peripheral workers who are hired as needed to provide the flexibility required in a rapidly changing environment and competitive marketplace. More and more companies will hire temporary workers to serve as a buffer for changes in demand for their products and services and to reduce expenditures for retirement, health care, and fringe benefits. Rather than upward mobility, there will be a variety of career paths, midcareer shifts, and a constant demand for new skill and knowledge development (Hall & Mirvis, 1995). As a result of these changes, employees will be (and are) less committed to the organization and will be much more mobile than in the past.

Organizations are also *out-sourcing*—or relying on contract workers to perform services once done by fulltime employees. Many workers *telecommute*—or work at home through computer networks. More and more firms are providing flextime, part-time jobs, job-sharing, and career breaks (Hall & Mirvis, 1995). Although such steps reduce organizational overhead, they also may reduce employee commitment.

If Drucker (1994) is correct in believing that workers will own the means for productivity and will have to engage in lifelong learning and that the nature of the employment contract has changed, there are some ominous possibilities for the future. Drucker emphasized, however, that this phenomenon will result in an increased responsibility of the individual to become a lifelong learner (Drucker, 1994). Many companies have reduced or eliminated their training departments and hired those already possessing the requisite knowledge and skills, while releasing those whose skills are no longer needed. Others rely on vendors. Given this change and the effects of downsizing, it may well be that training will have less importance in companies than at present (Hall

& Mirvis, 1995; Howard, 1995b). Some organizations are assigning responsibility for training to operating units and reducing central training staffs, not only to reduce staff size but also to achieve JIT solutions to performance problems (Howard, 1995b).

Hall and Mirvis (1995) have argued that organizations should consider discontinuing career planning and formal training to their workers, stating, "The best form of development is creative staffing, providing jobs that challenge and stretch workers over their life course" (p. 336). They have contended that such assignments promote self-training (Hall & Mirvis, 1995). One wonders if such a prescription will apply to every worker, regardless of the nature of their jobs.

For those who do provide training, however, it will be increasingly important to understand the link among knowledge, skills, and abilities so that workers can be directed to the appropriate kind and level of training. The creation of job families and career ladders with a clear indication of training-related knowledge, skills, and abilities will be essential (Harvey, 1991). Whether outside vendors will take this step is unknown, but it is not likely. Thus, it is prudent to be wary about hiring out training.

At the same time, trainers will need to be ready to provide training to those who telecommute, those who are assigned to remote geographic offices, those who work part-time, and those who work unusual hours. Modern technology involved in distance learning will be essential, whether the trainer is an organizational staff member or a service provider to the organization.

## The Changing Political Climate

Although there is much speculation regarding the shift in majority in the 1994 elections from a Democratic House and Senate to a Republication House and Senate in the U.S. Congress, there is a clear trend toward downsizing government at all levels and reducing support for training. It is possible that the pendulum will change direction, but at present there is increasing emphasis on budget cuts, some of which put federal support for training and education in jeopardy. Incentives to industry for training employees, especially the functionally illiterate, are at risk.

Although the major emphasis is on budget cuts, part of the problem in this area is that studies of the outcomes of various training programs for the unemployed, or those on welfare, have shown inconsistent results. Proponents and opponents can find support by citing the appropriate study. In a recent meta-analysis that was restricted to experimental or quasi-experimental designs, however, Fischer and Cordray (1995) found small but consistent positive effects of training programs on employment rates and reduction in welfare payments. These training programs involved job search, basic education, and vocational training programs. Effect sizes were great enough to justify the use of such programs. For employment status they were between 5% and 6%, whereas those for Aid to Families with Dependent Children 1 year after program enrollment were 4%.

Political views, legal decisions, and legislative climate are all questioning affirmative action. The impact of these changing views is unknown, but it will affect minorities, women, disabled, and older workers.

## Variations in Organizational Involvement in Training Employees

As we consider the future of training, it is important to look at the extent of training today. There is considerable variation in the use of training by U.S. organizations. Many companies rely on recruiting and selection to provide needed knowledge and skills, whereas others prefer to develop their own people. The need for new skills has been met in a variety of ways: Some companies hire people with advanced skills from other organizations, and others develop or purchase training. As to the latter, 71% of all establishments provided some sort of training in 1993, especially those with more than 50 employees. Almost half of these organizations provided job skills training, most commonly sales and customer relations, management skills, and computer skills. One third provided job orientation, safety and health information, and similar information (Bureau of Labor Statistics, 1995). The number of employees who benefit from such training is less clear. Secretary of Labor Robert Reich has stated that only 35% of employees get training and that most of these are college graduates (Marshall, 1995).

At present, large organizations are deemphasizing training while they attend to the problems of layoffs and restructuring. Small companies are hiring the already skilled older workers who have been laid off and see no need for training young people. Thus, little is being done in training the young workforce. The long-term effects of this neglect may be enormous.

Organizations are also confronted with problems of performance of young people who have been "passed" through or dropped out of the U.S. educational system (Goldstein & Gilliam, 1990). In 1991, more than 20% of Americans were high school dropouts (Howard, 1995a). Drucker (1994) has argued that the poor performance of the public schools in this country has been in part the result of the tendency to deviate from what many believe is their primary goal—teaching fundamental knowledge and skills—in order to meet requirements to implement myriad social policies. Whatever the cause, the evidence is clear that many who will enter the workforce, both young people and immigrants, suffer from a lack of language and computational knowledge and skills.

Some attention is being given to the lack of basic skills. In 1995, almost one fourth of the organizations with more than 50 employees provided formal training in basic reading, writing, and arithmetic skills (Bureau of Labor Statistics, 1995). If we consider the changes in the population, jobs, organizations, the employee–employer contract, and political changes, however, it seems clear that the availability of training to various segments of the workforce needs careful consideration.

## Conclusion

A vast number of changes are occurring: an increasingly diverse workforce, a shift in the employee–employer relationship, an increase in the number of high technology jobs, a shift to a service economy, the development of a knowledge society in which the worker owns the tools for production, a change in the political climate, and a shift in who trains and who is responsible for training.

Each of these developments have been treated one at a time. In reality, however, many of these will be occurring simultaneously or in sequence. It is difficult to anticipate how the interactions of these trends will affect training in the future. Add to these changes the many that are described in later chapters of this book.

Each of the developments described here and in later chapters will interact with others in unexpected ways, as well as with developments not mentioned. If employees will be increasingly responsible for their own growth and development, employees who are trainers and training researchers must keep up to date on these and other developments. It will be increasingly easy to become out of date. Those who rely on the latest training fad for their employment will be in great jeopardy. Breadth and depth of knowledge and skill will be essential for survival.

## References

Birren, J. E., & Fisher, L. M. (1995). Aging and speed of behavior: Possible consequences for psychological functioning. In J. T. Spence, J. M. Darley, & D. J. Foss. *Annual Review of Psychology, 46,* (pp. 329–353). Palo Alto, CA: Annual Reviews.

Bureau of Labor Statistics. (1995). Press release, February.

Cannon-Bowers, J. A., Tannenbaum, S. C. I., Salas, E., & Volpe, C. E. (1995). Defining competencies and establishing team training requirements. In R. C. A. Guzzo, E. Salas (Ed.), *Team effectiveness and decision making in organizations* (pp. 333–380). San Francisco: Jossey-Bass.

Charness, N. (1981). Search in chess: Age and skill differences. *Journal of Experimental Psychology: Human Perception and Performance, 2,* 467–476.

Charness, N., & Bosman, E. A. (1992). Human factors and age. In F. I. M. Craik & T. A. Salthouse (Eds.), *The handbook of aging and cognition* (pp. 495–551). Hillsdale, NJ: Erlbaum.

Davis, D. D. (1995). Form, function, and strategy in boundryless organizations. In A. Howard (Ed.), *The changing nature of work* (pp. 112–138). San Francisco, CA: Jossey-Bass.

Drucker, P. F. (1994). The age of social transformation. *The Atlantic Monthly, 274*(5), 53–80.

Filipczak, B. (1994, October). Looking past the numbers. *Training, 31,* 67–74.

Fischer, R. L., & Cordray, D. S. (1995). *Job training and welfare reform: A policy-driven synthesis (Research Summary).* Nashville, TN: Vanderbilt Institute for Public Policy Studies.

Francis, J. L. (1995). Training across cultures. *Human Resource Development Quarterly, 6,* 101–107.

Fullerton, H. N. (1989). New labor force projections, spanning 1988 to 2000. *Monthly Labor Review, 112*(11), 3–12.

Ghiselen, B. (1995). Work teams and diversity. *Issues & Observations, 15*(1), 1–5. Greensboro, NC: Center for Creative Leadership.

Goldstein, I. L., & Gilliam, P. (1990). Training system issues in the year 2000. *American Psychologist, 45,* 134–143.

Hage, J. (1995). Post-industrial lives: New demands, new prescriptions. In A. Howard (Ed.), *The changing nature of work* (pp. 485–512). San Francisco: Jossey-Bass.

Hall, D. T., & Mirvis, P. H. (1995). Careers as lifelong learning. In A. Howard (Ed.), *The changing nature of work* (pp. 323–362). San Francisco: Jossey-Bass.

Harvey, R. J. (1991). Job analysis. In M. D. Dunnette & L. M. Hough (Eds.), Vol. 2, *Handbook of industrial and organizational psychology* (2nd ed.) (pp. 71–163). Palo Alto: CA: Consulting Psychologists Press.

Horn, J. L., & Hofer, S. M. (1992). Major abilities and development in the adult period. In R. J. Sternberg & C. A. Berg (Eds.), *Intellectual development* (pp. 44–99). New York: Cambridge University Press.

Howard, A. (1995). Rethinking the psychology of work. In A. Howard (Ed.), *The changing nature of work* (pp. 513–556). San Francisco: Jossey-Bass.

Howell, W. C., & Cooke, N. J. (1989). Training the human information processor: A look at cognitive models. In I. L. Goldstein (Ed.), *Training and development in work organizations: Frontiers of industrial and organizational psychology* (pp. 121–182). San Francisco: Jossey-Bass.

Jackson, S. E., & Schuler, R. S. (1990). Human resource planning: Challenges for industrial/organizational psychologists. *American Psychologist, 45*, 223–239.

Kozlowski, S. W. J., Chao, G. T., Smith, E. M., & Hedlund, J. (1993). Organizational downsizing: Strategies, interventions, and research implications. In C. L. Cooper & I. T. Robertson (Eds.), *International review of industrial and organizational psychology 1993, Volume 8* (pp. 263–332). New York: Wiley.

Marshall, K. (1995, March 28). Labor chief checks out high-tech changes in textile industry. *The News & Observer*, D1–2.

Noe, R. A., & Ford, J. K. (1992). Emerging issues and new directions for training research. In G. Ferris & K. Rowland (Eds.), *Research in personnel and human resource management* (Vol. 10, pp. 345–384). Greenwich, CT: JAI Press.

Park, D. (1992). Applied cognitive aging research. In F. T. M. Craik & T. A. Salthouse (Eds.), *The handbook of aging and cognition*. Hillsdale, NJ: Erlbaum.

Ronen, S. (1989). Training the international assignee. In I. L. Goldstein (Ed.), *Training and development in organizations* (pp. 417–453). San Francisco: Jossey-Bass.

Rousseau, D. M., & Wade-Benzoni, K. A. (1995). Changing individual-organizational attachments: A two-way street. In A. Howard (Ed.), *The changing nature of work* (pp. 290–322). San Francisco: Jossey-Bass.

Rynes, S., & Rosen, B. (1995). A field survey of factors affecting the adoption and perceived success of diversity training. *Personnel Psychology, 48*, 247–270.

Salthouse, T. A. (1993). Attentional blocks are not responsible for age-related slowing. *Journal of Gerontology: Psychological Science, 48*, 263–270.

Sheridan, J. A. (1975, August). *Designing the work environment*. Paper presented at the annual meeting of the American Psychological Association, Chicago.

Stevens, M. J., & Campion, M. A. (1994, April). *Staffing teams: Development and validation of the Teamwork-KSA Test*. Paper presented at the annual meeting of the Society of Industrial and Organizational Psychology, Nashville, TN.

Turnage, J. J. (1990). The challenge of new workplace technology for psychology. *American Psychologist, 45*, 171–178.

Wall, T. D., & Jackson, P. R. (1995). New manufacturing initiatives and shopfloor design. In A. Howard (Ed.), *The changing nature of work* (pp. 139–174). San Francisco: Jossey-Bass.

Wallace, S. R., Jr., & Twichell, C. M. (1953). An evaluation of a training course for life insurance agents. *Personnel Psychology, 6*, 25–43.

Warr, P. (1994). Age and employment. In H. C. Triandis, M. D. Dunnette, & L. M. Hough (Eds.), *Handbook of industrial and organizational psychology* (Vol. 4, 2nd ed., pp. 485–550). Palo Alto, CA: Consulting Psychologists Press.

Wheeler, M. L. (1994). *Diversity training*. (Report Number 1083-94-RR). New York: Conference Board.

# Organizational Barriers to Implementing a Rational Model of Training

**Robert L. Dipboye**

The instructional systems design model (ISD) is a rational approach in which the design of training programs is based on needs assessment and the psychological research on learning and transfer. The program is subsequently retained, modified, or discarded on the basis of a rigorous evaluation of its utility to the organization. Most organizations, however, fail to follow the ISD approach in their employee training programs. As I write this chapter I am confronted with an example of this underutilization. A radio advertisement is hawking a "revolutionary" system of instruction in which the learner effortlessly assimilates instructional material by listening to tapes during sleep or while performing other tasks. More common than such obvious quackery are training programs that have potential merit but are unrelated to organizational needs, are implemented inefficiently, and are never evaluated. The sad state of training practices in industry led John Campbell (1971) to conclude that the training area was dominated by fads. Since Campbell's review, published more than 25 years ago, a useful body of knowledge has accumulated on how people learn in training programs and the factors influencing whether they use what they learn in the workplace (i.e., transfer of training). Moreover, methodologies have been proposed for systematically and scientifically guiding the training process. Despite the potential benefits of this knowledge base, however, a distressing gap still exists between the scholarly work and the actual conduct of training in organizations.

The purpose of this chapter is to explore why organizations so often fail to adopt and fully implement what the psychological literature would prescribe as effective training practices. I begin with a review of the practices that have been recommended and the ways in which organizations deviate from these recommendations. The remainder of the discussion examines the organizational factors that hinder the implementation of a rational, scientific approach to managing training processes. I argue that these factors include pressures to achieve the personal needs of users, a good person–organization fit, social justice, power, and the approval of important constituencies. Although these factors can lead organizations to stray from ISD, I believe that they are legitimate functions that should be considered in the design, implementation, and evaluation of training. A broader conception of the training process is advocated in which the role of training is expanded beyond providing a good fit to the knowledge, skills, and abilities of the job to include these other functions.

## Instructional Systems Design: A Rational Approach to Training

Human resource management (HRM) emerged from the fields of psychology and economics, and proponents assume that organizational effectiveness can be improved through people-oriented activities such as staffing, training, and wage and salary administration (Bolman & Deal, 1991; Ferris & Judge, in press). In an ideal situation, the management of the various HRM functions conforms to *norms of rationality* meaning that decisions are made that maximize the economic utility of the HRM programs (Murray & Dimick, 1978). To achieve this decision criterion, a careful evaluation is made of the goals of the organization and the desirability of alternative procedures for achieving these goals. A choice is then made of those procedures that maximize benefits and minimize costs. The rational approach to HRM that has evolved in personnel psychology consists of several characteristics. First and foremost it is scientific—rigorous research guides the design and evaluation of HRM functions. Second, top management's goals and values often serve as the ultimate standard against which programs are evaluated (Beer & Spector, 1984; Hinrichs, 1976). Third, the job is considered to be the building block of the organization (Ash, Levine, & Sistrunk, 1983), and the primary strategy for improving organizational effectiveness of the rational approach to HRM is to provide a good fit of the person's knowledge, skills, and abilities to the requirements of the job.

The best example of a rational approach to training is a genre of models that are referred to as the ISD approach (Goldstein, 1991; Hinrichs, 1976; Parker, 1976; Ryder, Redding, & Beckschi, 1987; Smith, 1971). The Human Resources Research Organization (HumRRO) appears to have first proposed this approach, but numerous versions of ISD have appeared over the past 3 decades (see Morrison, 1991). Goldstein's ISD model is perhaps the best known and most influential. According to his model, effective training is based on a careful needs assessment, is implemented through "precisely controlled learning experiences designed to achieve instructional objectives" (1991, p. 514), and is evaluated against performance criteria. The usual recommendation is to start with a formal job analysis to determine the knowledge, skills, and abilities required of incumbents and the criteria for measuring their performance. On the basis of this analysis, as well as a careful consideration of costs and benefits, techniques are chosen for implementation that are best suited for the situation. A formal evaluation follows. Those techniques that achieve the desired outcomes are retained whereas those that fail are either modified or discarded. The widespread acceptance of the ISD model as the best approach for managing the training process is shown in the frequent use of this model as the organizing schema in previous reviews of the training literature (Goldstein, 1993; Latham, 1988; Wexley, 1984). In a similar way, I will use this framework to arrange the discussion of how organizations have departed from rational approaches to training. Before doing this, however, I will describe in more detail the various steps of the ISD model.

## A Needs Assessment

The initial step in the model is to conduct a training needs assessment. At the heart of this assessment is an analysis of the tasks in the job and a determination of the relative importance of the knowledge, skills, and abilities required to perform these tasks. A person analysis is then conducted to evaluate how well current employees are performing and the type of instruction they need. Finally, an organizational analysis determines the factors in the situation that might help or prevent the transfer of what is learned in training to the job (Rouiller & Goldstein, 1993). A properly conducted needs assessment identifies the focus of the training and the basis for later evaluations of its effectiveness. Moreover, a needs analysis should provide clues on how to ensure that what is learned will be used on the job and how to choose the criteria that will be used in evaluating the training program's effectiveness.

## Incorporate Psychological Research in the Design and Implementation of the Instructional Program

The needs analysis should guide the second phase of the training cycle in which the instructional content of the program is chosen and implemented. In an ideal situation, the material, media, and procedures in a program are chosen because they are effective in facilitating learning and transfer. Among the instructional events that psychological research has shown to improve learning, practice, overlearning, spacing of material, advanced organizers, active participation of the learner, and refresher training (Druckman & Bjork, 1991). There are no universal principles of learning, however, and the best advice is to choose instructional events that are most appropriate to the capability that is the target of the training (Gagne, 1984). Perhaps the most important consideration in designing the training environment is to incorporate experiences that ensure the transfer to and maintenance on the job of what is learned in the classroom (Baldwin & Ford, 1988; Druckman & Bjork, 1991; Marx, 1982).

## Evaluate the Program

The last step in the training cycle is crucial and consists of a rigorous evaluation of the effectiveness of the training against criteria identified in the needs assessment phase. Goldstein (1991) described training as a closed-loop system in which the program is continuously evaluated and improved on the basis of results of the evaluation. An evaluation should allow an identification of which criteria have changed, whether these changes are the result of the training program, whether the same changes will occur in future replications of the program in the same organization with different participants, and whether the same changes will occur for new participants in the same program in a different organization. Kraiger, Ford, and Salas (1993) recommended in their model of training evaluation that the best method of evaluating training effectiveness is dictated by whether the learning outcome is cognitive, skill-based, or affective. In addition, the economic benefit of the training to the organization should be measured using utility estimation procedures (Cascio, 1989). The most rigorous evaluations are experiments that include pre- and posttesting, control groups, and random assignment (Cook & Campbell, 1979). Repeated experimentation may show that a training program is totally lacking in validity and utility or that its effectiveness varies with the situation and the type of trainee (Cronbach, 1975).

## Failure to Implement an ISD Model

Most of those who are responsible for HRM programs would probably endorse a rational approach, but the reality is that there is typically a "loosening of the relationship between the criterion of technical rationality and the choice of policies and programs by employers" (Murray & Dimick, 1978, p. 754). The failure to implement a rational approach is clearly shown in the amount and sophistication of the training that is conducted in most organizations. Despite the evidence that training is an effective means of enhancing organizational productivity (Burke & Day, 1986; Guzzo, Jette, & Katzell, 1985; Russell, Terborg, & Powers, 1985), most organizations give very little attention to training (Labor letter, 1991). According to one estimate, only 16% of American employees have ever received training from their employers (Carnevale, 1995). When training is provided, it often varies from the ISD model, as evidenced by the lack of thorough needs assessments, the neglect of psychological research on learning in the design of the program, the rarity of rigorous program evaluation, decision making that ignores utility considerations, and the prevalence of fads and the widespread use of unplanned and unsystematic on-the-job training.

### Thorough Needs Assessments Are Rare

Training programs are seldom preceded by thorough task, organization, and person analyses. More often they are adopted on the basis of a persuasive salesperson, a slick brochure, or testimonials from previous participants. Along these lines, Hinrichs observed in management training that decision makers seldom conduct thorough needs analyses. Instead,

> A typical reaction of the training department is to jump in with a "program" . . . there is seldom a determination of how to achieve proficiency in each component task or how to link tasks together to form proficiency in the total task. In effect, there is seldom a real rational analysis of how the training program should be constructed, much less any carefully controlled research. (1976, p. 844)

Goldstein noted that "many programs are doomed to failure because trainers are more interested in conducting training programs than in assessing needs of the organization'' (1993, p. 37). Some empirical evidence for what Hinrichs and Goldstein observed was provided by Saari, Johnson, McLauglin, and Zimmerle (1988) in a national survey of management training practices. Only 27% of the respondents indicated that a needs assessment was conducted, and when needs assessments were conducted, they were mostly restricted to training for lower levels of management. Possibly reflective of the lack of needs assessment, training too often appears to have little substance and little linkage to specific objectives of the organization (Wehrenberg, 1986).

## Psychological Research Is Often Ignored in Program Implementation

Training programs frequently omit instructional practices that could facilitate acquisition and transfer (Bjork, 1979). Dempster (1990) brought attention to one notable example—the prevalent use of *massed presentation* of instructional material rather than *spaced presentations*. In massed instruction, practice on the task occurs within a short period of time, whereas in spaced instruction practice is distributed across several periods of time. The finding that spaced presentations lead to better long-term retention is among the most replicated of learning phenomena, but the spacing effect is mostly ignored in the design of training. Possible reasons for the failure to apply spaced learning include the lack of theoretical understanding of the phenomenon and applied research demonstrating the effect in applied settings (Dempster, 1990). An even more compelling explanation is that massed practice yields more short-term evidence of learning and takes less time (Druckman & Bjork, 1991). Numerous other examples could be cited of how learning research is ignored in the design of training, such as the lack of careful attention to matching the instructional techniques to the learning objectives and the lack of any attempt to ensure transfer through follow-up training (Saari et al., 1988).

## Rigorous Evaluations Are Rare

Organizations frequently fail to evaluate their training programs, and when they do, these evaluations are rarely rigorous (cf., Kerr, 1975; Sackett & Mullen, 1993). True experiments or rigorous quasi-experiments are infrequent, with the predominant design consisting of either a simple pretraining–posttraining or a posttraining-only collection of data. Despite the potential problems of relying on self-reports (Dixon, 1987; Yancey & Kelly, 1990) and the admonitions to use multiple-level criteria (Kraiger et al., 1993), organizations typically use only "happy sheets" and ignore whether training has had an impact on learning, behavior, and the performance of the trainee on the job (Saari et al., 1988).

## Decisions About Training Often Deviate From Rationality

Contrary to the rational prescription that training programs should be evaluated on the basis of their monetary contribution to the organization (Kirrane, 1986), decisions on training seldom seem to reflect a rational analysis of costs and benefits. There is even some evidence that administrators reject information on the economic utility of HRM procedures. For instance, Latham and Whyte (1994) found that giving utility data to managers led them to express lower confidence in and commitment to a selection procedure relative to a condition in which no utility information was presented. The failure of decision makers to take an analytic approach is not unique to training but reflects the general reliance on intuitive decision making in organizations. A large amount of research and theory has demonstrated that managers and other organizational decision makers seldom conform to what would be expected under a rational model of decision making (Beach, 1990; Cohen, March, & Olsen, 1972; Isenberg, 1984; Komaroff, 1982; Lindblom, 1959; Mintzberg, Raisinghani, & Theoret, 1976; Weick, 1979). Even in situations in which decision makers *intend* to make rational decisions, they fall short of complete rationality because of cognitive limitations and the lack of information.

## Most Training Is Informal and On the Job

The failure to implement the ISD model is most clearly shown in the prevalence of unplanned, informal, and nonsystematic on-the-job training in organizations. The popularity of on-the-job training probably reflects its clear relevance to the job and the fact that the trainee is producing while learning. The apparent virtues of on-the-job training may be negated by the problems associated with this approach. On-the-job trainers may have no interest in developing the trainee and may even see training as a hindrance to performing their own duties. In addition, on-the-job trainers usually have no training or expertise in instructional methods and are not rewarded for performing their training duties effectively. On-the-job training could be more effective but often falls short of what could be achieved as the result of the sloppy manner in which it is implemented.

## Training Is Dominated by Fads and Fashions

A cursory review of the many "hot" trends in training that have dominated the industry provides additional evidence of how the ISD model has had only a limited impact on organizational training. Rather than carefully designing and implementing programs that fulfill specific needs, organizations follow fads and fashions without an adequate understanding of the theory and research relevant to the problems that they are attempting to solve (Levinson, 1992). This tendency to chase after popular programs seems especially prevalent in managerial training. In the 1960s, sensitivity training was one of the dominant trends. Despite the lack of evidence that such training benefited job performance (Campbell & Dunnette, 1968), a surprising number of organizations sent their employees off to sensitivity group sessions on the naive assumption that they would improve productivity back in the workplace. Sensitivity training eventually waned in popularity but was replaced by other fashionable programs. Among the contemporary fads are teambuilding (Dyer, 1987), diversity training (Hollister, Day, & Jesaitis, 1993; see also chapter 1, this volume), adventure training (Laabs, 1991; Noe & Ford, 1992), right brain training (Hines, 1987), and accelerated learning (Bretz & Thompsett, 1992). All of these types of training have worthy objectives and some are based on at least a modicum of legitimate theory and research. Unlike training that is driven by an ISD model, however, these programs tend to be adopted without assessing whether they meet specific instructional needs and without evaluating their effectiveness. Proponents of the various training fads often make extravagant claims for the effectiveness of the training. For instance, accelerated learning is purported to improve acquisition by 5 to 50 times above traditional instructional methods with no increased effort on the part of the trainee (Druckman & Bjork, 1991). Despite the lack of evidence to support this claim, accelerated learning has been adopted by numerous large and prestigious organizations in the public and private sectors (Bretz & Thompsett, 1992).

# The Barriers to Implementing a Rational Model of Training

The essential theme of this chapter is that the rational approach to training is underutilized because of factors in the organizational context that hinder its implementation. Several reviewers have brought attention to the need to consider the contextual factors in HRM (Beer & Spector, 1984; Dobbins, Cardy, & Carson, 1991; Goldstein, 1980; Johns, 1993; Latham, 1988; Tannenbaum & Yukl, 1992; Wiener, 1988). This chapter expands on this previous theorizing by examining some of the forces at work in the organizational system that can draw decision makers away from the prescriptions of an ISD model. These centrifugal forces include the attitudes of the persons who must actually implement the process, the desire to provide a better fit to the context of the job, norms for justice, political pressures, and the symbolic uses of training.

## Personal Attitudes of Users Toward a Rational Approach

Whether an innovation is adopted and successfully used depends on the attitudes of the individuals who implement it (Lewis & Seibold, 1993). In the same way, the attitudes of trainers and administrators are likely to influence whether an ISD model of training is attempted and fully implemented. Although most persons are likely to espouse support for many aspects of an ISD model, I think that the actual implementation of this approach is likely to evoke a variety of negative emotions on the part of both trainers and administrators.

The negative attitudes that I believe exist toward implementing an ISD model reflect several factors. An objective, data-based approach possibly conflicts with the personal characteristics of those who are drawn to the training profession. According to one survey of professional trainers, the best trainers were not perceived to be analytical or scientific but team oriented, warm, outgoing, positive, and humanistic (Leach, 1991). In addition, the HRM subculture appears to support a strong people orientation that may be at odds with the bottom-line approach characteristic of the ISD model. Some evidence of this was provided in a recent study of organizational stories gathered from HRM professionals in Fortune 500 companies (Hansen, Kahnweiler, & Wilensky). A dominant theme in the responses of those surveyed was a "genuine concern for group synergy and individual employee development," (1994, p. 264) whereas "financial and other bottom line business issues were not typical" (p. 263).

An objective, impersonal evaluation of training can also evoke anxiety and insecurity among those held accountable for the program. Just as trainees may learn less if they believe the program is a personal threat (Martocchio, 1992), an ISD model seems likely to fail if those who implement the program see the process as a threat to their self-esteem and career security. Argyris (1990) observed that organization development practitioners employ at least three patterns of defense in response to scientific scrutiny of their practices, and similar defensive responses can be seen in the implementation of an ISD model. In the first pattern, the practitioner reacts to scientific scrutiny by accusing the investigator of being inappropriately rational and insufficiently respectful of intuition. In the second pattern, the practitioner charges that rational dialogue and confrontation cause distress and interfere with personal learning styles. In the third pattern, the practitioner withdraws from the interaction and accuses skeptics of being judgmental and punishing.

Another source of negative attitudes about the model is the effort and cost associated with the ISD model. Conducting a needs analysis, carefully planning the content of the training program, taking steps to ensure positive transfer, and evaluating the effectiveness of the program all require time and effort that those involved in training may feel that they lack. It is usually easier and cheaper in the short-run to base decisions regarding training on gut feelings than to conduct elaborate analyses.

Still another source of negative attitudes is that the reliance on research and data in ISD may seem somewhat boring and tedious in contrast to the fun and excitement of some alternative approaches to training. Such fads as adventure training, integrated learning, sensitivity groups, and brain training all have strong entertainment value. For instance, a typical accelerated learning session devotes a substantial amount of time to exercises intended to evoke positive affect and produce a state of relaxation (e.g., listening to music, tossing a ball around the room, stating something "good or new" that one has experienced). It is not surprising, then, that instructors and trainees appear to report more enjoyment of accelerated learning than traditional lecture approaches (Bretz & Thompsett, 1992). Although there is some evidence that trainees who label a training program as fun learn more than trainees who label it as work (Webster & Martocchio, 1993), having fun too often becomes the primary indicator of the success of training programs (Dixon, 1987).

In addition to these factors, a final source of negative attitudes is the lack of respect for the special expertise of psychologists and others implementing ISD. Administrators and trainers often do not understand the scientific approach to training and its benefits. Administrators tend to view training as an administrative innovation that requires common sense rather than expertise (Johns, 1993) and as an expense rather than as an investment for the future (Labor letter, 1991). The lack of an integrated perspective to HRM also diminishes the credibility of not only the ISD approach but other HRM interventions. Beer and Spector (1984, pp. 270–271) observed that the low esteem that line managers have for personnel functions reflects their perceptions of these functions as disconnected, uncoordinated practices that are of more relevance to individual employees than to the organization as a whole. As a consequence, less expert power is likely to be attributed to psychologists and other HRM experts in the implementation of training than is attributed to an engineer or physical scientist in the implementation of a new machine or production process. If administrators and trainers are educated in needs assessment, the psychological research on learning and transfer, and program evaluation, they may come to appreciate the technical requirements of an effective training program and the benefits that a systematic, scientific approach can provide. Given the current state of ignorance, however, ISD may continue to be seen as an academic exercise in paper shuffling and number crunching with little payoff for the organization.

## Providing a Good Fit of the Trainee to the Job Context

Although ISD often makes some mention of the importance of considering the organizational context, especially in the needs assessment phase, the emphasis in ISD is on the job and its tasks. Contextual factors are becoming more important, however, and another reason that managers and trainees deviate from an ISD approach is in the interest of dealing with these factors. Borman and Motowidlo defined contextual activities as those that "support the organizational, social and psychological environment in which the technical core must function" (1993, p. 73). Different jobs require different task activities, but the job context requires such activities that are common to all jobs, such as volunteering, persisting, helping, cooperating, and organizational citizenship. Moreover, contextual performances are more likely to consist of discretionary activities than formally required job duties (Borman &

Motowidlo, 1993). As a result, contextual performances depend less on whether the job incumbent possesses the knowledge, skills, and abilities that fit the requirements of the tasks and more on the motivation, values, and personality predispositions of the job incumbent. To provide a good fit of the employee to the context, organizations may deemphasize the job and focus more on indoctrinating employees in the values and culture of the organization.

A sharp distinction is often made between training that is focused on the job and socialization that is typically described as the primary process by which employees are indoctrinated in the organizational culture (Fisher, 1986). In the socialization process, employees are often depicted as being subjected to intense experiences to encourage the giving up of old identities and the adoption of new attitudes and values (Schein, 1968). For instance, military recruits are not simply trained but are physically separated, shaved, stripped of their civilian clothes, and intimidated by drill instructors in the attempt to socialize them to military life. The distinction between training and socialization is becoming blurred, however, as training programs take on many of the qualities of socialization (Albert & associates, 1985; Alexander, 1987). Feldman has observed that training has become a lengthy process in many organizations in which

> Perceptions and expectations about the organization are formed, where norms about social behavior are developed, where corporate values and ideology are communicated, and where individuals formulate their career paths. Indeed, in many cases, training has gone beyond being part of the socialization process and has become synonymous with it. (1989, pp. 398–399)

The incorporation of contextual concerns into training seems to be accelerating as organizations attempt to cope with an increasingly complex, changing, and competitive environment. To adapt to their environments, organizations are restructuring and making dramatic changes in their work processes. As boundaries between jobs are becoming less distinct, employees are expected to work as team members, to share the values and goals of the organization, and to be good organizational citizens. In response to these changes, more organizations are adopting a competency-based model of HRM in which persons are selected and trained for organizational membership rather than for a fixed job (Lawler, 1994). Lado and Wilson (1994) are among the theorists who have suggested that an overemphasis on rational approaches to HRM functions may foster inflexibility and inhibit or destroy competencies that would provide an organization a competitive advantage. They have argued that even if an organization attains competitive advantage by adopting HRM practices that research has shown to be clearly linked to organizational outcomes, this advantage may be short-lived as other firms adopt the practices. They propose that sustained competitive advantage comes from adopting HRM practices that not only enhance competencies but that cannot be imitated as the result of being "unique, causally ambiguous, and synergistic" (p. 718). A training program at Disney Corporation is likely to contain unique aspects of the Disney culture (e.g., memorization of the Seven Dwarfs) that are transportable to other organizations.

Several elements of the ISD model appear inconsistent with attempts to develop employees for organizational membership. Needs assessment as described in the typical ISD approach incorporates the demands of the job context only to the extent that it is seen as a potential barrier to learning transfer. The context is infrequently judged to be a legitimate source of training content, and the focus is instead on the specific cognitive and motor skills required in the job. This narrow approach to assessing needs may prove inadequate if the intent is to shape attitudes, values, and norms. Likewise, the restriction of training evaluations to specific job criteria neglects criteria relevant to contextual performances. The training that is used in some organizations may appear inefficient and even irrelevant from the viewpoint of an ISD model but may be quite valuable in meeting contextual concerns.

## Maintaining Procedural and Distributive Justice

An ISD model of training also runs into trouble because of norms that exist within organizations and within society for social justice. With this in mind, training is approached as an instrument for achieving economic goals, but frequently training is evaluated more on the basis of the fairness with which it is implemented than for the efficient achievement of organizational objectives. Two approaches have dominated recent discussions of organizational justice. Distributive justice theories are concerned with the fairness with which outcomes are allocated to various organizational members (Bierhoff, Cohen, & Greenberg, 1986). Procedural justice is concerned with the fairness of the procedures used to distribute the outcomes (Folger & Greenberg, 1985).

## Norms for Distributive Justice

From a distributive justice perspective, as the term implies, decision makers judge the fairness of a procedure on the basis of how outcomes are distributed (Deutsch, 1975). An equity rule would lead decision makers to view a fair allocation as one in which outcomes are commensurate with contributions to the job. According to this rule, the fairness of allocations is judged by comparing the target person's ratio of inputs to outcomes to that of others. Inequity is defined as a state of affairs in which one person's ratio of inputs to outcomes is discrepant from the comparison person's ratio. Justice also can be defined on the basis of need. From this perspective, those who have the greatest need receive the largest outcomes regardless of their contributions or inputs. Finally, an equality norm would dictate that all persons receive the same outcome, regardless of inputs or contributions. The research shows that equity is the dominant rule but that the other two are salient in some circumstances (Bierhoff et al., 1986; Cohen, 1987).

All three distribution rules influence whether training is seen as fair or unfair. When equity norms are dominant, training could be seen as an outcome that is allocated to employees according to their qualifications or past performance. Equity norms could be violated, for example, if the employees who are admitted to a training program have lower test scores or poorer performance than employees who are rejected. When equality norms are dominant, all individuals in a situation are seen as deserving of training opportunities regardless of their inputs. An equality norm seems to drive training efforts in many situations. Some evidence of this was provided by Gray, Connor, and Decatur (1994), who found that leaders with a strong belief in equality put more funds into training their subordinates than leaders with a weak belief in equality. If need norms are salient, then the fairness of training allocations is evaluated on the basis of the personal needs of employees. For instance, employees with families may be seen as more deserving of training that would qualify them for promotion because of their financial needs.

ISD is likely to encounter resistance when training is perceived as an outcome and one or more of these distribution norms is salient. Concerns about equality and need may account for the fact that organizations seldom assess trainability, despite the existence of valid measures of trainability that can be used to predict success in training. Concerns about fairness also play havoc with attempts to rigorously evaluate training programs. Cook and Campbell (1979) listed several threats to the internal validity of experimental evaluations of interventions that appear to result from concerns over fairness. In the compensatory equalization of treatments, managers of the employees who are assigned to the no-treatment control group give them special treatment to make up for their inequitable treatment. In compensatory rivalry, the control group reacts to perceptions that they have been excluded from some beneficial treatment by attempting to prove that they can perform as well or better than the treatment group. In resentful demoralization the control group reacts with resentment that lowers their performance relative to the treatment condition. In all three cases the perceived unfairness of the outcome allocation leads to behaviors that confound comparisons between the control and experimental group and renders the evaluation of the program invalid.

### Norms for Procedural Justice

Perceptions of fairness are influenced not only by the distribution of outcomes but by the procedures used in allocating the outcomes. Perhaps the primary component of procedural justice is *voice* (Leventhal, 1980). Decisions are seen as fair to the extent that employees are allowed an opportunity to express their opinions and to the extent that policies and procedures are used consistently in making decisions. Procedural justice is an important determinant of the reactions of employees to HRM procedures such as training (Folger & Greenberg, 1985). For instance, Witt and Broach (1993) found that trainees were more satisfied with training when they perceived that there was procedural justice in the way the training was administered. This relationship was stronger for those with a strong exchange ideology defined by the belief that the organization's treatment of them should be reciprocated than for those with a weak exchange ideology.

In its reliance on scientific standards, the ISD model tends to violate norms for procedural justice in its authoritarian approach to designing, evaluating, and administering training. An objective analysis of training needs guides the design of a program. Moreover, the best approach to evaluating the effectiveness of training is through experimentation in which trainees are assigned randomly to training and no-training control conditions. The program can then be judged on the basis of whether it benefits learning, behavior, and performance (Kirkpatrick, 1977). In the actual implementation of the training, persons are assigned to programs if they have deficiencies that need correction and if they have the aptitude to benefit from the training.

In the interest of providing procedural justice, organizations deviate in several respects from these prescriptions. To the extent that systematic needs assessments are conducted, they tend to consist of self-reports of potential trainees. Although this practice could lead to more acceptance of the training (Noe & Schmitt, 1986), self-reports are vulnerable to biases and tend to differ from supervisor reports of training needs (McEnery & McEnery, 1987; Staley, Shockley-Zalaback, 1986; Tharenou, 1989). The most obvious way in which procedural fairness concerns can lead to violations of the ISD model is in the evaluation of training programs. The ISD approach presumes a rigorous evaluation of programs on the basis of criteria that are tightly linked to job specifications. However, as mentioned earlier, most organizations shun rigorous evaluations and rely instead on trainee testimonials. The use of happy sheets rather than hard data can lead to inaccurate conclusions but allows trainees a voice in the training process. For instance, student evaluations of teachers have many shortcomings as measures of teacher effectiveness but serve the important function of involving students in the instructional process.

Recent research suggests that providing trainees a voice is beneficial to achieving training objectives. Giving information to trainees on the nature of the training encourages use of what is learned in the program back on the job (Baldwin, Jagjuka, & Loher, 1991), engenders more positive reactions to the training (Alderfer, Alderfer, Bell, & Jones, 1992), and increases the motivation of trainees to learn (Hicks & Klimoski, 1987). Allowing trainees a choice in the types of training they receive also appears to yield a variety of positive outcomes (Baldwin et al., 1991; Hicks & Klimoski, 1987; Mathieu, Tannenbaum, & Salas, 1992; Ryman & Biersner, 1975). Despite these benefits, however, there is an inevitable tension between providing trainees with voice and the scientific objectivity that is essential to the ISD model. The concerns over providing voice may win out in the end over scientific concerns.

### The Potential Inflexibility of an ISD Approach

Organizations are complex social systems and both distributive and procedural justice could serve as the basis for fairness judgments. Moreover, these concerns can conflict with each other, and their strength can vary with the demands of the situation. Although the equity rule has received the most attention, need and equality also can become salient in some situations. For instance, when economic productivity is the primary goal, equity is the most salient rule, but when the primary goal is maintaining harmonious relationships, equality is dominant (Kabanoff, 1991). Those who design, implement, and evaluate training may desire sufficient flexibility to meet whatever norms are seen as dominant in the situation. An ISD model may strike some trainers and administrators as a threat to fairness as the result of being perceived as overly restrictive and impersonal.

## Acquiring and Maintaining Power

A fourth barrier to the rational approach derives from the political nature of organizations. Pfeffer has defined power as the ability to achieve desired outcomes and politics as the "activities taken within organizations to acquire, develop, and use power" (1981a, p. 7). Among the ways in which decision makers acquire power is by controlling the decision process and building coalitions (Pfeffer, 1981b) and through seeking situations that are sufficiently ambiguous that their actions cannot be closely scrutinized and monitored. These political behaviors can undermine rational HRM programs and can account at least in part for past failures of organizations to adopt rational practices (Ferris & Judge, in press; Johns, 1993). According to Kimberly, "no matter how impressive the performance characteristics of an innovation may be, its adoption and implementation will conflict with some interests and jeopardize some alliances" (1981, p. 93). This seems especially likely in training, in which politics can enter into the needs assessment, implementation, and evaluation of a program.

Politics occur in the assessment of needs because of the multiple and conflicting constituencies that invariably exist in complex organizations, including higher level managers, trainees, customers, and governmental agencies (Kossek, 1989; Tsui & Milkovich, 1987). In the attempt to deal with diverse constituencies, the design, implementation, and evaluation of training stray from the ISD model. Politics also occur insofar as training is used as an influence tactic. Training is not only a vehicle for imparting skills and knowledge required in the job but can be a reward or a punishment used to shape the behavior and attitudes of employees (Feldman, 1989; Nordhaug, 1989). The withholding of training can be used to thwart the career progress of some groups, as shown in discrimination in the allocation of training on the basis of gender and race. Informal, on-the-job training can be a means of coalition building. Politics are most apparent in the evaluation of training.

In an ideal situation, those responsible are continuously involved in evaluating and modifying training programs, but as discussed earlier, those involved in delivering and administering the training process too often fear public scrutiny of programs because of the potential threat to their careers. This threat increases as more money and effort are invested in the training program. Kerr noted, "The last thing many desire is a formal, systematic, and revealing evaluation. Although members of top management may actually hope for such systematic evaluation, their reward systems continue to reward ignorance in this area" (1975, p. 84). In the same vein, Cook and Shadish (1986) observed that the political nature of the real world has the effect of "forcing evaluators out of the cool world of pure analysis into a maelstrom of political and administrative complexity" (1986, p. 197). In this world,

> Policy makers, program officials, and project employees pursue their primary goals of keeping or improving their jobs and of promoting their beliefs, assigning these a higher priority than the evaluator's goal of identifying technically superior options for problem definition, program design, or problem amelioration. (pp. 197–198)

The failure to fully implement an ISD model of training in some cases reflects a lack of power on the part of those charged with implementing the training. The human resource department traditionally has little power in organizations relative to other departments. The trends toward the decentralizing and outsourcing of human resource functions may diminish even more the power of human resource professionals to take a systematic, scientific approach to training. For example, one of the largest insurance corporations recently found, unbeknownst to higher management, that a management training program based on Scientology and of dubious validity was being used as the basis for training supervisors (Sharpe, 1995), and the apparent explanation for the spread of this training was a restructuring of the company in which many of the responsibilities for human resource management were delegated to insurance agents rather than being dictated by a central department (Sharpe, 1995). The lack of central control and the unfamiliarity of agents in HRM led to the adoption and spread of the program. Even where there is a central training department that monitors training, training may be seen as a matter of administrative convenience for which there is no right or wrong approach (Johns, 1993). Training and development is not yet recognized as a profession that defines the expertise of its members through certification and formalized procedures (Hansen, Kahnweiler, & Wilensky, 1994, p. 265). As a consequence, expertise in needs assessment, measurement, and evaluation often go un-recognized while the opinions of outsiders with no formal expertise are seriously considered. Perhaps because they lack expert power, training professionals may be more concerned with providing programs that are fun and have a veneer of scientific credibility (e.g., right brain training) than in correcting deficiencies in knowledge, skills, and abilities. The powerlessness of training professionals and other change agents is exacerbated if they possess poor political skills and a poor understanding of organizational politics (Kumar & Thibodeaux, 1990). For instance, the ISD model seems likely to fail if professionals cannot convince top managers of the strategic advantages of using this approach (Dutton & Ashford, 1993).

## The Symbolic Functions of Training

The last and most inclusive reason that the training process deviates from prescriptions of a rational approach is the symbolic value of training to the organization. Dandridge, Mitroff, and Joyce (1980) described organizational symbols as actions, objects, and verbalizations used to represent the underlying values, beliefs, and feelings of the organization. Examples of organizational symbolism could include the company logo, the annual holiday party, an award presentation, the stories that are told about the past successes and failures of organizational members, and employee clothing. Organizational symbols frequently are extravagant, unrelated to the job, and even frivolous but can inspire, release tension, provide an interpretation of events, and direct the activities of organizational members (Dandridge et al., 1980).

If one looks beneath the manifest purpose of a training program, a rich variety of symbols can be discerned that are used in communicating important aspects of the organizational culture to employees. In some cases the training process consists of *rites,* which Trice and Beyer (1984) defined as unified events consolidating a number of cultural expressions in an elaborate and dramatic manner. In other cases they are ceremonials consisting of several rites in relation to an occasion or event. Other cultural forms that can occur in the training process are the telling of sagas (historical narratives about the accomplishments of the organization and its leaders), myths (dramatic descriptions of imagined events), stories (descriptions of true events containing some fiction and some truth), legends (an embellished recounting of an extraordinary event in the history of the group or organization), and folktales (completely fictitious stories). Trice, Belasco, and Alutto (1969) described managerial and supervisory training programs as rites of passage. In one company, candidates for supervisory positions took a 2-day battery of screening tests. Those who passed were placed in isolated training classes in which they were instructed in both the attitudes and techniques of supervision. Once they successfully completed these training courses, the trainees were promoted to supervisory rank and were honored in a ceremony in which the production superintendent gave a speech about the "ordeal" that the initiates had overcome. Although an evaluation by an objective third-party revealed that the training had failed to achieve its formal objectives, the authors found that the training persisted because it was perceived to be effective. The real function of this rite of passage, according to the authors, was not to improve task performance but instead to communicate the importance of the supervisory role and the competence of the new supervisor.

Training is not only used as a vehicle for communicating to members of the organization but also have symbolic value in managing the impressions that outsiders have of the organization. According to institutional theory, organizations engage in activities to gain the approval of important constituencies, and as a consequence, these activities often reflect "the myths of their institutional environments instead of the demands of their work activities" (Meyer & Rowan, 1977, p. 341). Thus, training procedures demonstrate to employees, professional organizations, potential customers, stockholders, competitors, and other audiences that the organization is doing the right things. This process of imitation can help explain the diffusion of training fads. For instance, Abrahamson (1991) has observed a pattern in the diffusion of administrative innovations in which a few large and prestigious organizations adopt the programs and then other organizations follow their lead to gain acceptance. Eventually the fashion fades as less prestigious organizations adopt the program and it loses its luster. A similar process is likely to occur in the waxing and waning of organizational training fads.

A cursory examination of training programs reveals a variety of images that organizations project in their training efforts. In all of these cases, the training has some substance but also is a vehicle for conveying desirable images of the organization to employees, shareholders, customers, and other stakeholders. The images conveyed include the following.

1. *This is an organization committed to diversity.* Diversity training communicates to employees, customers, shareholders, and other im-

portant constituencies the message that the organization is tolerant of differences in race, religion, and gender. Even where training fails in instilling this attitude, the program may succeed in communicating that the organization encourages diversity.

2. *Quality and customer service are our primary goals.* Organizations commonly espouse as a central value the importance of satisfying the needs of their customers and producing high quality goods and services. Training is frequently implemented to promote both of these values. Although specific skills are imparted, these types of training have the symbolic value of reinforcing the importance of these values to employees and to customers or clients.

3. *The employee is our most important asset.* Another common value espoused by organizations is support for the well-being and personal growth of its employees. Conveying this message in a dramatic and highly visible manner may be more important than actually instilling knowledge, skills, and abilities. For instance, the training efforts of organizations often are far removed from the immediate demands of the job and are more of a benefit or reward to the employee than an attempt to remedy task deficiencies.

4. *Management is in control and taking rational steps to solve our problems.* An organization may attempt to project an image that management is in control and taking rational steps to solve the problems facing the organization. Again, training is a visible symbol of such action. Floden and Weiner (1978) have noted that the evaluation of social programs serves as an important ritual that reduces anxieties and conveys the image of rationality even when it falls short on technical standards.

In the attempt to impress important constituents, organizations are likely to depart from many of the methods that are central to an ISD model of training. Scott and Meyer observed, "The tightly controlled training system, closely linked to very specific organizational tasks and purposes, is rarely to be found. Organizations tend to copy generally valued models, only loosely linked to their specific tasks and purposes" (1991, p. 322). In some cases the fulfillment of symbolic functions leads to the perpetuation of training that totally fails to fulfill its manifest purposes (Bolman & Deal, 1991; Trice et al., 1969). Training rituals can serve a variety of important objectives such as binding together the organization, firing the imagination, and deepening the beliefs of the participants, but they also can become a substitute for real action and effectively block innovation and change. Take, for example, the recent push to implement total quality management (TQM) in many organizations. Sending employees off to a week-long program in TQM symbolizes the commitment of the organization to the quality process, but the quality process often goes no further than the training program. The training can delude those inside and outside the organization into believing that something is being done to improve quality when in fact nothing of substance is being accomplished. Training programs are often labeled as if they were organization-wide interventions when they are actually very limited in scope (Golembiewski, 1992). The same substitution of training for action is found in a variety of programs such as training in leadership and diversity, motivation workshops, team building, and a variety of other programs. Kimberly (1981, p. 100) brought attention to the large gap that so often exists between the "rhetoric and the reality of managerial innovation." Kossek (1989) found that although management is more likely to see the symbolic value of HRM programs, those lower in the hierarchy see them as having more fluff than substance.

In summary, prescriptions of the ISD model are violated because training programs are used to express values important to both the culture and the institutional environment of the organization. In contrast, an ISD approach tends to restrict the program to knowledge, skills, and abilities that are job-related, and tends to discourage the rich mix of behaviors that are important to maintaining and communicating the values of the organization. Training is part of an impression management strategy in which organizations convince their constituencies and their employees that they are doing something that is beneficial. In many cases the symbolism is useful. When organizations confront poorly understood problems that require intuition, symbols provide a rich source of information that are used in understanding the situation (Daft, 1983; Pfeffer, 1981b). Managers use the training process to reduce uncertainty and build a consensus, but in some cases this symbolic use of training impedes effective action.

## When Is ISD Most Likely to Be Successfully Implemented?

The focus of this chapter is on deviations from the ISD model of training, but rational processes such as this are not always rejected and may succeed. Thompson (1967) proposed a topology of management control that suggests conditions in which a rational approach such as ISD is more likely to be successfully implemented than a nonrational approach. According to this topology, the management control used in an organization depends on both (a) the completeness of knowledge of cause–effect relationships, and (b) the degree to which there are crystallized standards of desirable performance that can be used to evaluate outcomes. When there is a high degree of knowledge of cause–effect relationships and crystallized standards, organizations find it easier to use rational procedures in their attempts at management control. To the extent that the standards for evaluating performance are unclear and the knowledge of cause–effect relations incomplete, organizations are more likely to deviate from rational standards. On the basis of Thompson's theory, one could propose that an ISD model is more likely to be adopted as knowledge of cause–effect relationships and agreement on standards for evaluating performance increase. When there is inadequate understanding of cause–effect relations and disagreement regarding performance standards, an ISD model is not only less likely to be adopted, but if it is implemented, may impose a false structure on an inherently unstructured situation. For instance, using a set of narrow criteria to evaluate training in a situation in which there is considerable disagreement on performance standards runs the risk of imposing an overly simplistic and deficient model of performance on trainers and trainees.

Similar arguments have been proposed by other theorists, although previous theories have not examined training specifically. Murray and Dimick (1978) built on Thompson's (1967) model to propose that the environment frequently presents serious impediments to rationally evaluating HRM procedures and as a consequence allows factors other than technical rationality to influence the choice of policy and program choices. Pfeffer (1981a, p. 70) has suggested that where there is disagreement among decision makers on goals as well as preferred outcomes, rational criteria cannot be used and politics is the only way to resolve disputes and make decisions (p. 70). Johns (1993) proposed that uncertainty is inherent in HRM practices and, as a consequence, organizational decision makers rely on politics and imitation rather than technical merit when choosing among alternative practices. The result is that organizations are prone to adopt the latest management fad and ignore practices that have been supported in the research. Where there is less uncertainty, decision makers are more receptive to technical arguments.

## Conclusion

In this chapter I have discussed a variety of forces that can hinder the application of an ISD model of training in organizations. I would not argue that the ISD model should therefore be discarded, however. To the contrary, organizations should make greater use of ISD models, especially where there is consensus as to the standards for evaluation and knowledge of cause–effect relationships. However, a more dynamic perspective is needed to replace the mechanistic approaches that seem to characterize the ISD approach to organizational training. This alternative view of training would incorporate the dynamic interplay among training programs, the larger social system, and the personal needs of those implementing the programs. The success of a program would be seen in this broader conceptualization as depending on more than fulfilling task-based criteria but also on whether the training fulfills functions defined by the larger system. These other functions would include the various factors that have been discussed here as barriers to ISD— that is, meeting the personal needs of those using the training, providing a good fit to the job context, maintaining power, complying with norms for justice, and conveying the values of the organizational culture. Rather than viewed as mere barriers, these other functions need to be recognized as legitimate concerns. The ISD approach to training can contribute to organizational effectiveness, but it is important to recognize that training serves a variety of legitimate organizational functions besides providing a good fit of the person to the job. Programs are often doomed to failure because these other functions are overlooked in the planning, implementation, and evaluation of the training.

Integrative solutions are needed in which training incorporates contextual concerns such as providing a good fit to the organization and satisfying the personal needs of users. To start with, needs assessment should go beyond the knowledge, skills, and abilities of a job to include the organizational system. I agree with Jackson and Schuler that " . . . future HRM research should elevate organization analysis (and perhaps extra-organization analysis) to a status equal to that currently enjoyed by job analysis" (1995, p. 18). An organizational analysis should be expanded to include an inventory of the attitudes of those who are actually implementing it, the values and norms of the culture, contextual performances, power dynamics, justice concerns, and the institutional environment. Efforts should be taken to develop an integrative conception of HRM in which training is not an isolated activity but a part of a coherent system that includes selection, appraisal, compensation, and other HRM functions. Psychologists involved in training perhaps need to redefine their roles so that they become change agents rather than technicians (Beer & Spector, 1984). Finally, those responsible for the design and implementation of training systems could learn from the research on sociotechnical systems interventions and involve those who will implement the training in the design of the programs.

The rational approach to training represents a major advance in HRM practice. Nevertheless, organizations often appear to stray from this model as the result of a variety of organizational factors. The ISD model needs to incorporate a broader view of the training process in which fulfilling these other functions is integrated with traditional concerns over correcting deficiencies in knowledge, skills, and abilities.

## References

Abrahamson, E. (1991). Managerial fads and fashions: The diffusion and rejection of innovations. *Academy of Management Review, 16*, 586–612.

Albert, S. and associates. (1985). Cultural development through human resource systems integration. *Training and Development Journal, 39*, 76–81.

Alderfer, C. P., Alderfer, C. J., Bell, E. L., & Jones, J. (1992). The race relations competence workshop: Theory and results. *Human Relations, 45*, 1259–1291.

Alexander, G. P. (1987). Establishing shared values through management training programs. *Training and Development Journal, 41*, 45–47.

Argyris, C. (1990). Inappropriate defenses against the monitoring of organization development practice. *The Journal of Applied Behavioral Science, 26*, 299–312.

Ash, R. A., Levine, E. L., & Sistrunk, F. (1983). The role of jobs and job-based methods in personnel and human resource management. In K. Rowland & G. Ferris (Eds.), *Research in personnel and human resources management* (pp. 45–84). Greenwich, CT: JAI Press.

Baldwin, T. T., & Ford, J. K. (1988). Transfer of training: A review and directions for future research. *Personnel Psychology, 41*, 63–105.

Baldwin, T. T., Magjuka, R. J., & Loher, B. T. (1991). The perils of participation: Effects of choice on training on trainee motivation and learning. *Personnel Psychology, 44*, 51–66.

Beach, L. R. (1990). *Image theory: Decision making in personal and organizational contexts.* Chichester, England: John Wiley.

Beer, M., & Spector, B. A. (1984). Human resources management: The integration of industrial relations and organization development. In K. Rowland & G. Ferris (Eds.), *Research in personnel and human resources management* (Vol. 2, pp. 261–298). Greenwich, CT: JAI Press.

Bierhoff, H. W., Cohen, R. L., & Greenberg, J. (1986). *Justice in social relations.* New York: Plenum Press.

Bjork, R. A. (1979). Information-processing analysis of college teaching. *Educational Psychology, 14,* 15–23.

Bolman, L. G., & Deal, T. E. (1991). Reframing organizations: Artistry, choice, and leadership. San Francisco: Jossey-Bass.

Borman, W. C., & Motowidlo, S. J. (1993). Expanding the criterion domain to include elements of contextual performance. In N. Schmitt & W. C. Borman (Eds.), *Personnel selection in organizations* (pp. 71–99). San Francisco: Jossey-Bass.

Bretz, R. D., Jr., & Thompsett, R. E. (1992). Comparing traditional and integrative learning methods in organizational training programs. *Journal of Applied Psychology, 77,* 941–951.

Burke, M. J., & Day, R. R. (1986). A cumulative study of the effectiveness of managerial training. *Journal of Applied Psychology, 71,* 232–245.

Campbell, J. P. (1971). Personnel training and development. In *Annual Review of Psychology.* Palo Alto: CA: Annual Reviews.

Campbell, J. P., & Dunnette, M. D. (1968). Effectiveness of T-group experiences in managerial training and development. *Psychological Bulletin, 70,* 73–104.

Carnevale, A. P. (1995). Enhancing skills in the new economy. In A. Howard (Ed.), *The changing nature of work* (pp. 238–251). San Francisco: Jossey-Bass.

Cascio, W. F. (1989). Using utility analysis to assess training outcomes. In I. L. Goldstein (Ed.), *Training and development in organizations* (pp. 63–89). San Francisco: Jossey-Bass.

Cohen, M. D., March, J. G., & Olsen, J. P. (1972). A garbage can model of organizational choice. *Administrative Science Quarterly, 17,* 1–25.

Cohen, R. L. (1987). Distributive justice: Theory and research. *Social Justice Research,* 1, 19–40.

Cook, T. D., & Campbell, D. T. (1979). *Quasi-experimentation: Design and analysis issues for field settings.* Chicago: Rand McNally.

Cook, T. D., & Shadish, W. R., Jr. (1986). Program evaluation: The worldly science. In M. R. Rosenzweig & L. W. Porter (Eds.), *Annual review of psychology* (pp. 193–232). Palo Alto, CA: Annual Reviews.

Cronbach, L. J. (1975). Beyond the two disciplines of scientific psychology. *American Psychologist, 30,* 116–127.

Daft, R. (1983). Symbols in organizations: A dual-content framework for analysis. In L. R. Pondy, P. J. Frost, G. Morgan, & T. C. Dandridge (Eds.), *Organizational symbolism* (pp. 197–207). Greenwich, CT: JAI Press.

Dandridge, T. C., Mitroff, I., & Joyce, W. F. (1980). Organizational symbolism: A topic to expand organizational analysis. *Academy of Management Review, 5,* 77–82.

Dempster, F. N. (1990). The spacing effect: A case study in the failure to apply the results of psychological research. *American Psychologist, 43,* 627–634.

Deutsch, M. (1975). Equity, equality, and need: What determines which value will be used as the basis of distributive justice? *Journal of Social Issues,* 31, 137–149.

Dixon, N. M. (1987). Meet training's goals without reaction forms. *Personnel Journal, 66,* 108–115.

Dobbins, G. H., Cardy, R. L., & Carson, K. (1991). Examining fundamental assumptions: A contrast of person and system approaches to human resource management. In G. R. Ferris & K. R. Rowland (Eds.), *Research in personnel and human resources management* (Vol. 9, pp. 1–38). Greenwich, CT: JAI Press.

Druckman, D., & Bjork, R. (1991). *In the mind's eye: Enhancing human performance.* Washington, DC: National Academy Press.

Dutton, J. E., & Ashford, S. J. (1993). Selling issues to top management. *Academy of Management Review, 18,* 397–428.

Dyer, W. G. (1987). *Team building: Issues and alternatives.* Reading, MA: Addison-Wesley.

Feldman, D. C. (1989). Socialization, resocialization, and training: Reframing the research agenda. In I. L. Goldstein (Ed.), *Training and development in organizations* (pp. 376–416). San Francisco: Jossey-Bass.

Ferris, G. R., & Judge, T. A. (in press). Personnel/human resources management: A political influence perspective. *Journal of Management.*

Fisher, C. D. (1986). Organizational socialization: An integrative review. In K. M. Rowland & G. R. Ferris (Eds.), *Research in Personnel and Human Resources Management* (Vol. 4, pp. 101–145). Greenwich, CT: JAI Press.

Floden, R. E., & Weiner, S. S. (1978). Rationality to ritual: The multiple roles of evaluation in governmental processes. *Policy Sciences, 9,* 9–18.

Folger, R., & Greenberg, J. (1985). Procedural justice: An interpretative analysis of personnel systems. In K. M. Rowland & G. R. Ferris (Eds.), *Research in personnel and human resources management* (Vol. 3, pp. 141–183). Greenwich, CT: JAI Press.

Gagne, R. M. (1984). Learning outcomes and their effects: Useful categories of human performance. *American Psychologist, 39,* 377–385.

Goldstein, I. L. (1980). Training in work organizations. In M. R. Rosenzweig & L. W. Porter (Eds.), *Annual review of psychology* (pp. 329–372). Palo Alto, CA: Annual Reviews.

Goldstein, I. L. (1991). Training in work organizations. In M. D. Dunnette & L. M. Hough (Eds.), *Handbook of industrial and organizational psychology* (2nd ed., pp. 507–619). Palo Alto, CA: Consulting Psychologists Press.

Goldstein, I. L. (1993). *Training in organizations: Needs assessment, development and evaluation.* Monterey, CA: Brooks/Cole.

Golembiewski, R. T. (1992). The "D" in organization development: Deepening a sense of the obvious. *Organization Development Journal, 10,* 11–14.

Gray, D. B., Connor, S., Decatur, M. (1994). The belief in equality inventory and leadership behavior: A construct validation. *Journal of Applied Social Psychology, 24,* 367–377.

Guzzo, R. A., Jette, R. D., & Katzell, R. A. (1985). The effects of psychologically based intervention programs on worker productivity: A meta-analysis. *Personnel Psychology, 38,* 275–292.

Hansen, C. D., Kahnweiler, W. M., & Wilensky, A. S. (1994). Human resource development as an occupational culture through organizational stories. *Human Resource Developmental Quarterly, 5,* 253–267.

Hicks, W. D., & Klimoski, R. J. (1987). Entry into training programs and its effects on training outcomes: A field experiment. *Academy of Management Journal, 30,* 542–552.

Hines, T. (1987). Left brain/right brain mythology and implications for management and training. *Academy of Management Review, 12,* 600–606.

Hinrichs, J. R. (1976). Personnel training. In M. D. Dunnette (Ed.), *The handbook of industrial and organizational psychology* (pp. 829–860). Chicago: Rand McNally.

Hollister, L. A., Day, N. E., & Jesaitis, P. T. (1993). Diversity programs: Key to competitiveness or just another fad? *Organization Development Journal, 11,* 49–59.

Isenberg, D. J. (November/December, 1984). How senior managers think. *Harvard Business Review, 62,* 81–90.

Jackson, S. E., & Schuler, R. S. (1995). Understanding human resource management in the context of organizations and their environments. In M. R. Rosenzweig and

L. W. Porter (Eds.), *Annual Review of Psychology* (p. 33). Palo Alto, CA: Annual Reviews.

Johns, G. (1993). Constraints on the adoption of psychology-based personnel practices: Lessons from organizational innovation. *Personnel Psychology, 46,* 569–592.

Kabanoff, B. (1991). Equity, equality, power, and conflict. *Academy of Management Review, 16,* 416–441.

Kerr, S. (1975). On the folly of rewarding A, while hoping for B. *Academy of Management Journal, 18,* 769–783.

Kimberly, J. R. (1981). Managerial innovation. In Paul C. Nystrom & W. H. Starbuck (Eds.), *Handbook of organizational design* (Vol 1., pp. 84–104). Oxford: Oxford University Press.

Kirkpatrick, D. L. (1977). Evaluating training programs: Evidence versus proof. *Training and Development Journal, 31,* 9–12.

Kirrane, D. E. (1986). Cost accounting today. *Training and Development Journal, 40,* 24–27.

Komaroff, A. L. (1982). Algorithms and the "art" of medicine. *American Journal of Public Health, 72,* 10–12.

Kossek, E. E. (1989). The acceptance of human resource innovation by multiple constituencies. *Personnel Psychology, 42,* 263–281.

Kraiger, K., Ford, J., & Salas, E. (1993). Application of cognitive, skill-based, and affective theories of learning outcomes to new methods of training evaluation. *Journal of Applied Psychology, 79,* 311–328.

Kumar, K., & Thibodeaux, M. S. (1990). Organizational politics and planned organizational change: A pragmatic approach. *Group and Organization Studies, 15,* 357–365.

Laabs, J. J. (1991, June). Team training goes outdoors. *Personnel Journal, 70,* 56–63.

Labor letter. (1991, October 22). *Wall Street Journal,* p. A1.

Lado, A. A., & Wilson, M. C. (1994). Human resource systems and sustained competitive advantage: A competency-based perspective. *Academy of Management Review, 19,* 699–727.

Latham, G. P. (1988). Human resource training and development. In M. R. Rosenzweig & L. W. Porter (Eds.), *Annual review of psychology* (pp. 545–582). Palo Alto, CA: Annual Reviews.

Latham, G. P., & Whyte, G. (1994). The futility of utility analysis. *Personnel Psychology, 47,* 31–46.

Lawler, E. E. III (1994). From job-based to competency-based organizations. *Journal of Organizational Behavior, 15,* 3–15.

Leach, J. A. (1991). Characteristics of excellent trainers: A psychological and interpersonal profile. *Performance Improvement Quarterly, 4,* 42–62.

Leventhal, G. S. (1980). What should be done with equity theory? New approaches to the study of fairness in social relationships. In K. G. Gergen, M. S. Greenberg, & R. H. Willis (Eds.), *Social exchange: Advances in theory and research* (pp. 27–55). New York: Plenum Press.

Levinson, H. (1992). Fads, fantasies and psychological management. *Consulting Psychology Journal: Practice and Research, 44,* 1–12.

Lewis, L. K., & Seibold, D. R. (1993). Innovation modification during intraorganizational adoption. *Academy of Management Review, 18,* 322–354.

Lindblom, C. E. (1959). The science of "muddling through." *Administration Review, 19,* 79–88.

Martocchio, J. J. (1992). Microcomputer usage as an opportunity: The influence of context in employee training. *Personnel Psychology, 45,* 529–552.

Marx, R. D. (1982). Relapse prevention of managerial training: A model for maintenance of behavior change. *Academy of Management Review, 7,* 433–441.

Mathieu, J. E., Tannenbaum, S. I., & Salas, E. (1992). Influences of individual and situational characteristics on measures of training effectiveness. *Academy of Management Journal, 35,* 828–847.

McEnery, J., & McEnery, J. M. (1987). Self-rating in management training needs assessment. A neglected opportunity? *Journal of Occupational Psychology, 60,* 49–60.

Meyer, J. W., & Rowan, B. (1977). Institutionalized organizations: Formal structure as myth and ceremony. *American Journal of Sociology, 83,* 340–363.

Mintzberg, H., Raisinghani, D., & Theoret, A. (1976). The structure of "unstructured" decision processes. *Administrative Science Quarterly, 21,* 246–275.

Morrison, J. E. (1991). Introduction. In J. E. Morrison (Ed.), *Training for performance: Principles of applied human learning* (pp. 1–10). Chichester, England: John Wiley.

Murray, V. V., & Dimick, D. E. (1978). Contextual influences on personnel policies and programs: An explanatory model. *Academy of Management Review, 3,* 750–761.

Noe, R. A., & Ford, J. K. (1992). Emerging issues and new directions for training research. In G. R. Ferris & K. M. Rowland (Eds.), *Research in personnel and human resources management* (pp. 345–385). Greenwich, CT: JAI Press.

Noe, R. A., & Schmitt, N. (1986). The influence of trainee attitudes on training effectiveness: Test of a model. *Personnel Psychology, 39,* 497–523.

Nordhaug, O. (1989). Reward functions of personnel training. *Human Relations, 42,* 373–388.

Pfeffer, J. (1981a). *Power in organizations.* Marshfield, MA: Pittman.

Pfeffer, J. (1981b). Management as symbolic action: The creation and maintenance of organizational paradigms. In L. L. Cummings & B. M. Staw (Eds.), *Research in organizational behavior* (pp. 1–52). Greenwich, CT: JAI Press.

Rouiller, J. Z., & Goldstein, I. L. (1993). The relationship between organizational transfer, climate, and positive transfer of training. *Human Resource Development Quarterly, 4,* 377–390.

Russell, J. S., Terborg, J. R., & Powers, M. L. (1985). Organizational performance and organizational level training and support. *Personnel Psychology, 38,* 849–863.

Ryder, J. M., Redding, R. E., & Beckschi, P. F. (1987). Training development for complex cognitive tasks. *Proceedings for the Thirty-first Annual Meeting of the Human Factors Society, 2,* 1261–1265.

Ryman, D. H., & Biersner, R. J. (1975). Attitudes predictive of diving success. *Personnel Psychology, 28,* 465–481.

Saari, L. M., Johnson, T. R., McLaughlin, S. D., & Zimmerle, D. M. (1988). A survey of management training and education practices in U. S. companies. *Personnel Psychology, 41,* 731–743.

Sackett, P. R., & Mullen, E. J. (1993). Beyond formal experimental design: Towards an expanded view of the training evaluation process. *Personnel Psychology, 46,* 613–627.

Schein, E. H. (1968). Organizational socialization and the profession of management. *Industrial Management Review, 9,* 1–16.

Scott, W. R., & Meyer, J. W. (1991). The rise of training programs in firms and agencies: An institutional perspective. In L. L. Cummings and B. Staw (Eds.), *Research in Organizational Behavior, 13,* 297–326.

Sharpe, R. (1995, March 22). How Allstate applied Scientology methods to train its managers. *Wall Street Journal,* pp. A1, A4.

Smith, R. G. (1971). *The engineering of educational and training systems.* Lexington, MA: Heath Lexington Books.

Staley, C. C., & Shockley-Zalabak, P. (1986). Communication proficiency and future training needs of the female professional: Self-assessment vs. superior's evaluation. *Human Relations, 39,* 891–902.

Tannenbaum, S. I., & Yukl, G. (1992). Training and development in work organizations. In M. R. Rosenzweig & L. W. Porter (Eds.), *Annual review of psychology* (pp. 399–441). Palo Alto, CA: Annual Reviews.

Tharenou, P. (1989). Management training needs analysis by self-report questionnaire: Managers' identified needs and preferred training strategies. *Academy of Management Best Paper Proceedings* (pp. 137–141).

Thompson, J. D. (1967). *Organizations in action.* New York: McGraw-Hill.

Townley, B. (1993). Foucault, power/knowledge, and its relevance for human resource management. *Academy of Management Review, 18,* 518–545.

Trice, H. M., Belasco, J., & Alutto, J. A. (1969). The role of ceremonials in organizational behavior. *Industrial and Labor Relations Review, 23,* 40–51.

Trice, H. M., & Beyer, J. M. (1984). Studying organizational cultures through rites and ceremonials. *Academy of Management Review, 9,* 653–669.

Tsui, A. S., & Milkovich, G. T. (1987). Personnel department activities: Constituency perspectives and preferences. *Personnel Psychology, 40,* 519–537.

Webster, J., & Martocchio, J. J. (1993). Turning work into play: Implications for microcomputer software training. *Journal of Management, 19,* 127–146.

Wehrenberg, S. B. (1986). The vicious circle of training and organizational development. *Personnel Journal, 65,* 98–100.

Weick, K. E. (1979). *The social psychology of organizing.* Reading, MA: Addison-Wesley.

Wexley, K. N. (1984). Personnel training. In M. R. Rosenzweig & L. W. Porter (Eds.), *Annual Review of Psychology, 34,* 519–551.

Wiener, Y. (1988). Forms of value systems: A focus on organizational effectiveness and cultural change and maintenance. *Academy of Management Review, 13,* 534–545.

Witt, L. A., & Broach, D. (1993). Exchange ideology as a moderator of the procedural justice-satisfaction relationship. *Journal of Social Psychology, 133,* 97–103.

Yancey, G. B., & Kelly, L. (1990). The inappropriateness of using participants' reactions to evaluate effectiveness of training. *Psychological Reports, 66,* 937–938.

# Part Two

# Optimizing Learning by Structuring Training

The major objective in designing training is to optimize transfer to the job environment. Traditional instruction programs have focused on the knowledge required to perform a job, but this may be done at the expense of integrating knowledge and skill. An increasing trend to organize workers into groups that perform a function or that are process-based rather than task-based, makes it even more critical that the requisite knowledge is well-integrated with required procedural skills. The three chapters in this section examine experimental support for different principles of training design that focus on how skill is acquired and how easily knowledge will be retrieved and used when job performance demands it.

In chapter 3, Ghodsian, Bjork, and Benjamin provide a survey of the literature that focuses on the essential distinction between learning and performance and discuss ways of structuring the learning environment to provide optimal transfer (i.e., learning), rather than just good performance during training. They tackle the difficult problem of satisfying the various goals of the individuals providing the training (to get positive feedback from the individuals and organization), the goals of the organization (having better trained employees), and the goals of the trainees (feeling of accomplishment, that they are better equipped to perform the work). Thus, in this chapter we see cognitive psychologists considering organizational, as well as individual, problems.

One of the goals of this book was to bring together the perspectives of the cognitive psychologist, the human factors engineer, and the industrial–organizational psychologist. In chapter 4, Smith, Ford, and

Kozlowski satisfy this objective by bringing the industrial–organizational view to bear on much research in cognitive and educational psychology. The chapter outlines a framework in which to apply principles of learning, such as those outlined by Ghodsian and colleagues in chapter 3 and by Carroll and Atlas and colleagues in a later section (see chapter 12).

In a sense, all three chapters challenge the common assertion that "practice makes perfect." In chapter 5, Ehrenstein, Walker, Czerwinski, and Feldman survey research that shows that, even in some relatively simple tasks, there seem to be fundamental limitations in what people can learn. In particular, the chapter shows that a simple associationistic view, in which it is presumed that people learn to associate particular stimuli with particular responses, fails to capture some basic properties of human learning. The chapter demonstrates the importance of both stimulus and practice context, while exposing some basic characteristics of task performance.

The three chapters in this section point to important research findings in learning and skill acquisition. Moreover, they suggest ways that these research findings can shape and improve programs of training and job design.

# Evaluating Training *During* Training: Obstacles and Opportunities

**Dina Ghodsian, Robert A. Bjork, and Aaron S. Benjamin**

The conditions of training can be manipulated in a great variety of ways, producing multiple possible configurations of a given training program. Trainees' posttraining performance, in turn, is heavily influenced by such manipulations: Some configurations of the conditions of training are far better than others. It is of obvious importance to choose those configurations that optimize the conditions of training, but doing so depends on accurate assessment, which itself can pose formidable difficulties.

One problem is that trainees' performance *during* training is an unreliable indicator of posttraining performance. Manipulations that enhance performance during training can yield poor long-term posttraining performance, and other manipulations that seem to create difficulties and slow the rate of learning can be optimal in terms of long-term performance (see Christina & Bjork, 1991; Schmidt & Bjork, 1992). Another problem is that trainees' own subjective evaluations of their knowledge and capabilities can be misguided, leading them to prefer nonoptimal training regimens (see Bjork, 1994b; Jacoby, Bjork, & Kelley, 1994).

Given those problems, it may seem obvious that one should assess training programs in terms of trainees' posttraining performance in the real-world settings that are the target of training. Optimizing on-the-job performance is, after all, the goal of typical training programs. For a variety of institutional reasons, however, assessing on-the-job performance in a meaningful way is often impractical, if not impossible.

It is the mission of this chapter to consider a question of theoretical interest and practical importance: Are there some measures of performance obtainable during training that might serve as viable indicators of the degree to which the long-term goals of training are being met? In part to motivate the consideration of such measures, should they exist, we first summarize the difficulties and disadvantages of trying to use on-the-job performance as a measure of training. We then summarize the reasons why typical measures of in-training performance, both objective and subjective, are unreliable indicators of learning. We conclude by proposing some innovations in training programs that might provide more reliable measures of learning.

## Impediments to Posttraining Assessment

Posttraining measures of on-the-job performance are potentially the most valid measures of a training program's effectiveness, but in practice, obtaining such measures is often difficult. There are both practical difficulties and institutional impediments that can preclude the collection or timely acquisition of posttraining data. We summarize a few of those difficulties and impediments in this section. (For a more complete discussion, see Bjork, 1994a.)

*Practical Difficulties.* In some cases, training is administered by an independent entity or by a training division so isolated from the rest of the organization that trainers simply do not have access to trainees once training is completed. In other cases, the lag between completion of the training program and receipt of posttraining data by training personnel is too long for the information to be of use in modifying the training regimen. Further, organizational units responsible for posttraining operations may lack the staff and resources necessary for extensive on-the-job assessment, or they may be deterred by the sensitive nature of such assessment. Testing in the work environment can cause significant apprehension by those being evaluated and may hinder normal operations.

*Institutional Impediments.* In addition to such relatively passive deterrents of adequate posttraining assessment, there are a number of more active institutional impediments. Often, there is resistance to the collection of field data, driven by a fear of liability. If an analysis of performance on the job reveals inadequate training, the training institution could face legal and financial penalties. Hence, management settles on a policy of ignorance. Another source of resistance to the measurement of posttraining proficiency relates to the cost of retraining. If it is determined that an individual is performing at a substandard level, there is a pressure to retrain (or release) that individual. However, each time a person is sent back for retraining, there are costs to the organization. Again, in such an instance, the solution settled on is simply to remain unaware of the deficiency, under the assumption that what you don't know will probably hurt you less than what you might find out.

The numerous financial, organizational, and political deterrents just enumerated can eliminate posttraining assessment as a practical option in many settings. The other option is to assess training *during* training. As mentioned earlier, however, current methods of in-training assessment often provide unreliable indicators of long-term performance. Nevertheless, we believe that it is worth looking again at the potential for in-training assessment in the light of certain salient characteristics of human learning and memory.

## Obstacles to In-Training Assessment

Individuals attempting to assess a training program's effectiveness can draw on two categories of measures—objective measures and subjective measures. *Objective measures* include tests of performance during training and tests administered at the end of training. *Subjective measures* include trainees' evaluations of training, often assessed on "smile sheets" or "happy sheets" administered at the end of training, and a trainer's own sense of satisfaction with the program (see Goldstein, 1993, for a discussion of evaluation techniques). Both objective and subjective measures of training effectiveness can be flawed indicators. They can be tainted or misinterpreted in ways that may lead to dramatic errors in assessment.

### Interpreting Objective Performance

Of primary importance in the evaluation of the efficacy of a particular training regimen is assessing the *objective* state of a trainee's learning. Because performance on seemingly "objective" tests during learning can be biased by factors that will not be influential at a later time or in different circumstances, it is important to delineate those confounds known to obscure the relationship between actual long-term learning and performance on tests administered during learning.

## Learning Versus Performance

Probably the most fundamental oversight on the part of a trainer is a failure to recognize the distinction between observed performance and actual learning. *Learning* is meant to refer to relatively permanent changes underlying behavior, brought about by manipulations of the conditions of training. The overt characteristics of behavior, which at a given time may or may not reflect such permanent changes, are referred to as *performance*. As Schmidt (1988) pointed out, performance during training can be propped up or impaired by short-term factors that are unique to the conditions of training and that may mask the actual level of learning that has been achieved.

One simple example is the effect of fatigue. Several studies have shown that although fatigue may depress performance during the acquisition of a skill, its effects on learning—as measured on delayed tests of retention—are frequently negligible (e.g., Alderman, 1965; Carron, 1969; Cotten, Thomas, Spieth, & Biasiotto, 1972; Schmidt, 1969; for a review, see Chamberlin & Lee, 1993). Schmidt (1969), for example, investigated the effect of fatigue on learning a ladder-climbing skill. All research participants performed a series of trials that involved climbing and balancing a free-standing ladder with an unfamiliar spacing between rungs. They were instructed to climb the ladder until it toppled over, as many times as possible in ten 30-second trials. Between trials, participants rode a stationary bicycle. The intensity of the exercise between trials was varied to induce different levels of fatigue. Whereas performance on the ladder-climbing task suffered with increased fatigue during the acquisition of the skill, there was no significant effect of fatigue on later ladder-climbing performance as measured by a retention test administered 2 days after the end of training. This experiment and others suggest that in the absence of knowledge about retention performance, an instructor observing the training performance of fatigued learners could easily and erroneously deem the training ineffective. It is thus crucial for an instructor to recognize that a given manipulation of the conditions of training can have vastly different short-term and long-term consequences.

## Short-Term Versus Long-Term Consequences of Training

Just as fatigue acts to depress performance levels temporarily, other factors can artificially enhance training performance. Massing practice in a relatively short period of time often results in rapid improvement and high levels of performance during training (see, e.g., Bahrick, 1979;

Estes, 1955). Trainers are encouraged by such impressive results and can thereby be shaped into providing massed practice to keep performance levels high. Also, dividing a to-be-learned task into subtasks, which can seem a good idea to trainers, can result in massed practice on one subtask before the next subtask is introduced. For these reasons, there is a motivation for those responsible for training to implement massed training sessions. This motivation rests on the assumption— often false—that high levels of performance during training reflect high levels of learning.

There is evidence that during massed practice, learners can use the multiple, immediate repetitions to bypass some of the processes normally involved in producing a behavior: They simply repeat their performance from previous attempts (see, e.g., Jacoby, 1978). As a consequence, performance appears good during training, but little learning is actually achieved. In fact, after massed practice, performance tends to fall dramatically over periods of disuse. The opposite effect results from spaced practice. Trainees following a spaced practice schedule usually look worse than their counterparts engaging in massed practice during training but show significantly higher levels of retention at a delay (see, e.g., Baddeley & Longman, 1978; Bahrick, 1979; and Melton, 1970).

If a trainer can recognize that high levels of performance do not necessarily imply a high degree of learning, the goals of training can be shifted to a deeper level, at which future capabilities are given precedence over present functioning. Indeed, research on learning conducted in multiple domains suggests that instructors should introduce "desirable difficulties" for the learner during training in order to enhance long-term retention and transfer of skills to novel situations (Bjork, 1994b). Some examples of practice manipulations that depress performance during training but lead to a high level of long-term retention are discussed in the next paragraphs. (Also see Schmidt & Bjork, 1992.)

***Reduced Feedback Frequency.*** One particularly counterintuitive learning effect is the effect of reducing the frequency of feedback provided to the learner. Here, the finding is that individuals who receive feedback about their performance after every attempt during training tend to perform more poorly on subsequent tests of retention than do individuals receiving less frequent feedback. Of course, there are limits to this generalization, as it is clear that some feedback is almost always better than no feedback.

The clearest evidence for an effect of reduced feedback frequency comes from motor-learning experiments, where feedback is often termed KR (knowledge of results). In an extensive review of the early literature on KR, Salmoni, Schmidt, and Walter (1984) noted the opposite effects of reduced feedback on performance during the acquisition of a skill and on retention performance. Winstein and Schmidt (1990) subsequently reported a set of experiments that nicely illustrated the effect. They used a horizontal lever moving task, in which individuals were to reproduce as accurately as possible a goal trajectory and movement time. They showed that reduced feedback at acquisition resulted in better performance on a no-KR retention test than did 100% feedback. Perhaps more interesting to note, however, was that the same effect was obtained when the retention test was conducted under conditions of 100% feedback (Experiment 3). That is, the benefits of reduced feedback frequency seemed to operate independently of the superficial similarity between acquisition and test conditions.

In a somewhat more applied study, Schooler and Anderson (1990) studied the effects of reducing feedback in the context of learning the computer language LISP. Training was to a large extent self-paced, and in addition to the enforced feedback differences between groups (high versus low frequency), there was some variation in the frequency of feedback administered within groups, depending on the specific nature of the errors made by individuals. Under these more relaxed conditions, retention was still facilitated by a decrease in the number of feedback presentations.

*Variable Practice.* Another effect that is robust across multiple domains is the advantage of variable practice. Experience with several versions of a task or materials during practice (variable practice), as opposed to only one version (constant practice), is often advantageous for learning as measured on a subsequent retention or transfer test. One characteristic of variable practice less marked in the other practice manipulations discussed here is that it results in a greater capability to generalize the knowledge or skills acquired during training to novel situations (see Lee, Magill, & Weeks, 1985; Van Rossum, 1990, for reviews).

The effects of variable practice are illustrated in an experiment by Catalano and Kleiner (1984). Participants in their experiment were seated perpendicular to a column of lights that, when illuminated in sequence, simulated movement toward the individual. The participants' task was to push a button coincident with the arrival of the "moving" lights. Participants in the variable–practice condition performed ten trials at each of four different light speeds—5, 7, 9, and 11 mph—whereas participants in the constant-practice condition performed all 40 training trials at one of those four speeds. The transfer test consisted of five trials at either 1, 3, 13, or 15 mph (all outside the range of speeds experienced during training). Whereas during training participants in the constant group showed lower error scores than participants in the variable group, the reverse was true on the transfer test. On that test, participants in the variable group produced a significantly lower mean error score than participants in the constant group, supporting the claim that variable practice enhances a learner's capability to generalize from specific training tasks to novel conditions.

There is also some evidence that it may be beneficial to induce more variability during training than one expects to encounter in the setting that is the target of that training (see Bjork, 1994b). Consider a study conducted by Kerr and Booth (1978), who used children as participants. They asked 8-year-old children to toss miniature beanbags to a target. Children in the variable group practiced throwing from 2 ft and 4 ft, and children in the constant group always practiced 3 ft from the target. After completing the same number of training trials, children in both groups were given a test in which they were required to toss the beanbag at a target 3 ft away. Children in the variable group produced smaller error scores than did children in the constant group. This result is striking, because the criterion distance was exactly the distance (3 ft) at which the constant-practice group, by conventional wisdom, should have excelled. In this experiment and many others, however, conventional wisdom is a poor guide; the advantages of variable practice, such as learning to modulate the distance of a throw, apparently more than compensated for any specific practice advantage that accrued to the constant group.

***Random Practice.*** The random practice effect is an effect of task-ordering within training sessions. In a typical experiment, one group of participants practices a set of tasks under *blocked conditions*—that is, multiple trials of one task (a block) are performed before moving on to the next task. Another group practices the same tasks under *random conditions*, with the same number of trials per task, but the order of performance of the tasks on successive trials is more or less random. Participants in the random-practice group are therefore continually switching from task to task, and they tend to perform more poorly than participants in the blocked condition, who spend a majority of the time repeating the task from the previous trial. Despite this negative effect on acquisition performance, the random schedule ultimately results in better performance on delayed tests of retention and transfer. Note that studies of the effects of random practice differ from those of the variable–practice effect in that (a) learners are engaged in training on several distinct tasks, not multiple versions of a single task, and (b) the only factor that varies between groups in studies of blocked versus random practice is the order in which the tasks are practiced; the number of tasks practiced and the number of trials per task are identical for all learners.

The first clear demonstration of the random practice effect was presented in a paper by Shea and Morgan (1979). Three tasks were performed by each participant during the acquisition phase. Participants were to knock down three of six barriers with a tennis ball, in a specified order, as fast as possible. The specific set of three barriers to be knocked down was different for each task. Half of the participants practiced the three tasks under a blocked schedule, and the other half practiced them under a random schedule. Although performance of participants in the random group suffered relative to the blocked group during acquisition, they performed better on retention and transfer tests, regardless of whether those tests were administered with random or blocked schedules. (However, the advantage of random practice on the blocked retention test was not statistically significant.) Numerous studies on the random-practice effect were conducted subsequent to Shea and Morgan's study, confirming its robustness (see Magill & Hall, 1990, for a review).

Hall, Domingues, and Cavazos (1994) replicated Shea and Morgan's (1979) results and extended them, using a real-world sport (baseball) and skilled players as participants. They split a set of 30 collegiate baseball players into three groups, all of whom participated in normal batting practice. Two of the groups received two additional batting-practice sessions each week for 6 weeks, each consisting of 45 pitches—15 fastballs, 15 curveballs, and 15 change-up pitches. The third group, a control group, received no additional practice sessions. During the additional batting-practice sessions, one group (the blocked group) received 15 pitches of one type, then 15 pitches of the next type, followed by 15 pitches of the third type. The other group (the random group) received the same number of pitches of each type, but in a random order. At the end of the 6-week period, all 30 players received two 45-trial transfer tests, one in a blocked order and one in a random order.

Whereas during training, players in the blocked group produced a higher mean number of solid hits than did players in the random group, the opposite was true on the transfer tests. Players who trained under a random schedule performed significantly better at test, regardless of whether the test was administered under a blocked or random schedule.

Shea and Morgan (1979) and Hall and colleagues (1994) explored the effects of blocked versus random practice using motor skills. The effects of random practice are not, however, restricted to motor tasks. Carlson and Yaure (1990) tested the effects of blocked versus random practice on problem-solving efficiency and found results remarkably consistent with those found in the motor learning literature. Indeed, all of the practice effects discussed in the preceding sections—spaced practice, reduced feedback frequency, variable practice, and random practice—are quite general. They have been demonstrated using motor, verbal, and problem-solving tasks, diverse participant populations, and a wide range of retention intervals (for example, see Baddeley & Longman, 1978; Bahrick, 1979; and Dempster, 1990, on the spacing effect; see Salmoni et al., 1984, and Schooler & Anderson, 1990, on the effects of reduced feedback frequency; see Bird & Rikli, 1983; Gick & Holyoak, 1983; and Hunt, Parente, & Ellis, 1974, on variable practice; and see Carlson & Yaure, 1990; Landauer & Bjork, 1978; and Lee & Magill, 1983, on the random-practice effect).

Generality across domains and the tendency to produce opposite effects on short-term and long-term performance are not the only features shared by these practice manipulations. Note that the results of Hall and colleagues (1994) are in a general sense parallel to those observed by Kerr and Booth (1978) in their experiment on variable practice and to the results of Winstein and Schmidt (1990) in their study on reduced feedback frequency. In all three cases, performance at test was independent of the superficial similarities between practice and testing conditions. Recall that Kerr and Booth (1978) found an advantage of variable practice over constant (fixed) practice even when testing was conducted under formerly experienced fixed conditions. Winstein and Schmidt (1990) showed that practice with feedback after every trial produced poorer retention performance than practice with reduced feedback even when feedback was given after every trial at test. Also, Hall and colleagues (1994) demonstrated the superiority of random practice over blocked practice even when testing was blocked by task. Whereas intuitively one might expect that the ideal training conditions would overlap maximally with testing conditions, these studies suggest that perhaps such superficial similarities are not as important as the underlying processes invoked at practice and the tendency of those processes to support long-term performance at test.

## Interpreting Subjective Experience

Awareness of the limitations of objective performance measures is a crucial first step in assessing the effectiveness of training. However, equally important is a proper interpretation of subjective measures of training performance. There are at least two aspects of the training situation that can be assessed improperly—the performance of the learner and the effectiveness of the instructor. These two aspects can be viewed both from the perspective of the instructor and from the perspective of the learner, and the resulting subjective assessments can have a profound impact on the quality of training.

### Interpreting the Learner's Performance

There are obviously two sides of an evaluation of training success: the instructor's and the learner's.

*The Instructor's Perspective.* Perhaps the most common misconception in the consideration of a learner's performance is that errors are always bad and successes are always good. To the contrary, inducing errors during training can be highly beneficial for learning. People *do* learn from their mistakes. In fact, one could argue that new learning only occurs after errors demonstrate the need for change. In research on concept identification, for example—in which participants are required to learn the rule or principle that determines whether a given multidimensional stimulus is or is not an instance of an experimenter-defined concept—there is clear evidence that learning only occurs after errors. As Trabasso and Bower (1968) put it,

> Opportunities for learning (entering the solution state from the presolution state) occur only in trials in which the participant makes an error, whereas correct response trials provide no opportunity to exit from the presolution state. (p. 46)

The broader point is that errors provide the stimulus for reassessment and discovery in a variety of learning contexts. Correct responding, which can often be the product of local cues—or of a conceptualization that works in the present situation, but not in general—offers no stimulus for change.

Individuals responsible for training can inadvertently structure training such that trainees can respond correctly based on a superficial understanding, or, worse, so that constraints in the training situation shield trainees from exhibiting misunderstandings. Training conditions that keep performance levels artificially high—frequent feedback, massed practice, practice under fixed conditions—prevent learners from making mistakes, and are therefore likely to prevent significant learning.

Jacoby and colleagues (1994) warned that trainers who work to prevent errors during training may simply be deferring those errors to the posttraining environment, where errors can be costly. Yet even when trainers are aware of the value of mistakes during learning, management practices can serve to perpetuate substandard training practices. Trainers themselves are typically evaluated based on the performance of their trainees during training or at the end of training. This method of evaluation encourages trainers, consciously or unconsciously, to use training and testing methods that produce rapid improvement and high scores during training, which can, in turn, work in direct opposition to the long-term goals of training.

*The Learner's Perspective.* Bjork (1994b) and Jacoby and colleagues (1994) have argued that a learner's own subjective reading of the level of learning achieved is as important as the actual learning achieved. Whether trainees choose to engage in further practice or volunteer for other tasks depends on the reading they take of their own skills and knowledge. In certain work environments, such as air-traffic control, police operations, or the operation of nuclear power plants, individuals who do not possess critical skills and knowledge but think they do pose a special problem. In those environments, on-the-job learning can be hazardous not only to the individual, but to society as a whole. (For a thorough discussion of the importance of trainees' subjective experience during training and its effects on learning, see chapter 8, this volume.)

Learners, like their instructors, can also fall prey to an anti-error bias. As long as they are performing well and improving at a fast pace, they conclude that they must be learning; but when they make mistakes and improvement slows, they get discouraged and doubtful about the value of their training. Misunderstandings of this sort can lead learners to reject beneficial training programs in favor of less optimal instruction (Jacoby et al., 1994).

Baddeley and Longman (1978), for example, in an experiment that manipulated the practice schedules of British postal workers who had to learn a new keyboard skill, observed a striking discrepancy between subjective preferences and objective measures. They varied the distribution of training sessions across time and found, consistent with earlier work, that distributing training sessions in time produced better learning per hour of instruction. At the end of the study, they asked the postal workers to rate how satisfied they were with their schedules. They found a negative relationship between those ratings and the actual efficiency of the different schedules. Left to their own judgment, the learners would have chosen the training condition that produced the smallest amount of learning per hour of instruction.

Misconstrual of the meaning of errors and successes is not the only type of misinterpretation demonstrated by learners when assessing their own level of learning. A related problem is that many people are not aware of the complex, multidimensional nature of human memory (Bjork, 1994b). Memory can be indexed in a variety of ways. Suppose we wish to test someone's memory for a particular episode—for example, exposure to a new song on the radio. There are several ways in which the testing can be carried out. One option is to simply ask: What was the new song you heard on the radio last week? Another method is to ask the person to choose from a list of alternatives. A more subtle approach is to find evidence of prior exposure by replaying the song and checking to see if the person can hum along. All three measures are valid options, but one cannot substitute for another.

A common error on the part of learners is to use one type of index to predict another (Bjork, 1994b; Jacoby et al., 1994). Most people can remember an occasion when, as a student, they walked into an exam highly confident of their mastery of the material and walked out equally sure that they had failed to master it. There is a good chance that a majority of our study time was spent rereading book chapters and class notes and nodding privately in agreement. If the exam had tested recognition of course material, that strategy might have been a successful one. On an exam that requires one to generate information from memory, however, such a strategy is ineffective; in effect, the exam requires a skill that may have been neglected during study. In other words, the feeling of familiarity experienced during study may have been inappropriately used to predict retrieval capability.

Experimental research conducted over the past 10 years has revealed numerous ways in which learners can use inappropriate indicators to judge their own knowledge. In many of these studies, researchers have been interested specifically in discovering whether learners' assessments of their own knowledge could be affected by increased familiarity with certain types of information. One method of increasing a learner's feeling of familiarity for a piece of information is simply to expose the learner to that information. Prior exposure causes the information to become *activated,* or primed, in memory so that it is processed more easily if encountered again a short time later, and ease or fluency of processing is often experienced by the learner as a feeling of familiarity (see Jacoby, Kelley, Brown, & Jasechko, 1989). Thus, a common technique used by researchers has been to test the effects of prior exposure to information (and thus, familiarity for that information) on learners' judgments of their own related knowledge.

For instance, Reder (1987) conducted an experiment in which she used a game show paradigm to test the effects of prior exposure to parts of questions on feelings of knowing the answers to those questions. In her paradigm, participants quickly scanned a general-information question and indicated by pressing a button whether or not they thought they could answer the question. They were asked to base their response on a first impression rather than actually trying to retrieve the answer. After each trial, they attempted to answer the question and were subsequently shown the correct response. She showed that prior exposure to key words in a general-information question (such as the words *golf* and *par* in the question, "What is the term in golf for scoring one under par?") inflates the probability that participants feel they know the answer. It is interesting to note that such exposure to portions of the questions did not actually result in increased accuracy of the answers; the exposure only affected participants' *predictions* about their accuracy. In a similar vein, Reder and Ritter (1992) were able to influence participants' speeded judgments as to whether they could retrieve the answer to an arithmetic problem simply by exposing them to some of the terms of the problem. Given the problem "23 × 17," participants were more likely to judge the answer as retrievable if they had been previously presented the numbers 23 and 17 in the context of another mathematically distinct task. Thus, ease or fluency of processing of a question can sometimes be mistaken for knowledge of the answer.

Glenberg and Epstein (1987) demonstrated yet another form of faulty prediction on the part of learners. They had participants read text passages and rate their comprehension of the material. The participants were either experts or novices in the content domain of the passages (e.g., physics or music), but had no prior experience with the specific passages themselves. Later, all participants were asked to answer questions about the passages. Experts were less accurate in assessing their comprehension than were novices; apparently, they were unable to separate their general familiarity with a domain from their comprehension of a specific piece of text.

It is interesting to note that even current ease of retrieval can be a misleading guide to judgments of a later capability to retrieve. Benjamin, Bjork, and Schwartz (1996) asked participants to answer each of a series of general-information questions and then to predict for each answer whether they would be able, at the end of the experiment, to recall that answer in the absence of the question. They found that participants' predictions of recall for a given answer correlated negatively with the time it initially took them to answer the question. Participants expected to recall an answer easily if they could answer the question quickly, and conversely, they expected to have difficulty with recall if answering the question required more time. In actuality, the probability of recalling an answer in the absence of cues was greater when more time was spent answering the original question, possibly because greater initial difficulty in arriving at an answer made for a more memorable episode. Participants' failure to appreciate this relationship reflects an underlying misconception about the degree to which performance on one memory retrieval task (recalling general information) can be used to predict performance on another (retrieving details of a particular episode).

## Evaluating the Instructor's Effectiveness

Misinterpretations of the sort just described are not limited to inferences about the trainees' performance. The effectiveness of a trainer's instructional performance can also be misjudged. The consequences of incorrect appraisal can be serious, as perceptions of an instructor's effectiveness affect training in a number of ways. Trainers often use their own sense of success, or lack thereof, as a way of determining how much time to spend on different portions of the program. Errors in their judgment can lead to a suboptimal allocation of time and, therefore, suboptimal levels of learning. The perceptions of learners can also have a large impact on the training process. In many situations, evaluations of instructors by trainees are an important part of the review of training staff and practices. If those evaluations are misguided, they can result in changes that are detrimental to the training program.

*The Instructor's Perspective.* Research conducted by Newton (1990) bears on the issue of instructor effectiveness. Her studies are a powerful demonstration of the effects of perspective on judgments of the comprehension of others. She separated participants into two groups—the "tappers" and the "listeners." The tappers' job was to choose a song from a list of 25 common titles and to tap the rhythm of that song for a listener. The listeners' task was to guess the name of the song. In addition, before the listeners responded, the tappers were asked to predict the likelihood that the listeners would identify the song correctly. The tappers estimated a 50% probability that listeners could identify the songs. In actuality, the listeners were correct only 2.5% of the time! Here, it is important to realize that the tappers probably heard much more in their own heads than the simple rhythms they were producing. Coversely, they may have heard a full rendition, complete with melody and harmony. Griffin and Ross (1991) suggested that the tappers were unable to adjust their estimates to take into account the differences between their perspective and the perspective of the listeners.

Instructors can easily suffer the same problems of perspective. Their expertise in an area of instruction can color their judgment of the clarity with which they communicate information. Extensive experience with training materials can also cause trainers to misjudge the difficulty of learners' tasks. Goranson (1976) provided people with a series of puzzles and asked them to judge the difficulty of the puzzles for others. Half of the people were given the answers from the outset and were asked to generate a judgment by pretending to solve the puzzle step by step. The other half were not given the answers and actually solved the puzzles themselves. The people who were given the answers to the puzzles grossly underestimated the time it would take to solve the problems as compared to those who actually solved them. Exposure to the answers subjected people to a hindsight bias (Fischoff, 1975) that prevented them from generating accurate assessments.

In another set of studies, Jacoby and Kelley (1987) asked participants to rate how difficult anagrams (such as FSCAR) would be for other participants to solve. Some of the anagrams were shown with the solution (FSCAR = SCARF), and others were shown without the solution (FSCAR = ?????). In the latter condition, participants' judgments of difficulty were considerably more accurate in predicting others' performance than in the former condition. Participants apparently used their own subjective experience (i.e., the ease with which they solved the anagrams) as an index for generating predictions about others. Exposure to the solutions robbed them of that subjective experience and therefore adversely affected their perceptions.

Jacoby and Kelley (1987) conducted another experiment using the same procedures, but instead of presenting some of the solutions beside the anagrams, they presented a list of half of the solutions to participants before they attempted to solve the anagrams. Exposure to the list made the solution of those items easier, but participants failed to take that prior experience into account in making their predictions. They judged anagrams for which they had seen the solutions as easier than those for which they had not. In short, they continued to base judgments of difficulty on their own subjective experience and therefore underestimated the difficulty of some items for others.

*The Learner's Perspective.* Learners can also be fooled when judging a trainer's effectiveness. They often mistake good presentation style for good teaching. Some providers of training seminars capitalize on this misperception. They put together an entertaining package—an instructor who resembles a stand-up comedian, a few cute illustrations, and some amusing activities—and thereby trade a little information for a lot of money. In a similar way, students in a classroom usually prefer an entertaining teacher to an effective, nonentertaining one. Of course, learners are probably more receptive to a trainer who makes things easy to understand, but if the content is lacking, training amounts to nothing more than a "feel good" session.

In a different vein, Jacoby and colleagues (1994) noted that learners can misattribute their own improvement for an improvement in instruction. As they accumulate knowledge and skill, they may find suggestions more useful and lectures easier to understand. However, instead of attributing their ease of understanding to their own level of proficiency, they might assume that the instructor is more organized or better prepared. Misattributions of this sort can open the door to abusive training practices. If the difficulty of the training materials is manipulated so that later tests are constructed to be easier than early ones, learners can be misled into believing that their improved performance reflects effective instruction.

## In-Training Assessment Reconsidered

The multitude of misconceptions identified in the preceding sections may make the task of in-training assessment seem daunting. However, we offer some possible innovations that could make assessment during training a more realistic option. As evidenced by the findings reported previously, research on the general principles of learning and memory, together with investigations within specific domains, constitute a resource to trainers in all types of organizations and industries. Research can aid in the design of training programs and in the interpretation of observed performance.

## Making Subjective Experience More Diagnostic

Two of the major sources of difficulty in the previous assessment involve the use of subjective experience as a basis for assessment. Both trainers and learners often rely on subjective experience—rather than more objective measures—in forming opinions about the quality of training and in predicting future performance. (See Jacoby et al., 1994, for a more extensive treatment of this topic.) In general, the use of subjective experience in forming judgments is probably a good heuristic—especially in the absence of good objective methods of judgment (see, e.g., Wilson & Schooler, 1991). But as we have seen, subjective experience can sometimes be misleading in ways that can result in dramatic errors in assessment. However, it is fortunate that recent research suggests that training conditions can be structured in ways that better educate the subjective experience of learners and instructors.

### Educating the Learner's Subjective Experience

In a previous section, we illustrated a number of ways in which learners sometimes base judgments of their comprehension or proficiency on inappropriate indices. For example, a learner might mistakenly use feelings of familiarity to predict performance on a test of recall. This phenomenon can be considered a misuse of subjective experience. Learners confuse their feelings of familiarity with an ability to recall information.

There are at least two ways to adjust for this effect. One is to educate learners about the nature of human learning, making them aware of the differences between recall, recognition, familiarity, and so on. Even when this is a viable option, however, it may not prevent learners from misjudging their own level of knowledge. Learners may not be able to adjust sufficiently for their subjective experience. For example, Strack, Schwarz, Bless, Kübler, and Wänke (1993) have shown that informing participants that they have been primed with information that will influence their assessments does little more than bias those later assessments in a direction opposite to that expected by the priming. Thus, it seems that such a proviso makes participants aware of their ruined subjective experience but provides them no way to correct for it.

A second way to adjust for the deleterious effects of misleading subjective experience is to use objective measures of learning periodically during the course of training (Fischoff, 1975). Frequent tests that challenge the learners' understanding can serve to recalibrate their judgments of their own skill level. When faced with poor performance on a reliable test, learners will be much more likely to take steps to upgrade their skills or knowledge. Testing during training is, in fact, doubly advantageous. Tests themselves can be potent learning events. The very act of retrieving information from memory makes that information more recallable in the future (see, e.g., Anderson, Bjork, & Bjork, 1994; Bjork, 1975, 1988), and there is considerable evidence that a successful retrieval can be more advantageous than an additional study opportunity, particularly at a long retention interval (see, e.g., Allen, Mahler, & Estes, 1969; Hagman, 1983; Hogan & Kintsch, 1971; Landauer & Bjork, 1978).

### Educating the Instructor's Subjective Experience

The steps that can be taken to educate an instructor's subjective experience are similar to those for the learner. The difference lies in the fact that the learners' attempts at assessment are directed toward themselves, whereas instructors attempt to gauge the learning of others. Consider the anagram study conducted by Jacoby and Kelley (1987). The task of participants was to rate the difficulty of the anagrams for others, and participants' ability to do so was negatively influenced by prior exposure to the solutions. In follow-up experiments, participants were informed of the effects of prior exposure to solutions before making their judgments, but they were still unable to compensate for their ruined subjective experience. The only manipulation that resulted in some adjustment of ratings was one in which participants were informed of the effect and asked to attempt to recognize the solutions as having been on the list before making their judgments.

Given instructors' difficulties in adopting the perspective of the learners, it may be wiser for instructors as well to rely on more objective measures of learning. However, one serious problem arises with the use of tests during the acquisition of a skill. Those tests can be extremely unreliable measures of long-term learning. This point was made at the outset, in the discussion of the distinction between learning and performance. There are several examples across domains of conditions of practice that produce high levels of performance during training but yield poor retention and transfer performance at a delay (see, e.g., Schmidt & Bjork, 1992). For accurate assessment during training, tests need to be devised that are both (a) sensitive to the type of learning and comprehension that supports long-term performance and (b) relatively free of the fleeting influences of short-term factors.

## Making Objective Performance More Diagnostic

The task of assessing long-term learning given performance on tests administered in the short term is clearly a daunting one, but it can be simplified by using measures in those assessments that are more diagnostic of the desired aspects of stable, long-term learning. What follows are some general characteristics to be considered when evaluating measures of performance on this dimension.

### Assessing Transfer-Appropriate Processing

One general guideline for the selection of reliable tests of long-term learning rests on the concept of transfer-appropriate processing (Morris, Bransford, & Franks, 1977). Within the transfer-appropriate processing framework, a training manipulation is assumed to enhance retention or transfer to the extent that the processes exercised during training overlap with those required at retention. An implication of the foregoing statement is that instructors should employ tasks that require the learner to use the processes that will later be required to perform well in the target situation. Training regimens that encourage practice under fixed conditions—or that involve blocking skills by subtasks—work precisely against such a goal. However, practice that is carried out under variable conditions and schedules that require quasi-random switching from subtask to subtask are probably more similar to what trainees will encounter on the job and therefore are more desirable conditions for training.

In previous sections, we noted that typical measures of training performance do not always reflect long-term learning. If they did, conditions producing superior training scores would always produce superior retention scores. As noted previously, exactly the opposite is true of manipulations such as blocked versus random practice and full versus reduced feedback frequency. In pursuit of the goal of measuring learning during training, one solution is obvious: Use measures sensitive primarily to the factors contributing to enhanced retention.

In studies of blocked versus random practice, a common interpretation as to why blocked practice appears good is that participants can bypass some memory retrieval processes in producing repetitions. In order to reveal the true level of competence being achieved, a trainer periodically could administer trials on a probe task that requires efficient retrieval of a training task, perhaps by embedding one of the old tasks in a more complex new task. In teaching kids to play basketball, for example, a coach could interrupt training drills periodically in order to assess whether his or her players have learned to perform different types of shots under random, rather than blocked, conditions. A test that simulated time pressure, varied positions of receiving the ball prior to shooting, varied defender positions, and so forth, would not allow the players to forgo those aspects of learning to retrieve and initiate the shot that are not exercised under blocked conditions.

This prediction implies yet another interesting prediction. By the logic just presented, the acquisition performance of participants in the random group is already reflective of processes supporting long-term retention. It is the performance of the blocked group that is potentially misleading. A similar conclusion applies to interpretations of the spacing effect. Because measurements of training performance for a spaced practice group are always taken after longer intertrial intervals, they are more similar to measures of retention than are measures of training performance for a massed practice group. Thus it seems that conditions that are better for learning are more likely to be the cases in which performance reflects learning. Put differently, those conditions of practice that enhance learning should also yield more accurate measures of learning.

### Tests of Transfer During Training

Most tests administered during training can be considered tests of retention. They usually require the learner to reproduce the same information or skills that were experienced during instruction. Because retention tests consist of the same tasks practiced during training, their results are subject to the effects of the temporary influences alluded to earlier. Tests of retention are therefore almost always administered after a delay, when the temporary influences have dissipated. Transfer tests, by contrast, require learners to somehow transfer what they have learned to a novel task or altered conditions. Learners may be asked to draw inferences based on their knowledge or to perform a more complex version of a given task. Transfer tests composed of tasks similar to the training tasks are considered tests of near transfer, whereas tests using very different tasks constitute tests of far transfer (for discussions of similarity and transfer, see Gick & Holyoak, 1987; Mayer & Greeno, 1972; Osgood, 1949).

Unlike the case for retention tests, it is generally acceptable for transfer tests to be administered immediately after the acquisition of skills. Exceptions would be those cases in which temporary factors present during acquisition, such as fatigue, might be expected to affect transfer tasks as well. In the typical cases in which this is not an issue, it also should be possible to administer transfer tests as probe tasks during training. The transfer tests would presumably provide purer measures of learning. And if, as Christina and Bjork (1991) have suggested, retention tests can be thought of as tests of very near transfer, then the probe tasks should be predictive of later retention performance.

To illustrate, consider a training task consisting of the repair of a certain type of machinery. Suppose further that the piece of machinery exists in several different sizes. In training, the instructor has a limited time to teach a somewhat complex repair skill and is faced with the choice of using machines of several sizes or of only one size throughout training. Realizing that the process of switching to new versions of a task almost always causes an increase in errors, the instructor decides to use a single size only. What the instructor does not realize is that the increase in errors during practice with several versions of a task is only a temporary performance decrement. Indeed, variable practice of this sort tends to enhance the flexibility of learners in performing a skill and allows greater generalization to new conditions.

If, during training, learners were given short tests requiring them to anticipate the effects of a change in the size of the machine—for example, difficulties in reaching certain parts or changes in the amount of force to be used in manipulating components—the advantage of variable practice might be revealed immediately. Learners engaging in variable practice would probably have more elaborate and flexible mental representations with which to approach the new task. Practice under fixed conditions would likely result in inferior performance on such a test. In other words, transfer tests like the one suggested previously would give trainers a much better sense of the capabilities of their trainees than would conventional tests of training performance. In this particular example, typical methods of assessment during training would have led the instructor to prefer a nonoptimal training plan.

The aforementioned methods of testing during training are, in fact, likely to be triply advantageous. In addition to allowing more re-liable assessment, they should potentiate future learning and induce desirable scheduling conditions during practice. As noted previously, successful attempts at retrieval tend to make information more recall-able in the future (see Bjork, 1975, 1988) and can retard forgetting (Izawa, 1970). The effects of tests on practice scheduling should also be positive. By inserting short tests between training sessions, trainers will induce spaced and random practice—two conditions of practice that produce well-documented retention benefits (see Dempster, 1990; Magill & Hall, 1990). Thus it seems that testing during training, if care-fully engineered, can have multiple beneficial effects on learning and evaluation.

## Conclusion

We noted at the outset that, in general, the most desirable measure of training effectiveness is performance in the posttraining environment. The higher fidelity of tests in the real world coupled with the lack of short-term contaminating influences makes posttraining assessment a top choice in the evaluation of training. It is unfortunate, however, that posttraining assessment is very often out of the reach of those respon-sible for training. For this reason, our focus in this chapter has been on exploring the possibility of measuring effectiveness during training itself.

In identifying the numerous pitfalls one can encounter in assessing training performance—misleading performance, problems of perspec-tive, misinterpretations of subjective experience, and so forth—we ar-rive at the conclusion that intuition and standard practice are often poor guides to the training process. The capability to evaluate training programs in progress rests in large part on educating ourselves about the nature of learning and its implications for performance. We have reached a point at which research findings provide the potential for significant improvements in the assessment of training.

We have suggested procedures that might upgrade the extent to which subjective experience is a valid measure of training, and we have suggested objective measures that might be more reliable indicators of long-term learning. Should those and related innovations prove viable as guides for selecting optimal configurations of training, in-training evaluation, with its practical advantages over posttraining evaluation, may prove to be the assessment method of choice.

## References

Alderman, R. (1965). Influence of local fatigue on speed and accuracy in motor learning. *Research Quarterly, 36,* 131–140.

Allen, G. A., Mahler, W. A., & Estes, W. K. (1969). Effects of recall tests on long-term retention of paired associates. *Journal of Verbal Learning and Verbal Behavior, 8,* 463–470.

Anderson, M. C., Bjork, R. A., & Bjork, E. L. (1994). Remembering can cause forgetting: Retrieval dynamics in long-term memory. *Journal of Experimental Psychology: Learning, Memory, and Cognition, 20,* 1063–1087.

Baddeley, A. D., & Longman, D. J. A. (1978). The influence of length and frequency of training session on the rate of learning to type. *Ergonomics, 21,* 627–635.

Bahrick, H. P. (1979). Maintenance of knowledge: Questions about memory we forgot to ask. *Journal of Experimental Psychology: General, 108,* 296–308.

Benjamin, A. S., Bjork, R. A., & Schwartz, B. L. (1996). *The mismeasure of memory: When retrieval fluency is misleading as a metamnemonic index.* Manuscript submitted for publication.

Bjork, R. A. (1975). Retrieval as a memory modifier. In R. Solso (Ed.), *Information processing and cognition: The Loyola Symposium* (pp. 123–144). Hillsdale, NJ: Erlbaum.

Bjork, R. A. (1988). Retrieval practice and the maintenance of knowledge. In M. M. Gruneberg, P. E. Morris, & R. N. Sykes (Eds.), *Practical aspects of memory: Current research and issues, Vol. 1: Memory in everyday life* (pp. 396–401). New York: John Wiley.

Bjork, R. A. (1994a). Institutional impediments to effective training. In D. Druckman & R. A. Bjork (Eds.), *Learning, remembering, believing: Enhancing human performance.* Washington, DC: National Academy Press.

Bjork, R. A. (1994b). Memory and metamemory considerations in the training of human beings. In J. Metcalfe & A. P. Shimamura (Eds.), *Metacognition: Knowing about knowing* (pp. 185–205). Cambridge, MA: MIT Press.

Bird, A. M., & Rikli, R. (1983). Observational learning and practice variability. *Research Quarterly for Exercise and Sport, 54*(1), 1–4.

Carlson, R. A., & Yaure, R. G. (1990). Practice schedules and the use of component skills in problem solving. *Journal of Experimental Psychology: Learning, Memory, & Cognition, 16*(3), 484–496.

Carron, A. V. (1969). Performance and learning in a discrete motor task under massed vs. distributed practice. *Research Quarterly, 4,* 481–489.

Catalano, J. F., & Kleiner, B. M. (1984). Distant transfer in coincident timing as a function of variability of practice. *Perceptual & Motor Skills, 58,* 851–856.

Chamberlin, C., & Lee, T. D. (1993). Arranging practice conditions and designing instruction. In R. Singer, M. Murphy, & L. K. Tennant (Eds.), *Handbook of research on sport psychology* (pp. 213–241). New York: MacMillan.

Christina, R. W., & Bjork, R. A. (1991). Optimizing long-term retention and transfer. In D. Druckman & R. A. Bjork (Eds.), *In the mind's eye: Enhancing human performance.* Washington, DC: National Academy Press.

Cotten, D. J., Thomas, J. R., Spieth, W. R., & Biasiotto, J. (1972). Temporary fatigue effects in a gross motor skill. *Journal of Motor Behavior, 4,* 217–222.

Dempster, F. N. (1990). The spacing effect: A case study in the failure to apply the results of psychological research. *American Psychologist, 43,* 627–634.

Estes, W. K. (1955). Statistical theory of distributional phenomena in learning. *Psychological Review, 62,* 369–377.

Fischoff, B. (1975). Hindsight is not equal to foresight: The effects of outcome knowledge on judgment under uncertainty. *Journal of Experimental Psychology: Human Perception and Performance, 1,* 288–299.

Gick, M. L., & Holyoak, K. J. (1983). Schema induction and analogical transfer. *Cognitive Psychology, 15,* 1–38.

Gick, M. L., & Holyoak, K. J. (1987). The cognitive basis of knowledge transfer. In S. M. Cormier & J. D. Hagman (Eds.), *Transfer of learning: Contemporary research and applications* (pp. 9–46). San Diego, CA: Academic Press.

Glenberg, A. M., & Epstein, W. (1987). Inexpert calibration of comprehension. *Memory & Cognition, 15*(1), 84–93.

Goldstein, I. L. (1993). *Training in organizations: Needs assessment, development, and evaluation.* Pacific Grove, CA: Brooks/Cole.

Goranson, R. E. (1976). A paradox in educational communication. In I. Kusyszyn (Ed.), *Teaching and learning process seminars* (Vol. 1, pp. 63–76). Toronto, Ontario: York University Press.

Griffin, D. W., & Ross, L. (1991). Subjective construal, social inference, and human misunderstanding. In M. Zanna (Ed.), *Advances in experimental social psychology* (Vol. 24, pp. 319–359). New York: Academic Press.

Hagman, J. D. (1983). Presentation- and test-trial effects on acquisition and retention of distance and location. *Journal of Experimental Psychology: Learning, Memory, and Cognition, 9,* 334–345.

Hall, K. G., Domingues, D. A., & Cavazos, R. (1994). Contextual interference effects with skilled baseball players. *Perceptual and Motor Skills, 78,* 835–841.

Hogan, R. M., & Kintsch, W. (1971). Differential effects of study and test trials on long-term retention and recall. *Journal of Verbal Learning and Verbal Behavior, 10,* 562–567.

Hunt, R. R., Parente, F. J., & Ellis, H. C. (1974). Transfer of coding strategies in free recall with constant and varied input. *Journal of Experimental Psychology, 103*(4), 619–624.

Izawa, C. (1970). Optimal potentiating effects and forgetting-prevention effects of tests in paired-associate learning. *Journal of Experimental Psychology, 83,* 340–344.

Jacoby, L. L. (1978). On interpreting the effects of repetition: Solving a problem versus remembering a solution. *Journal of Verbal Learning and Verbal Behavior, 17,* 649–667.

Jacoby, L. L., Bjork, R. A., & Kelley, C. M. (1994). Illusions of comprehension, competence, and remembering. In D. Druckman & R. A. Bjork (Eds.), *Learning, remembering, believing: Enhancing human performance.* Washington, DC: National Academy Press.

Jacoby, L. L., & Kelley, C. M. (1987). Unconscious influences of memory for a prior event. *Personality and Social Psychology Bulletin, 13,* 314–336.

Jacoby, L. L., Kelley, C. M., Brown, J., & Jasechko, J. (1989). Becoming famous overnight: Limits on the ability to avoid unconscious influences of the past. *Journal of Personality and Social Psychology, 56,* 326–338.

Kerr, R., & Booth, B. (1978). Specific and varied practice of motor skill. *Perceptual & Motor Skills, 46,* 395–401.

Landauer, T. K., & Bjork, R. A. (1978). Optimum rehearsal patterns and name learning.

In M. M. Gruneberg, P. E. Morris, & R. N. Sykes (Eds.), *Practical aspects of memory* (pp. 625–632). London: Academic Press.

Lee, T. D., & Magill, R. A. (1983). The locus of contextual interference in motor skill acquisition. *Journal of Experimental Psychology: Learning, Memory, and Cognition, 9*(4), 730–746.

Lee, T. D., Magill, R. A., & Weeks, D. J. (1985). Influence of practice schedule on testing schema theory predictions in adults. *Journal of Motor Behavior, 17,* 283–299.

Magill, R. A., & Hall, K. G. (1990). A review of the contextual interference effect in motor skill acquisition. *Human Movement Science, 9,* 241–289.

Mayer, R. E., & Greeno, J. G. (1972). Structural differences between learning outcomes produced by different instructional methods. *Journal of Educational Psychology, 63,* 165–173.

Melton, A. W. (1970). The situation with respect to the spacing of repetitions and memory. *Journal of Verbal Learning and Verbal Behavior, 9,* 596–606.

Morris, C. D., Bransford, J. D., & Franks, J. J. (1977). Levels of processing versus transfer appropriate processing. *Journal of Verbal Learning and Verbal Behavior, 16*(5), 519–533.

Newton, L. (1990). *Overconfidence in the communication of intent: Heard and unheard melodies.* Unpublished doctoral dissertation, Department of Psychology, Stanford University, Stanford, CA.

Osgood, C. E. (1949). The similarity paradox in human learning: A resolution. *Psychological Review, 56,* 132–143.

Reder, L. M. (1987). Selection strategies in question answering. *Cognitive Psychology, 19,* 90–138.

Reder, L. M., & Ritter, F. E. (1992). What determines initial feeling of knowing? Familiarity with question terms, not with the answer. *Journal of Experimental Psychology: Learning, Memory, and Cognition, 18,* 435–451.

Salmoni, A. W., Schmidt, R. A., & Walter, C. B. (1984). Knowledge of results and motor learning: A review and critical reappraisal. *Psychological Bulletin, 95*(3), 355–386.

Schmidt, R. A. (1969). Performance and learning a gross muscular skill under conditions of artificially induced fatigue. *Research Quarterly, 40*(1), 185–191.

Schmidt, R. A. (1988). *Motor control and learning: A behavioral emphasis* (2nd ed.). Champaign, IL: Human Kinetics.

Schmidt, R. A., & Bjork, R. A. (1992). New conceptualizations of practice: Common principles in three paradigms suggest new concepts for training. *Psychological Science, 3*(4), 207–217.

Schooler, L. J., & Anderson, J. R. (1990). The disruptive potential of immediate feedback. *The Twelfth Annual Conference of the Cognitive Science Society* (pp. 702–708). Hillsdale, NJ: Erlbaum.

Shea, J. B., & Morgan, R.L. (1979). Contextual interference effects on the acquisition, retention, and transfer of a motor skill. *Journal of Experimental Psychology: Human Learning and Memory, 5*(2), 179–187.

Strack, F., Schwarz, N., Bless, H., Kübler, A., & Wänke, M. (1993). Awareness of the influence as a determinant of assimilation versus contrast. *European Journal of Social Psychology, 23,* 53–62.

Trabasso, T., & Bower, G. H. (1968). *Attention in learning: Theory and Research.* New York: Wiley.

Van Rossum, J. H. (1990). Schmidt's schema theory: The empirical base of the variability of practice hypothesis: A critical analysis. *Human Movement Science, 9*(3–5), 387–435.

Wilson, T. D., & Schooler, J. W. (1991). Thinking too much: Introspection can reduce the quality of preferences and decisions. *Journal of Personality and Social Psychology, 60*, 181–192.

Winstein, C. J., & Schmidt, R. A. (1990). Reduced frequency of knowledge of results enhances motor skill learning. *Journal of Experimental Psychology: Learning, Memory, and Cognition, 16*(4), 677–691.

# Building Adaptive Expertise: Implications for Training Design Strategies

Eleanor M. Smith, J. Kevin Ford,
and Steve W. J. Kozlowski

**A** critical component of any training system is determining how to design training environments and experiences to enhance learning and the transfer of trained knowledge and skills to the job. A review of training design research in the industrial–organizational psychology literature identified a number of design characteristics that should lead to the training outcomes of acquisition, retention, maintenance, and generalization of skills (Baldwin & Ford, 1988). Design characteristics such as overlearning, the conditions of practice, feedback, variability, and the incorporation of identical elements have been used in training programs to facilitate learning and transfer. A limitation of the industrial–organizational training design literature is that the majority of the research has used simple tasks, and training has been evaluated using criteria of immediate reproduction and short-term retention (Baldwin & Ford, 1988). As a consequence, the design strategies currently in use are most relevant when trainees must reproduce behaviors or motor skills as closely as possible to the training material.

However, jobs today require individuals to become more adaptable in performing tasks. Advances in technology have created jobs that are more cognitively complex and demanding. The shift from manufacturing to service jobs has increased the importance of "softer" skills such as interpersonal and problem solving skills (Goldstein & Gilliam, 1990). As a consequence, the problems faced in many jobs are unstructured and ill-defined. As task demands become less predictable, the traditional industrial–organizational perspective to training design has diminishing relevance (Ford & Kraiger, 1995; Howell & Cooke, 1989).

In contrast, research in cognitive and instructional psychology, which focuses on the mental processes and changes that occur during learning, has great potential for improving training design given today's complex workplace. It has been argued that training research would benefit from the rich theoretical work emerging from cognitive and instructional psychology (Goldstein, 1993; Tannenbaum & Yukl, 1992). Applied psychologists have thus begun to suggest ways to apply cognitive principles and concepts to training. In particular, Kraiger, Ford, and Salas (1993) reviewed advances in cognitive and instructional psychology and developed a classification scheme for evaluating learning outcomes. The classification scheme revolves around three key learning outcomes—cognitive (verbal knowledge, knowledge organization, and metacognitive strategies), skill-based (compilation and automaticity), and affective (attitudes and motivation). Kraiger and colleagues (1993) identified a critical future step to be the development of a nomological network relevant to the learning outcomes. This would include the identification of training interventions that lead to learning and the relationship of learning outcomes to transfer outcomes.

The purpose of this chapter is to apply some of the instructional constructs being actively investigated in other domains to training design research. A particular focus of this chapter is the design of a learning environment that prepares the trainee for adapting to changing task demands. We build on the work of Kraiger and colleagues (1993) and identify a nomological network that links specific design strategies to the learning constructs of knowledge structure and metacognition. These learning constructs were chosen as the leading candidates to be closely linked to the building of adaptability.

The major premise of this chapter is that training for the twenty-first century requires more creative design strategies to build knowledge structures and metacognitive skills that allow for a deeper understanding of job demands and enhance adaptability to novel or changing demands. We first review the emerging cognitive research on building adaptive expertise and contrast it with the typical focus on building what has been called "routine" expertise. We then identify characteristics of adaptive expertise. We describe two learning constructs that provide a logical link to building adaptive expertise. We also describe design strategies from the cognitive and instructional psychology literatures that have particular relevance for building effective knowledge structures and enhancing metacognitive skills. In the final section we discuss needed research on this nomological network of relationships among design strategies, learning outcomes, and adaptive expertise for improving training effectiveness.

## Adaptive Expertise

*Positive transfer of training* is usually defined as the degree to which trainees effectively apply the knowledge, skills, and attitudes gained in a training context to the job context. Expected outcomes of the transfer process include both the generalization of trained skills to the job and the maintenance or long-term retention of trained knowledge and skills (Baldwin & Ford, 1988). Generalization involves more than mimicking trained responses to events that occurred in training, because it requires trainees to exhibit trained behaviors in response to different settings, people, and situations from those trained. Maintenance issues focus on the changes that occur in the form or level of knowledge, skills, or behaviors exhibited in the transfer setting as a function of time elapsed from completion of the training program.

As noted by Ford and Kraiger (1995), applied research has tended to limit our understanding of the transfer process to easily obtainable measures of knowledge (e.g., declarative knowledge tests) and behavioral change (e.g., performance ratings). Few attempts have been made to understand transfer from the perspective of what it means to learn. In fact, the applied psychology literature has viewed learning and transfer as conceptually distinct constructs, with learning viewed as a precursor to transfer. In contrast, researchers in cognitive and instructional psychology often conceptualize learning and transfer as two ends of the same continuum. Proponents of this perspective argue that the effectiveness of learning is revealed by or measured by the level of retention shown. Thus, a critical assumption of cognitive research on transfer is that the psychological processes underlying transfer and learning are largely inseparable (Gick & Holyoak, 1987). For example, the capability to generalize can be thought of as one indicator of learning (Schmidt & Bjork, 1992).

An emerging literature in cognitive psychology contends that another key indicator of learning is the extent to which an individual can adapt to novel or changing situational demands. This research has important implications for developing design strategies to train individuals to handle jobs that are less structured and defined.

## Routine Versus Adaptive Expertise

Holyoak (1991) identified three generations of theories on building expertise. The first generation is best captured by the work of Newell and Simon (1972). They considered problem-solving skill and general heuristic search to be the definition of expertise. Several heuristic search methods (e.g., means–end analysis) were identified that could be applied across domains with minimal knowledge of the content of a specific domain.

Examination of experts in knowledge-rich domains such as chess and physics called this definition of expertise into question. In addition, research provided little evidence that training in general problem-solving skills transferred across content domains. Instead, research comparing the performance of experts and novices found that expertise depended on detailed domain knowledge and the ability to represent and understand problems in terms of deeper, structural features (Chi, Feltovich, & Glaser, 1981; Proctor & Dutta, 1995). Novices were found to rely on the surface features of problems and to use heuristic search strategies. Expertise also involved extensive time invested in domain learning. Experts were found to store more information, which was better organized, in long-term memory (Anderson, 1993a).

This research led to the second generation of expertise theories. Holyoak (1991) cited Anderson's ACT* (1983) theory as a clear example. Because expertise was defined as knowing how to do something well, this approach focused on studying procedural as well as declarative knowledge. According to ACT* theory, practice at a task leads to compilation of declarative knowledge into procedural, condition–action rules. Compilation leads to larger, integrated chunks of procedural knowledge, whereas continued practice leads to automatic and efficient performance (see Fitts & Posner, 1967).

Holyoak (1991) described this second generation of theories as a simple picture of the development of expertise. He linked this approach to the concept of routine expertise. Routine experts quickly apply solutions or strategies to well-learned and familiar contexts (Hatano & Inagaki, 1986). Holyoak noted, however, that serial production theories of expertise comprising specific condition–action rules cannot account for the ability of experts to integrate simultaneously multiple sources of knowledge.

Holyoak (1991) introduced the notion of a third generation of theories that corresponds to the concept of adaptive expertise. Although routine experts can solve familiar problems quickly and accurately, they have difficulty with novel problems. In contrast, adaptive experts can invent new procedures based on their knowledge and make new predictions (Hatano & Inagaki, 1986). The key to their ability to adapt to novel problems is a deeper conceptual understanding of the target domain. In addition to learning procedural knowledge of what to do, individuals must also learn why procedures are appropriate for certain conditions. Mindful processing and abstraction are critical to the development of adaptive expertise (Hatano & Inagaki, 1986; Salomon & Perkins, 1989). This allows adaptive experts to recognize when current procedures must be changed to respond to novel circumstances.

Adaptability or adaptive expertise is evidenced when the individual responds successfully to changes in the nature of the trained task. Novelty has been a component in several definitions of transfer that requires adaptability (Butterfield & Nelson, 1989; McDaniel & Schlager, 1990). Adapting one's skills to novel tasks requires an understanding of deeper principles underlying the task, executive-level capabilities to recognize and identify changed situations, and knowledge of whether or not the existing repertoire of procedures can be applied. If a transfer situation requires individuals to reconfigure procedures, extensive knowledge about a variety of procedures, as well as how to select and combine them, is necessary. If learned procedures are no longer appropriate, individuals must be able to identify an existing procedure as insufficient, as well as to create a new, more appropriate one.

Research in cognitive and instructional psychology provides suggestions on how to train individuals to become adaptive experts. A critical factor in training for adaptive expertise is to encourage active and mindful learning during training. Two learning outcomes that are particularly relevant to building these adaptive capabilities are knowledge structures and metacognition.

## Learning Outcomes and Adaptive Expertise

Training research and practice have focused on a narrow range of learning outcomes to evaluate training effectiveness. Learning is usually assessed with measures of declarative knowledge such as achievement tests. In the case of skills, learning has often been measured by observing trainee performance in simulations or on the job (Kraiger et al.,

1993). When the objective of training is to develop adaptive capabilities, outcomes such as declarative knowledge and proceduralization of skills are only partial indicators of training effectiveness.

Two learning processes are critical for individuals to become adaptive experts. First, individuals must develop detailed knowledge about the task domain that is effectively organized in memory. The quality and content of the knowledge structure that is developed during training determines the capability to adapt to novel circumstances. Second, individuals must build skills in metacognition that allow for planning, monitoring, and evaluation. The development of these skills aids learners in understanding when there is a need for adaptability. The next sections discuss these two learning outcomes and link them to adaptive expertise. For a discussion of techniques and procedures for measuring these learning outcomes see Royer, Cisero, and Carlo (1993) or Kraiger and colleagues (1993).

## Knowledge Structure

As individuals gain experience with a task through formal training programs, on-the-job training, and job performance, their declarative knowledge not only becomes compiled into procedural rules, it also becomes meaningfully structured in memory (Kraiger et al., 1993). Researchers have developed various concepts to describe this knowledge structure such as *scripts, schema, mental models,* and *cognitive maps.* Research has found that experts and novices differ in the organization and content of their knowledge structures. For example, experts possess knowledge structures that contain both problem definitions and solutions, whereas novices tend to possess separate knowledge structures for problem definition and problem solution (Glaser & Chi, 1989). Thus, expert structures contain strong links between problem types and specific solutions. In addition to the organization of knowledge, the content of expert knowledge structures is broader and deeper compared to novices. For example, experts represent the task in terms of its deeper, structural features, whereas novices tend to represent the task on surface features (Chi, Feltovich, & Glaser, 1981).

Patel and Groen made a finer distinction between experts, intermediates, and novices. "A distinguishing trait of experts, even outside their domain of specialization, is knowledge of what not to do" (1991, p. 121). Intermediates possess the domain knowledge that experts possess (i.e., what to do given a particular task situation), but they do not know what *not* to do. This leads them to conduct irrelevant searches, be distracted by irrelevant clues, and access unnecessary knowledge from their memory. Novices do not conduct these irrelevant searches because they do not know what to do. This suggests that experts possess more complex knowledge structures that not only contain information on correct task strategies but also information on strategies that would be errors. Individuals learn why a particular strategy is appropriate in a given situation, when it is inappropriate, and errors that may occur in its application. This deeper conceptual understanding and greater range of responses can lead to better adaptability to novel circumstances.

Sternberg and Frensch (1992) have identified a potential cost of expertise related to the highly structured organization of their knowledge. They found that experts were less able to adapt when deep, structural principles of the task were changed. When knowledge structures become routinized and automatized, it leads to less flexibility if the task contains elements incompatible with the individual's knowledge structure. Adaptive expertise requires not only highly developed knowledge structures, but also skills at a conscious, executive level. In this way, individuals are able to override their automatic routines when the situation requires it.

## Metacognition

Metacognition is the awareness and control of one's cognition (Flavell, 1979; Nelson & Narens, 1990). Metacognition is an executive-level function that includes an awareness and understanding of the relationship between task requirements and individual capabilities (Pressley, Snyder, Levin, Murray, & Ghatala, 1987). Metacognition also includes a control function of planning, monitoring, and regulating strategies or mental activities (Bereiter & Scardamalia, 1985).

Research indicates that experts possess superior metacognitive capabilities compared to novices. Larkin (1983) found that experts in physics were more likely to discontinue ineffective problem-solving strategies compared to novices. Etelapelto (1993) found that expert computer programmers had superior metacognitive understanding of the programming task, of ideal working strategies, and a better awareness of their own performance strategies. Dorner and Scholkopf (1991) characterized experts as individuals who analyze the facts of a situation and program their actions based on self-instructions. Experts do not follow these self-instructions blindly; instead, they use self-reflection to repeatedly check their actions. Experts pay particular attention to failures, modifying their strategies when appropriate.

Individuals who possess superior metacognitive skills are able to engage in the mindful and deliberate learning that leads to adaptive expertise. These self-regulatory capabilities enable individuals to recognize novelty or change, select potential responses, monitor and evaluate progress, and modify or create different responses to the task if necessary. Lack of metacognitive skill may lead to failure to transfer trained strategies (Day, 1986), as well as an inability to identify when trained strategies no longer apply.

In sum, individuals must develop detailed and organized knowledge about the task domain, as well as the capability to monitor and control their knowledge and behavior, in order to adapt to novel or changing task demands. Research in cognitive and instructional psychology suggests several processes through which knowledge structures and metacognition can develop. These processes lead us to consider innovative approaches to training design that can facilitate the development of adaptive expertise.

## Training Design Strategies

Industrial–organizational training researchers traditionally have agreed on a set of learning principles that can be incorporated into a plan of instruction and guide training design. Learning principles such as overlearning, reinforcement schedules, and frequent feedback have been focused on building declarative knowledge and highly efficient, proceduralized, and routinized skills. Training research and practice have focused less on strategies to develop more complex knowledge structures and skills so as to enhance adaptable and flexible capabilities in the transfer environment.

Drawing on work in the cognitive and instructional psychology literatures offers two advances that have implications for improving training design. First, recommendations have been developed that improve our understanding of how and when traditional design principles may affect particular learning outcomes. Second, new design strategies have been developed to build the capacity for adaptive expertise.

## Advances to Traditional Design Strategies

New theoretical approaches have provided a cognitive explanation for many of the traditional design principles. For example, the major behaviorist theory for transfer is the *theory of identical elements* (Thorndike & Woodworth, 1901). From this perspective, identical elements were viewed as relationships between stimuli and responses (Butterfield & Nelson, 1989; Patrick, 1992). This view led to principles of learning that were focused on how to shape the behavior of individuals during learning.

Cognitive theories of learning focus on how individuals attend to, encode, store, and retrieve information. For example, Anderson (1993a, 1993b) described the stages through which individuals develop problem-solving and other cognitive skills. According to ACT-R theory, the identical elements that must be shared between learning and transfer environments are production rules that specify the conditions for which an action is appropriate. Cormier (1987) described the encoding specificity principle as important to transfer. Stimulus cues in the transfer environment must be encoded with information learned during training for the cues to aid later retrieval. Gick and Holyoak (1987) argued that it is the perceived similarity between the training and transfer environments, not necessarily the actual similarity, that determines the amount of transfer. Thus, cognitive explanations for the theory of identical elements emphasize the mental processes of recognizing, storing, and retrieving the stimulus information that indicates that the training and transfer environments share similar features.

Cognitive research has also enriched existing design principles by making their application contingent on stages of the learning process. For example, stimulus variability as a design principle is the idea that positive transfer is more likely when a variety of examples are employed during training. Providing varied examples allows individuals to induce more general rules by abstracting the features that are shared by the examples (Gick & Holyoak, 1987). However, cognitive research suggests that high variability of examples, although enhancing transfer, may hinder initial learning (Schmidt & Bjork, 1992). If individuals are provided with a highly diverse set of examples early in acquisition, they may have difficulty in abstracting general rules. Thus, presenting low variability examples early in learning, followed by greater variability later in training, may be effective for transfer while at the same time creating less confusion during acquisition (Gick & Holyoak, 1987). Sequencing of variability may also depend on the learning approach taken by trainees. For example, Elio and Anderson (1984) found that transfer was more effective when low-variability examples were introduced first, but only when individuals took an implicit approach to learning. When individuals were instructed to use an explicit hypothesis-testing approach to learning rules for category membership, transfer was greater if high-variability examples were introduced first.

In addition, Gick and Holyoak (1987) have differentiated two components of a situation that might be varied during training—its surface and structural components. Structural components are functionally related to outcomes or goal attainment, whereas surface components are not causally related. Thus, varying the surface components of a situation can lead to the abstraction of generalized rules that facilitate transfer. In contrast, varying the structural components of a situation will not facilitate transfer.

Finally, the principle of overlearning achieves a more theoretical explanation and more specific application in cognitive research. The notion that continued practice beyond the point of successful task performance is critical for transfer is closely related to the concept of skill automaticity (Shiffrin & Schneider, 1977). Automatic processing occurs when few attentional demands are required for task performance. Research has shown that extensive practice on task components that are consistent across conditions allows automaticity for these components to develop (Myers & Fisk, 1987; Proctor & Dutta, 1995). Schneider (1985) suggested that training should focus on automatizing the consistent components of tasks so that attentional and memory resources are available for the inconsistent portions of the task.

In summary, cognitive research forces us to consider the dynamic processes underlying individual learning and how traditional design principles can be applied differently at various stages of learning. Nevertheless, these revised design principles are more useful for building routine rather than adaptive expertise. For example, allowing for overlearning assumes a task that requires some consistency of action. The use of stimulus variability assumes that one is able to identify the range of situations for which the knowledge or skill is applicable. Finally, these principles are more effective when the relationship between situation and action is clear to the trainee, and the task environment is fairly stable over time.

## Design Strategies to Build Adaptive Expertise

The traditional training perspective assumes that work environments are largely predictable and that training designs can be identified to prepare trainees to respond appropriately across routine job situations. An alternative approach is to assume that the changing elements in the workplace lead to a fair amount of unpredictability (Ford & Kraiger, 1995). Training can facilitate learning through the development of mental processes that increase flexibility for dealing with this unpredictability. Adaptive expertise requires more than the acquisition of response repertoires. It requires the systematic development in training of meaningful structures for organizing knowledge and self-regulatory skills that enhance the capacity for learning from on-the-job experience.

### Linking Previous Knowledge

This section describes a number of recent advances to design strategies that concentrate on linking previous knowledge with new knowledge, creating well-defined knowledge structures, and building executive-level (metacognitive) skills for greater flexibility and adaptability. Figure 1 is a general heuristic that shows how these design strategies affect adaptive expertise through their impacts on learning outcomes.

The trainee's background knowledge is an important factor to consider in the learning process (Gick & Holyoak, 1987). Individuals faced with acquiring a new set of materials routinely attempt to relate it to previous knowledge and thus try to provide their own structure to the material (Clark & Voogel, 1985). Training design can take advantage of this active information-processing by providing initial structure to the training that links new knowledge to previous knowledge. The use of advance organizers and analogies are two examples of this approach.

### Advance Organizers

*Advance organizers* are materials presented at the beginning of training that are at a high level of abstraction, generality, and inclusiveness (Ausubel, 1968). Advance organizers provide an initial organizing structure or framework that clarifies trainees' expectations and allows them to organize and retain the material to be learned (Mayer, 1975). Advance organizers can facilitate learning because they explicitly draw on relevant anchoring concepts already in the learner's cognitive structure and make them part of the organizing framework. This facilitates the inte-

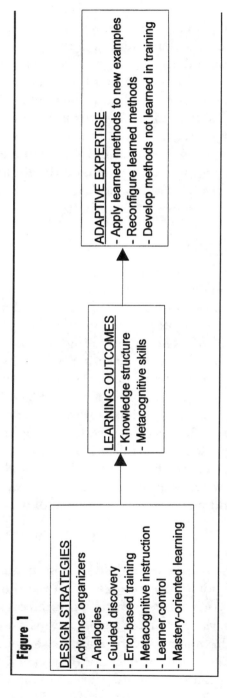

**Figure 1**

Designing training environments to build adaptive expertise.

gration of fundamental conceptual ideas with existing knowledge and can lead to transfer to new situations. In an ideal situation, comparative organizers that explicitly delineate similarities and differences between two sets of ideas should be used. The advance organizers should also include a demonstration of the end goal, with reasoning processes implicitly or explicitly available (Glaser & Bassok, 1989).

DiVesta and Peverly (1984) examined learner-generated organization of examples. They found that an advance organizer condition, in which individuals created their own organization of concept examples, led to the greatest adaptive transfer. The benefit of the self-organized examples was that they were more decontextualized than instructor-provided examples (Clark & Voogel, 1985). Decontextualized and abstracted knowledge has been emphasized as an important learning outcome leading to adaptive expertise (Salomon & Perkins, 1989). Kraiger and his associates (Jung & Kraiger, 1994; Kraiger, Salas, & Cannon-Bowers, 1995) have conducted a series of studies in which trainees were provided advance organizer information (objectives and how to attain objectives) prior to or after completion of an introductory training session on a tactical decision-making simulation. They found that the quality of trainees' knowledge structures was correlated with performance after training for trainees who received the advance organizers but not for control group members.

Advance organizers have sometimes been operationalized by using an analogous model from an individual's previous experience that provides the appropriate structure for learning new material. For example, Mayer (1975) presented an advance organizer to individuals learning how to program a computer that was based on past experiences with scoreboards, ticket windows, shopping lists, and other ideas familiar to most individuals. Individuals provided this advance organizer were better at solving problems requiring interpretation compared to individuals provided with other types of models.

This approach is closely linked to work by Gick, Holyoak, and colleagues on the retrieval and use of analogies in problem solving. Some of their research has varied the surface and structural features of the analogy. When the surface features of two tasks were different, individuals had difficulty spontaneously transferring what was learned from one task to a second task. For example, Gick and Holyoak (1980) found that training on one example in which a certain strategy was applicable led to very little transfer to a second example in which the surface features were different. In a subsequent study, individuals were exposed to two examples in which the strategy applied and had to write a description of their similarity. Gick and Holyoak (1983) found that the quality of the description predicted transfer to a third example that also varied on surface features. Thus, it appears that involving the learner in actively processing the meaning of the analogy is important for the transfer of the analogy to a different problem. Holyoak and Koh (1987) varied the surface and structural features of the analogy and transfer tasks and found that individuals had difficulty in transfer when either the surface or structural similarity was reduced. After hints about the analogy were given, only structural dissimilarity significantly impaired total transfer.

Advance organizers and analogies can lead individuals to learn and retain knowledge in a more abstract form. Rather than learning rules that are applied automatically in specific circumstances, individuals can learn the relationship between decontextualized representations and the specific instances to which they apply (Salomon & Perkins, 1989). This abstracted knowledge provides a framework that can lead to greater adaptive transfer in novel situations.

## Creating Well-Defined Knowledge Structures

Researchers have examined ways to build high quality knowledge structures to aid retention and transfer. We will examine two such strategies—one that promotes inductive learning and another that focuses on error management strategies.

The *traditional learning approach* explicitly instructs individuals on the complete task and its concepts, rules, and strategies. This *deductive approach* is in contrast to recent efforts that have examined an inductive or discovery learning process. In a discovery learning environment, individuals must explore and experiment with the task to infer and learn the rules, principles, and strategies for effective performance.

An early review of discovery learning studies indicated that it leads to greater transfer, especially for tasks that are more complex or novel, compared to rule–example (deductive) methods of instruction (Hermann, 1969). A key factor in the effectiveness of discovery learning methods is the amount and type of guidance provided to learners. Guidance can include the following types: giving answers to problems; providing leading questions or hints to learners; varying the size of steps in instruction; and providing prompts without giving solutions (Hermann, 1969; Kamouri, Kamouri, & Smith, 1986).

Several theoretical reasons for the benefits of discovery learning have been described. Individuals in a discovery learning setting may be more motivated because they are responsible for learning and generating correct task strategies, and thus are more actively engaged in learning (Singer & Pease, 1976). Discovery learning allows learners to use hypothesis-testing and problem-solving learning strategies, which require more conscious attention for their application (McDaniel & Schlager, 1990; Veenman, Elshout, & Busato, 1994). The development of these strategies for discovering information can help individuals to identify when a transfer situation is novel and to search for an appropriate new response (McDaniel & Schlager, 1990). In addition, because individuals generate optimal methods on their own, the knowledge they acquire can become better integrated with their existing knowledge (Egan & Greeno, 1973; Frese et al., 1988). Active processing during learning can lead to more flexible knowledge, because it is acquired at a higher level of regulation (Frese & Zapf, 1994).

Research has examined several ways to operationalize guided discovery for perceptual-motor and problem-solving tasks. In general, guided discovery is operationalized as either reducing the variability of possible responses (Greenockle & Lee, 1991) or providing the general strategy to the trainee and having him or her discover the specific moves (McDaniel & Schlager, 1990). Some research has found that discovery learning leads to greater transfer of training to novel transfer tasks compared to procedural instruction (Kamouri et al., 1986). Other research has found that more traditional instruction with memory aids leads to greater transfer than discovery learning (Carlson, Lundy, & Schneider, 1992). Researchers have found also that pure discovery is better than guided discovery for adaptive transfer (McDaniel & Schlager, 1990), whereas other researchers have shown the two methods to have similar results (Singer & Pease, 1976) or that guided discovery is more effective (Greenockle & Lee, 1991).

Although hypothesis testing and problem solving are viewed as the hallmark of discovery learning, instructional research has not based operationalizations of guided discovery on this theoretical foundation. This may be one reason for the inconsistency of research comparing pure discovery, guided discovery, and traditional learning approaches. Providing guidance to learners in forming hypotheses about the learning material and testing these ideas may be an effective way to provide more structure to a discovery learning environment (Smith, 1995). Individuals who are not used to having full responsibility for learning, or who do not possess skills in systematic learning and problem solving, may benefit from receiving guidance in these approaches. Frese and colleagues (1988) provided some evidence that guiding people in hypothesis-testing leads to greater knowledge, which can be used in later situations that require the learning of a new task strategy. Hypothesis testing and the capability to make predictions and devise new strategies is a key component of adaptive expertise (Hatano & Inagaki, 1986).

In addition, from an organizational perspective, pure discovery learning may not be a realistic option for promoting adaptability. Pure discovery requires more instructional time, and learners differ in their capability and desire for unstructured learning environments. Guided discovery provides an alternative that enables individuals to think more actively about the training content and develop richer knowledge structures.

A design strategy closely related to discovery learning is *error-based learning* (Frese et al., 1988; Ivancic & Hesketh, 1995/1996). Although some training approaches have sought to minimize incorrect responses (e.g., Skinner, 1987), other researchers have argued that error-making is beneficial. From this perspective, learning environments can be designed to be an "error-filled" experience. As has been discussed earlier in this book, errors are beneficial because they allow for more controlled processing by the learner. Errors can get the learner's attention because they signal unexpected events. Errors can also alert individuals to incorrect assumptions in their knowledge structure (Ivancic & Hesketh, 1995/1996). In this way, making mistakes can lead to a better operative mental model of the task (Frese et al., 1988).

A distinction between error-training and discovery learning is that error-training contains error management elements (Frese et al., 1991). Providing error management strategies allows learners to cope with and recover from error situations that may have negative motivational consequences (Ivancic & Hesketh, 1995/1996). Frese and Altmann (1989) have identified methods to assist trainees in managing errors. Instruction should focus trainees on the beneficial aspects of errors for learning and the information that these errors provide. Trainees must be able to learn what caused an error and how it can be avoided in the future. Making errors should also be emphasized as a goal of the training. Because most people view errors as negative, training should provide heuristics that remind individuals of the benefits of errors and that change their learning goal to one of trying to learn from errors (Frese & Altmann, 1989).

Ivancic and Hesketh (1995/1996) raised the possibility of training individuals about the likely errors they would commit, examples of what they should not do, or information about the limits of a model or strategy. This type of intervention would then address the problems faced by intermediate experts who do not know what not to do (Patel & Groen, 1991). This approach may provide the same benefits as a discovery learning method, but trainees would not actually have to make many mistakes. However, if transfer requires the types of hypothesis-testing and problem-solving skills that are learned and used during discovery learning, then this direct presentation of error information may not lead to effective transfer.

In sum, research on discovery learning and error-based training suggests that allowing individuals latitude to explore the training content and develop their own understanding of it can lead to the development of higher quality knowledge structures. These knowledge structures contain information not only on optimal strategies but also information on mistakes and procedures that are not optimal for a given situation. Individuals who engage in exploratory learning are also likely to try out a greater range of strategies that become integrated with their existing knowledge. This additional knowledge is then available to try when faced with a novel situation. Thus, these individuals should be more successful when faced with adaptive transfer situations.

## Building Executive-Level Skills

Researchers have noted that a critical component of adaptive expertise is the capability to select from alternate strategies, monitor the use of strategies, and revise or select a different strategy if the current approach is not successful (Butterfield & Nelson, 1989; Salomon & Perkins, 1989). The most successful performers are more aware of their cognitive processes and are more effective at monitoring and evaluating their strategies while performing tasks (Etelapelto, 1993). This suggests that training for adaptive expertise should include attention to metacognitive awareness and regulatory processes.

Research on teaching individuals metacognitive skills has tended to focus on children and those with learning disabilities. However, research has also provided evidence that incorporating metacognitive activities into instruction can facilitate learning in older or adult samples

(Meloth, 1990; Veenman, Elshout, & Busato, 1994). Volet (1991) found that undergraduate students who were taught metacognitive activities during an introductory computer programming course received better grades at the end of the course compared to the control group. In addition, the experimental group was better at applying this knowledge to solving new problems (Volet, 1991). The metacognitive treatment consisted of instruction on a planning strategy that included monitoring and evaluation components. Lundeberg (1987) identified the strategies used by experts (lawyers and law professors) in reading legal cases and developed guidelines based on these strategies. Instruction combining guidelines (similar to advanced organizers) and self-control training led to higher test performance compared to training on just guidelines, which led to greater performance compared to no training.

Greiner and Karoly (1976) conducted a study to teach college students a standard method to improve their study habits. Students were instructed on this study method alone or in combination with instruction on various components of self-regulation, as follows: (a) self-monitoring; (b) self-monitoring with self-reward; or (c) self-monitoring, self-reward, and planning strategies. Results indicated that training on self-monitoring or self-monitoring with self-reward did not lead to significantly different learning outcomes compared to training on the study method alone. In contrast, the group receiving instruction on self-monitoring, self-reward, and planning strategies spent significantly more time studying than the other two self-regulatory groups, and they spread their study time out more evenly over the academic quarter. The planning group also performed significantly better than other groups on a second quiz compared to a first quiz (Greiner & Karoly, 1976).

For the most part, research has examined the role of metacognitive instruction in relatively structured or traditional learning environments (Seabaugh & Schumaker, 1994, provides an exception). It is likely that metacognitive skills may be even more critical when individuals are faced with greater responsibility for learning on their own. Metacognitive processing can be facilitated during training by encouraging and prompting the learners to identify goals, generate new ideas, elaborate on existing ideas, and strive for greater understanding (Scardamalia, Bereiter, & Steinbach, 1984). Two approaches for encouraging the development of metacognitive skills are increasing learner control over the learning process and directing the learner to take a mastery orientation to the learning task.

The research on learner control (e.g., Steinberg, 1989) contends that giving learners some choice or control over instructional elements provides greater opportunities for metacognitive monitoring and control (Ford & Kraiger, 1995). Learner control can include choice over the content, the sequence, and the pace of learning. Allowing learners to have control over instruction can lead them to be more motivated and more involved in learning (Steinberg, 1989). Because individuals can focus more time on material that is difficult for them, it has been hypothesized that learner control leads to better learning than instructor-controlled situations. Individuals have the opportunity to explore the task and develop strategic behavior (Wilson & Cole, 1991). Research has shown, however, that advice should be provided to individuals to help them make informed choices about their learning needs (Tennyson, 1981). This advice should include information on the learner's progress, as well as advice on what to do next to improve understanding.

Mastery-oriented training is another method for promoting metacognitive processing. Dweck (1986) has identified two types of goal orientations to learning activities. A *mastery orientation* includes the belief that effort leads to improved outcomes, and that ability is malleable. Individuals with a mastery orientation focus on developing new skills, attempt to understand their tasks, and successfully achieve self-referenced standards for mastery (Dweck, 1986). In contrast, individuals with a performance orientation believe that ability is demonstrated by performing better than others, surpassing normative-based standards, or succeeding with little effort. Mastery and performance orientations, therefore, represent different ideas of success and different reasons for engaging in learning (Ames, 1992).

Research has found that classroom settings emphasizing mastery goals lead students to use more effective learning strategies, prefer challenging tasks, have a more positive attitude toward the class, and have a stronger belief that success comes out of effort. In contrast, classrooms emphasizing performance goals lead students to focus on their abilities, evaluate their ability negatively, and attribute their failures to lack of ability (Ames & Archer, 1988). Research has shown that mastery goals lead to persistence in the face of difficulties, whereas performance goals lead to the avoidance of challenging tasks (Dweck, 1986; Dweck & Leggett, 1988; Elliott & Dweck, 1988).

Kozlowski, Gully, Smith, Nason, and Brown (1995) suggested that mastery-oriented training should lead individuals to engage in metacognitive processes such as monitoring and evaluating comprehension and trying out different strategies for task performance. They examined the sequencing of increasingly complex mastery goals on various learning outcomes and generalization. Research participants who were provided mastery goals were instructed to focus on learning components of the task, trying out skills, and exploring new strategies. Individuals in the performance goal condition were instructed to achieve a difficult, specific outcome goal. Results indicated that, compared to performance goals, mastery goals positively influenced the formation of metacognitive structure across training sessions, as well as the development of self-efficacy for the task. Both learning outcomes were significant predictors of generalization after controlling for cognitive ability, training performance, and declarative knowledge.

In sum, strategies for building executive-level skills can be effective in increasing learning and transfer of knowledge and skills. Results indicate that teaching both self-regulatory strategies and a specific learning strategy for the task being learned are important for retention (Lundeberg, 1987) and generalization of learning (Sawyer, Graham, & Harris, 1992). There is also evidence that individuals trained in self-regulatory skills are better able to apply their knowledge to solving new problems (Volet, 1991). Finally, learning environments that encourage learner control and mastery orientation can be effective in enhancing metacognitive processing, which then aids in adaptive transfer.

## Discussion and Future Directions

This chapter has described the constructs derived from cognitive and instructional psychology that we feel have much potential to advance our understanding and improve the practice of workplace training. We contend that building well-integrated, high quality knowledge structures and developing metacognitive skills in planning, monitoring, and evaluation are important prerequisites for adaptive expertise. Also, the design strategies of advance organizer information, analogical reasoning, guided discovery learning, error-based learning, metacognitive training, learner control, and mastery-oriented training are expected to influence adaptability through their impact on knowledge structures and metacognition.

The findings we reviewed from cognitive and instructional psychology, though, are not directly generalizable to workplace training issues. There are key differences between the research goals of cognitive psychology and the issues faced in workplace training relevant to issues of learning and the transfer of that learning to the job context (Kraiger, 1995). Because of these differences in goals, Ford and Kraiger (1995) stressed the need to bridge the gap between research domains. By identifying the gaps, one can begin to determine how the study and conduct of workplace training can be appreciably different by applying new constructs to training design. There are four critical research gaps that need to be addressed by applied psychologists to advance our understanding of the constructs in this chapter.

*1. How is adaptability defined and investigated?* One research gap concerns the way the construct of adaptability has been studied. Adaptability has been defined as the capability to adjust knowledge and skills in the face of novel situations or requirements. The weakest form of adaptability involves a task that requires the same method learned in training that is applied to a new exemplar. A second, somewhat stronger, form of transfer occurs when an individual can use the same procedures or methods learned in training but the methods must be reconfigured (adapted) to handle the transfer task. The third and strongest form of transfer occurs when effectiveness in the transfer environment requires adapting different methods from those learned in training and using existing knowledge to generate new approaches and strategies (Patrick, 1992).

Much of the research cited in this chapter on design strategies have measured adaptability consistent with the first two forms. As an example of the first type of transfer, Gick and Holyoak (1983) examined how the same strategy learned in training could be transferred to a problem containing different surface features than the trained problem. As an example of the second type, Butterfield and Nelson (1991) taught individuals to combine pieces of information additively, but a transfer task required them to combine the information multiplicatively. Thus, the more basic research has tended to examine how the learner generalizes skills from training to situations that are roughly at the same level of complexity.

From a training perspective, the changing workplace places a premium on the acquisition of knowledge and skills that prepare individuals to make continuous improvements in their jobs. Thus, the strongest form of adaptability is most relevant for training in the twenty-first century as individuals must recognize when trained methods are not appropriate or effective, new methods must be learned, or new strategies must be considered given an increasing level of task complexity. This is consistent with an earlier call by Royer (1979) for psychologists to study more intensely the design and transfer strategies that facilitate an individual's capacity for "learning to learn." Research is needed that identifies high performance skills and examines how to effectively train these skills in a way that facilitates adaptability rather than rote application.

*2. What is the task to be learned?* A second research gap on adaptive expertise is that this literature has been less interested in the type of task the participant is learning (Kraiger, 1995). The tasks chosen often have little relevance to real-world tasks in work settings. For example, much of the research reviewed in this chapter has focused on tasks such as word problems (Gick & Holyoak, 1983), ball-tossing tasks in which individuals must throw a volleyball off a circle marked on a wall to hit a target on the floor (Greenockle & Lee, 1991), serial manipulation tasks (Singer & Pease, 1976), and water jar problems in which individuals have to obtain a specific amount of water using a number of jars of different sizes (McDaniel & Schlager, 1990). These tasks have well-defined parameters (which allows for a clear focus on the learning processes of interest) and one best solution for accomplishment. In addition, this research has focused on single-task situations; little attention has been paid to how design strategies might affect behavior across multiple tasks.

The changing nature of work has led to task domains that are increasingly dynamic and unbounded. Problems are becoming less structured, with multiple paths to a single solution and several potential solutions. We need research on tasks that include these characteristics, as adaptability is most relevant in jobs in which individuals face these complex, ill-structured problems. Thus, the type of task being trained becomes a critical concern in applying design strategies to organizational training (Gagné, Briggs, & Wager, 1993). Research must examine whether design strategies effective for well-structured tasks generalize to dynamic and ill-defined tasks. In applied settings we are also interested in how individuals behave across a range of tasks that must be performed each day. We need to understand how to build adaptive capabilities that affect performance across these varied tasks.

*3. When are design strategies effective?* The research on design strategies has focused on basic issues of whether one type of design is effective for learning and transfer. Research on discovery learning is conducted separate from research on learner control or research on mastery-oriented training. A third research gap is that we know little about the possible additive or interactive effects of combining design strategies in a single training program. Some of these design elements may work in different ways to build knowledge structures or metacognitive skills. For example, it is not clear from present research whether mastery-oriented training provides a unique pathway for building metacognitive skills and adaptability when compared to learner control strategies, or whether both techniques operate through a common psychological mechanism.

There is also a concern about the utility of developing training programs that incorporate multiple design elements. Design strategies such as guided discovery may be more time-intensive methods for building adaptive expertise. Developing training in organizations requires a balance between the cost of complex training designs and their possible benefits. It is important to determine whether certain design strategies are more effective than others, or if certain design elements can be substituted for one another depending on the content to be learned. In addition, existing research on training design has focused more attention on normative results. Less attention has been paid to how individual differences may impact the effectiveness of particular design strategies. If design strategies show differential effectiveness based on trainee characteristics, then research must consider and measure these factors. Some attention has been paid to the interaction between cognitive ability and design strategies (e.g., Cronbach & Snow, 1977); however, personality and motivational factors may also be important. For example, a recent study found that an individual's mastery orientation had a positive impact on metacognitive activity, which in turn was related to knowledge and skill acquisition under learner control conditions (Smith, Ford, Weissbein, & Gully, 1995). More research on individual difference factors can assist applied psychologists concerned with developing training programs that are effective for many types of learners.

*4. Why is the transfer environment important for building adaptability?* Much of the research on adaptability cited in this chapter has examined whether learning on a particular task generalizes to more complex aspects of the same task or to tasks similar to the learned task. These differences in task performance are typically investigated within the same type of learning environment (Kraiger, 1995). A fourth research gap, therefore, is the low emphasis placed on examining environmental impacts on transfer.

The transfer environment in which work tasks are performed is rarely the same as the training environment. Trainees must not only apply learned knowledge and skills to similar or different tasks but must also adapt behaviors to a more complex and demanding environment. For example, training may emphasize skills in problem solving and encourage the development of new and innovative solutions. In the work setting, though, the immediate pressures for short-term gains may not allow for careful consideration of alternative methods or strategies. Without changes in the work setting to build in more time for innovative thinking and pursuing alternative courses of action, it is likely that individuals will return to more familiar ways of accomplishing tasks.

In addition, the transfer environment may or may not be supportive of the knowledge and skills obtained during training. Kozlowski and Salas (in press) have argued that the environmental context must be aligned with trained skills for transfer to be effective. For example, a traditional authoritarian organization may not be supportive of individuals who attempt to take risks and try out new strategies. Mistakes and errors may be viewed as problems rather than as opportunities to learn and continuously develop. This situational context may overwhelm any desire on the part of an individual to build adaptive expertise. Thus, we need research that examines how contextual factors can support or inhibit the continued development of adaptive expertise. One option is to shift interventions and experiences that enhance adaptive expertise to the job setting (Kozlowski, Gully, McHugh, Salas, & Cannon-Bowers, in press). Then strategies or interventions in the transfer environment can be designed to enhance the development of a continuous learning orientation.

## Conclusion

The need to build adaptive expertise certainly resonates in the minds of training researchers and practitioners given the changing nature of the workplace. We have identified several design strategies that have much relevance for building such expertise. We have also presented a model linking these design strategies to adaptability through their impact on the key learning outcomes of knowledge structures and metacognitive skills. Research should begin to bridge the gap between more basic issues of learning and the applied issues of interest to training researchers concerning design strategies, learning, and adaptability.

An examination of the design strategies suggests the likelihood of common psychological mechanisms that mediate the link to learning outcomes. For example, learner control, error-based training, and mastery-oriented training are presumed to influence learning through metacognitive and self-regulatory processes. In contrast, advance organizers are presumed to affect the assimilation and organization of new knowledge—a different psychological mechanism. As a consequence, one thrust in theoretical development is to identify the common and the distinct mediating mechanisms that lead to learning outcomes. There are three potential benefits for conducting this type of research. For interventions that have a common mechanism, one can identify the most effective design intervention. Interventions that make unique contributions to a common mechanism can be combined to yield a more effective and integrative intervention. And, where interventions operate through differential mechanisms, they can be combined to have additive effects on learning and adaptability.

The learning outcomes discussed here are only a portion of the outcomes that are likely to be relevant for adaptability. The cognitive and applied psychological literatures certainly recognize that learning is not a simple function of information processing and its organization in memory. Indeed, there is a long history in psychological theory and research that links motivation and learning in common models and frameworks. As a consequence, a second research thrust would be to integrate more explicitly learning and motivational outcomes that result from design interventions. For example, mastery-oriented training may have a positive impact on an individual's self-efficacy, as well as on building metacognitive skills. Research suggests that self-efficacy perceptions enhance resilience to stress and lead to a willingness to try new or innovative strategies to challenging problems (Kozlowski et al., 1995; Smith et al., 1995). This is the essence of adaptability.

## References

Ames, C. (1992). Classrooms: Goals, structures, and student motivation. *Journal of Educational Psychology, 84*, 261–271.

Ames, C., & Archer, J. (1988). Achievement goals in the classroom: Students' learning strategies and motivation processes. *Journal of Educational Psychology, 80*, 260–267.

Anderson, J. R. (1983). *The architecture of cognition.* Cambridge, MA: Harvard University Press.

Anderson, J. R. (1993a). Problem solving and learning. *American Psychologist, 48*, 35–44.

Anderson J. R. (1993b). *Rules of the mind.* Hillsdale, NJ: Erlbaum.

Ausubel, D. P. (1968). *Educational psychology: A cognitive view.* New York: Holt, Rinehart, & Winston.

Baldwin, T. T., & Ford, J. K. (1988). Transfer of training: A review and directions for future research. *Personnel Psychology, 41,* 63–105.

Bereiter, C., & Scardamalia, M. (1985). Cognitive coping strategies and the problem of "inert" knowledge. In S. Chipman, J. W. Segal, & R. Glaser (Eds.), *Thinking and learning skills: Vol 2. Research and open questions* (pp. 65–80). Hillsdale, NJ: Erlbaum.

Butterfield, E. C., & Nelson, G. D. (1989). Theory and practice of teaching for transfer. *Educational Technology Research and Development, 37,* 5–38.

Butterfield, E. C., & Nelson, G. D. (1991). Promoting positive transfer of different types. *Cognition and Instruction, 8,* 69–102.

Carlson, R. A., Lundy, D. H., & Schneider, W. (1992). Strategy guidance and memory aiding in learning a problem-solving skill. *Human Factors, 34,* 129–145.

Chi, M. T. H., Feltovich, P. J., & Glaser, R. (1981). Categorization and representation of physics problems by experts and novices. *Cognitive Science, 5,* 121–152.

Clark, R. E., & Voogel, A. (1985). Transfer of training principles for instructional design. *Educational Communication and Technology Journal, 33,* 113–123.

Cormier, S. M. (1987). The structural processes underlying transfer of training. In S. M. Cormier & J. D. Hagman (Eds.), *Transfer of learning: Contemporary research and applications* (pp. 152–182). San Diego, CA: Academic Press.

Cronbach, L. J., & Snow, R. E. (1977). *Aptitudes and instructional methods.* New York: Irvington.

Day, J. D. (1986). Teaching summarization skills: Influences of student ability level and strategy difficulty. *Cognition and Instruction, 3,* 193–210.

DiVesta, F. J., & Peverly, S. T. (1984). The effects of encoding variability, processing activity, and rule-example sequence on the transfer of conceptual rules. *Journal of Educational Psychology, 76,* 108–119.

Dorner, D., & Scholkopf, J. (1991). Controlling complex systems; or, Expertise as "grandmother's know-how." In K. A. Ericsson & J. Smith, *Toward a general theory of expertise* (pp. 218–239). Cambridge: Cambridge University Press.

Dweck, C. S. (1986). Motivational processes affecting learning. *American Psychologist, 41,* 1040–1048.

Dweck, C. S., & Leggett, E. L. (1988). A social-cognitive approach to motivation and personality. *Psychological Review, 95,* 256–273.

Egan, D. E., & Greeno, J. G. (1973). Acquiring cognitive structure by discovery and rule learning. *Journal of Educational Psychology, 64,* 85–97.

Elio, R., & Anderson, J. R. (1984). The effects of information order and learning mode on schema abstraction. *Memory and Cognition, 12,* 20–30.

Elliott, E. S., & Dweck, C. S. (1988). Goals: An approach to motivation and achievement. *Journal of Personality and Social Psychology, 54,* 5–12.

Etelapelto, A. (1993). Metacognition and the expertise of computer program comprehension. *Scandinavian Journal of Educational Research, 37,* 243–254.

Fitts, P. M., & Posner, M. (1967). *Human performance.* Monterey, CA: Brooks/Cole.

Flavell, J. H. (1979). Metacognition and cognitive monitoring: A new area of cognitive-developmental inquiry. *American Psychologist, 34,* 906–911.

Ford, J. K., & Kraiger, K. (1995). The application of cognitive constructs to the instructional systems model of training: Implications for needs assessment, design and transfer. In C. L. Cooper & I. T. Robertson (Eds.), *The international review of industrial and organizational psychology* (Vol. 10, pp. 1–48). Chichester, England: Wiley.

Frese, M., Albrecht, K., Altmann, A., Lang, J., Papstein, P. V., Peyerl, R., Prumper, J., Schulte-Gocking, H., Wankmuller, I., & Wendel, R. (1988). The effects of an active development of the mental model in the training process: Experimental results in a word processing system. *Behaviour and Information Technology, 7*, 295–304.

Frese, M., & Altmann, A. (1989). The treatment of errors in learning and transfer. In L. Bainbridge & S. A. R. Quintanilla (Eds.), *Developing skills with new technology.* Chichester, England: John Wiley.

Frese, M., Brodbeck, F., Heinbokel, T., Mooser, C., Schleiffenbaum, E., & Thiemann, P. (1991). Errors in training computer skills: On the positive function of errors. *Human-Computer Interaction, 6*, 77–93.

Frese, M., & Zapf, D. (1994). Action as the core of work psychology: A German approach. In H. C. Triandis, M. D. Dunnette, & L. M. Hough (Eds.), *Handbook of industrial and organizational psychology* (Vol. 4, pp. 271–340). Palo Alto, CA: Consulting Psychologists Press.

Gagné, R. M., Briggs, L. J., & Wager, W. W. (1992). *Principles of instructional design.* New York: Harcourt Brace.

Gick, M. L., & Holyoak, K. J. (1980). Analogical problem solving. *Cognitive Psychology, 12*, 306–355.

Gick, M. L., & Holyoak, K. J. (1983). Schema induction and analogical transfer. *Cognitive Psychology, 15*, 1–38.

Gick, M. L., & Holyoak, K. J. (1987). The cognitive basis of knowledge transfer. In S. M. Cormier & J. D. Hagman (Eds.), *Transfer of training: Contemporary research and applications* (pp. 9–46). New York: Academic Press.

Glaser, R., & Bassok, M. (1989). Learning theory and the study of instruction. *Annual Review of Psychology, 40*, 631–666.

Glaser, R., & Chi, M. T. (1989). Overview. In M. T. Chi, R. Glaser, & M. J. Farr (Eds.), *The nature of expertise* (pp. xv–xxviii). Hillsdale, NJ: Erlbaum.

Goldstein, I. L. (1993). *Training in organizations.* Pacific Grove, CA: Brooks/Cole.

Goldstein, I. L., & Gilliam, P. (1990). Training system issues in the year 2000. *American Psychologist, 45*, 134–143.

Greenockle, K. M., & Lee, A. (1991). Comparison of guided and discovery learning strategies. *Perceptual and Motor Skills, 72*, 1127–1130.

Greiner, J. M., & Karoly, P. (1976). Effects of self-control training on study activity and academic performance: An analysis of self-monitoring, self-reward, and systematic-planning components. *Journal of Counseling Psychology, 23*, 495–502.

Hatano, G., & Inagaki, K. (1986). Two courses of expertise. In H. Stevenson, H. Azuma, & K. Hakuta (Eds.), *Child development and education in Japan* (pp. 262–272). San Francisco: Freeman.

Hermann, G. (1969). Learning by discovery: A critical review of studies. *Journal of Experimental Education, 38*, 58–72.

Holyoak, K. J. (1991). Symbolic connectionism: Toward third-generation theories of expertise. In K. A. Ericsson & J. Smith (Eds.), *Toward a general theory of expertise* (pp. 301–336). Cambridge: Cambridge University Press.

Holyoak, K. J., & Koh, K. (1987). Surface and structural similarity in analogical transfer. *Memory & Cognition, 15*, 332–340.

Howell, W. C., & Cooke, N. J. (1989). Training the human information processor: A review of cognitive models. In I. L. Goldstein (Ed.), *Training and development in organizations* (pp. 121–182). San Francisco: Jossey-Bass.

Ivancic, K., & Hesketh, B. (1995/1996). Making the best of errors during training. *Training Research Journal, 1*, 103–125.

Jung, K., & Kraiger, K. (1994, April). *Structural assessment as a predictor of transfer perfor-*

*mance.* Paper presented at the annual Air Force Symposium of Applied Behavioral Sciences, Colorado Springs, CO.

Kamouri, A. L., Kamouri, J., & Smith, K. H. (1986). Training by exploration: Facilitating the transfer of procedural knowledge through analogical reasoning. *International Journal of Man-Machine Studies, 24,* 171–192.

Kozlowski, S. W. J., Gully, S. M., McHugh, P. P., Salas, E., & Cannon-Bowers, J. A. (1996). A dynamic theory of leadership and team effectiveness: Developmental and task contingent leader roles. In G. R. Ferris (Ed.), *Research in personnel and human resource management* (Vol. 14). Greenwich, CT: JAI Press.

Kozlowski, S. W. J., Gully, S. M., Smith, E. M., Nason, E. R., & Brown, K. G. (1995, May). *Learning orientation and learning objectives: The effects of sequenced mastery goals and advance organizers on performance, knowledge, meta-cognitive structure, self-efficacy, and skill generalization for complex tasks.* Paper presented at the Tenth Annual Conference of the Society for Industrial and Organizational Psychology, Orlando, FL.

Kozlowski, S. W. J., & Salas, E. (1996). An organizational systems approach for the implementation and transfer of training. In J. K. Ford and Associates (Eds.), *Improving training effectiveness in work organizations.* Hillsdale, NJ: Erlbaum.

Kraiger, K. (1995, August). *Paradigms lost: Applications and misapplications of cognitive science to the study of training.* Invited Address presented at the 103rd Annual Convention of the American Psychological Association, New York, NY.

Kraiger, K., Ford, J. K., & Salas, E. (1993). Application of cognitive, skill-based, and affective theories of learning outcomes to new methods of training evaluation. *Journal of Applied Psychology, 78,* 311–328.

Kraiger, K., Salas, E., & Cannon-Bowers, J. A. (1995). Measuring knowledge organization as a method for assessing learning during training. *Human Factors, 37,* 804–816.

Larkin, J. H. (1983). The role of problem representation in physics. In D. Gentner & A. L. Stevens (Eds.), *Mental models* (pp. 75–98). Hillsdale, NJ: Erlbaum.

Lundeberg, M. A. (1987). Metacognitive aspects of reading comprehension: Studying understanding in legal case analysis. *Reading Research Quarterly, 22,* 407–432.

Mayer, R. E. (1975). Different problem-solving competencies established in learning computer programming with and without meaningful models. *Journal of Educational Psychology, 67,* 725–734.

Mayer, R. E. (1979). Can advance organizers influence meaningful learning? *Review of Educational Research, 49,* 371–383.

McDaniel, M. A., & Schlager, M. S. (1990). Discovery learning and transfer of problem-solving skills. *Cognition and Instruction, 7,* 129–159.

Meloth, M. S. (1990). Changes in poor readers' knowledge of cognition and the association of knowledge of cognition with regulation of cognition and reading comprehension. *Journal of Educational Psychology, 82,* 792–798.

Myers, G. L., & Fisk, A. D. (1987). Training consistent task components: Application of automatic and controlled processing theory to industrial task training. *Human Factors, 29,* 255–268.

Nelson, T. O., & Narens, L. (1990). Metamemory: A theoretical framework and new findings. *The Psychology of Learning and Motivation, 26,* 125–141.

Newell, A., & Simon, H. A. (1972). Human problem solving. Englewood Cliffs, NJ: Prentice-Hall.

Patel, V. L., & Groen, G. J. (1991). The general and specific nature of medical expertise: A critical look. In K. A. Ericsson & J. Smith, *Toward a general theory of expertise* (pp. 93–125). Cambridge: Cambridge University Press.

Patrick, J. (1992). *Training: Research and practice.* London: Academic Press.

Pressley, M., Snyder, B. S., Levin, J. R., Murray, H. G., & Ghatala, E. S. (1987). Perceived

Readiness for Examination Performance (PREP): Produced by initial reading of text and text containing adjunct questions. *Reading Research Quarterly, 22,* 219–236.

Proctor, R. W., & Dutta, A. (1995). *Skill acquisition and human performance.* Thousand Oaks, CA: Sage.

Royer, J. M. (1979). Theories of transfer of learning. *Educational Psychologist, 14,* 53–69.

Royer, J. M., Cisero, C. A., & Carlo, M. S. (1993). Techniques and procedures for assessing cognitive skills. *Review of Educational Research, 63,* 201–243.

Salomon, G., & Perkins, D. N. (1989). Rocky roads to transfer: Rethinking mechanisms of a neglected phenomenon. *Educational Psychologist, 24,* 113–142.

Sawyer, R. J., Graham, S., & Harris, K. R. (1992). Direct teaching, strategy instruction, and strategy instruction with explicit self-regulation: Effects on the composition skills and self-efficacy of students with learning disabilities. *Journal of Educational Psychology, 84,* 340–352.

Scardamalia, M., Bereiter, C., & Steinbach, R. (1984). Teachability of reflective processes in written composition. *Cognitive Science, 8,* 173–190.

Schmidt, R. A., & Bjork, R. A. (1992). New conceptualizations of practice: Common principles in three paradigms suggest new concepts for training. *Psychological Science, 3,* 207–217.

Schneider, W. (1985). Training high-performance skills: Fallacies and guidelines. *Human Factors, 27,* 285–300.

Seabaugh, G. O., & Schumaker, J. B. (1994). The effects of self-regulation training on the academic productivity of secondary students with learning problems. *Journal of Behavioral Education, 4,* 109–133.

Shiffrin, R. M., & Schneider, W. (1977). Controlled and automatic human information processing: II. Perceptual learning, automatic attending, and a general theory. *Psychological Review, 84,* 127–190.

Singer, R. N., & Pease, D. (1976). A comparison of discovery learning and guided instructional strategies on motor skill learning, retention, and transfer. *The Research Quarterly, 47,* 788–796.

Skinner, B. F. (1987). What ever happened to psychology as the science of behavior? *American Psychologist, 42,* 780–786.

Smith, E. M. (1995). *The effects of individual differences, discovery learning, and metacognition on learning and adaptive transfer.* Unpublished dissertation proposal, Michigan State University.

Smith, E. M., Ford, J. K., Weissbein, D. A., & Gully, S. M. (1995, May). *The effects of goal orientation, metacognition, and practice strategies on learning and transfer.* Paper presented at the Tenth Annual Conference of the Society for Industrial and Organizational Psychology, Orlando, FL.

Steinberg, E. R. (1989). Cognition and learner control: A literature review, 1977–1988. *Journal of Computer Based Instruction, 16,* 117–121.

Sternberg, R. J., & Frensch, P. A. (1992). On being an expert: A cost-benefit analysis. In R. R. Hoffman (Ed.), *The psychology of expertise* (pp. 191–203). New York: Springer-Verlag.

Tannenbaum, S. I., & Yukl, G. (1992). Training and development in work organizations. *Annual Review of Psychology, 43,* 399–441.

Tennyson, R. D. (1981). Use of adaptive information for advisement in learning concepts and rules using computer-assisted instruction. *American Educational Research Journal, 18,* 425–438.

Thorndike, E. L., & Woodworth, R. S. (1901). The influence of improvement in one mental function upon the efficiency of other functions. *Psychological Review, 8,* 247–261.

Veenman, M. V. J., Elshout, J. J., & Busato, V. V. (1994). Metacognitive mediation in learning with computer-based simulations. *Computers in Human Behavior, 10,* 93–106.

Volet, S. E. (1991). Modeling and coaching of relevant metacognitive strategies for enhancing university students' learning. *Learning and Instruction, 1,* 319–336.

Wilson, B., & Cole, P. (1991). A review of cognitive teaching models. *Educational Technology Research & Development, 39,* 47–64.

# Some Fundamentals of Training and Transfer: Practice Benefits Are Not Automatic

**Addie Ehrenstein, Bruce N. Walker,
Mary Czerwinski, and Evan M. Feldman**

Common wisdom has it that "practice makes perfect," but those of us who study human performance know that this is far from the truth. In this chapter we review a number of studies from our own laboratories and a few others to provide insight into practice effects in some relatively basic task domains. We consider two types of tasks: choice–reaction and visual search tasks. These tasks are fundamental to the performance of many jobs and have been the subject of a great deal of research. For example, problems in the mapping of action goals (e.g., in the field of aviation, lowering the landing gear) to control devices (e.g., a specific cockpit lever) were largely responsible for the development of the field of human factors in the 1940s. Other examples of choice–reaction tasks range from selecting the correct pedal to depress in order to stop a car to tasks as complex as operating a backhoe. Among jobs that rely heavily on visual search capabilities are observing traffic signals and monitoring the status indicators in process control. A concern in both task domains is whether there are some behaviors that can be executed automatically—that is, whether there are tasks that can be performed in a seemingly effortless fashion, bypassing more time-consuming processes and allowing attention to be allocated elsewhere.

In this chapter we consider two major ways in which automaticity can been conceptualized. One way is as an innate process that does not rely on time-consuming cognitive processes. Evidence for this type of automaticity is found in some studies of response selection and in visual search for basic features of stimuli. Perhaps more interesting to training researchers is whether automatic performance can be acquired, such that initially time-consuming processes come to be executed automatically with practice. We will evaluate accounts of acquired automaticity in light of the data on training basic performance and, in particular, examine the implications for training regimes based on the ideal of automatized performance.

In almost any task, no matter how simple, initial performance is characterized by relatively slow, inefficient, and error-prone responding. With practice, performance becomes more efficient and fluid, and less effort is required to carry out the task. Logan (1988) described the shift from controlled, effortful performance to more fluid, efficient performance as a shift from reliance on rules or algorithms for task completion to direct retrieval of appropriate responses from memory. On a more basic level, Welford (1968, 1976) proposed that the primary influence of practice is on the processes that translate stimuli into responses (i.e., response–selection processes), and this contention has been supported in numerous studies (e.g., Pashler & Baylis, 1991; Teichner & Krebs, 1974). However, changes in the efficiency of response selection cannot account for the major practice effects in all cases. In particular, perceptual learning of stimulus features and the context in which they are presented may be an important component of learning in many of the tasks that workers normally encounter. Thus, we discuss studies that attempt to address response–selection processes directly by minimizing the contribution of stimulus–identification and motoric processes. We also discuss studies that specifically address the role of stimulus-feature structure in learning.

## Skill at Responding in Choice–Reaction Tasks

Studies of response–selection processes have typically used choice–reaction tasks in which two or more stimuli are assigned to two or more responses. On any trial, only a single stimulus is presented, and the response assigned to it is to be made as quickly as possible. As with virtually any task, practice in choice–reaction tasks leads to performance improvements, with the speedup in reaction times (RTs) following a power function (Newell & Rosenbloom, 1981).

## Spatial Compatibility Practice Effects

One factor that exerts a robust influence on the ease with which responses can be selected is the spatial correspondence between the stimulus and the response, and problems in performance arise when this correspondence cannot be maintained. An example of the failure to maintain spatial correspondence that is familiar to all too many of us concerns the mapping of electric car window controls to the driver's side control buttons. We probably all have pushed the wrong buttons to lower a passenger side window because of poor mapping of controls to desired actions.

Spatial choice–reaction tasks in which the stimuli are defined by their spatial locations and the responses are keypresses made at assigned locations have been studied extensively (e.g., see Proctor & Dutta, 1995). Stimulus–response compatibility effects are usually found such that responses are faster when the mapping of stimulus locations to response locations is direct (e.g., in a two-choice task the left stimulus is mapped to the left response and the right stimulus to the right response) than when it is indirect (i.e., left stimulus to right response and right stimulus to left response). Compatibility effects are obtained regardless of how the responses are actually executed (e.g., whether the left response key is operated by the left index finger and the right response key by the right index finger, or vice versa; Brebner, Shephard, & Cairney, 1972), suggesting that response selection is based on abstract spatial codes and not on the correspondence of stimuli with an anatomical distinction. As with most other stimulus–response compatibility effects, the compatibility effect in the spatial two-choice task is thought to reflect additional processing required to determine the correct response under the indirect mapping as opposed to the direct mapping (Proctor & Reeve, 1990). The primary concerns for training researchers should include the extent to which asymptotic performance depends on initial conditions (e.g., whether spatial coding will cease to be a factor after extended practice, perhaps because direct associations between stimuli and the hands or fingers used to make the responses are created and strengthened), how to optimize performance, and the extent to which the benefits of practice transfer to altered task conditions. The notion that training results in a qualitative change in processing is at the core of models of automaticity (e.g., Logan, 1988; Schneider & Shiffrin, 1977) and models of skill that propose that task-specific procedures are acquired when the stimulus–response mapping is kept constant across the period of practice (e.g., Anderson, 1982). Thus, it might be expected that stimulus–response compatibility effects would be eliminated with practice. However, research shows that this is not the case for a range of compatibility tasks.

Initial investigations of practice effects in the two-choice spatial compatibility task by Brebner (1973) suggested that the benefit for the spatially direct mapping relative to the indirect mapping does not disappear with practice. Even after 1,200 trials of practice, a significant compatibility effect of approximately 50 milliseconds remained (albeit somewhat reduced from its initial 70-ms level). However, Brebner's experiment required that participants switch between four different stimulus–response mapping conditions each day, such that the mapping of stimuli to responses varied within each session. Thus, the apparent failure to develop automatic responding may have been a result of the switching between stimulus–response assignments. To optimize any benefits of practice, Dutta and Proctor (1992) conducted an experiment in which each participant performed exclusively with either the direct or indirect spatial mapping for 2,400 trials distributed over 8 days. The initial compatibility effect was 72 ms, and the magnitude of the effect decreased reliably across the first few sessions but little thereafter. In the eighth session, the RTs were still 46 ms faster for the direct mapping than for the indirect mapping. Thus, Dutta and Proctor's results are similar to those of Brebner (1973) and indicate that, even when conditions of practice are consistent, performance with the indirect spatial mapping remains at a disadvantage relative to that with the direct spatial mapping.

Although there was no sign of the compatibility effect disappearing with extended practice in the studies just mentioned, it could be argued that with additional incentives to improve performance, the effect would disappear. Feedback that supports setting or attainment of more stringent performance goals is one factor that has been shown to facilitate performance (e.g., Tubbs, 1986). Thus, Dutta and Proctor (1993) conducted two additional experiments that allowed such goals to be set. In the first experiment, summary feedback in the form of mean RT and percentage of correct responses was provided at the completion of each 40-trial block of the experiment. As found previously, there was a reduction in the compatibility effect (from 91 ms to 52 ms) but no sign that the effect would disappear. Because summary feedback alone was not sufficient to eliminate the spatial compatibility effect, a deadline procedure was introduced in the second experiment. Across ten sessions of 240 trials each, the deadline was decreased in successive steps of 15 ms from 500 ms to 365 ms. The deadline procedure was effective at decreasing the mean RTs. Even in the initial session, responses were relatively fast, and the compatibility effect (30 ms) was smaller than in the previous experiments. Despite the reduced magnitude of the initial effect, it decreased reliably with practice to a value of 11 ms in the last session, which was still significant. Moreover, considerably more incorrect responses and missed deadlines occurred for the indirect condition than for the direct condition. The disparity in missed deadlines increased significantly, and the disparity in incorrect responses increased by a nonsignificant amount as the deadline decreased, suggesting that the greater reduction in the compatibility effect relative to other studies was a result in part to the imposed deadline. In short, the basic two-choice spatial compatibility effect is a phenomenon that persists throughout extended practice, even when summary feedback and deadlines are used to enable the setting of strict performance goals.

The implications for training that come out of these results are clear. Whereas certain training approaches (e.g., provision of feedback and the use of deadlines) may reduce RTs slightly, performance decrements resulting from a lack of stimulus–response compatibility will not be practiced away.

The persistence of spatial compatibility effects despite extended practice suggests that translation processes continue to mediate response selection, contrary to the view that stimuli come to automatically activate their assigned responses. To assess whether any qualitative changes in these processes occur as participants become practiced or whether the changes are strictly quantitative, Proctor and Dutta (1993) conducted a series of transfer experiments using the two-choice spatial task. In addition to using direct and indirect mappings, the hands were placed on the response keys in a crossed or uncrossed position. With this procedure, three different relations for which compatibility may be crucial can be isolated (Brebner, 1973): (a) Response locations can be compatibly mapped to stimulus locations (e.g., the left key is pressed in response to a stimulus presented on the left), (b) the hand used to make the response can be compatibly mapped to the response location (e.g., a left finger is used to press the left key), and (c) response hands can be compatibly mapped to stimulus locations (e.g., the left hand is used to respond to a stimulus presented on the left). Predictions for the ordering of RTs can be made based on these relationships between stimulus locations, response locations, and the hand used to make the response. The general logic is that if a particular relation is important,

RTs should depend on whether that relation is compatible or incompatible. Thus, faster RTs for the direct mapping than for the indirect mapping would indicate an effect of the relation between stimulus and response locations, and faster RTs for the uncrossed placement than for the crossed placement would indicate an effect of the relation between response locations and response hand. If the relation between stimulus locations and hands is important, the effects of spatial mapping and hand placement should be underadditive (i.e., the effect of both an incompatible mapping and crossed hand placement should be less than the sum of the effect of crossed hands plus the effect of an incompatible mapping), because this relation is compatible for the indirect mapping–crossed hands condition.

However, the typical finding is that RTs are slower with the indirect spatial mapping than with the direct mapping and when the hands are crossed than when they are uncrossed, with these effects being additive (e.g., Brebner, 1973; Brebner et al., 1972). This pattern of results implicates spatial coding as the basis for the difference in compatibility between the direct and indirect mappings, with an additional contribution of the compatibility between the response location and the hand used to respond. It suggests no role of the stimulus location to response hand relation. To determine whether participants continue to rely on spatial coding as they become practiced, rather than directly associating stimuli with manual responses, Proctor and Dutta (1993) had participants practice for three sessions of 300 trials each with one of the four conditions created by factorially combining direct versus indirect spatial mapping and crossed versus uncrossed hand placement.

As in previous studies, the two variables of spatial mapping and hand placement exerted independent effects on RT in the initial session. More important, the relation between the conditions held across the three sessions of practice. In other words, there was no evidence of a shift from spatial coding to direct specification by a stimulus of the responding finger. After the three sessions of practice, equal numbers of the participants in each of the practice groups were tested in a transfer session with one of the four mapping × placement conditions. Thus, one fourth of the participants continued to perform in the same condition in which they had practiced, and the rest participated in a different condition. Positive transfer was evident in those conditions for which the spatial mapping was the same in the transfer session as in practice, with no evidence for transfer based on either the stimulus–response hand or response key–response hand relations. It is clear, then, that this finding indicates that the benefit of practice involves primarily the relation between stimulus and response locations. This is consistent with the proposal that there are limits on the extent to which the task environment can be restructured by the performer.

Although studies of practice effects in stimulus–response compatibility tasks fail to show evidence of an acquired automaticity in response selection, some results from studies using stimulus–response ensembles that contain a mixture of compatible and incompatible responses suggest a role for automatic processing. Dutta and Proctor (1996) conducted several experiments that compared performance with mixed mappings of compatible and incompatible stimulus–response relations. In each experiment, four horizontally aligned stimulus locations were assigned to a row of four response keys such that two stimuli were assigned to spatially compatible responses (i.e., two stimuli were mapped to responses in a direct manner) and two stimuli were assigned incompatibly (i.e., the mapping of stimulus to response was indirect). Other studies (e.g., Proctor & Reeve, 1985), in which all stimuli were mapped compatibly to responses, have shown that response selection is easier if salient features in the stimulus set correspond to salient features in the response set. For example, if the letter stimuli {O, o, z, and Z} are assigned to keypress responses, performance will be better if the salient feature "letter identity" (i.e., whether the letter is "o" or "z") corresponds to the salient feature "left versus right." In order to determine whether correspondence between salient features in the stimulus and response sets would facilitate the selection of a mapping rule, and not just the selection of a response, Dutta and Proctor examined assignments in which compatible and incompatible mappings either coincided with a salient feature of the stimulus–response ensemble (i.e., the distinction between compatible and incompatible mappings coincided with either the left–right or inner–outer location distinction) or did not (i.e., alternate locations were compatibly mapped). Dutta and Proctor's objective was to test the suggestion of Duncan (1977) that performance in such mixed tasks requires two stages—selection of the appropriate mapping rule and application of that rule—by examining whether rule selection is subject to the influence of the same factors as is the selection of a response.

Dutta and Proctor's (1996) first experiment compared performance with three different mixed-mapping conditions. In the left–right assignment the two right stimuli were mapped directly to responses and the two left stimuli were indirectly mapped. Thus, the compatible–incompatible mapping distinction was consistent with the salient left–right feature of the stimulus–response ensemble. The inner–outer assignment had either the two inner or the two outer stimuli mapped compatibly and the remaining two incompatibly. Finally, in the alternate-location assignment every other stimulus was directly mapped, so that the distinction between compatible and incompatible mappings did not coincide with a salient feature of the stimulus–response ensemble. Dutta and Proctor found that performance was better with the left–right and inner–outer assignments than with the alternate-location assignment. This is consistent with the prediction that salient-feature correspondence should facilitate the selection of a mapping rule. Both compatible and incompatible responses were relatively slow with the alternate-location assignment, but the incompatible responses were most affected. This suggests that in addition to rule-selection being more difficult, selection of the incompatible response is more difficult under this assignment than the others.

In another experiment, Dutta and Proctor (1996) compared performance with the left–right and alternate-location assignments across eight sessions of practice. Performance with both assignments improved with practice, but the improvement for the compatible stimulus–response pairs in the left–right assignment was relatively slight. As a result of this differential improvement, the compatibility effect (incompatible RT − compatible RT) was reduced to a greater extent in the left–right than in the alternate-location condition. The major finding, then, is that not only is the compatibility effect robust with respect to practice, but so is the difference between the assignments. Thus, selection between rules appears to be subject to the same basic constraints as selection of a response to a stimulus. The persistent difference between the compatibly mapped stimulus–response pairs with the left–right and alternate-location assignments indicates that the difficulty of selecting the response does not fully account for the results, because in both assignments, the same, corresponding response is made to the compatibly mapped stimuli.

Dutta and Proctor (1996) also conducted an experiment using the four-choice task with both compatible and incompatible stimulus–response pairs in which the possible responses were reduced from four to two by precuing two of the stimulus positions on most trials (e.g., for the left–right precue either the two right or the two left positions were precued). On one fourth of the trials, the precue indicated only compatible or only incompatible responses (e.g., for the left–right assignment, precuing either the two right or the two left positions would leave two compatibly or two incompatibly mapped alternatives). The point of this experiment was to contrast the relative benefit of the possible precues for the left–right versus the alternate-location assignment. It was predicted that when only stimulus–response pairs of one type (compatible or incompatible) were precued, responses would be relatively fast. This prediction was found to hold only for the left–right assignment. That is, precuing benefits were approximately equal for all the precues with the alternate-location assignment, but the left–right precue produced the fastest RTs for the left–right assignment. Moreover, for the left–right assignment, the left–right precue produced larger and more consistent benefits for the compatible than for the incompatible stimulus–response pairs. One explanation for this is that response–selection can proceed according to a fast, automatic route when all stimulus–response pairs are known to be compatible. However, this appears to be true only when the distinction between compatible and incompatible pairs is salient.

These experiments can be used to evaluate accounts of stimulus–response compatibility that propose that some of the processing that occurs is automatic. In particular, van Duren and Sanders's (1988) suggestion of an additional, automatic route for response selection that can be used when all possible responses are compatible receives some support from the finding of relatively fast response times to compatibly mapped stimuli with the left–right assignment and left–right precue—but the complexity of the stimulus–response ensemble still must be considered. It seems that when the distinction between compatible and incompatible stimulus–response pairs is more difficult to make, as with the alternate-location assignment, task performance is biased to depend on a more time-consuming response–selection process. The precuing results showed this bias in the lack of an advantage for the alternate-location precue with the alternate-location assignment. Response–selection in these tasks is perhaps best characterized by both rule-selection and alternative-selection routes. When all responses in a stimulus–response ensemble are compatible, or when the subset of compatible responses follows a salient distinction in the stimulus–response set (thus allowing rapid selection of the appropriate mapping rule) response selection can proceed rapidly in an automatic manner.

## Skill at Responding to Symbolic Stimuli

Many of the findings with spatial compatibility tasks have been replicated with tasks involving nonspatial, symbolic stimuli. For example Dutta and Proctor (1992; see also Miller, 1982; Proctor & Reeve, 1985) used a four-choice task in which two-dimensional, symbolic stimuli (e.g., the letters O, o, Z, z) are assigned to four keypress responses. In this task, RTs are faster if the more salient letter-identity feature of the stimulus set corresponds to the salient distinction between left and right in the horizontal row of response keys (e.g., a left-to-right mapping of O, o, z, Z—the OozZ mapping) than if there is no systematic relation between stimulus features and the left–right feature of the response set (e.g., a left-to-right assignment of O, z, o, Z—the OzoZ assignment). This symbolic compatibility effect seems to reflect differences in the amount of required stimulus–response translation in much the same way that the spatial compatibility effects do (De Jong, Wierda, Mulder, & Mulder, 1988; Proctor & Reeve, 1985). Dutta and Proctor (1992) tested participants for eight sessions of 310 trials and found compatibility effects of 88 ms in the first session, 42 ms in the third session, and 47 ms in the eighth session. Thus, as with the spatial compatibility effects discussed previously, practice reduces but does not seem to eliminate the symbolic compatibility effect. The broader point in this study is that features of the stimulus and response sets significantly influence both initial and asymptotic performance.

One way to assess the contribution of stimulus and response features to learning is through transfer experiments that test for generalization of learning. Pashler and Baylis (1991) introduced a paradigm in which the stimuli were selected from categories (letters, digits, and non-alphanumeric symbols), and the responses were keypresses made with the index, middle, and ring fingers of the right hand. Following practice for 15 blocks of 50 trials each with a subset of category members, both old and new category members were tested for five additional transfer blocks. In experiments for which the mapping of stimuli to responses was categorizable (e.g., digits were assigned to one response, letters to a second, and symbols to a third), a high degree of transfer to new items in the category and little disruption of responding to the old items were observed in the transfer session. In contrast, when the mapping was uncategorizable (i.e., all stimuli were letters or both letters and digits were assigned to each of the three fingers), little transfer was evident and responses to old items were almost as slow as those to new items. These data led Pashler and Baylis to conclude that when symbolic stimuli are assigned to keypress responses, what is learned is the relation between the category representations and the responses. This learning could involve the relations between categories and fingers or between categories and response locations. To evaluate these possibilities, Pashler and Baylis (1991) conducted an experiment with a categorizable mapping in which the hand used for responding (right or left) was changed for the transfer blocks. As with spatial stimulus–response compatibility, considerable transfer to the new hand was evident. This suggests that the relation learned is between the categories and response locations, rather than between categories and specific fingers used to respond.

Another outcome of interest in Pashler and Baylis's (1991) study was that with noncategorizable mappings adding new stimuli to responses disrupted responding to the stimuli with which participants had practiced. Most accounts of practice effects, such as the development of automaticity, would seem to predict little effect of new stimuli on responses to the old stimuli. Because only a relatively small amount of practice—750 trials—was given in these experiments, it is possible that the disruptive influence of new items would decrease with more extended practice. Dutta (1993) gave participants 1,200 trials of practice (25 blocks of 48 trials each) and found, to the contrary, that RTs for the old items were virtually identical to those for the new items in the first transfer block, as well as in the other transfer blocks. Moreover, when the amount of practice was varied within a single experiment, the magnitude of interference for old items in the first transfer block, relative to the last practice block, increased monotonically (increases in RT of 37, 57, 98, 100, and 121 ms for groups receiving 5, 10, 15, 20, and 25 blocks of practice, respectively). Thus, the disruptive influence of new stimuli on responses to old stimuli clearly is not a result of insufficient practice with the old stimuli. Pashler and Baylis (1991) hypothesized an ad hoc category node to account for the disruption in responding to old stimuli. According to this hypothesis, ad hoc category nodes are created to encompass groups of stimuli that were unrelated prior to the experiment but that are related within the experiment by being assigned to the same responses. The addition of new stimuli in the transfer blocks renders the original ad hoc categories inapplicable and requires that new category nodes be created. Hence, responding to the old stimuli is disrupted.

One implication of the ad hoc category node hypothesis is that if new members are introduced for only some of the three stimulus–

response sets in the transfer blocks, no new ad hoc category nodes would have to be created for the unchanged sets. As a result, there should be no disruption of responding to old stimuli for unchanged sets. Dutta (1993) tested this implication by introducing a new stimulus item for either one or two of the three stimulus sets during the transfer blocks. In contrast to this prediction, performance was disrupted for both changed and unchanged sets when either one or two of the sets were changed.

The fact that introduction of new stimuli produces disruption in responding even for stimuli in other sets that remain unchanged suggests that some learning of the entire stimulus set in relation to the response set occurs. This finding poses problems not only for the ad hoc category node hypothesis but also for associationistic accounts in which a stimulus–response bond is strengthened by the co-activation of a stimulus and response. It seems that the efficiency of response selection depends also on the similarity between a specific stimulus and the alternative members of the stimulus set. That is, just as stimulus–response compatibility effects depend on the ensemble of stimuli assigned to a response set, so does the entire set of stimuli influence choice reactions when multiple stimuli are assigned to each response. Only if the stimulus set has some structure to it [e.g., letters, numbers, and nonalphanumeric stimuli (Pashler & Baylis, 1991) or groups of visually similar stimuli assigned categorically (Dutta, 1993)] does category-based translation seem to occur.

## Summary of Response–Selection Effects

Performance of choice–reaction tasks at early stages of practice relies on processes that translate stimulus codes into response codes (e.g., Umiltà & Nicoletti, 1990). The codes for keypress responses are presumed to be spatial, with the stimulus codes also being spatial if location is the defining stimulus property, and symbolic if the stimuli are alphanumeric. Regarding the question whether the response–selection processes are the same initially and after practice, or whether direct associations between stimuli and fingers are acquired, most of the evidence suggests that there is no qualitative change in the nature of response selection. In the two-choice compatibility task, the role of spatial coding does not seem to diminish and direct associations between stimuli and fingers apparently are not learned. This is evidenced by the findings of Proctor and Dutta (1993) that RTs for the four conditions created by the combinations of direct–indirect spatial mappings and crossed–uncrossed hands maintain the same ordering across three sessions of practice, and that transfer occurs only for conditions in which the spatial mapping used in practice is maintained. The studies with symbolic stimuli paint a similar picture. The symbolic compatibility effect obtained with two-dimensional stimuli assigned to four keypress responses apparently does not disappear with extended practice (Dutta & Proctor, 1992). Also, after practicing with a categorizable mapping of stimuli to responses, the hand with which the responses are executed can be changed with little consequence (Pashler & Baylis, 1991), suggesting that the relation between categories and response locations is crucial. With a noncategorizable mapping, adding a new stimulus member to the set of stimuli assigned to one or two of three responses increases the RTs of the responses for which the stimulus sets have not been changed (Dutta, 1993), implying that direct associations between the stimuli and the response are not the basis of response–selection skill.

The finding of disruption in these simple tasks points to possible problems in the training of task performance. First, care must be taken to design displays to capitalize on the structure of the display contents that serve as stimuli for a task. Second, retraining will likely be necessary to get performance up to an acceptable level when new tasks, or even new stimuli, are introduced. Finally, if, even in these simple tasks, a shift to automatic performance does not occur, we should be aware that there is only so much that training can accomplish.

## Stimulus Characteristics and Training in Visual Search

The research we have discussed to this point tends to consider the stimulus as a unitary "object" that has certain contextual properties such as display location, symbolic meaning, or membership in a specific category. In each of the studies reported previously the task was to respond to one item presented in the display. Many tasks, however, require that search be performed for the relevant task information. Thus, we address search performance in this section, and we discuss evidence for what has been the major concern in search studies—automatization of performance. Moreover, we concentrate on research that focuses on analyzing the various dimensions or features that make up the elements in the display. The interactions of the various features of a stimulus, such as the visual dimensions of size, shape, and color, have been found to play a significant role in the processing and classification of stimuli. It is accepted that different dimensions of stimuli can be used to improve performance, a fact that is well known to interface designers who use these dimensions to group items in displays, but how the constitution of stimuli interacts with training in search for those stimuli has received little attention.

Three major classes of stimulus dimensions have been reported in the literature: separable, configural, and integral (e.g., Pomerantz & Garner, 1973; Pomerantz, Pristach, & Carson, 1989). The dimensions (or features) in a given stimulus set or display are defined relative to other features, with the classification depending on how the dimensions interact with each other.

Separable dimensions are those dimensions that can easily be attended to selectively; in this case, we say that the features themselves do not group. In a classification task in which stimuli must be sorted on the basis of the value of one or more stimulus dimensions, it is relatively easy to attend to one separable dimension while ignoring the other. It is much harder to perform a classification task that depends on the processing of both stimulus dimensions (i.e., it is difficult to divide attention across separable dimensions; Pomerantz et al., 1989). For example, color and shape are separable dimensions. The color of a stimulus does not influence judgments of its shape, nor does shape affect judgments of the stimulus color.

Integral dimensions have been operationally defined as those dimensions for which variation on one dimension influences the processing of the other (Garner, 1974). In other words, it is essentially impossible to attend to one integral dimension of a stimulus and ignore the other. For example, saturation and brightness, components of color, are integral dimensions. Classification performance is poor when discrimination of saturation must be made in the face of random variations of brightness.

For stimuli made up of configural dimensions, it is difficult to process either or both of the constituent stimulus dimensions because of an emergent feature produced by the interaction of stimulus features. For example, Pomerantz and Garner (1973) showed that it was more difficult to sort the stimulus set { ( (, ( ), ) ( and ) ) } into the two groups { ( ( and ( ) } versus { ) ( and ) ) }, than into the two groups { ( ) and ) ( } versus { ( ( and ) ) }. The discrimination in the first case requires attention only to the parenthesis in the left-hand position and can thus be considered a measure of selective attention to that position.

The second set, however, seems to require that attention be divided between the constituent parentheses, yet leads to better classification performance. It has been argued that the combination of the two parentheses creates an emergent feature to which participants attend when classifying the stimuli. Pomerantz, Carson, and Feldman (1994) have shown that two letters placed side by side also group configurally, with the degree to which the letters group depending mainly on the frequency of co-occurrence of the letters in the English language and other linguistic properties of the letter pairs. For example, the letter stimulus pairs AA, AN, NA, and NN show strong properties of grouping, such that it is much easier to discriminate AA and AN from NA and NN than it is to discriminate AA and NA from AN and NN. In the first example, it is the left-hand letter that needs to be attended to, whereas in the second example, the right-hand letter must be attended. Thus, it appears that it is easier to ignore the right-hand letter when attending to the left, than it is to ignore the left-hand letter when attending to the right, owing to the manner in which the English language is read. In contrast, the letter pairs FF, FQ, QF, and QQ, which normally do not occur in language, show relatively reduced grouping properties.

Real-world search tasks usually involve complex stimuli in complex backgrounds. Thus, it is almost guaranteed that the underlying dimensions of the stimuli and the training context will have the potential to interact (for examples of such interaction, see Fisk & Eggemeier, 1988; Klein, Calderwood, & Clinton-Cirocco, 1986; Rogers, Lee, & Fisk, 1995; Schneider, Vidulich, & Yeh, 1982). Understanding these interactions becomes paramount for predicting the ease of visual search and the effects of visual search training in real-world applications. The method of training and the particular stimulus characteristics may affect the performance benefits associated with automatic processing—or determine whether automaticity can even be achieved. Studying search training effects with configural stimuli is a step toward examining the effects of context and stimulus interactions in task performance. We will discuss training experiments using such configural stimuli after a brief review of some of the research relevant to examining the effects of stimulus dimensions on training efficacy.

Much of the recent research on training conducted by experimental psychologists has used search tasks (e.g., Fisk, Lee, & Rogers, 1991; Kramer, Strayer, & Buckley, 1990; Rogers et al., 1995; Schneider & Detweiler, 1987, 1988; Schneider & Fisk, 1982; Schneider & Shiffrin, 1977). The task is typically to search a display of one or more visually presented letters or digits for the presence of one or more items currently held in working memory. On target–present trials, one item from the memory (or target) set is present in the display, whereas on target–absent trials, none of the items in the display is a member of the target set. The general finding in such tasks is that initial performance is best characterized as serial, relatively slow, and sensitive to attentional demands. One of the most robust characteristics of visual search performance is the set-size effect, such that search time increases as set size increases (i.e., as the number of items held in working memory or present in the display increases). Under some conditions, this slow, serial performance gives way to relatively fast, seemingly automatic performance. For example, Schneider and Shiffrin (1977; Shiffrin & Schneider, 1977) found that the set-size effect virtually disappeared when the items searched for were never used as distractors [i.e., target items were used consistently as targets and distractor items only appeared as distractors; the consistent mapping (CM) condition]. However, this was not the case when the target on one trial could be used as a distractor on other trials [i.e., in the varied mapping (VM) condition]. Another characteristic of visual search performance is the target–presence effect. This effect, often taken as evidence of self-terminating search through each element in the display, is that the set-size effect is greater for target–absent than for target–present trials (see Sternberg, 1969; Van Zandt & Townsend, 1993). As with set-size effects, the target–presence effect tends to disappear with practice in the CM condition but not the VM condition (Schneider & Shiffrin, 1977; Shiffrin & Schneider, 1977). These performance changes observed in CM search have been described, in part, as being a result of consistently mapped targets "calling" attention, so that attentional limitations are bypassed. In this case, as the number of items in the display increases beyond one, there is no detriment to a person's ability to find the target in the visual display (Shiffrin & Schneider, 1977).

The differential training advantage for CM over VM conditions has been observed in tasks more complex than search for single digits or letters. For example, in a task similar to one performed by telecommunications workers, Myers and Fisk (1987) had observers search for conjunctions of letters (e.g., "MVK") embedded in an array of letters. Myers and Fisk found greater performance improvements for letter conjunctions that were consistently used as targets, and the lack of set-size and target presence effects was taken as evidence that performance became automatic in that condition. However, the trainees also showed greater than normal improvement in the varied mapping condition. Myers and Fisk explained this improvement by noting that even in the VM condition there were certain regularities in task performance that could be learned (e.g., the same configurations of letters were used as targets repeatedly and hence could be learned). This same point—that even partial consistencies in stimulus conditions may be learned—was demonstrated by Kramer and colleagues (1990) in a complex search task in which rules had to be applied to the stimulus display in order to determine the correct response. Kramer and colleagues found that consistent mapping of specific stimuli to responses was not required for training to be beneficial, as long as higher order consistencies (e.g., the conjunctions between stimulus features and the rules applied to them) are present.

The development of automaticity with consistent practice conditions has received much attention from human factors researchers. For instance, Schneider (e.g., Schneider, 1985; Schneider et al., 1982) has taken steps toward validating training programs based on the development of automatic task components. In a similar applied vein, Fisk and his colleagues have moved toward developing general principles of training based on this line of research (e.g., Fisk & Eggemeir, 1988). If we are to accept consistent practice as a general principle of training, it is important to determine the range of conditions under which automaticity can be expected to develop. For example, we have already seen that there are limits to how "automatic" responding can become in choice–reaction tasks. Therefore, we discuss some alternative views of automaticity and constraints on the development of automaticity, and we consider the role of stimulus composition in the development of automatic responding.

## Searching for Stimulus Features

The results of training in visual search tasks are often described as the development of automatic performance. Thus, it makes sense to consider how automaticity is treated in theories of visual performance. Most current theories of attention and visual search assume search through a display of stimuli to be serial unless the target item is defined by a unique, separable feature, such as the color red (Carter, 1982; Egeth, Virzi, & Garbart, 1984; Treisman, 1982; Treisman & Gelade, 1980). Many of these theories emphasize stimulus characteristics and have addressed the role of processing of stimulus displays. However, there are theorists who have focused on the significant role that both training and stimulus features can play in the pattern of results obtained in visual search paradigms (see Shiffrin, 1988, for a review).

Treisman and her colleagues have investigated stimulus characteristics in visual search and developed the feature integration theory (FIT) to account for the characteristics of visual search for stimulus sets composed of separable features such as orientation, shape, and color (Treisman & Gelade, 1980; Treisman & Gormican, 1988). In FIT, search for a target is described as automatic (or preattentive) when search RT or accuracy is not affected by the number of items in the display. Such performance is found when a target can be distinguished from distractors by a unique feature (e.g., when search is for a red stimulus among green distractors). The underlying reason for better search for single features is thought to be that low-level detectors for simple features (called feature detectors) are present in the visual system. When a target can only be differentiated from the surrounding distractors by a conjunction of features (e.g., when search is for a red square in a display of red circles and green squares), search RT depends on the number, and not just the nature, of the distractors and is described by Treisman as serial and attentive (Treisman & Gelade, 1980; see Treisman & Gormican, 1988, for an alternative version of the theory).

Treisman, Vieira, and Hayes (1992) considered whether performance improvements in conjunctive search should be characterized as automatic in the same sense that search for features is. They performed an extensive series of training experiments to see whether "feature detectors" would develop for conjunctive targets. Although they observed significant performance improvements, transfer tasks revealed that the performance improvements were restricted not only to the specific stimuli used, but also to the context in which these stimuli had occurred. Thus, it did not appear that a new way of processing configural targets had developed (i.e., automaticity did not develop). Rather, it appeared that performance improvements were dependent on the recall of previous instances (Logan, 1988) or specific occurrences of target displays.

Some alternative theories (e.g., Duncan & Humphreys, 1989) predict that the same search processes underlie search for both single features and conjunctions of features. For example, Duncan and Humphreys's (1989) emphasis is on the set-level similarity relations between targets and distractors. According to their account, search will be more efficient when target–distractor similarity is low and the distractor–distractor similarity is high. Increasing similarity within the target set also increases search efficiency. Although most of Duncan and Humphreys's studies used stimuli that would be classified as separable, the fact they do not ascribe any special role to the specific features of the stimuli leads to a prediction of no difference in search for separable versus configural features.

Duncan and Humphreys (1989) have contended that training alters the similarity relationships in the target and distractor sets and, thus, affects search performance. However, although changes in similarity relationships can account for many of the effects of practice on search performance, they do not explain all of the data. For example, Duncan and Humphreys's model does not account for the finding of Shiffrin and Schneider (1977) that reversing the roles of targets and distractors after CM training results in a drop in performance (i.e., such that the items that were treated as distractors are now classified as targets). If all features were treated equally, there should be no effects of switching targets and distractors beyond those associated with changing the stimulus–response mapping.

Finally, Fisher (1986; Fisher & Tanner, 1992), in his feature overlap model, proposed that with practice an optimal order of feature matching is learned, thus increasing the efficiency of search. The model consists of a partly parallel, limited capacity hierarchy of feature detectors. For example, if the task is to search for the letter "A" in a display of other letters, one might first search for a small horizontal line in each letter of the display. If such a feature is not found, all of the items compared at that level in the hierarchy can be eliminated from search in parallel. If such a feature is found in any of the letters, that display item is passed to a higher level of analysis. If any of the items has been passed to this higher level, another feature is chosen from the letter "A" and compared to the members of the selected set. This sort of feature analysis continues until an item containing all the same features as "A" is found (resulting in the classification judgment, "target present"), or until all items are rejected ("target absent"). Performance improves as the most efficient order in which to match target features to display items is learned. Again, it is not clear how stimulus composition (e.g., whether they are made up of separable or configural dimensions) would affect search training.

## The Problem of Unequal Training and Search for Configural Stimuli

The evidence seems compelling that practice with a consistent mapping produces qualitatively different performance improvements than does practice with a varied mapping. However, it is important to note that whereas the number of stimulus items in CM and VM conditions has been controlled in many visual search experiments, the number of training trials a given stimulus has received as a target item has not always been equated for the two conditions. In the CM condition, the targets always come from the same set, so practice with each stimulus and its corresponding response is more frequent than in the VM condition. Thus, for example, when each of the stimuli in a four-item stimulus set can be either target or distractor (VM condition), each stimulus–response pair is encountered only one fourth as many times as in the CM condition. When Czerwinski (1988) equated the training trials for alphanumeric target items in CM and VM conditions, both conditions showed virtually no increase in the time to find the target as the display size increased.

Czerwinski's (1988) results, in combination with later work, partially support the feature overlap model put forward by Fisher (1986; Fisher & Tanner, 1992) in that specific target training against particular background or distractor items has a strong effect on search performance. Such training diminishes the difference between CM and VM conditions [although it should be noted that there was still evidence for automatic processing in Czerwinski's (1988) visual search tasks when the search sets were large or when a secondary task was added to the search task]. Fisher's model does not predict the results obtained from Czerwinski's transfer tasks, however, in which performance suffered when old CM targets were used as distractors to be ignored among other old display items. These results are better explained as support for automatic processing in which the target calls attention to itself. It is important to note that these findings are based on stimulus items that were comprised of separable dimensions.

The question arises whether similar search results will be obtained when configural, rather than separable, stimuli are used in the visual search CM and VM training conditions, with the proper controls for equal target training across the two conditions. This is an important concern if we are to extend search results to training in general, because stimulus dimensions in the real world are often configural (e.g., as when items are grouped to form "good" figures in a display). Moreover, if search for configural stimuli is different from that for separable dimensions, theories of visual search will have to address these differences.

Czerwinski, Feldman, and Cutrell (1994) sought to generalize the issue of how training affects visual search in a series of experiments using configural letter pair stimuli. As mentioned earlier in the chapter, letter stimuli can group configurally, with the magnitude of the effect depending primarily on frequency of co-occurrence of the letters in language. In Czerwinski and colleagues' (1994) visual search experiment, targets and distractors were single consonants preceded by an additional consonant. For example, if the target was N and the distractors were C, Y, and S, then with the prefix letter M the display could contain the elements {MN, MC, MY, and MS}. For each participant, four consonants were assigned as CM items, with one of these four designated as the CM target and the other three designated distractors. One of four other possible letters was assigned as a prefix for each set of items. On each trial, the prefix letter was displayed to the left of each of the CM items. A separate set of four letters served as VM items; prefixes were assigned to the target and distractor consonants as in the CM condition. None of the prefix items served as CM or VM items, nor did any of the CM items serve as prefixes or VM items (and vice versa) within a participant's stimulus set, thus the prefix letter was irrelevant to the visual search task and should have been ignored for optimal performance. One, two, or four items were shown on each trial (distractor items could be repeated in the display), and target-present and target-absent trials were equally probable for each display size. Four times as many VM blocks (36) as CM blocks (9) were conducted in order to equate the number of target trials for each letter across the two conditions.

Prior to the first session of training, participants performed a visual classification experiment (see Pomerantz et al., 1989, for detailed methodology of the visual classification paradigm) in order to verify that the particular stimulus pairs used did indeed display the characteristics of configural dimensions. After the initial visual classification experiment in Session 1, participants were given five blocks of 100 trials of training in the visual search task.

The typical power function speed-up in RTs across sessions was observed for both CM and VM conditions, but there was a significant CM mapping advantage ($M$ RT = 687 and 745 ms for CM and VM, respectively). Although the difference between the CM and VM conditions decreased over sessions, search RTs in the CM condition were still about 40 ms faster than in the VM condition in the last session. Typical effects of target presence and display size were found. Most important, however, set size, session, and mapping interacted, such that although the set-size effect was reduced for both mapping conditions as a function of session, there was more of a reduction for the CM condition. Thus, the CM condition showed one of the primary characteristics of automatic processing: an almost complete lack of dependence of search RT on the number of letter-pair stimuli in the display.

Based on these results, it appears that search for one letter of a configural pair of letters is different from search for a single alphanumeric stimulus in a display of other single stimuli. Czerwinski (1988; Czerwinski, Lightfoot, & Shiffrin, 1992) showed in earlier studies that when the number of stimulus exposures was controlled, there was no evidence of a significant search advantage for the CM condition over the VM condition. Thus, there appear to be differences in how configural and single alphanumeric stimuli are processed. The discrepancy between the results of Czerwinski and colleagues (1994), using configural stimuli and previous studies that used separable stimuli, poses a challenge to theories of visual search. One cannot simply consider the features in the display items without considering the relation of those items to each other.

The major difference between Czerwinski and colleagues' (1994) study and previous studies investigating CM mapping advantages was that Czerwinski and colleagues used pairs of letters that combined configurally, rather than single letters. Therefore, it is of interest to ask whether performance would change if, after practice, the prefix letters were dropped so that the search was for single-letter stimuli. This was tested in transfer sessions to determine whether the CM search advantage would disappear or not. If participants continued to show a CM search advantage after the prefix letter was dropped, it could be argued that automatic processing of the individual CM target letters had been maintained.

The same people that participated in the search training described previously also participated in two additional sessions with no prefix letters. Contrary to previous studies in which single, alphanumeric stimuli were used in CM and VM visual search tasks with the number of CM and VM presentations equated (Czerwinski, 1988), a significant effect of mapping was found. Although there was an initial disruption of both CM and VM search performance early in the first transfer session, search performance quickly recovered and a significant CM search advantage was evident by the second transfer session. It should be noted that these results were obtained using the same type of stimuli and the same procedure as those used in Czerwinski (1988) and Czerwinski and colleagues (1992), in which no CM search advantage was obtained. To test the hypothesis that search for CM targets was automatic, an additional transfer task (the *diagonal transfer task*) was used. In this task, participants were instructed to attend to only two items of the four presented, those occupying the upper-left and lower-right positions, and to ignore the other two items (those in the upper-right and lower-left positions). This was similar to a task used by Shiffrin and Schneider (1977).

For each participant, a previously trained VM target was selected as the target for CM search on the relevant diagonal, and the other VM items were used as distractors (on both the relevant and irrelevant diagonals). In other words, one VM item was now searched for in a CM condition; no VM condition existed for this task. The important comparison for evaluating whether search had become automatic was between trials on which the old CM target appeared on the irrelevant diagonal and trials on which it did not. If automaticity had developed with CM search, such that the CM stimuli came to "call" attention, then presenting the CM target item on the irrelevant diagonal should have interfered with target detection on the relevant diagonal. Indeed, this is what was found: When old CM targets appeared on the to-be-ignored diagonals, a significant disruption in finding the target on the relevant diagonal occurred. This finding provides converging evidence that participants had developed an automatic attention response to CM targets.

To review, it appears that automatic attending to consistently mapped targets can occur under the proper conditions. Most notably, when the processing load is high (as in hybrid memory–visual search tasks or in dual-search paradigms with multiple-item displays; Czerwinski, 1988; Schneider & Shiffrin, 1977; Shiffrin & Schneider, 1977), or when configural stimulus items are used, a CM search advantage emerges fairly quickly with training. It may be that the processing of configural stimulus sets incurs a higher processing load than does the processing of stimuli that are separable. This question awaits further research. Regardless, when mental load is relatively low (e.g., with visual search for separable stimuli or under conditions of low similarity between the targets and distractors), and when the amount of target training is equated between CM and VM conditions, no significant advantage for consistently mapped target items is observed. Future research will need to focus on other configural stimulus items in visual search training paradigms to test the generalizability of these results.

## Implications for Training

Visual search is an important component of a variety of jobs, including assembly line inspection, monitoring nuclear control panels, radiological diagnosis, and air traffic control. In some of these visual search environments, components to be searched for are consistently classified (e.g., there may be a hallmark sign of a certain disease that radiologists search for in an X ray film to diagnose patients). In other visual search tasks, a search item's classification changes depending on the context. For example, given the observable symptoms of a patient, a radiologist may classify a particular finding in an X ray film as evidence of a certain disease. In the absence of these symptoms, a different classification may result. The study by Czerwinski and colleagues (1994), together with previous work, shows that certain stimulus items may be easier or harder to train to the level of automaticity, depending on their dimensional structure. The present research suggests that configural target items will show a larger difference in performance benefits (i.e., evidence of automatic processing) under consistent, as opposed to varied, training conditions.

These findings also have implications for the principles of training outlined by Fisk and colleagues (1991). In the research they used to generate their training principles, CM and VM training conditions were not equated across target–distractor pairings. It is now clear that simply equating the number of training trials for individual targets in CM and VM conditions results in a minimization of the CM search advantage when stimuli are separable and there is a low task workload. However, configural CM target items show strong evidence of automatic processing early in training (Czerwinski et al., 1994), even when the number of search items is relatively low. Fisk and colleagues (1991) stated that any increase in consistency in training will cause a direct improvement in performance. However, the nature of the stimulus dimensions may influence the degree to which performance is improved during consistent training. Any training principles generalized from visual search studies will need to account for the nature of the stimulus dimensions used during training and the different results obtained when using separable, configural, or integral training items. It appears to be important for attention and training researchers to classify their stimuli and to vary their stimulus sets in order to enhance our understanding of how the dimensional composition of training materials can influence the development of automatic processing.

# Conclusion

Perhaps the major message from this chapter is that whereas practice can certainly improve performance, the performance gains to be expected depend heavily on the structure of the task environment. In other words, although training is important, and can be structured in optimal ways (see chapters 3 and 12, this volume), training can accomplish only so much. Several empirical generalizations regarding practice in basic tasks emerge from the research we have presented. First, practice effects in a range of choice–reaction tasks develop during the initial 500 to 1,000 trials and remain relatively stable thereafter. Both spatial and symbolic compatibility effects are reduced during this period but show little change with further practice (Dutta & Proctor, 1992). For a limited range of tasks—that is, where all stimulus–response mappings are known to be compatible and that compatibility is a salient feature of the task—response selection can proceed in a seemingly automatic fashion. Relations between symbolic stimuli and their assigned responses for both categorizable and noncategorizable mappings show evidence of having been learned (Pashler & Baylis, 1991), and strong positive transfer to altered task conditions occurs when certain conditions are met. In general, so long as the salient features of the stimulus set are kept in correspondence with the response set, transfer will occur even when the hand or finger used to make the response is changed (Procter & Dutta, 1993).

In studies of visual search performance, results are often very similar to those obtained with choice–reaction tasks. Practice effects develop quickly over the first few sessions, with RT functions following the typical power law speed-up. In addition, practice benefits are well retained; after a disruptive transfer session, very short periods of retraining bring performance up to the level obtained originally.

Researchers initially concentrated on simple stimuli that were composed of separable dimensions. Consistent mapping (CM) conditions, where targets are always targets and distractors are always distractors, will often lead to response times that can be described as automatic. One hallmark of this automaticity is the elimination of any set-size effects, so that RTs no longer depend on the number of items in a display. This CM training showed a distinct advantage over VM conditions, where targets and distractors could exchange roles (Czerwinski, 1988; Fisk & Ackerman, 1988; Schneider & Shiffrin, 1977; Shiffrin & Schneider, 1977). This implied that the best training method was multiple presentations of the same stimulus–response pairs. However, when the actual number of presentations of a stimulus were equated, this CM advantage disappeared (Czerwinski, 1988). Thus it seemed that it was only the amount of practice with a given search item that really mattered. Many real-world search tasks, though, involve more complex stimuli, and initial work suggests that with configural stimuli (e.g., letter pairs; Czerwinski et al., 1994), the CM advantage returns. Thus it seems that whereas easy tasks and simple stimuli do not show a CM advantage, in certain circumstances, such as when tasks involve high processing loads or configural stimuli, CM training produces reliable benefits.

In summary, both choice–reaction and visual search experimental results show that the composition of both the individual stimuli and the stimulus set as a whole (as well as the stimulus–response mapping) exert strong effects on asymptotic performance. Thus, the specifics of the stimuli, be they lights, sounds, or letters on a screen, and the global nature of the task environment (e.g., the degree of stimulus–response compatibility and cognitive load) must be considered. With more research at each of these levels, in both of these fields, a simpler picture of how much can be done automatically should emerge.

## References

Anderson, J. R. (1982). Acquisition of cognitive skill. *Psychological Review, 89,* 369–406.

Brebner, J. (1973). S-R compatibility and changes with practice. *Acta Psychologica, 37,* 93–106.

Brebner, J., Shephard, M., & Cairney, P. (1972). Spatial relationships and S-R compatibility. *Acta Psychologica, 36,* 1–15.

Carter, R. C. (1982). Visual search with color. *Journal of Experimental Psychology: Human Perception and Performance, 8,* 127–136.

Czerwinski, M. P. (1988). *Differences between visual and memory search: Implications for models of attention.* Unpublished doctoral dissertation, Indiana University, Bloomington, IN.

Czerwinski, M. P., Feldman, E. M., & Cutrell, E. (1994). The influence of stimulus dimensions and training on visual search performance. In *Proceedings of the Human Factors and Ergonomics Society 38th Annual Meeting* (pp. 1266–1270). Santa Monica, CA: Human Factors and Ergonomics Society.

Czerwinski, M., Lightfoot, N., & Shiffrin, R. M. (1992). Automatization and training in visual search. Special Issue: Views and varieties of automaticity. *American Journal of Psychology, 105,* 271–315.

De Jong, R., Wierda, M., Mulder, G., & Mulder, L. J. M. (1988). Use of partial information in response processing. *Journal of Experimental Psychology: Human Perception and Performance, 14,* 682–692.

Duncan, J. (1977). Response selection rules in spatial choice reaction tasks. In S. Dornic (Ed.), *Attention and performance VI* (pp. 49–61). Hillsdale, NJ: Erlbaum.

Duncan, J., & Humphreys, G. W. (1989). Visual search and stimulus similarity. *Psychological Review, 96*, 433–458.

Dutta, A. (1993). *Categorical learning in choice-reaction tasks.* Unpublished doctoral dissertation, Purdue University, West Lafayette, IN.

Dutta, A., & Proctor, R. W. (1992). Persistence of stimulus–response compatibility effects with extended practice. *Journal of Experimental Psychology: Learning, Memory, and Cognition, 18*, 801–809.

Dutta, A., & Proctor, R. W. (1993). The role of feedback in learning spatially indirect choice reaction tasks: Does it have one? In *Proceedings of the Human Factors and Ergonomics Society 37th Annual Meeting* (pp. 1320–1324). Santa Monica, CA: Human Factors and Ergonomics Society.

Dutta, A., & Proctor, R. W. (1996). *Selecting rules and responses in mixed compatibility four-choice tasks.* Manuscript submitted for publication.

Egeth, H. E., Virzi, R. A., & Garbart, H. (1984). Searching for conjunctively defined targets. *Journal of Experimental Psychology: Human Perception and Performance, 10,* 32–39.

Fisher, D. L. (1986, August). *Programmable perceptrons: Serial and parallel search.* Paper presented at the Annual Meeting of the Society for Mathematical Psychology, Cambridge, MA.

Fisher, D. L., & Tanner, N. S. (1992). Optimal symbol set selection: A semiautomated procedure. *Human Factors, 34,* 79–96.

Fisk, A. D., & Ackerman, P. L. (1988). Effects of type of response on memory/visual search: Responding just "yes" or just "no" can lead to inflexible performance. *Perception & Psychophysics, 43,* 373–379.

Fisk, A. D., & Eggemeier, F. T. (1988). Application of automatic/controlled processing theory to training tactical command and control skills: 1. Background and task analytic methodology. In *Proceedings of the Human Factors Society 32nd Annual Meeting* (pp. 1227–1231). Santa Monica, CA: Human Factors and Ergonomics Society.

Fisk, A. D., Lee, M. D. & Rogers, W. A. (1991). Recombination of automatic processing components: The effect of transfer, reversal and conflict situations. *Human Factors, 33,* 267–280.

Garner, W. R. (1974). *The processing of information and structure.* Potomac, MD: Erlbaum.

Klein, G. A., Calderwood, R., & Clinton-Cirocco, A. (1986). Rapid decision making on the fire ground. In *Proceedings of the Human Factors Society 30th Annual Meeting* (pp. 576–580). Santa Monica, CA: Human Factors and Ergonomics Society.

Kramer, A. F., Strayer, D. L., & Buckley, J. (1990). Development and transfer of automatic processing. *Journal of Experimental Psychology: Human Perception and Performance, 16,* 505–522.

Logan, G. D. (1988). Toward an instance theory of automatization. *Psychological Review, 95,* 492–527.

Miller, J. (1982). Discrete versus continuous stage models of human information processing: In search of partial output. *Journal of Experimental Psychology: Human Perception and Performance, 8,* 273–296.

Myers, G. L., & Fisk, A. D. (1987). Training consistent task components: Application of automatic and controlled processing theory to industrial task training. *Human Factors, 29,* 255–268.

Newell, A., & Rosenbloom, P. (1981). Mechanisms of skill acquisition and the law of practice. In J. R. Anderson (Ed.), *Cognitive skills and their acquisition* (pp. 1–56). Hillsdale, NJ: Erlbaum.

Pashler, H., & Baylis, G. (1991). Procedural learning: 1. Locus of practice effects in speeded choice tasks. *Journal of Experimental Psychology: Learning, Memory, and Cognition, 17,* 20–32.

Pomerantz, J. R., Carson, C. E., & Feldman, E. M. (1994). Interference effects in perceptual organization. In S. Ballesteros (Ed.), *Cognitive approach to human perception* (pp. 123–152). Hillsdale, NJ: Erlbaum.

Pomerantz, J. R., & Garner, W. R. (1973). Stimulus configuration in selective attention tasks. *Perception and Psychophysics, 14,* 565–569.

Pomerantz, J. R., Pristach, E. A., & Carson, C. E. (1989). Attention and object perception. In B. Shepp & S. Ballesteros (Eds.), *Object perception: Structure and process* (pp. 53–89). Hillsdale, NJ: Erlbaum.

Proctor, R. W., & Dutta, A. (1993). Do the same stimulus–response relations influence choice reactions initially and after practice? *Journal of Experimental Psychology: Learning, Memory, and Cognition, 19,* 922–930.

Proctor, R. W., & Dutta, A. (1995). Acquisition and transfer of response selection skill. In A. F. Healy & L. E. Bourne, Jr. (Eds.), *Learning and memory of knowledge and skills: Durability and specificity* (pp. 300–319). Thousand Oaks, CA: Sage.

Proctor, R. W., & Reeve, T. G. (1985). Compatibility effects in the assignment of symbolic stimuli to discrete finger responses. *Journal of Experimental Psychology: Human Perception and Performance, 11,* 623–639.

Proctor, R. W., & Reeve, T. G. (Eds.) (1990). *Stimulus–response compatibility: An integrated perspective.* Amsterdam: North-Holland.

Rogers, W. A., Lee, M. D., & Fisk, A. D. (1995). Contextual effects on general learning, feature learning, and attention strengthening in visual search. *Human Factors, 37,* 158–172.

Schneider, W. (1985). Training high-performance skills: Fallacies and guidelines. *Human Factors, 27,* 285–300.

Schneider, W., & Detweiler, M. (1987). A connectionist/control architecture for working memory. In G. H. Bower (Ed.), *The psychology of learning and motivation* (Vol. 21, pp. 53–119). San Diego, CA: Academic Press.

Schneider, W., & Detweiler, M. (1988). The role of practice in dual-task performance: Toward workload modeling in a connectionist/control architecture. *Human Factors, 30,* 539–566.

Schneider, W., & Fisk, A. D. (1982). Concurrent automatic and controlled visual search: Can processing occur without resource cost? *Journal of Experimental Psychology: Learning, Memory, and Cognition, 8,* 261–278.

Schneider, W., & Shiffrin, R. M. (1977). Controlled and automatic human information processing: I. Detection, search, and attention. *Psychological Review, 84,* 1–66.

Schneider, W., Vidulich, M., & Yeh, Y-Y. (1982). Training spatial skills for air-traffic control. In *Proceedings of the Human Factors Society 26th Annual Meeting* (pp. 10–14). Santa Monica, CA: Human Factors Society.

Shiffrin, R. M. (1988). Attention. In R. C. Atkinson, R. J. Herrnstein, & R. D. Luce (Eds.), *Stevens's handbook of experimental psychology: Volume 2. Learning and cognition* (2nd ed., pp. 739–811). New York: Wiley.

Shiffrin, R. M., & Schneider, W. (1977). Controlled and automatic human information processing: II. Perceptual learning, automatic attending, and a general theory. *Psychological Review, 84,* 127–190.

Sternberg, S. (1969). Memory scanning: Mental processes revealed by reaction time experiments. *American Scientist, 57,* 421–457.

Teichner, W. H., & Krebs, M. J. (1974). Laws of visual choice reaction time. *Psychological Review, 81,* 75–98.

Treisman, A. (1982). Perceptual grouping and attention in visual search for features and for objects. *Journal of Experimental Psychology: Human Perception and Performance,* *8,* 194–214.

Treisman, A. M., & Gelade, G. (1980). A feature integration theory of attention. *Cognitive Psychology, 12,* 97–136

Treisman, A. M., & Gormican, S. (1988). Feature analysis in early vision: Evidence from search asymmetries. *Psychological Review, 95,* 15–18.

Treisman, A., Vieira, A., & Hayes, A. (1992). Automaticity and preattentive processing. *American Journal of Psychology, 105,* 341–362.

Tubbs, M. E. (1986). Goal setting: A meta-analytic examination of the empirical evidence. *Journal of Applied Psychology, 71,* 474–483.

Umiltà, C., & Nicoletti, R. (1990). Spatial stimulus-response compatibility. In R. W. Proctor & T. G. Reeve (Eds.), *Stimulus–response compatibility: An integrated perspective* (pp. 89–116). Amsterdam: North-Holland.

van Duren, L. L., & Sanders, A. F. (1988). On the robustness of the additive factors stage structure in blocked and mixed choice reaction designs. *Acta Psychologica, 69,* 83–94.

Van Zandt, T., & Townsend, J. T. (1993). Self-terminating versus exhaustive processes in rapid visual and memory search: An evaluative review. *Perception & Psychophysics, 53,* 563–580.

Welford, A. T. (1968). *Fundamentals of skill.* London: Methuen.

Welford, A. T. (1976). *Skilled performance: Perceptual and motor skills.* Glenview, IL: Scott, Foresman.

# Part Three

# Designing Effective Training Systems

Once a decision has been made to design and implement a new training program, the next set of questions tends to revolve around the issue of training media. For example, the use of videotaped training sessions versus lectures may occupy a disproportionate amount of the training developer's attention and time. Although important, the concern for the type of media to be used is usually considered too early in the process. As Gagne once put it, the most critical decision to be made in training is what is to be learned. Only after that question has been answered should the host of other design issues be considered.

The problem of deciding what is to be learned is exacerbated by changes in the work environment from using specialists to handle tight clusters of similar tasks to giving responsibility to individuals or groups for more loosely bound bundles of interconnected tasks. As the tasks to be performed become more diverse and interconnected, so the problems of defining required knowledge, skills, and abilities become more difficult to solve. In addition, a number of situational factors must be considered when considering the best way to train these critical knowledge, skills, and abilities. This section presents three chapters that address the thorny issue of training program design.

In chapter 6, Kraiger and Jung present a framework for linking training objectives to training evaluation criteria. This is perhaps the most crucial, yet most difficult problem encountered by training developers. The authors present three processes by which learning outcomes may be derived from the instructional objectives of training. They are an examination of the goals of training; identification of instructional strategies, and an examination of the performance domain. Using this approach, the trainer must consider a number of training evaluation measures to find those that are consistent with the goals of the training program and that can be used to evaluate the overall success of the program.

Quiñones draws attention to a number of contextual factors that must be considered in the design and implementation of a training program. These include participation by trainees in the training process, framing of training assignments, and organizational climate. In addition, the author presents a conceptual model linking these contextual factors with training and transfer outcomes. Quiñones argues that trainee characteristics such as motivation to learn, self-efficacy, and fairness perceptions are particularly sensitive to contextual influences.

Finally, in chapter 8 Gist reviews recent developments in training design and pedagogy and offers new perspectives on the learning process. She presents a review of motivational theories and highlights the link between motivation and learning. From this review, three factors that influence training design are identified. These are the phases involved in cognitive learning, the level of learning required for effective performance, and the task being trained. Finally, training design issues are linked with learning outcomes of initial skill acquisition, maintenance, and generalization.

# Linking Training Objectives to Evaluation Criteria

## Kurt Kraiger and Katharine M. Jung

**T**raining can be used to confer new information, skills, or attitudes to employees. Because of this, management often views training as a tool to remain flexible and to correct for the deficiencies of its workforce (Cascio, 1991). In addition, management may elect to use training to achieve organizational objectives. For example, training in customer-focused selling may be offered if an organization intends to improve customer service. Programs aimed at employee and organizational development are growing in popularity, leading to a greater demand for training resources (Tannenbaum & Woods, 1992).

The role of the training department within the typical organization is also changing. Training departments are being asked to operate as profit centers; as budgets are decreased, training departments are required to supplement their budgets with funding from other organizational units. Therefore, they are being asked to provide documentation of the value added as a result of their services. Thus, the increased importance of training coupled with decreased fixed funding has accentuated the need for effective training evaluation. In this chapter, we first discuss the importance of evaluation to effective training programs, while noting the deficiencies of prior approaches to training evaluation. We note the contributions of a new, learning outcomes approach to evaluation. However, this newer approach may be limited too because training programs are often designed around instructional objectives, not learning outcomes. Thus, we discuss the relationship between learning outcomes and instructional objectives, illustrate how learning outcomes may be generated from knowledge of the training, provide an example of how to design outcomes-based evaluation measures, and make suggestions for future research.

## Evaluation of Training

It is an unfortunate fact that there is no consensus among experts about how to determine the effectiveness of training. Experts have suggested a variety of methods for evaluating training. In particular, they assert that evaluation should answer any of the following questions: Does the training target the knowledge, skills, and abilities critical to job performance (Ford & Wroten, 1984)? Does learning occur during training (Kraiger, Ford, & Salas, 1993)? Does learning transfer to job performance (Baldwin & Ford, 1988)? Does the training result in a positive return-on-investment (London, 1989)? Because the goal of training is to confer knowledge and skills to trainees, we contend that the most valuable evaluations assess whether learning has occurred or has been applied to the job. Evaluations are useful in the determination of the level of learning and transfer and the identification of obstacles to those processes. Thus, the results of evaluation can be used to provide feedback to trainees, instructors, or program designers; aid decision makers in deciding whether to keep, expand, or reduce training offerings; and help training departments market the benefits of their courses to additional organizational units or future trainees.

### Kirkpatrick's Approach

Despite the need for effective evaluation, there are no clear guidelines for developing measures of learning during training. The most commonly used evaluation model is Kirkpatrick's (1976) hierarchy, which delineates four levels of training criteria: *reaction, learning, behavior,* and *results. Reactions* refer to trainees' affective response to the quality or relevancy of the training. *Learning* refers to the extent to which trainees' mastered the knowledge and skills disseminated in training. *Behavior,* according to Kirkpatrick, refers to either the extent to which skills learned in training are applied on the job or the extent to which these skills resulted in superior on-the-job performance. Finally, *results* refer to either the extent to which training resulted in superior on-the-job performance, or the extent to which training resulted in some bottom-line impact on the organization, such as high productivity. The model prescribes only that organizations follow the four steps in the specified order, stopping after any level that yields unfavorable results. This process was developed with the hope that administrators of training programs would "gradually progress from a simple subjective reaction sheet to a research design that measures tangible results" (Kirkpatrick, 1976, p. 26) when evaluating the success of their programs.

Although Kirkpatrick's hierarchy has served as a useful framework to assist practitioners in thinking about *how to evaluate,* it is a limited tool for guiding decisions about *what to evaluate* or *how to link* evaluation results to strategic decision making about training. There are several shortcomings to the Kirkpatrick approach that limit its value as a theoretical or practical model. These include (a) its assumption that evaluation levels are causally or sequentially linked (data and common sense challenge Kirkpatrick's assumption of causality; see Alliger & Janak, 1989); (b) its ambiguity about how to operationalize measurement levels (e.g., Kirkpatrick uses performance ratings as examples of both behavioral and results criteria); and (c) its failure to incorporate recent psychological findings on learning and skill acquisition (Kraiger et al., 1993). With regard to the latter point, Kirkpatrick's hierarchy reflects the behaviorist stimulus–response models of learning prevalent in the 1950s and 1960s. Given that training in the twenty-first century will make greater use of computerized technologies grounded in modern cognitive learning theory (Ford & Kraiger, 1995), it will become increasingly obvious that the behavioral perspective of Kirkpatrick is outdated.

## Learning Outcomes Approach

Initial progress toward a prescriptive model of *what to evaluate* in a training program comes from Kraiger and colleagues (1993). They provided a theoretically driven definition of learning along with a preliminary classification scheme for selecting evaluation measures given knowledge of learning outcomes. In the field of educational psychology, a similar typology of cognitive outcomes and measures has been proposed by Royer, Cisero, and Carlo (1993). Learning outcomes indicate the type of categories that describe the anticipated results of instruction (Gagne, 1984). One contribution made by both Kraiger and colleagues (1993) and Royer and colleagues (1993) was the reemphasis of the importance of linking training evaluation to learning outcomes and of extending previous thinking on this link by postulating a broader range of possible learning outcomes. Kraiger and colleagues proposed that learning during training may be classified into one of three types of outcomes: cognitive, skill-based, and affective outcomes. Each type of outcome includes particular categories of learning outcomes—for example, verbal knowledge or cognitive strategies are categories of cognitive outcomes. In addition, for each type, Kraiger and colleagues suggest specific foci of measurement and specific evaluation measures linked to those. Thus, they proposed that cognitive outcomes may be assessed via measures of *verbal knowledge* (factual and propositional knowledge), *knowledge organization* (how *information*—concept attributes and relationships—is mentally arranged), and *cognitive strategies* (allocation and regulation of cognitive resources). Skill-based outcomes may be assessed through measures of *compilation* (proceduralization—routine development—and composition—procedure linkage) and *automaticity* (ability to perform a task without conscious monitoring and with additional tasks). Finally, affective outcomes may be assessed through measures of *attitudinal and motivational measures* (motivational disposition—attitude about learning—self-efficacy—perception about ability to perform—and goal setting).

Though the focus of the Kraiger and colleagues (1993) typology is on the link of learning outcomes to training evaluation, these outcomes have considerable import in the instructional design process as well. For example, once learning outcomes are identified, they can be used to develop instructional strategies (e.g., establishing how problem solving is taught) or to guide needs assessment processes (e.g., discovering what must be known in order to apply proper problem-solving techniques). And, as discussed in the following section, they also can be used to generate instructional objectives.

The learning outcomes typology of Kraiger and colleagues (1993) is a significant step toward a methodology to guide researchers and practitioners in the selection and design of evaluation measures. In contrast to Kirkpatrick (1976), who neither defined learning nor suggested construct-based measures of learning, Kraiger and colleagues recommended specific measures of learning outcomes based on a theoretically driven model of learning. However, whereas Kraiger and colleagues' typology is helpful for linking measures to learning outcomes, it does not provide much guidance about how to *identify* learning outcomes given a set of instructional objectives. Note that *currency* of the typology is learning outcomes; it is these learning outcomes that determine the selection and design of evaluation measures. The currency of traditional training systems models (e.g., Dick & Carey, 1990; I. L. Goldstein, 1993) is instructional *objectives*; the objectives are derived from a needs assessment and are used to determine the design of training. Therefore, in order to provide guidance to training evaluators in the selection of construct-valid evaluation measures given a set of instructional objectives, it is necessary to explicate the links among instructional objectives, learning outcomes, and evaluation measures. Thus, the purpose of this chapter is to further develop a process by which researchers and practitioners may select and design evaluation measures given knowledge of instructional objectives and training content.

## Framework for Developing Evaluation Measures

In this section, we distinguish between instructional objectives and learning outcomes and describe three processes by which learning outcomes can be derived with or without knowledge of the specific instructional objectives.

### Distinction Between Objectives and Outcomes

Before discussing a framework for developing evaluation measures, it is important to distinguish instructional objectives from learning outcomes.

#### Instructional Objectives

Instructional objectives serve a central role in most models of instructional systems design (e.g., Dick & Carey, 1990; I. L. Goldstein, 1993). Instructional objectives act as the link between the results of a needs assessment and the design of training. These objectives specify what the trainee can accomplish on completion of training, as well as indicate the standards by which the trainee will be evaluated (I. L. Goldstein, 1993; Mager, 1984). Because instructional objectives are derived from the needs assessment of an organization, they are considered to be content based. Thus, instructional objectives are invaluable as input to the design of training, the selection of instructional strategies, and the content of evaluation measures.

#### Learning Outcomes

Learning outcomes have also served an important role in theories of learning and instruction, although they have served a less central role in the instructional design process than have instructional objectives (Gagne, 1984; Krathwohl, Bloom, & Masia, 1964). Because categorization is executed by the instructional designer, learning outcomes reflect the educational goals of trainers or designers. Therefore, the learning outcomes attainable from a lecture-style training course may be different than those attainable from an intelligent tutoring system with opportunities for practice and feedback. In sum, learning outcomes are category based and are intricately linked to the design of training and selection of instructional strategies.

It may be helpful to draw an analogy between the role of instructional objectives and outcomes in training development and the role of task statements and knowledge, skills, and abilities in test development. *Task statements* are descriptions of what workers do. Like instructional objectives, they reflect the content of the job or test domain. *Knowledge, skills, and abilities* are characteristics or attributes of workers that enable them to accomplish the activities described in the task statements. Knowledge, skills, and abilities are similar to outcomes in that they reflect the underlying attributes of workers required for job performance. Just as knowledge, skills, and abilities typically address core requirements in a selection context, learning outcomes (cognitive, affective, or skill-based) identify end states of training. For example, categories such as procedural knowledge or automaticity may identify desired end states of trainees that are believed to underlie effective job performance.

For a test such as a work sample to be *content valid* (representative of the conceptual domain it was designed to represent; Kaplan & Saccuzzo, 1993), the tasks that are assessed must reflect core job tasks. This is accomplished in test development through the use of task statements. However, for the same test to be construct valid, the underlying constructs should reflect the core knowledge, skills, and abilities required for the job. In the same way, instructional objectives should influence the content of both the training program and the evaluation instruments. If this is true, then the evaluation instruments will be content valid. However, through the systematic process of needs assessment, training design, and criterion specification, learning outcomes are typically implicitly or explicitly linked to the stated instructional objectives. By designing evaluation measures that assess these learning outcomes, we can create construct-valid instruments that can determine if trainees have achieved the desired end states of training (see Merrill, Reigeluth, & Faust, 1979).

It is crucial to understand the relationship between instructional objectives and learning outcomes, as well as the processes by which outcomes can be derived from objectives. This understanding can provide insight to the training evaluator about how to operationalize the learning constructs from the typology of Kraiger and colleagues (1993).

An example will illustrate these relationships. For a sales training course, instructional objectives might include (a) "The learner should be able to identify cues that determine the customer's readiness to buy" or (b) "Given knowledge of a customer's needs, the learner should be able to write a proposal that presents the most cost-effective solution to those needs." Note that depending on the goals and methods of training, any of several learning outcomes may be generated for each instructional objective. Categories of learning outcomes for the first objective may include verbal knowledge and knowledge organization. An evaluator may want to determine if the trainee acquired bodies of knowledge by evaluating his or her ability to recall the types of cues that a willing customer gives or his or her ability to respond to cued propositional information (ability to recognize the cues that a willing customer gives). The evaluator also may want to determine if the learner developed appropriate knowledge structures by evaluating the learner's ability to form a schema of sales situations or infer problem difficulty from situational cues.

Possible categories of outcomes for the second learning objective may include knowledge organization and cognitive strategies. Here the evaluator may want to focus on applying knowledge to new situations, applying principles of proposal writing, problem solving, or evaluating the quality of several possible solutions. Only after trainers or instructional designers are able to articulate intended learning outcomes for their instructional objectives are they able to implement the evaluation measures presented by Kraiger and colleagues (1993), select instructional strategies, or write test items.

## Generating Outcomes From Objectives

Because identification of learning outcomes is critical to designing relevant evaluation measures, and because those outcomes are often not articulated by instructional designers, it is important that there be methods for generating learning outcomes from whatever is known about the training. In the following sections, we provide an historical overview of how learning outcomes may be generated and suggest three perspectives for writing outcomes given knowledge of the training.

## Historical Approaches

Identifying learning outcomes from instructional objectives is implicit in most instructional systems design models. Common approaches to training design articulate only the process of writing instructional objectives—the results of a needs analysis are expressed as expectations for what learners will be able to *do* with the training in the context of their jobs. For each behavioral expectation, the instructional designer specifies the conditions of performance and the standards by which learner performance will be evaluated (Mager, 1984). Note, however, that these objectives should communicate "the educational intent" (I. L. Goldstein, 1993, p. 80) of training. *Educational intent* implies learning outcomes and suggests the means by which training events are linked to intended learner states. For example, I. L. Goldstein (1993) suggested that depending on the intention of instruction, the objective of *appreciate safety* could be realized in a variety of ways. The objective might be considered attained if trainees pass a safety knowledge test or if trainees modify their behavior so they maintain a certain distance from a dangerous machine. These types of objectives emphasize only behavioral outcomes rather than taking into account the other types of learning outcomes as detailed in Kraiger and colleagues' (1993) typology. Whereas behaviorally based learning outcomes are generated by writing instructional objectives that are observable and by specifying criteria in terms of behaviors, cognitive and affective learning outcomes rely on inference.

## A New Approach

The scope of learning outcomes suggested by Kraiger and colleagues (1993) is much broader than those conceived by I. L. Goldstein (1993), Dick and Carey (1990), and others. Therefore, new methods are needed for generating these learning outcomes given a set of instructional objectives. Because the generation of outcomes is a mental (and creative) act, it is difficult to specify a set methodology for how this may be done. Instead, we propose three different "lenses" through which instructional objectives may be viewed: (a) examination of the goals of training, (b) identification of instructional strategies, and (c) examination of the performance domain. By considering objectives from each of these perspectives, the act of generating learning outcomes may be facilitated. Note that because each activity is being undertaken for the same purpose (to identify learning outcomes from objectives), each lens should lead to identical conclusions about those learning outcomes. However, because each lens implies a different perspective, these activities may or may not generate identical outcomes in practice. In addition, depending on situational constraints (e.g., the availability and clarity of training goals or instructional strategies), one lens may be easier to apply than another. We present all three as alternative tools available to the training evaluator who wants to implement construct-valid measures from Kraiger and colleagues' (1993) typology.

## Examination of the Goals of Training

Training programs may be conducted for any number of purposes, and these purposes often shape the way instructional objectives are enacted. One common way of characterizing training is by distinguishing training for developmental purposes, from training for enabling purposes (e.g., to correct performance deficiencies; London, 1989). Instructional objectives written for the latter will be more likely to specify cognitive or skill-based learning outcomes. Moreover, within those categories, learning outcomes will be oriented more toward acquisition outcomes (e.g., attaining automaticity) than toward application, generalization, or maintenance outcomes. Instructional objectives written for developmental training may be more likely to specify *higher-order* knowledge or skill-based outcomes (e.g., developing a mental model) and more likely to specify affective outcomes. For example, acquiring a mastery orientation toward a subject matter may be an affective outcome desirable for trainees in a developmental training program (Dweck, 1986).

Another way of characterizing training purposes is by the predominant instructional paradigm used in that training. Educational psychologist Farnham-Diggory (1994) has proposed that there are only three core instructional paradigms—behavior, development, and apprenticeship. These paradigms may be defined by the differentiating factor between novices (learners) and experts and by how novices are transformed into experts and by the goals of these instructional paradigms.

In the behavior paradigm, novices and experts are differentiated by the quantity of knowledge or skill that they possess. Novice and expert states represent points on a (hypothetical) quantitative scale, and novices are transformed into experts through a process of incrementation (aligning instructional events so that learners make successive steps toward the desired goal; Farnham-Diggory, 1994). Behaviorally oriented training (e.g., Decker & Nathan, 1985) usually employs the behavior paradigm, although the term *behavior* does not mean the same as *behaviorism* as it is classically defined. The goal of this type of instructional paradigm is to facilitate movement from the novice state to the expert state. Such a goal is difficult to monitor in many situations. It is therefore necessary to examine the learning outcomes desired. Learning outcomes related to this style of training include skill-based outcomes. Experts believe that there are stages in skill development. These stages are necessarily sequential, and learning progresses incrementally within them. Among skill-based outcomes are *composition* (step grouping), *proceduralization* (routine building), *automatic processing*, and *tuning* (process refining; Kraiger et al, 1993). Cognitive and affective outcomes are less likely to be achieved in this context, though there may be some implicit outcomes associated with trainees' identification with, or attraction to, a behavioral model (Decker & Nathan, 1985).

In the development paradigm, novices and experts are distinguished on the basis of their personal beliefs or qualitative models of events or experiences. Novices are transformed to experts through a process of *perturbation* (creating instructional events that intrude on or contradict learners' models). The goal of this type of instructional paradigm is to transform novices to experts by forcing them to formulate new models (Farnham-Diggory, 1994). Again, depending on the learning outcomes desired, this type of instructional paradigm may or may not be appropriate. An example in which this paradigm is appropriate follows: A student driver may believe that the necessary force to apply to a brake pedal in order to stop a car is determined solely by the speed of the car. A driving instructor may take the student to a snowy parking lot and ask the student to apply a normal amount of force. The result of this experience should perturb this belief. Learning outcomes related to this style of learning include attitudinal outcomes. Attitudes are often established by experience and are difficult to change. Often it is through events experienced by the learner and changes in behavior patterns that attitudes and values become internalized (A. P. Goldstein & Sorcher, 1974; Kraut, 1976).

In addition, cognitive outcomes may also be elicited through the developmental paradigm. In particular, the development of mental models may be affected by perturbation. Related to schemas, *mental models* influence the interpretation of events and acquisition of knowledge (Messick, 1984). By subjecting learning to contradictory events, the instructor perturbs the trainees' mental models and causes the learners to modify their beliefs. In addition, instructors may ask questions or pose problems that cause learners to question the effectiveness or breadth of their cognitive strategies. Therefore, the desired outcomes (affective and cognitive) are consistent with the goals of the developmental paradigm, whereas skill-based outcomes are not.

Finally, in the apprenticeship model, novices and experts are distinguished in terms of context-based, tacit models of practice. Novices can become experts only by participating in the experts' domain and by receiving nurturance, guidance, and feedback from expert instructors (Farnham-Diggory, 1994). Farnham-Digory used the metaphor of cultures to characterize the differences between novices and experts. For example, when we travel from culture to culture, much of what is important is implicit and not easily discernible. In the same way, the differences between the knowledge and skills of experts and novices are also implicit and difficult to distinguish. Studies of expert problem solving in cognitive psychology depict expert–novice differences in this manner (e.g., Gitomer, 1988). Within industrial–organizational psychology, team training research captures some of these distinctions (e.g., see chapter 10, this volume), and within the field of instructional psychology, models of cognitive apprenticeship and situated learning share this orientation (Brown, Collins, & Duguid, 1989; Collins, Brown, & Newman, 1985). Cognitive apprenticeship and situated learning are examples of formal instructional strategies based on principles of the apprenticeship model. Therefore, the goal of this type of instructional paradigm is to facilitate the transformation of novice to expert by *inculturating* the learner. This type of goal lends itself to attaining particular learning outcomes. Learning outcomes related to this style of learning include cognitive outcomes like the formation of mental models and the development of metacognitive skills. By embedding learning in realistic contexts or by modeling behavior, the instructor facilitates the development of mental models (Glaser & Bassok, 1989) by allowing the learner to incorporate situationally specific information into his or her model (Ford & Kraiger, 1995). In addition, such a learning style could aid in a learner's acquisition of metacognitive skills. Having a learner listen to think-aloud protocols by an expert during problem solving may lead the learner to identify gaps in his or her own problem-solving strategies. The guidance and feedback provided by the instructor would be instrumental to the learner's understanding of the process. Therefore, the desired outcomes—like the formation of mental models and the development of metacognitive skills—would be better attained by employing an instructional paradigm with the goal of inculturating the learner. In sum, it is clear that instructional paradigms with particular goals are more conducive to attaining associated learning outcomes than are instructional paradigms with goals that do not facilitate attaining desired learning outcomes.

## Identification of Instructional Strategies

A second lens for generating learning outcomes is the identification of the instructional strategies used in training. Related to instructional paradigms, *instructional strategies* are narrower in scope. For example, situated learning is an instructional strategy that is encompassed within the apprenticeship paradigm. Examples of instructional strategies include performance coaching (learners receive feedback on performance), performance scaffolding (combined with coaching, learners receive suggestions, cues, and so forth, to help in task accomplishment), exploration (learners actively formulate or test hypotheses), and concept learning (learners are presented concepts and the attributes and relationships associated with those concepts; Ford & Kraiger, 1995).

In an ideal situation, learning outcomes are set first, and these influence the selection of instructional strategies. However, in situations in which learning outcomes are unknown, it is more likely the case that the determination of instructional strategies occurred after the derivation of instructional objectives and before the design of training (selection of media, writing course content, etc.). Thus, the instructional strategy chosen implicitly suggests the intended outcomes of training. If the selected strategy is more directive on the part of the trainer (or passive on the part of the learner) then lower order cognitive outcomes are the likely end states of training. For example, if the instructional strategy employs a lecture format, little more than declarative knowledge (measured by multiple-choice tests) may be expected as a learning outcome.

Other instructional strategies may target higher order cognitive outcomes or various behavioral and affective outcomes. Concept learning is an example of an instructional strategy specifically oriented toward developing a conceptual knowledge or understanding in trainees (Klausmeier, 1992). Conceptual knowledge is based on the relatedness or link among pieces of information. When targeting conceptual knowledge, learners are expected to be able to identify examples and nonexamples of the concept, understand the principles surrounding the concept, understand the taxonomic and other relationships involving the concept, and use the concept in solving problems (Klausmeier, 1992). In addition, strategies may also be taught that aid learners in discriminating among the attributes of the concept. Thus, when concept learning is used as an instructional strategy, likely learning outcomes might include better knowledge organization, semantic mapping of constructs, and cognitive strategies for learning and categorizing new information.

As a second example, cognitive apprenticeship is a relatively new instructional strategy designed to target a number of different learning outcomes (Brown et al., 1989; Collins et al., 1985). Cognitive apprenticeship includes three instructor activities (modeling, coaching, and scaffolding) and three learner actions (articulation, reflection, and exploration). Cognitive apprenticeship has been adapted from traditional apprenticeship models used to teach craftspeople, and their intended outcomes include procedural knowledge, cognitive strategies, compilation and proceduralization, mastery orientation, and self-efficacy.

Similar analyses may be conducted for different instructional strategies. Regardless of training content, each strategy will be more likely to elicit some learning outcomes and less likely to elicit others. By considering the instructional strategies carefully, training evaluators can make better decisions about the intended outcomes of training and better choices of appropriate evaluation measures. In addition, the process of examining the learning outcomes that were generated for particular instructional strategies may lead one to reconsider the appropriateness of those strategies. In this way, the training program may be improved through successive iteration of instructional strategies and generating learning outcomes.

### Examination of the Performance Domain

A third lens for generating learning outcomes is the examination of the performance domain. This might be done by observing trainees during their first assignment or interviewing their peers and supervisors on the job. During this examination, it is important to determine which learning outcomes would be most effective to job performance. This can be done by reviewing job descriptions, observing incumbents, or interviewing subject-matter experts with knowledge of the design or content of training. In some ways, this process mirrors the earlier needs assessment; however, it is accomplished with reference to learning outcomes rather than instructional objectives.

One might argue that this is the most critical lens of the three. Without knowledge of the performance domain, it would be very difficult to ascertain the learning outcomes that are important for the job.

Given that the training designer is uncertain of the desired outcomes of training, it would be nearly impossible to then select an appropriate instructional strategy or design evaluation measures.

Tools for determining desired learning outcomes based on the performance domain would be similar to those used by applied cognitive psychologists or knowledge engineers building expert systems. In general, specialists such as these proceed by identifying subject-matter experts, analyzing characteristics of expert competence, and depicting those characteristics in a form amenable to instruction or measurement (Glaser, 1966). Specific questions can be asked of subject-matter experts to elicit the precise learning outcomes from the perspective of job performance. Sample questions might include (a) is this something incumbents should know or be able to do? (b) If it is something they must know, how is this knowledge used on the job? (c) Do they recall facts, use their knowledge to determine whether a job event is familiar or unfamiliar? Once these characteristics have been elicited, they can be compared to the instructional objectives to determine learning outcomes.

There are various typologies for categorizing the tools or strategies for eliciting and depicting domain-specific characteristics of expertise. For example, McGraw and Harbison-Briggs (1989) identified nine families of knowledge elicitation techniques including concept analysis, unstructured interviews, structured interviews, task analysis, process tracing and protocol analysis, and simulations. Regardless of the method of analysis, the key to this process is identifying, through the subject-matter expert, the *form* in which knowledge, skills, or affect is to be held. For example, if a subject-matter expert indicates that a trainee should be able to *do* something, follow-up questions can determine whether the trainee should be able to execute the action with a coach present, on his or her own, or on his or her own under conditions that permit inferences of automaticity. A completed set of instructional objectives coupled with a current job description may be used as a starting point for generating learning outcomes based on the performance domain.

After viewing the instructional objectives through the three lenses, training designers are better able to determine which learning outcomes they want to measure. Once the desired outcomes are identified, it becomes easy to apply the framework provided by Kraiger and colleagues (1993). Training designers may use Kraiger and colleagues' typology to select or develop the most appropriate measures for particular outcomes.

## An Example

Imagine that a major computer corporation, in an effort to remain competitive, contracts with a software designer to make its word processing program more user friendly. After an analysis of customer needs and complaints, the designer determines that a training program is necessary. The designer writes a CD-ROM interactive program to teach word processing to home users. She starts by writing instructional objectives. Here is a sampling of the types of instructional objectives that may be expected:

1. The learner would be expected to know all fonts available.
2. The learner would be expected to know what a mouse can do.
3. The learner would be expected to be able to state the function of *autocorrect*.
4. The learner would be expected to know which commands can be found on the edit menu.

Given these objectives, the learner would also be expected to perform certain tasks and learn particular skills. Note also that there would be numerous objectives in addition to these four. However, for purposes of illustration, we will apply the three lens discussed previously to these four instructional objectives.

### Goals of Training

The designer notes that the customers in her analysis were ignorant of the basic terminology of the word processing program. She assumes that people acquire definitions incrementally, therefore she is using the behavior paradigm. The learning outcome that the designer is targeting is verbal knowledge; in particular, she is interested in declarative knowledge. *Declarative knowledge* consists of propositions and the "knowledge about facts and things" (Anderson, 1985, p. 199; Wideman & Owston, 1993); and it is generally considered the simplest form of knowledge. Further examination of the results of the analysis lead the designer to recognize that the customers lack a roadmap for a word processing screen. The designer decides that she wants to explain where things might be found on a screen or give customers a method for locating items within the program. In addition, she realizes that the best instructional paradigm to use in this situation would be the apprenticeship paradigm, because the CD-ROM format will enable learners to see and mimic how expert word processors use the system. In this case, the learning outcome is knowledge organization. As knowledge becomes more advanced, organization of that knowledge becomes increasingly important. The learner will be expected to develop knowledge structures (Ford & Kraiger, 1995) to aid in the interpretation of events by organizing information (Messick, 1984).

## Instructional Strategies

After specifying the desired objectives of training, it is then necessary to design a program in which those objectives are attained. By selecting an instructional strategy, events may be specified that link learning processes to the instructional objectives (Gagne & Dick, 1983).

Instructional methods for declarative knowledge could consist of lectures or some other narrative process. An effective presentation of declarative knowledge would be sufficient to facilitate the learners' ability to recognize or recall information presented. Given the CD-ROM format, the designer found that this strategy would be easy to incorporate into the training.

In contrast, incorporating knowledge organization into the program would be more challenging. Given that knowledge organization is an important learning outcome, instruction should also include structural knowledge (Jonassen, Beissner, & Yacci, 1993). Within the apprenticeship paradigm, concept learning is a method of instruction in which the conceptual level of understanding is targeted (Klausmeier, 1992). The designer needs to build in both the presentation of items (providing clear definitions using examples and nonexamples) and feedback to the learners in their acquisition of the knowledge. Again, the format of the program would be conducive to the achievement of these goals. Learners would be able to learn about the items and receive feedback because of the interactive nature of the CD-ROM program.

Using concept learning as the instructional strategy will lead to the learners' ability to attach definitions to attributes and link attributes in a meaningful way. Thus, because this ability is associated with knowledge organization, knowledge organization is again revealed as an intended learning outcome. Also, the attaching of definitions to attributes suggests the acquisition of declarative knowledge.

## Performance Domain

By embedding the training in the realistic context of the actual word processing program, the designer will be better able to elicit knowledge organization in her learners. She intends to build in activities within training that use the problem-solving skills of the learners. Word processing can be challenging because users need to learn how to format their documents, how to change fonts, or perform other functions to ensure an attractive product, which can be complicated. The nature of this performance domain aids in the development of knowledge organization because of the nature of the attributes that should be included (e.g., linking problems to solutions, etc.). Interviews with word processing experts may provide insights into how the training may be applied on the job or to accomplish actual word processing tasks. For example, an expert might note that the use of the *autocorrect* function can be used to increase typing efficiency by substituting code words (that are automatically retyped) for longer words that may be difficult to type without error.

After viewing her instructional objectives through the three lenses, the training designer determined that she was interested in two learning outcomes: verbal knowledge and knowledge organization. Using Kraiger and colleagues's typology (1993), she learned that in order to target verbal knowledge, she should use recognition and recall tests. Use of more elaborate measures would be superfluous for such a simple form of knowledge.

For knowledge organization, more complex measures are necessary to assess the quality of the learners' knowledge structures. This may be accomplished through a number of techniques, each requiring comparison of the trainee's knowledge structure with that of an expert. Given that experts' knowledge structures differ from those of novices (Glaser & Chi, 1989), increased similarity between the structures of experts versus novices would indicate learning.

The training designer could elect to use relatedness tasks in which learners rate pairs of concepts based on their relatedness to each other (Kraiger et al., 1993). Or the designer could use spatial representations of knowledge structures as units of comparison. The evaluation technique would involve comparing the representation of the learner's knowledge structure to that of an expert. Structural assessment may be achieved through such activities as *free-sort tasks* (learners physically arrange concepts on cards) or cognitive mapping tasks (Cooke, 1992).

## Implications and Summary

The importance of identifying learning outcomes and linking outcomes to evaluation measures will be increasingly important as new training technologies enable instructional designers to train a broader range of cognitive skills and types of knowledge. Some implications of these training technologies for measurement are discussed in the next section.

## Implications of New Training Technologies

The process of generating learning outcomes from instructional objectives and constructing evaluation measures will be affected by advancements in training technologies. It is clear that various forms of computer-based training (CBT) will become increasingly popular as we approach the next century. Two forms of CBT that are already popular are intelligent tutoring systems (ITS) and hyper-text or hypermedia training (HMT). *Intelligent tutoring systems* base instruction on an expert model, a student model, a tutor capable of multiple instructional strategies, and a domain-specific knowledge base (Polson & Richardson, 1988). The ITSs diagnose student models and select instructional strategies design to reduce the discrepancy between the expert and student models. *Hypermedia* refers to a computer-driven interactive training system in which textual, graphic, video, and auditory information is integrated for easy access by users (Tessmer, 1995). Students learn through HMT systems by accessing multiple forms of information to solve problems or complete assignments.

These training technologies will affect the training processes described previously to the extent that they constrain the domain of instructional strategies available to trainers. In this sense, the popularity of these technologies may make the process of designing evaluation measures easier as evaluation experts are continually confronted with the same types of training. It is thus instructive to consider the unique aspects of instructional strategies inherent in either technology and suggest the types of evaluation measures that may be designed for those technologies.

## Evaluation and the New Training Technologies

Compared to other forms of training, intelligent tutoring systems are characterized by (a) situated or case-based learning, (b) incorporation of expert models, and (c) the need for the learner to understand both the training content and the instructional model (e.g., how layering with the system enables the learner to study training material at different levels of difficulty). Hypermedia training systems are characterized by (a) exposure to multiple forms of knowledge (i.e., declarative, procedural, structural) presented in different media, and (b) the need for the learner to exert control over the process by which knowledge or information is obtained from the system.

There are a number of implications of these systems for the design of construct-valid evaluation measures. When assessing the knowledge acquisition of trainees, it will be important to assess multiple forms of knowledge. For both systems, it may be helpful to assess trainees' understanding of system functioning as well as of training content. The former may be used as a covariate during statistical analysis. Because HMT systems may cover declarative, procedural, and structural knowledge, separate measures may be developed for each learning construct.

Because intelligent tutoring systems incorporate an expert model in their design, it is appropriate to assess trainee learning against an external standard. For example, representations of the knowledge organization of trainees can be scored by comparing them to experts' structures (Goldsmith & Kraiger, in press), or experts' problem-solving processes can be determined by think-aloud protocols and compared to those of trainees. For HMT systems, learning is more individually oriented, and comparisons to experts may not be appropriate without a theoretical foundation. A constructivist approach to trainee learning may be warranted in which the criterion for training effectiveness is the utility of the knowledge for the unique needs of each trainee (Jonassen, 1995). Thus, if one trainee has fewer but more focused learning needs than a second trainee, training for the former trainee *may* be effective even if he or she learns less than the second trainee.

Finally, various forms of attitudinal measures may be appropriate with either training system. Particularly in the case of HMT, it may be appropriate to assess trainee attributes such as self-efficacy or mastery orientation. Through repeated exposure to the training system, trainees' may develop greater confidence in their ability to master new material and become more interested in the learning process. In the case of ITS, trainees' self-efficacy should be more task-focused. Because problem difficulty increases with student learning and because of the case-based approach of ITS, its trainees should come to be more confident that they can solve similar problems in the field.

## Implications for Research Designs

As training evaluation becomes more prevalent, training researchers and practitioners eventually will face the same problem that has baffled selection researchers—the *criterion problem* (Wallace, 1965). In the area of personnel selection, predictors are often validated against performance criteria. However, the veracity of this evidence is limited because there is often nothing against which the criteria may be validated. In the same way, as researchers and practitioners continue to implement measures such as those suggested by Kraiger and colleagues (1993) and Royer and colleagues (1993), they eventually must be able to show that these measures are construct valid. The evaluation paradox becomes this: If a new measure is to be used to evaluate training, it must first be validated, but the primary means of validation is to determine if it is sensitive to training.

Construct validation is a multistep process of defining the attribute measured by a psychological instrument and determining through rational and empirical verification procedures whether the instrument measures the intended construct (J. P. Campbell, 1976). The process of construct validation traditionally has been conceived of as a strategy of specifying and testing a nomological network in which the net contains a set of hypotheses about the measure of interest and other measures or experimental factors (J. P. Campbell, 1976; Cronbach & Meehl, 1955). Three strategies for investigating the construct validity of training evaluation measures in the design discussed next are convergent validity, discriminant validity, and predictive validity. In a general sense, evidence of convergent validity occurs whenever measures of like constructs are correlated, evidence of discriminant validity occurs whenever measures of dissimilar constructs are uncorrelated, and evidence of predictive validity occurs whenever test scores predict a criterion in a different environment from which the test was administered (see J. P. Campbell, 1976; D. T. Campbell & Fiske, 1959).

It is fortunate that the training researcher operates in a more controlled environment than the selection researcher and so has a greater opportunity to resolve the "criterion problem." Consider the traditional research design shown in Figure 2 in which a pretest and posttest of a single learning construct are administered to a training group and a control (no training) group. In this design, evidence that pre- and posttest change is greater for the training group than for the control group *may* indicate that the training is effective. However, these pre- and posttest changes may occur even if the training measures are not valid. For example, trainees may have received feedback on their test scores and reviewed pretest items, but control group members will not. More important, if pre- and posttest differences *do* occur, there is no

**Figure 2**

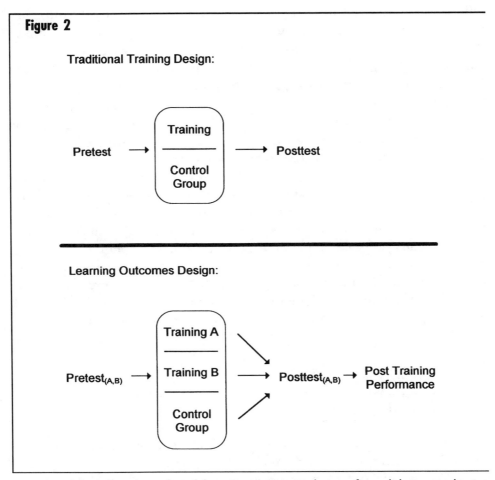

Traditional Training Design:

Pretest → | Training / Control Group | → Posttest

Learning Outcomes Design:

Pretest$_{(A,B)}$ → | Training A / Training B / Control Group | → Posttest$_{(A,B)}$ → Post Training Performance

Comparison of traditional and learning outcomes designs for validating evaluation measures.

way of determining whether the measure is a valid assessment of the intended construct (e.g., knowledge organization rather than procedural knowledge).

In contrast, consider the research opportunities available in the other design in Figure 2. A second training group is added; Training A and B may differ either in terms of instructional strategies (e.g., cognitive apprenticeship versus situated learning) or may be similar training strategies with a key component manipulated (e.g., practice with or without feedback). Because only the training goals or instructional strategies differ, Training A and Training B can have identical instructional objectives but different intended learning outcomes. Two pretests are administered to both training groups as well as the control group. Key to the design is tailoring one test to the learning outcomes of Training A, and tailoring the second to the learning outcomes of Training B. For example, although the content of training is identical, Training A could be a form of concept learning, and Training B could be in the form of problem-based learning. Two types of pre- and posttests could be administered, a measure of knowledge organization (hypothesized to be more sensitive to Training A) and a measure of declarative knowledge (hypothesized to be more sensitive to Training B).

The same or parallel tests are then administered to all groups on posttest. In addition, some measure of posttraining performance is collected to assess transfer of training. In this design, there are at least three opportunities to assess the construct validity of the measures: convergent validity, discriminant validity, and predictive validity. In an ideal situation, results would show that pretest and posttest scores are more highly correlated within training groups than across groups; scores on Test A change more for members of Training A than Training B, whereas scores on Test B change more for members of Training B; and posttest scores are correlated with measures of posttraining performance.

## Conclusion

As training technologies become more sophisticated, there is greater potential to achieve more complex learning outcomes. However, there is no current model of training evaluation to guide evaluators in assessing whether these outcomes were achieved. The predominant framework for training evaluation, Kirkpatrick's (1976) hierarchy, has several shortcomings that limit its value as a theoretical or practical model. The typology of learning outcomes presented by Kraiger and colleagues (1993) was a significant step forward toward a methodology to guide researchers and practitioners in the selection and design of evaluation measures for a variety of learning outcomes. However, this model is also of limited value because it relates evaluation measures to learning outcomes, but most training programs are described in terms of instructional objectives.

This chapter describes three processes by which learning outcomes may be derived from the instructional objectives of training. Once these outcomes are identified, then Kraiger and colleagues' (1993) typology may be applied to generate potential evaluation measures. Special considerations for evaluating intelligent tutoring systems and hypermedia training systems were also discussed, as were strategies for investigating the construct validity of the new evaluation measures.

The potential of the new training technologies for improving how we learn is tremendous. For that potential to be realized, training and system designers must receive feedback on the extent to which newly developed systems succeed or fail relative to *all* learning outcomes.

## References

Alliger, G. M., & Janak, E. A. (1989). Kirkpatrick's levels of training criteria: Thirty years later. *Personnel Psychology, 42,* 331–342.

Anderson, J. R. (1985). *Cognitive psychology and its implications* (2nd ed.). New York: Freeman.

Baldwin, T. T., & Ford, J. K. (1988). Transfer of training: A review and directions for future research. *Personnel Psychology, 41,* 63–105.

Brown, J. S., Collins, A., & Duguid, P. (1989). Situated cognition and the culture of learning. *Educational Researcher, 18,* 32–42.

Campbell, D. T., & Fiske, D. W. (1959). Convergent and discriminant validation by the multitrait-multimethod matrix. *Psychological Bulletin, 56,* 81–105.

Campbell, J. P. (1976). Psychometric theory. In M. D. Dunnette (Ed.), *Handbook of industrial and organizational psychology* (pp. 122–185). Chicago: Rand-McNally.

Cascio, W. F. (1991). *Applied psychology in personnel management.* Englewood Cliffs, NJ: Prentice-Hall.

Collins, A., Brown, J. S., & Newman, S. E. (1985). Cognitive apprenticeship: Teaching the crafts of reading, writing, and mathematics. In L. B. Resnick (Ed.), *Knowing, learning and instruction: Essays in honor of Robert Glaser* (pp. 453–494). Hillsdale, NJ: Erlbaum.

Cooke, N. J. (1992). *A taxonomy and evaluation of elicitation techniques* (Contract No. NAS9-17900). Houston, TX: NASA.

Cronbach, L. J., & Meehl, P. E. (1955). Construct validity in psychological tests. *Psychological Bulletin, 62,* 281–302.

Decker, P. J., & Nathan, B. R. (1985). *Behavior modeling training.* New York: Praeger.

Dick, W., & Carey, L. (1990). *The systematic design of instruction* (3rd ed.). Glenview, IL: Scott, Foresman.

Dweck, C. S. (1986). Mental processes affecting learning. *American Psychologist, 41,* 1040–1048.

Farnham-Diggory, S. (1994). Paradigms of knowledge and instruction. *Review of Educational Research, 64,* 463–477.

Ford, J. K., & Kraiger, K. (1995). The application of cognitive constructs and principles to the Instructional Systems Model of Training: Implications for needs assessment, design, and transfer. *The International Review of Industrial and Organizational Psychology, 10,* 1–35.

Ford, J. K., & Wroten, S. P. (1984). Introducing new methods for conducting training evaluation and for linking training evaluation to program redesign. *Personnel Psychology, 11,* 651–665.

Gagne, R. M. (1984). Learning outcomes and their effects: Useful categories of human performance. *American Psychologist, 39,* 377–385.

Gagne, R. M., & Dick, W. (1983). Instructional psychology. In *Annual Review of Psychology.* Palo Alto, CA: Annual Reviews.

Gitomer, D. H. (1988). Individual differences in technical troubleshooting. *Human Performance, 1*(2), 111–131.

Glaser, R. (1966). Psychological bases for instructional design. *AV Communication Review, 14,* 433–449.

Glaser, R., & Bassok, M. (1989). Learning theory and the study of instruction. *Annual Review of Psychology, 40,* 631–666.

Glaser, R., & Chi, M. T. (1989). Overview. In M. T. Chi, R. Glaser, & M. J. Farr (Eds.), *The nature of expertise* (pp. xv–xxviii). Hillsdale, NJ: Erlbaum.

Goldsmith, T., & Kraiger, K. (in press). Applications of structural knowledge assessment to training evaluation. In J. K. Ford & Associates (Eds.), *Improving training effectiveness in work organizations.* Hillsdale, NJ: Erlbaum.

Goldstein, A. P., & Sorcher, M. (1974). *Changing supervisory behavior.* New York: Pergamon Press.

Goldstein, I. L. (1993). *Training in organizations: Needs assessment, development, and evaluation.* (3rd ed.). Pacific Grove, CA: Brooks/Cole.

Jonassen, D. H. (1995). Constructivist evaluation of distance learning. In *Proceedings of the advancements in integrated delivery technologies conference.* Available on-line.

Jonassen, D. H., Beissner, K., & Yacci, M. (1993). *Structural knowledge: Techniques for representing, conveying, and acquiring structural knowledge.* Hillsdale, NJ: Erlbaum.

Kaplan, R. M., & Sacuzzo, D. P. (1993). *Psychological testing: Principles, applications, and issues* (3rd Ed.) Pacific Grove, CA: Brooks/Cole.

Kirkpatrick, D. L. (1976). Evaluation of training. In R. L. Craig (Ed.), *Training and development handbook: A guide to human resource development.* New York: McGraw-Hill.

Klausmeier, H. J. (1992). Concept learning and concept teaching. *Educational Psychologists, 27,* 267–286.

Kraiger, K., Ford, J. K., & Salas, E. (1993). Application of cognitive, skill-based, and affective theories of learning outcomes to new methods of training evaluation. *Journal of Applied Psychology, 78,* 311–328.

Krathwohl, D. R., Bloom, B. S., & Masia, B. B. (1964). *Taxonomy of educational objectives: The classification of educational goals.* New York: David McKay.

Kraut, A. I. (1976). Developing managerial skills via modeling techniques: Some positive research findings—A symposium. *Personnel Psychology, 29,* 325–328.

London, M. (1989). *Managing the training enterprise.* San Francisco: Jossey-Bass.

Mager, R. F. (1984). *Preparing instructional objectives.* Belmont, CA: Pitman Learning.

McGraw, K. L., & Harbison-Briggs, K. (1989). *Knowledge acquisition: Principles and guidelines.* Englewood Cliffs, NJ: Prentice-Hall.

Merrill, M. D., Reigeluth, C. M., & Faust, G. W. (1979). The instructional quality profile: A curriculum evaluation and design tool. In H. K. O'Neill, Jr. (Ed.), *Procedures for instructional systems development.* New York: Academic Press.

Messick, S. (1984). Abilities and knowledge in educational achievement testing: The assessment of dynamic cognitive structures. In B. S. Plake (Ed.), *Social and technical issues in testing: Implications for test construction and usage* (pp. 156–172). Hillsdale, NJ: Erlbaum.

Polson, M. C., & Richardson, J. J. (1988). *Foundations of intelligent tutoring systems.* Hillsdale, NJ: Erlbaum.

Royer, J. M., Cisero, C. A., & Carlo, M. S. (1993). Techniques and procedures for assessing cognitive skills. *Review of Educational Research, 63*, 201–243.

Tannenbaum, S. I., & Woods, S. B. (1992). Determining a strategy for evaluating training: Operating within organizational constraints. *Human Resource Planning, 15*, 63–81.

Tessmer, M. (1995). Formative multimedia evaluation. *Training Research Journal, 1*, 127–149.

Wallace, S. R. (1965). Criteria for what? *American Psychologist, 20*, 411–417.

Wideman, H. H., & Owston, R. D. (1993). Knowledge base construction as a pedagogical activity. *Journal of Educational Computing Research, 9*, 165–196.

# Contextual Influences on Training Effectiveness

**Miguel A. Quiñones**

**A**ll indicators point to the fact that the pace of technological innovation will continue to accelerate in the future (Adler, 1991; Van der Spiegel, 1995). Organizations often rely on technological innovations to improve their efficiency and gain profitability (Rosow & Zager, 1988; Wall & Jackson, 1995). However, organizations have also begun to realize that they cannot reap the full benefits of technological innovation without considering the human element (Laumann, Nadler, & O'Farrell, 1991). The implementation of new technologies into organizations, the employees of which lack the proper knowledge, skills, and other characteristics needed to make full use of that technology, can often lead to disappointing results (Rosow & Zager, 1988).

It is clear that in an environment of rapid change, individuals must be able to adapt in order to meet new challenges. Training is the tool most often used to prepare individuals for this change. In fact, training is perhaps the most important component of any technological innovation in the workplace (Goldstein & Gilliam, 1990; Rosow & Zager, 1988). However, in an era of high-technology changes, organizations often focus solely on the technology involved in training. This is evidenced by the increased use of computerized intelligent tutoring systems, virtual reality, interactive CD-ROM, and other training technologies (chapters 9 and 11, this volume).

Although the applications of new technologies to training hold great promise, research demonstrating their advantage over traditional training methods is lacking (Lippert, 1989). In spite of this gap in evaluation information, the rapid pace of development of these high-technology methods continues unabated (Tannenbaum & Yukl, 1992). It is ironic to note that it is often the mundane and low-technology factors of a training system that make the difference between a successful training program and wasted organizational resources. However, these factors are often ignored in the design and implementation of training systems (Goldstein, 1993).

Traditional training design focuses on determining the appropriate training content (e.g., Ford & Wroten, 1984), establishing instructional objectives and conditions of practice (e.g., Gagné, Briggs, & Wager, 1992), and identifying evaluation measures that are consistent with the objectives of training (e.g., Kraiger, Ford, & Salas, 1993; see also chapter 6, this volume). However, even if these steps are performed correctly, a training program can fail as a result of inappropriate implementation (chapter 2, this volume). Because training occurs within a larger organizational context, other factors in addition to traditional design considerations can influence training outcomes.

Noe (1986) suggested that individual trainee characteristics such as attitudes and motivation are critical, but often neglected, factors that can have a direct impact on the effectiveness of a training program. A number of researchers have begun to examine organizational context factors such as support (e.g., Rouillier & Goldstein, 1993), participation (e.g., Baldwin, Magjuka, & Loher, 1991), and framing of training (e.g., Martocchio, 1992; Quiñones, 1995), which have been implicated in the development of trainee attitudes and motivation. In spite of increasing evidence pointing toward the importance of organizational contextual effects in training, a comprehensive review and integrative analysis of this literature has not been forthcoming (for an overview, see Latham & Crandall, 1991; Tannenbaum & Yukl, 1992).

In this chapter I will address the gap in the training literature by reviewing studies examining contextual influences on training effectiveness. First, I will present a general framework specifying the hypothesized role of contextual factors on training effectiveness. Second, I will discuss trainee factors relevant for training effectiveness. Third, I will review the available empirical evidence supporting the framework. Fourth, I will discuss conclusions and directions for future research concerning contextual influences on training effectiveness.

## General Framework

The goal of any training program is to impart to individuals a new set of skills, knowledge, behaviors, or attitudes (Goldstein, 1993). Training effectiveness refers to the extent to which the stated objectives of training are met. To be specific, training programs are typically evaluated by measuring a number of training and transfer outcomes. Training outcomes are measures gathered during or immediately after training, whereas transfer outcomes are gathered at a later point in time, typically in a different setting (Baldwin & Ford, 1988).

Kirkpatrick (1967) identified learning, behavior, results, and reactions as four measures relevant for evaluating training outcomes. Although some controversy has emerged regarding the appropriate relationships among these measures (e.g., Alliger & Janak, 1989), they still represent a valuable heuristic for evaluating training outcomes. Kraiger and colleagues (1993) have expanded the learning construct to include cognitive, affective, and skill-based measures of learning. Transfer outcomes, however, are typically assessed by measuring the maintenance and generalization of trained skills after the trainee has been on the job for some time (Baldwin & Ford, 1988).

Training researchers have focused on identifying factors related to one or several of these training and transfer outcomes. Much of this research has concentrated on training design factors related to training effectiveness. For example, Thorndike and Woodworth (1901) proposed the principle of identical elements as a central feature of training design. This principle suggests that transfer will be maximized to the extent that there are similar stimulus and response elements present in the training and transfer settings (see also Royer, 1979). Other design issues such as training content (e.g., Gagné, 1962), delivery (e.g., Kearsley, 1991), and conditions of practice have proven to be reliable predictors of training effectiveness (Baldwin & Ford, 1988; Goldstein, 1993).

In addition to training design factors, individual differences among trainees have also been found to be related to training and training outcomes (e.g., Fleishman & Mumford, 1989; Ford, Quiñones, Sego, & Sorra, 1992; Noe & Schmitt, 1986; Ree & Earles, 1991). To be specific, numerous studies have found that trainee differences in variables such as cognitive ability, motivation, self-efficacy, attributions, and attitudes can determine the amount of information learned during training and

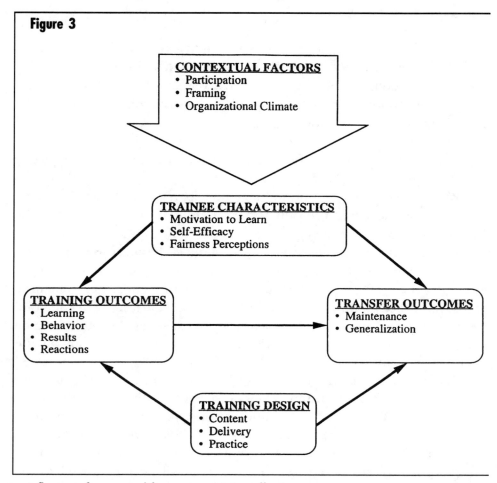

**Figure 3**

Influence of contextual factors on training effectiveness.

transferred to the work site. These effects have been shown to be independent from training design factors (Fleishman & Mumford, 1989).

Researchers are beginning to realize that factors beyond training design and individual differences can also have an indirect impact on training and transfer outcomes. These factors evolve out of the organizational context in which training programs exist. Thus, they are often neglected during the design and implementation of training systems (Goldstein, 1993). In spite of the identification of these contextual factors, their exact roles in training effectiveness have not been addressed explicitly.

Quiñones (1995) proposed that contextual factors have their influence through trainee characteristics prior to training. Contextual factors represent higher order variables that are perceived by individuals and influence their thoughts and actions. The characteristics a trainee brings to the training setting are then likely to influence their training and transfer outcomes (Baldwin & Ford, 1988; Noe, 1986). Figure 3 presents a depiction of this conceptual framework describing the role of contextual factors on training effectiveness in relation to training design and trainee factors. The framework suggests that trainee characteristics and training design factors have independent effects on training and transfer outcomes. Furthermore, contextual factors influence training and transfer outcomes through their effect on trainee characteristics.

Although it is possible for individual and situational factors to have reciprocal influences (e.g., Ross & Nisbett, 1991), the temporal ordering of the training process makes the framework presented in Figure 3 more plausible. However, in situations in which individuals go through training prior to entering the organization (e.g., as in the military) it is possible that trainee characteristics can have an influence on contextual factors (Quiñones, Ford, Sego, & Smith, 1995). But in typical training situations in which individuals are already in the organization, a levels-of-analysis perspective suggests that higher level constructs, such as contextual factors, are more likely to have their influence on lower level constructs (e.g., trainee characteristics) than the other way around (Klein, Dansereau, & Hall, 1994; Rousseau, 1985). Finally, empirical support for these theoretical links has been found by researchers examining contextual factors. The specifics of these studies are discussed later in this chapter. However, because trainee characteristics play a central role in linking contextual influences with training and transfer outcomes, more discussion of these is presented in the next section.

## Trainee Characteristics

Consistent with Noe's (1986) call for further research into the role of trainee characteristics, Mumford, Weeks, Harding, and Fleishman (1988) conducted a comprehensive study to examine the relative contributions of trainee characteristics and design characteristics on training effectiveness. The results of their study revealed that trainee characteristics such as aptitude and motivational levels were among the most consistent predictors of trainee performance. In fact, they found that the effects of trainee characteristics were stronger than course–content variables (see also Fleishman & Mumford, 1989).

A number of other studies have found support for the role of individual differences among trainees and subsequent training performance. For example, Fleishman and Hempel (1955) compared the learning curves of groups high or low on ability measures such as reaction time, spatial orientation, and speed of arm movement. Their results clearly show that individuals high on these abilities reached higher levels of performance in fewer trials and exhibited superior overall asymptotic performance than their low-ability counterparts. Ackerman (1987) as well as Cronbach and Snow (1977) have also found significant effects of individual differences in abilities on training performance. Finally, Ree and Earles (1991) found that general cognitive ability was a better predictor of training performance than specific abilities for a number of Air Force jobs.

Such studies have tended to focus on the role of human abilities on training performance. Abilities are generally regarded as relatively enduring attributes of individuals related to the performance of a set of tasks (Fleishman, 1972; Fleishman & Mumford, 1989). Thus, the implications of this line of research relates more to the selection of individuals for training and the design of training in a manner consistent with the ability levels of individuals. By contrast, organizational contextual factors are more likely to affect malleable differences among trainees. These include variables such as trainee motivation to learn, self-efficacy, and fairness perceptions.

## Motivation to Learn

Noe (1986) suggested that whereas trainees may have the ability (e.g., cognitive, spatial, or psychomotor ability) to benefit from training, they may fail to do so because of low motivation. Countless studies in the field of education and educational psychology have shown that classrooms that foster student motivation are often the ones in which the largest amount of learning take place (Ames, 1992). In organizational settings, the empirical evidence has upheld the importance of motivation as a determinant of training effectiveness (Quiñones, 1995; Ryman & Biersner, 1975).

*Motivation* is typically defined as variability in behavior not attributable to stable individual differences (e.g., cognitive ability) or strong situational coercion (Kanfer, 1990). Thus, motivation involves a choice by an individual to expend energy toward one particular set of behaviors over another. In a training setting, motivation to learn can express itself in a number of ways. Motivation can affect whether or not an individual decides to attend a training session in the first place (Maurer & Tarulli, 1994; Noe & Wilk, 1993). It can also influence the amount of effort exerted during the training session (Ryman & Biersner, 1975). Finally, motivation can affect whether or not an individual chooses to apply the trained skills on the job (Baldwin & Ford, 1988).

An individual's level of motivation is dependent on a number of internal and external factors (Kanfer, 1990). As a consequence, a change in the external environment can affect a person's level of motivation. In fact, a number of theories exist linking environmental factors to motivational levels (Kanfer, 1990; Vroom, 1964). In the same way, motivation to learn is likely to arise from contextual factors surrounding the training event (Clark, Dobbins, & Ladd, 1993; Mathieu, Tannenbaum, & Salas, 1992). As the studies described hereinafter will show, the fluid nature of motivation to learn makes it an ideal conduit for contextual influences on training effectiveness.

## Self-Efficacy

*Self-efficacy* refers to an individual's expectations regarding his or her future level of performance on a task (Bandura, 1977; Gist & Mitchell, 1992). In the past few years, there has been an explosion in the number of studies showing the relationship between self-efficacy and various aspects of training effectiveness (see chapter 8, this volume). It has been implicated in all stages of the training process, from participation in training activities (e.g., Noe & Wilk, 1993), to acquisition of knowledge and skills during training (e.g., Gist, 1989; Gist, Schwoerer, & Rosen, 1989; Martocchio & Webster, 1992; Quiñones, 1995), to transfer of trained skills to the job setting (Ford et al., 1992). The educational literature has also embraced the construct of self-efficacy as a way of explaining differences in classroom performance (e.g., Schunk, 1982).

Individuals rely on many situational cues to establish their level of self-efficacy (Gist & Mitchell, 1992). Perhaps most important is feedback from past performance of the same or similar tasks. Successful past performance leads to high levels of self-efficacy, whereas failure results in lower levels. Attributional evaluations of this feedback can enhance or mitigate the effects of feedback on self-efficacy (Quiñones, 1995). Individuals also rely on their evaluation of the task requirements as well as their level of ability when forming self-efficacy perceptions.

Organizational contextual factors can serve as a source of information on which individuals base their level of self-efficacy. Individuals can directly acquire or infer information from the environment regarding their level of performance, difficulty of training materials, appropriate attributional inferences, and even the organization's expectations of the trainee's likelihood of success in training. Therefore, self-efficacy represents another potential link between contextual factors and training effectiveness.

## Fairness Perceptions

Training is fast becoming an important commodity for an individual's survival within an organization. In fact, labor contracts often include training as a benefit for union members. As organizations adjust to technological changes, it is often skills, as opposed to tenure, that determine who will remain in the organization (Kozlowski, 1987). Therefore, it is likely that organizational members will be sensitive to the fairness of access to, and distribution of, training opportunities.

Quiñones (1995) proposed that trainees may be sensitive to the process used to arrive at training decisions (procedural fairness) as well as the actual training decisions themselves (distributive fairness). The perceived fairness of human resource practices has been shown to have far reaching effects such as changes in commitment, motivation, satisfaction, and performance (Folger & Greenberg, 1985; Folger & Konovsky, 1989; Gilliland, 1993). In a training setting, fairness perceptions have been shown to be related to motivation to learn, actual learning, and reactions to training (Quiñones, 1995).

Although individuals may use different criteria for evaluating fairness (e.g., Witt & Broach, 1993), several general rules exist. Fair procedures are those that (a) follow consistent rules, (b) are based on accurate information, (c) employ safeguards against bias, (d) allow for appeals to be heard, and (e) are based on prevailing moral and ethical standards (Leventhal, 1980). It is possible for individuals to accept an outcome judged to be unfair if they perceive the process used to determine that outcome as fair (Leung & Li, 1990). Organizational contextual factors can supply information regarding the process used to arrive at training decisions and directly affect trainee's fairness perceptions. These perceptions are likely to have an impact on training and transfer outcomes.

## Contextual Factors

The discussion thus far has revolved around establishing a mechanism by which organizational contextual factors can affect training effectiveness. It has been argued that contextual factors are likely to affect malleable individual differences (motivation to learn, self-efficacy, and fairness perceptions), which have been shown to lead to differences in training and transfer outcomes. Having established this mechanism, I will now discuss organizational contextual factors relevant to training.

### Participation in Training Decisions

The process of developing and implementing a training system is complex and involves a series of systematic steps, each requiring a number of decisions (Goldstein, 1993). The first and perhaps most important decision to make is whether or not training is even needed. Once it has been established that training is necessary, it is important to decide what is to be learned (Gagné, 1962). Often these questions are answered through a systematic process of training needs assessment (Ostroff & Ford, 1989). Other choice points in the development of a training program may involve the type of media to be used, criterion measures, and training site, among others.

In light of these myriad choices required for the development and implementation of training programs, a critical contextual factor that can influence the efficacy of this process is the degree of participation given to trainees. Although the issue of participation in decision making is not new, its application to training decisions is relatively recent. Proponents of participation point to increases in decision acceptance, commitment, motivation, and productivity as the main impetus for increasing the level of participation within organizations (see Wagner & Gooding, 1987, for a review). Others argue in favor of participation on philosophical and moral grounds, appealing to issues of equality and democracy (see Locke & Schweiger, 1979, for an excellent discussion).

Participation implies the sharing of responsibility for reaching a decision. However, participation can vary along a number of dimensions (Cotton, Vollrath, Froggatt, Lengnick-Hall, & Jennings, 1988). Participation can be formally established through organizational rules or it can be informal (e.g., consulting a colleague down the hall before reaching a decision). Direct participation occurs when a person has immediate personal involvement in the decision making, whereas indirect participation involves representation in the process. Finally, participation can vary in the level of access, or influence, an individual has over the final decision.

An important decision in the implementation of a training program involves the voluntary or compulsive nature of trainee attendance. Allowing trainees to decide whether or not to attend training may run counter to an organization's need to impart critical knowledge to organizational members (e.g., how to use the new E-mail system). However, forcing individuals to attend training may create resentment among trainees. In perhaps the earliest attempt to examine this question, Ryman and Biersner (1975) evaluated volunteers for a Navy SCUBA training course. One of the measures in this study assessed trainee attitudes toward volunteering for the course. The results showed that trainees who expressed the most concern over their involvement in the experiment were more likely to drop out of the course. In addition, highly concerned trainees who remained in the course were less likely to pass.

A more direct examination of trainee participation or choice in training attendance was conducted by Hicks and Klimoski (1987). These researchers randomly assigned groups of managers and supervisors in a large research and development firm to one of two choice conditions. One group of individuals was presented with a memo from their supervisor requiring their attendance at the training session and a second group received a memo from the training department describing the training program along with information about the dates, times, and location of the sessions. Consistent with the framework presented in Figure 3, the study found that trainees who were given a choice to attend training reported higher levels of motivation to learn, were more satisfied with the training program, and received higher scores on an objective achievement test of the training material than trainees without a choice to attend.

Often large organizations offer employees a menu of training programs for their choosing. Thus, in addition to having a choice to attend, trainees may also have the option to select the actual content of the training course. However, the reality is that some training courses may become so popular that they fill up quickly. Trainees who signed up for these popular courses but do not get in may be forced to attend a less desirable course that they actually did not choose. This scenario provided the backdrop for a study conducted by Baldwin and colleagues

(1991), which examined what the authors referred to as the *perils of participation.*

Baldwin and his colleagues were interested in finding out whether it was better to give trainees a choice to attend training—and risk the possibility of not being able to honor that choice— instead of providing no choice. These researchers argued that the scenario just described is consistent with past research on organizational justice and fairness (e.g., Folger & Greenberg, 1985). Providing a choice may have beneficial effects because trainees see the process as fair and become more motivated and committed to doing well during training. However, providing a choice is also likely to raise expectations regarding the outcome of that choice. When their choice is not honored, individuals may actually become frustrated and be less satisfied than if they had not had a choice to begin with.

The results of their study, again, were consistent with the framework developed in this chapter. Baldwin and his colleagues found the highest levels of motivation to learn among those trainees who received their choice in courses. By contrast, trainees who were allowed to choose which course, among several, they wanted to attend but did not receive their choice had the lowest level of motivation to learn and received the lowest scores on a short-answer learning measure. This study highlights the subtle effects of contextual factors on training effectiveness. First, organizations may not even consider the potential effects of forcing individuals to attend training. However, enlightened organizations that allow trainees to choose the type of training they wish to attend may actually do more harm than good if they are not able to honor those choices.

In another test of the effects of choice on training effectiveness, Mathieu, Tannenbaum, and Salas (1992) asked employees in a large state university who were attending a proofreading training course whether they had volunteered for the program or had been signed up by their supervisors. Although the study failed to find a direct link between choice and motivation to learn, choice was found to affect post-test training scores indirectly through trainee reactions. Furthermore, an interaction between trainee motivation to learn and reactions on learning was found. This study highlights the complex role of trainee attitudes and motivation in the training process. It is clear that contextual influences on training effectiveness can travel along many pathways.

Mathieu, Martineau, and Tannenbaum (1993) speculated that the choices trainees make are likely to reflect their self-assessed ability to benefit from the training program chosen. Therefore, trainees who voluntarily choose to attend a particular training program should have relatively high levels of self-efficacy compared to trainees who have been forced to attend training by their supervisors or because of organizational policies. In support of this finding, Mathieu and his colleagues (1993) found that students who enrolled in a bowling class to fulfill a requirement had lower levels of pretraining self-efficacy and received lower course grades than students who chose to be in the class.

Taken together, these studies lend support to the proposed conceptual model linking contextual factors to trainee characteristics. Participation in training attendance has been found to be related to pretraining motivation to learn and self-efficacy. In addition to these motivational influences, an organizational justice perspective has also proved relevant for predicting participation effects. Thus, trainees respond to the amount of participation they are afforded and react accordingly during training.

## Framing of Training

Organizations can also create the context for training through the information they provide trainees about a training program. This information can *frame* the training situation by providing cues that can be used by trainees to construct and interpret events (Martocchio, 1992; Salancik & Pfeffer, 1978). For example, during a corporate downsizing, training can be framed as an employee's only way of remaining in the organization. Organizations can also convey information suggesting that training is a punishment for inadequate behavior. This framing of training is likely to affect pretraining trainee characteristics and subsequent learning.

Perhaps the most obvious way in which organizations can frame a training program is by providing information regarding the content of training. Thus, a training program titled Sexual Harassment Training elicits expectations that the training will deal with the definition, identification, and eradication of sexually harassing behavior. However, oftentimes trainee expectations are formed from inaccurate information or reflect internal assumptions on the part of trainees. In any case, it is the perceived framing of the training program that will determine how a trainee reacts.

Tannenbaum and his colleagues conducted a study to examine the potentially negative effects of unmet trainee expectations (Tannenbaum, Mathieu, Salas, & Cannon-Bowers, 1991). A training fulfillment measure incorporating trainee expectations of training content, perceptions of actual training content, and desired training content was created in this study. The researchers found that high levels of training fulfillment were associated with increased training motivation, self-efficacy, and organizational commitment (see also Cannon-Bowers, Salas, Tannenbaum, & Mathieu, 1995). These findings suggest that organizations should be aware of the information they communicate to trainees and ensure that expectations are in line with actual training content.

The competencies gained in training can often have positive outcomes for individual trainees (Nordhaug, 1989). For example, training can be a way of increasing one's competitiveness in the labor market. This is certainly the case for learning to use microcomputers (Turnage, 1990). However, the implementation of computer technology in the workplace can also be perceived as a threat to job security. A study by Martocchio (1992) examined the effects of framing a microcomputer training program as an opportunity for advancing trainees' careers on computer efficacy beliefs and actual learning. Martocchio hypothesized that an opportunity frame would represent the presence of personal control and result in acceptance of the training event by trainees (Thompson, 1981). This acceptance was expected to lead to lower levels of anxiety and higher efficacy beliefs. These, in turn, should lead to better learning. The results of the study were consistent with these hypotheses. An opportunity frame resulted in lower computer anxiety, higher efficacy beliefs, and higher scores on a multiple-choice test of the training material. Quiñones (1995) suggested that framing can provide feedback information regarding past performance. This may happen if organizations develop separate training programs for low and high ability individuals (Cronbach & Snow, 1977). Statistics suggest that our educational system is failing, thus leaving work organizations to provide remedial education in basic skills such as reading, writing, and arithmetic (Rosow & Zager, 1988). Training programs are likely to acquire different frames as training assignments become associated with different types of trainees. Therefore, the organization may be perceived as giving feedback to individuals through their training assignments. Quiñones (1995) hypothesized that this feedback would affect trainee self-efficacy and motivation to learn. In addition, he hypothesized that individual's expected training assignments would interact with actual training assignments to influence fairness perceptions. The assignment process was anticipated to be perceived as fair if trainees received the training assignments they expected. The results of this study supported the hypothesized relationships.

In sum, these studies suggest that information available to trainees concerning training programs frames training assignments and has an impact on various measures of training effectiveness. Trainees can use this information to form expectations about the content of the training course, infer their past level of performance, and make judgments about the fairness of the process used to make training assignments. How a program is framed can also influence expectations of success in completing training. Perhaps the most important aspect of framing effects is that organizations are potentially unaware of how the information they provide trainees is perceived and interpreted. Because of the ubiquitous nature of framing effects, the key is to find frames that serve to improve training effectiveness.

## Organizational Climate

Organizational theorists have long recognized that individuals tend to behave according to their perceptions of the external environment instead of the objective environmental characteristics. These perceptions form what has come to be referred to as *climate* (e.g., James & Jones, 1974). Schneider and Reichers (1983) argued that climates are perceptions of the environment that evolve out of the interaction among organizational members. During these interactions, individuals attach meaning to organizational features and events as they engage in a process of sense-making. A distinction is typically made between psychological climate, or perceptions held by an individual, and organizational or group climate (James, James, & Ashe, 1990). Organizational climate is said to exist when a group of individuals share a common perception of the work context (Joyce and Slocum, 1984). Thus, analyses typically involve aggregation to a meaningful level of analysis (e.g., work group) and comparisons are made between these aggregate units (James, Demaree, & Wolf, 1984). A substantial body of evidence exists linking both psychological and organizational climate to many outcomes of interest (see Schneider, 1990).

The climate construct is not a generic measure that applies to all aspects of the perceptual domain but rather a broad multidimensional construct that derives its content from the criterion of interest (Schneider, 1985). Research that has attempted to relate broad measures of organizational climate with specific behavioral dependent measures have met with little success (e.g., Pritchard & Karasick, 1973). However, narrowly defined measures of climate (e.g., climate for safety) should relate to criterion measures of a relevant construct (e.g., accidents). In a training context, researchers have examined updating climate and climate for transfer.

Kozlowski and Hults (1987) examined the updating climate of various engineering organizations to predict involvement in courses and programs related to the improvement of technical skills. A positive updating climate was defined as one that encourages individuals to maintain their technical skills, provides opportunities for growth and development through formal and informal courses, and has supervisors who are supportive of their subordinate's updating activities. Several dimensions of climate for updating were measured in this study including general updating climate, updating support, supervisor support, and job assignments. Their results showed that organizations with a climate that was supportive of updating activities, provided incentives for participating in updating activities, and promoted innovation and creativity had engineers who took more courses and attended seminars, training programs, and professional meetings (see also Kozlowski & Farr, 1988).

Further support for the role of organizational climate on participation in development activities has been found by Noe and Wilk (1993) as well as Maurer and Tarulli (1994). Researchers in both of these studies found that individuals who reported working in a supportive environment were more likely to take part in formal and informal training programs related to their primary job duties. In addition, these studies examined the relationship between organizational climate and trainee characteristics. Noe and Wilk (1993) found significant positive correlations between measures of social support and motivation to learn. However, regression analyses failed to find a mediating role for trainee characteristics. Maurer and Tarulli (1994) found a relationship between supervisor support and trainee self-efficacy. These findings lend some support to the general framework presented in this chapter (see Figure 3) within the context of training attendance.

A second line of research has focused on organizational transfer climate. Rouiller and Goldstein (1993) defined organizational *transfer climate* as situations and consequences that inhibit or help trainees apply the skills gained in training to the job setting. In their study, two dimensions of transfer climate were measured. These included situational cues, which helped remind trainees to use their training, and consequences such as feedback from peers or supervisors. Using a sample of graduates from an assistant manager training program in a fast food chain, Rouiller and Goldstein (1993) found that the organizational climate measures explained a significant portion of variance in transfer behavior above trainee learning and organizational productivity. Consistent with these findings, Ford and colleagues (1992) discovered that recent Air Force trainees reporting a high degree of supervisory and coworker support were also performing the most challenging and difficult of the trained tasks after returning to the work site. More recently, Tracey, Tannenbaum, and Kavanagh (1995) examined the transfer climate of departments within a number of supermarkets. They found that managerial trainees from departments with more positive transfer climates showed the largest increases in performance after attending a 3-day training seminar covering basic supervisory skills.

Although not completely unequivocal, there is limited evidence to suggest that organizational transfer climate affects transfer outcomes through its effect on trainee characteristics. Trainees tend to be more motivated when they know that they can count on help from their coworkers or supervisors as they try to incorporate the training material into their behavioral repertoire. In addition, supportive transfer climates create an environment in which trainees feel that the skills gained in training will help them perform their jobs more efficiently (Clark et al., 1993). However, trainees are likely to be unmotivated if they know that a number of situational constraints will impede their ability to transfer what they have learned (Mathieu et al., 1992; Mathieu et al., 1993). Situational constraints such as insufficient materials and supplies, time, information, or equipment, can frustrate a trainee's attempt to translate knowledge and motivation into performance (Peters & O'Connor, 1980). Furthermore, situation impediments to transfer can lower self-efficacy if trainees are convinced that these constraints will not allow them to perform the tasks taught during training once they return to the workplace (Mathieu et al., 1993).

It is clear that trainee perceptions of the work environment, or climate, can have an impact on the success of a training program. Climates can affect whether organizational members attend training as well as their use of the trained skills on the job. Goldstein (1993) recommended performing a thorough organizational assessment to identify potentially negative perceptions that can interfere with the successful implementation of an otherwise well-designed training program. The research by Mathieu and his colleagues suggests that this assessment should also examine situational constraints such as the availability of supplies and equipment. It would be a waste of time to train organizational members on how to use the latest computer equipment if all they have on their desks are antiquated systems and a promise of upgrades in some distant future.

## Conclusion

In this chapter, I have integrated a growing number of studies in the training literature examining the role of contextual influences in training effectiveness. I proposed a framework linking contextual factors with training and transfer outcomes. A key feature of the framework is the central role played by trainee characteristics, such as motivation to learn, self-efficacy, and fairness perceptions. The results of the studies reviewed were generally consistent with the framework I developed in this chapter.

Perhaps the most obvious conclusion that can be drawn from the research presented is that context matters. Training does not operate in a vacuum. This is not to say that training design issues such as instructional methods, course content, and training media are not important. Individuals will only learn what is taught in training. However, trainees arrive at the training site with expectations, attitudes, and motivational levels, and these can act as limiting factors on the effectiveness of a well-designed training program. Highly motivated trainees are not likely to benefit from a poorly designed training program, however. Thus, training must be thought of as a system embedded within a larger organizational system, each level of which influences the other (Goldstein, 1993; Noe & Ford, 1992).

Because various factors can influence training effectiveness, it is critical that a thorough training evaluation be conducted. It is not only important to find out if training worked, but also *why* it worked. A knowledge test at the end of training may reveal serious gaps in learning. However, the test does not say whether it was poor training materials, insufficient practice, or low trainee motivation that resulted in deficient scores. Evaluation techniques must become more sophisticated if they are to provide useful information for improving training. It may become important to collect evaluation data before training even occurs to ensure that trainees are ready for training. Such an analysis can help identify negative contextual influences conspiring against an effective training intervention.

Perhaps the most pressing research need is the identification and classification of other contextual factors. A qualitative analysis based on interviews with trainers, trainees, supervisors, and others involved in the training process should help identify broad themes. These can be followed up with more rigorous correlational and experimental methods to determine the actual contributions to training effectiveness.

Most of the literature dealing with contextual effects in training has focused on the pre- and posttraining environment. It is unfortunate that there is little information about what happens during training. Examining the interactions between trainer and trainees as well as among trainees themselves will help identify other important issues. For example, a study by Thoms and Klein (1994) examined the degree of participation during training on trainee reactions and learning. They found that trainees who participated more during training reported more positive reactions to the training program. Other studies could examine, for example, the types of climate characterizing most training programs. In addition to degree of participation, climates could vary along dimensions of support, competition, or challenge. The role of the trainer is also one that has received little attention.

Given the increasing role of training for maintaining competitiveness, issues revolving around fairness and justice are likely to become more important in the future. For example, we know little about what organizational members consider to be a fair system for distributing training opportunities. Some may believe that poor performers are most deserving of training opportunities in order to bring their performance up to par with other organizational members. Others may think that training opportunities should be reserved for those who have proven their abilities. Perhaps a more fundamental question is whether individuals believe that organizations are morally obligated to provide training every time they introduce a technological innovation into the workplace. Some might hold a more Darwinian view in which those who adapt to the new system on their own should be the ones who survive.

It is perhaps comforting to know that the only constant in life is change. Training is likely to remain the method of choice for dealing with change. Organizations may no longer have to ask whether they need training but rather what type of training they need. Psychological science is ideally positioned to answer these critical questions as we prepare for the challenges of the twenty-first century.

# References

Ackerman, P. L. (1987). Individual differences in skill learning: An integration of psychometric and information processing perspectives. *Psychological Bulletin, 102*, 3–27.

Adler, P. S. (1991). Capitalizing on new manufacturing technologies: Current problems and emergent trends in U.S. Industry. In *National academy of engineering and national research council, people and technology in the workplace* (pp. 59–88). Washington, DC: National Academy Press.

Alliger, G. M., & Janak, E. A. (1989). Kirkpatrick's levels of training criteria: Thirty years later. *Personnel Psychology, 42*, 331–342.

Ames, C. (1992). Classrooms: Goals, structures, and student motivation. *Journal of Educational Psychology, 84*, 261–271.

Baldwin, T. T., & Ford, J. K. (1988). Transfer of training: A review and directions for future research. *Personnel Psychology, 41*, 63–105.

Baldwin, T. T., Magjuka, R. J., & Loher, B. T. (1991). The perils of participation: Effects of choice of training on trainee motivation and learning. *Personnel Psychology, 44*, 51–65.

Bandura, A. (1977). Self-efficacy: Toward a unifying theory of behavioral change. *Psychological Review, 84*, 191–215.

Cannon-Bowers, J. A., Salas, E., Tannenbaum, S. I., & Mathieu, J. E. (1995). Toward theoretically based principles of training effectiveness: A model and initial empirical investigation. *Military Psychology, 7*, 141–164.

Clark, C. S., Dobbins, G. H., & Ladd, R. T. (1993). Exploratory field study of training motivation. *Group and Organization Management, 18*, 292–307.

Cotton, J. L., Vollrath, D. A., Froggatt, D. A., Lengnick-Hall, M. L., & Jennings, K. R. (1988). Employee participation: Diverse forms and different outcomes. *Academy of Management Review, 13*, 8–22.

Cronbach, L. J., & Snow, R. E. (1977). *Aptitudes and instructional methods: A handbook for research on interactions.* New York: Irvington. Fleishman, E. A. (1972). On the relation between abilities, learning, and human performance. *American Psychologist, 27*, 1017–1032.

Fleishman, E. A., & Hempel, W. E. (1955). The relation between abilities and improvement with practice in a visual discrimination reaction task. *Journal of Experimental Psychology, 49*, 301–312.

Fleishman, E. A., & Mumford, M. D. (1989). Individual attributes and training performance. In I. L. Goldstein (Ed.), *Training and development in organizations* (pp. 183–255). San Francisco: Jossey-Bass.

Folger, R., & Greenberg, J. (1985). Procedural justice: An interpretive analysis of personnel systems. In K. Rowland & G. Ferris (Eds.), *Research in personnel and human resources management* (Vol. 3, pp. 141–183). Greenwich, CT: JAI Press.

Folger, R., & Konovsky, M. A. (1989). Effects of procedural and distributive justice on reactions to pay raise decisions. *Academy of Management Journal, 32*, 115–130.

Ford, J. K., Quiñones, M. A., Sego, D., & Sorra, J. (1992). Factors affecting the opportunity to perform trained tasks on the job. *Personnel Psychology, 45*, 511–527.

Ford, J. K., & Wroten, S. P. (1984). Introducing new methods for conducting training evaluation and for linking training evaluation to program redesign. *Personnel Psychology, 37*, 651–665.

Gagné, R. M. (1962). Military training and principles of learning. *American Psychologist, 17*, 83–91.

Gagné, R. M., Briggs, L. J., & Wager, W. W. (1992). *Principles of instructional design.* Fort Worth, TX: Harcourt Brace Jovanovich.

Gilliland, S. W. (1993). The perceived fairness of selection systems: An organizational justice perspective. *Academy of Management Review, 18,* 694–734.

Gist, M. E. (1989). The influence of training method on self-efficacy and idea generation among managers. *Personnel Psychology, 42,* 787–805.

Gist, M. E., & Mitchell, T. R. (1992). Self-efficacy: A theoretical analysis of its determinants and malleability. *Academy of Management Review, 17,* 183–211.

Gist, M. E., Schwoerer, C., & Rosen, B. (1989). Effects of alternative training methods on self-efficacy and performance in computer software training. *Journal of Applied Psychology, 74,* 884–891.

Goldstein, I. L. (1993). *Training in organizations: Needs assessment, development, and evaluation.* (3rd ed.). Monterey, CA: Brooks/Cole.

Goldstein, I. L., & Gilliam, P. (1990). Training system issues in the year 2000. *American Psychologist, 45,* 134–143.

Hicks, W. D., & Klimoski, R. J. (1987). Entry into training programs and its effects on training outcomes: A field experiment. *Academy of Management Journal, 30,* 542–552.

James, L. R., Demaree, R. G., & Wolf, G. (1984). Estimating within-group interrater reliability with and without response bias. *Journal of Applied Psychology, 69,* 85–98.

James, L. R., James, L. A., & Ashe, D. K. (1990). The meaning of organizations: The role of cognition and values. In B. Schneider (Ed.), *Organizational climate and culture* (pp. 40–84). San Francisco: Jossey-Bass.

James, L. R., & Jones, A. P. (1974). Organizational climate: A review of theory and research. *Psychological Bulletin, 81,* 1096–1112.

Joyce, W. F., & Slocum, J. W. (1984). Collective climate: Agreement as a basis for defining aggregate climates in organizations. *Academy of Management Journal, 27,* 721–742.

Kanfer, R. (1990). Motivation theory and industrial/organizational psychology. In M. D. Dunnette & L. M. Hough (Eds.), *Handbook of industrial and organizational psychology* (Vol. 1, pp. 75–170).

Kearsley, G. (1991). Training media and technology. In J. E. Morrison (Ed.), *Training for performance: Principles of applied human learning* (pp. 231–257). Chichester, England: Wiley.

Kirkpatrick, D. L. (1967). Evaluation of training. In R. L. Craig & L. R. Bittel (Eds.), *Training and development handbook* (pp. 87–112). New York: McGraw-Hill.

Klein, K. J., Dansereau, F., & Hall, R. J. (1994). Levels issues in theory development, data collection, and analysis. *Academy of Management Review, 19,* 195–229.

Kozlowski, S. W. J. (1987). Technological innovation and strategic human resource management: Facing the challenge of change. *Human Resource Planning, 10,* 69–79.

Kozlowski, S. W. J., & Farr, J. L. (1988). An integrative model of updating and performance. *Human Performance, 1,* 5–29.

Kozlowski, S. W. J., & Hults, B. M. (1987). An exploration of climates for technical updating and performance. *Personnel Psychology, 40,* 539–563.

Kraiger, K., Ford, J. K., & Salas, E. (1993). Application of cognitive, skill-based, and affective theories of learning outcomes to new methods of training evaluation. *Journal of Applied Psychology, 78,* 311–328.

Latham, G. P., & Crandall, S. R. (1991). Organizational and social factors. In J. E.

Morrison (Ed.), *Training for performance: Principles of applied human learning* (pp. 259–285). Chichester, England: Wiley.

Laumann, E. O., Nadler, G., & O'Farrell, B. (1991). Designing for technological change: People in the process. In National Academy of Engineering and National Research Council, *People and technology in the workplace* (pp. 59–88). Washington, DC: National Academy Press.

Leung, K., & Li, W. (1990). Psychological mechanisms of process-control effects. *Journal of Applied Psychology, 75,* 613–620.

Leventhal, G. S. (1980). What should be done with equity theory? In K. J. Gergen, M. S. Greenberg, & R. H. Willis (Eds.), *Social exchange: Advances in theory and research* (pp. 27–55). New York: Plenum Press.

Lippert, R. C. (1989). Expert systems: Tutors, tools, and tutees. *Journal of Computer Based Instruction, 16,* 11–19.

Locke, E. A., & Schweiger, D. M. (1979). Participation in decision making: One more look. *Research in Organizational Behavior, 1,* 265–339.

Martocchio, J. J. (1992). Microcomputer usage as an opportunity: The influence of context in employee training. *Personnel Psychology, 45,* 529–552.

Martocchio, J. J., & Webster, J. (1992). Effects of feedback and cognitive playfulness on performance in microcomputer software training. *Personnel Psychology, 45,* 553–578.

Mathieu, J. E., Martineau, J. W., & Tannenbaum, S. I. (1993). Individual and situational influences on the development of self-efficacy: Implications for training effectiveness. *Personnel Psychology, 46,* 125–147.

Mathieu, J. E., Tannenbaum, S. I., & Salas, E. (1992). Influences of individual and situational characteristics on measures of training effectiveness. *Academy of Management Journal, 35,* 828–847.

Maurer, T. J., & Tarulli, B. A. (1994). Investigation of perceived environment, perceived outcome, and person variables in relationship to voluntary development activity by employees. *Journal of Applied Psychology, 79,* 3–14.

Mumford, M. D., Weeks, J. L., Harding, F. D., & Fleishman, E. A. (1988). Relations between student characteristics, course content, and training outcomes: An integrative modeling effort. *Journal of Applied Psychology, 73,* 443–456.

Noe, R. A. (1986). Trainees' attributes and attitudes: Neglected influences on training effectiveness. *Academy of Management Review, 11,* 736–749.

Noe, R. A., & Ford, J. K. (1992). Emerging issues and new directions for training research. *Research in Personnel and Human Resources Management, 10,* 345–384.

Noe, R. A., & Schmitt, N. (1986). The influence of trainee attitudes on training effectiveness: Test of a model. *Personnel Psychology, 39,* 497–523.

Noe, R. A., & Wilk, S. L. (1993). Investigation of the factors that influence employees' participation in development activities. *Journal of Applied Psychology, 78,* 291–302.

Nordhaug, O. (1989). Reward functions of personnel training. *Human Relations, 42,* 373–388.

Ostroff, C., & Ford, J. K. (1989). Assessing training needs: Critical levels of analysis. In Goldstein (Ed.), *Training and development in organizations* (pp. 25–62). San Francisco: Jossey-Bass.

Peters, L. H., & O'Connor, E. J. (1980). Situational constraints and work outcomes: The influences of a frequently overlooked construct. *Academy of Management Review, 5,* 391–398.

Pritchard, R. D., & Karasick, B. W. (1973). The effect of organizational climate on managerial job performance and job satisfaction. *Organizational Behavior and Human Performance, 9,* 126–146.

Quiñones, M. A. (1995). Pretraining context effects: Training assignment as feedback. *Journal of Applied Psychology, 80,* 226–238.

Quiñones, M. A., Ford, J. K., Sego, D. J., & Smith, E. M. (1995). The effects of individual and transfer environment characteristics on the opportunity to perform trained tasks. *Training Research Journal, 1,* 29–48.

Ree, M. J., & Earles, J. A. (1991). Predicting training success: Not much more than g. *Personnel Psychology, 44,* 321–332.

Rosow, J. M., & Zager, R. (1988). *Training—The competitive edge.* San Francisco: Jossey-Bass.

Ross, L., & Nisbett, R. E. (1991). *The person and the situation.* New York: McGraw-Hill.

Rouillier, J. Z., & Goldstein, I. L. (1993). The relationship between organizational transfer climate and positive transfer of training. *Human Resource Development Quarterly, 4,* 377–390.

Rousseau, D. M. (1985). Issues of level in organizational research: Multi-level and cross-level perspectives. In L. L. Cummings and B. M. Staw (Eds.), *Research in Organizational Behavior, 7* (pp. 1–37). Greenwich, CT: JAI Press.

Royer, J. M. (1979). Theories of the transfer of learning. *Educational Psychologist, 14,* 53–69.

Ryman, D. H., & Biersner, R. J. (1975). Attitudes predictive of diving success. *Personnel Psychology, 28,* 181–188.

Salancik, G. R., & Pfeffer, J. (1978). A social information processing approach to job attitudes and task design. *Administrative Science Quarterly, 23,* 224–243.

Schneider, B. (1985). Organizational behavior. *Annual Review of Psychology, 36,* 573–611.

Schneider, B. (1990). *Organizational climate and culture.* San Francisco: Jossey-Bass.

Schneider, B., & Reichers, A. E. (1983). On the etiology of climates. *Personnel Psychology, 36,* 19–39.

Schunk, D. H. (1982). Effects of effort attributional feedback on children's perceived self-efficacy and achievement. *Journal of Educational Psychology, 74,* 548–556.

Tannenbaum, S. I., Mathieu, J. E., Salas, E., & Cannon-Bowers, J. A. (1991). Meeting trainees' expectations: The influence of training fulfillment on the development of commitment, self-efficacy, and motivation. *Journal of Applied Psychology, 76,* 759–769.

Tannenbaum, S. I., & Yukl, G. A. (1992). Training and development in work organizations. *Annual Review of Psychology, 43,* 399–441.

Thompson, S. C. (1981). Will it hurt less if I can control it? A complex answer to a simple question. *Psychological Bulletin, 90,* 89–101.

Thoms, P., & Klein, H. J. (1994). Participation and evaluative outcomes in management training. *Human Resource Development Quarterly, 5,* 27–39.

Thorndike, E. L., & Woodworth, R. S. (1901). The influence of improvement in one mental function upon the efficiency of other functions. *Psychological Review, 8,* 247–261.

Tracey, J. B., Tannenbaum, S. I., & Kavanagh, M. J. (1995). Applying trained skills on the job: The importance of the work environment. *Journal of Applied Psychology, 80,* 239–252.

Turnage, J. J. (1990). The challenge of new workplace technology for psychology. *American Psychologist, 45,* 171–178.

Van der Spiegel, J. (1995). New information technologies and changes in work. In A. Howard (Ed.), *The changing nature of work.* San Francisco: Jossey-Bass.

Vroom, V. H. (1964). *Work and motivation.* New York: Wiley.

Wagner, J. A., & Gooding, R. Z. (1987). Shared influence and organizational behavior: A meta-analysis of situational variables expected to moderate participation-outcome relationships. *Academy of Management Journal, 30,* 524–541.

Wall, T. D., & Jackson, P. R. (1995). New manufacturing initiatives and shopfloor job design. In A. Howard (Ed.), *The changing nature of work.* San Francisco: Jossey-Bass.

Witt, L. A., & Broach, D. (1993). Exchange ideology as a moderator of the procedural justice-satisfaction relationship. *The Journal of Social Psychology, 133,* 97–103.

# Training Design and Pedagogy: Implications for Skill Acquisition, Maintenance, and Generalization

## Marilyn E. Gist

**B**arely more than a decade ago, it was difficult to know with much certainty which training methods were most effective and why. Much of the relevant literature presented nonexperimental comparisons, case-oriented studies, or anecdotal perspectives on training approaches. A few studies (e.g., behavioral modeling; Latham & Saari, 1979) involved well-controlled designs, but comparatively limited theoretical development existed to clarify why some methods worked. Reviews of the training literature called repeatedly for more rigorous empirical work that was theory driven (cf. Goldstein, 1980; Wexley, 1984).

Since then, the field has advanced markedly. A substantive body of evidence exists to guide practitioners in designing training programs more effectively. There also exists a more rigorous scientific basis for continued theoretical and empirical development in the area of training design. In this chapter I review these developments in training design and pedagogy and offer new perspectives on individual learning. I begin by discussing motivation theory in order to illustrate its increasing relevance for training research. Following this review, I emphasize three factors that influence training design: (a) the phases involved in cognitive learning, (b) the level of learning required for effective performance, and (c) the tasks being trained. I then review advances in training design for each of the following learning outcomes: initial skill acquisition, maintenance, and generalization.

# Human Motivation and Learning

One of the more exciting developments related to training has been the contribution of contemporary motivation theories to conceptions of human learning. Advances in the motivation arena have been applied to learning contexts; in turn, findings in the area of training design have added to the body of knowledge about human motivation.

## Evolution of Motivational Theory

The earliest views of human motivation focused on noncognitive variables. In drive theories (Hull, 1943, 1952), motivation was viewed as a force of energy (i.e., a drive) within individuals that directed their behavior. Drive theories assumed that humans and other organisms had a resting, balanced, or homeostatic state. As organisms diverged from homeostasis, tension arose in the form of drives (e.g., hunger, sexual urges) that activated the organism to pursue homeostasis. In other words, tension could be temporarily satisfied by behaving in ways that the drive directed.

Following drive theories, a perspective on needs emerged. Unlike drives that were rather vaguely defined as energies, *needs* were articulated as fundamental requirements for healthy existence. Maslow's (1943) well-known hierarchy of five physical and psychological needs (physiological, safety–security, belongingness, self-esteem, and self-actualization) was never fully validated; however, the presence of innate needs for existence, relatedness, and growth has been supported (Alderfer, 1969). McClelland (1965) later illustrated that certain needs could be acquired or learned (e.g., needs for achievement, power, affiliation). Although need theories represented a conceptual advance over drive theories, both perspectives emphasized factors within the individual, frequently operating below the level of consciousness, that induced behavior.

A differing perspective emerged with behaviorists (Skinner, 1971) who introduced the view that behavior was shaped or conditioned by the external environment. Classical conditioning referred to an associative relationship whereby behavior becomes related to some external stimulus. Of greater general interest was operant conditioning in which external reinforcement was shown to influence behavioral responses. In operant conditioning, individuals learned to operate on their environment—to adapt their behaviors in order to gain a desirable environmental stimuli (often a reward or positive reinforcement) or stop an undesirable one (e.g., noise, punishment). Thus, reinforcement schedules (i.e., the timing and form of external stimuli) were studied in an effort to determine optimal learning conditions.

As operant conditioning became synonymous with learning, the individual was viewed increasingly as a *respondent* to the learning process. However, because both need and operant conditioning theories received some empirical validation, a debate ensued over the appropriate causal direction of behavior (external stimuli–behavior vs. internal need state–behavior).

While the search for unidirectional causality continued, a third perspective emerged involving human cognition. Among the contributors who were studying behavior in organizational contexts were (a) Locke and Latham (1990) and their early work showing that goal setting influenced behavior—particularly when goals are challenging, specific, and attainable; (b) Vroom (1964), who introduced expectancy theory whereby expectations about the probability that effort would lead to performance and the probability that performance would lead to specific outcomes, along with the value placed on those outcomes, would jointly influence behavior; and (c) Adams (1963) who proposed equity theory, which clarified that individuals identify referent persons for self–other comparisons with respect to work contributions and benefits, and that the result of these comparisons influences subsequent behavior. Again, all these approaches received some empirical support, but they differed from earlier theories in that they demonstrated that human cognition influenced behavior.

These competing perspectives on what motivates behavior (i.e., innate factors, external stimuli, cognition) were integrated by Bandura in social learning theory—a model of reciprocal determinism whereby "behavior, other personal factors, and environmental factors all operate as interlocking determinants of each other" (1977, pp. 9–10). Bandura clarified that behavior is learned both from response consequences (i.e., reinforcement) and from modeling (i.e., vicarious or social learning), but that all such learning occurs through cognitive processes such as cognitive representation, recall, and interpretation. Further, self-regulatory capacities (e.g., cognitive evaluation and control) were posited as having a prominent role in determining behavior.

> By arranging environmental inducements, generating cognitive supports, and producing consequences for their own actions, people are able to exercise some measure of control over their own behav-

ior. To be sure, the self-regulatory functions are created and occasionally supported by external influences. Having external origins, however, does not refute the fact that, once established, self-influence partly determines which actions one performs. (Bandura, 1977, p. 13)

As cognition received greater empirical validation in determining human behavior, the model has been expanded and renamed *social cognitive theory* (Bandura, 1986).

## The Self as Motivator

As recognition grew for the importance of social cognition in studies of human performance, an interest arose in the self as a contender in motivation. Self-conceptions emerged in the work–motivation literature in Korman's work on self-consistency theory. In this view, individuals were seen as having views of themselves (self-image) with which they tried to align their behavior (Korman, 1970, 1971). A more recent formulation, image theory, has emerged from studies of decision making. Although it appears related to Korman's view, the focus of image theory on decision processes has led to an improved articulation of the stages involved in making decisions that are consistent with self-image (cf. Beach, 1993; Beach & Mitchell, 1987). These theories hold some appeal, and partial support has been found for each. However, they have not figured prominently in literature on learning and performance—partly because the complexity of their tenets mitigates against strong predictive validity where specific tasks are involved.

By contrast, self-efficacy is a construct involving an individual's belief in his or her capability of performing a specific task. Self-efficacy originally showed promise for motivation and mastery in studies related to overcoming phobias (Bandura & Adams, 1977). Self-efficacy was subsequently related to faculty research productivity (Taylor, Locke, Lee, & Gist, 1984) indicating its predictive potential as a motivator in work performance settings. Later, Gist (1987) suggested that self-efficacy held promise for research on motivation and articulated the construct's theoretical implications for organizational behavior and human resource management.

A relation between self-efficacy and performance has since been supported through a number of studies in the organizational training arena. For example, Frayne and Latham (1987) found that self-efficacy was related to job attendance following self-management training, and Gist (1989) found a similar association between self-efficacy and idea generation among managers following cognitive modeling training. The significance of those findings lay in the positive influence that self-management and modeling were anticipated to have on trainee self-efficacy based on Bandura's insight that self-efficacy could be influenced by guided mastery and modeling. Gist, Schwoerer, and Rosen (1989) clarified that self-efficacy did mediate the training method–performance relationship in a study of computer software training that contrasted video-based behavioral modeling (which exerted the expected, positive influence on self-efficacy) with diskette tutorial methods (which provided comparable instruction but did not enhance self-efficacy).

## Self-Regulation

Before elaborating on more contemporary findings, it is useful to provide a definition and model of a larger self-regulatory process. Self-regulation pertains to the management of psychological processes involved in performance and includes cognitive variables that are implicated in human motivation. Figure 4 shows a heuristic of the self-regulatory hub in which self-efficacy is the lead variable.

Although the reciprocal influence of many variables suggests that the model could begin at other points, this discussion positions self-efficacy first because it is the most fundamental perception about self as the performer.

Thus, moving forward in Figure 4, evidence shows that self-efficacy influences the goal level chosen on experimental tasks (Locke, Frederick, Lee, & Bobko, 1984). Those high in initial self-efficacy tend to set higher goals than individuals who are low in self-efficacy. This finding also has been validated in the training context (Gist, Stevens, & Bavetta, 1991). Goals, in turn, are widely known to influence performance (Locke & Latham, 1990). During self-regulation, goals direct attention and effort toward the task through a process that involves self-monitoring with respect to the goals and adjustment of effort to achieve desired outcomes.

Following performance, studies suggest that feedback is necessary for accurate self-regulation (Feltz, 1982). Some tasks may provide direct feedback on performance (e.g., typing), whereas others (e.g., diving performance, interpersonal behavior) more typically require that feedback be provided by outside observers.

Regardless, the effect of feedback on subsequent self-regulatory attempts may not be direct. Silver, Mitchell, and Gist (1995) showed

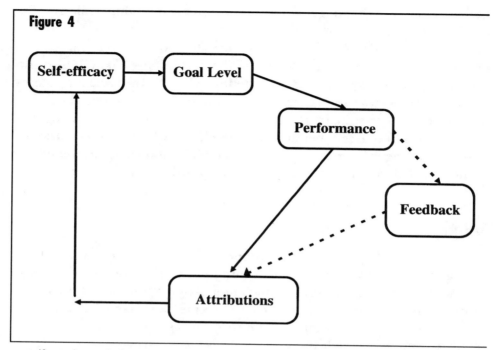

**Figure 4**

Self-regulatory hub.

that self-efficacy moderates the feedback–attribution relationship. Under conditions of unsuccessful performance, low self-efficacy individuals tend to make self-effacing attributions (e.g., more stable and internal) for their performance, whereas high self-efficacy individuals make self-serving attributions (more external and variable). Thus, high self-efficacy individuals may be more resilient—they shield themselves from declines in confidence with an ego-supportive attributional pattern—whereas low self-efficacy individuals tend to be more sensitive to early cues for failure.

Attributions about the causes of past performance, combined with actual past performance levels, accounted for more than half the variance in subsequent self-efficacy in the Silver and colleagues (1995) study. Apart from this direct evidence, substantial indirect evidence supports the role of feedback and attributions in self-regulation. For example, Wood and Bandura (1989) and Martocchio (1994) showed that individuals tend to perform better when they are led to believe that task performance is an acquirable skill versus a fixed ability. Based on Gist and Mitchell's (1992) conceptualization, and Silver and colleagues (1995) study, attributions about the causes of weak initial performance being variable (e.g., acquirable skill) as opposed to stable (e.g., fixed entity) should sustain positive self-efficacy leading to better performance.

Additional support for this is suggested by extensive evidence of Pygmalion effects (i.e., self-fulfilling prophecy; Eden & Ravid, 1982; Eden & Shani, 1982) in which subordinates perform better when leaders hold positive expectations for subordinates' performance than when leaders expect them to fail. In a similar way, subordinates for whom low expectations are held tend to perform worse (i.e., Golem effects; Oz & Eden, 1994). The mechanisms by which Pygmalion and Golem effects occur appear consistent with those known to be involved in self-regulation. The degree of instruction and verbal persuasion offered by leaders holding favorable (or unfavorable) expectations should influence self-efficacy (Bandura, 1977). Also, the favorable leader communication observed in the Pygmalion phenomenon should contribute to more positive attributions about early performance attempts; this, in turn, should sustain reasonable levels of subordinate self-efficacy and induce better overall performance. The reverse is likely under Golem effects.

Contemporary thought links motivation to learning as well as behavior. Social cognitive theory integrates concepts of operant conditioning by acknowledging that external reinforcement can influence learning and behavior. Social cognitive theory also specifies that learning occurs vicariously (i.e., through cognitive processes) as well as experientially, and that cognitive self-regulation is an important motivational force in determining human behavior. Of the many self-constructs in the literature, self-efficacy has been the most effective in predicting performance on specific tasks. With respect to training, we also know now that: (a) self-efficacy varies across individuals when faced with new tasks, and (b) some training methods yield better performance than others at least partly because they enhance self-efficacy (or affect other self-regulatory variables) while simultaneously stressing content instruction.

Nonetheless, these developments in motivation are only one factor to consider in training design. Other important factors pertain to the processes involved in learning and the nature of the tasks being trained.

## Perspectives on Human Learning

An early model proposed by Kirkpatrick (Kirkpatrick, 1967) recognized the need for focusing on both learning and behavior (among other factors) when evaluating training. Although the validity of the under-lying assumptions of the model has been questioned (Alliger & Janak, 1989), few training scholars would discount the centrality of learning to success with most other training goals.

## Cognitive Skill Acquisition

As recognition grew that cognitive processes are indeed involved in learning, attention turned to how cognitive learning occurs. Anderson (1982) identified three stages involved in cognitive skill acquisition. The first is *declarative knowledge* in which trainees learn the facts and data that relate to task performance. This stage appears to be memory-based, yet performance at this time tends to be awkward and requires frequent review to see if recall of information is correct. During the next stage, *knowledge compilation*, trainees are more adept at recalling information but now work at sequencing the steps required for performance in an appropriate way. Although performance often improves during the knowledge compilation stage, mistakes are still common. During the final stage, termed *procedural knowledge*, performance becomes auto-mated; less effort is required to recall facts or to think about the se-quencing involved. Some evidence for distinction across phases was pro-vided by Kanfer and Ackerman (1989), who showed that during the early phase of learning performance suffered if individuals were cog-nitively distracted from attending strictly to task demands. In particular, they found that goals (which trigger self-regulation by prompting self-comparisons against an intended level of performance) appeared to draw cognitive resources away from the task itself such that individuals who were assigned goals performed less well than those without goals at this stage. As tasks became better learned, goal setting led to better performance.

In the same way, Mitchell, Hopper, Daniels, George-Falvy, & James (1994) found that people reported reductions in cognitive processing for working on a task and for making self-regulatory assessments. Ack-erman (1988) introduced a model of cognitive ability determinants that are associated with the commonly accepted phases of learning. He clar-ified that cognitive abilities (i.e., verbal, quantitative, and figural) influ-ence knowledge acquisition during Phase 1; this more explicit formu-lation is compatible with Anderson's declarative knowledge phase but offers the advantage of clarifying both the learning tasks involved at this stage (i.e., memory-based) and the specific abilities related to those tasks. Ackerman suggested that perceptual speed influences learning in the associative phase (i.e., Phase 2). This phase was described as a stimulus–response phase and again appears consistent with Anderson's knowledge compilation phase while clarifying the learning task involved and the ability demanded by it. Finally, in the autonomous Phase 3, psychomotor abilities influence performance as learning is complete and performance becomes automatic (similar to Anderson's phase involving proceduralization of knowledge).

Ackerman (1992) offered empirical support for this conceptualization of learning, implicating individual ability significantly in the learning process. Still, in a subsequent investigation, Ackerman, Kanfer, and Goff (1995) noted that, although individual differences in abilities influence learning, individual's perceptions of these abilities may mediate ability–performance relationships.

Thus, contemporary learning theory incorporates some of the earlier operant conditioning view (i.e., stimulus response during the knowledge compilation or associative phase). However, learning theory now stresses both the cognitive demands and attendant abilities related to early stage learning and the confidence-based requirements that may exist throughout learning but remain influential even after controlling for ability during the final stage of automated learning. Finally, by articulating that learning is progressive (i.e., occurs in sequential phases), current theories imply that the timing of a cognitive learning assessment may determine the phase of learning that is actually assessed.

## Levels of Learning

The conceptualizations described thus far focus primarily on cognitive learning; thus, they offer only limited insight into how people learn behavioral skills. Noting that there is a distinction between knowing what to do and being able to do it, Gist and Stevens (1996) distinguished several operational levels of learning. These levels are viewed as a hierarchy that begins at a cognitive level and proceeds through demonstrated behavior (see Table 1). As a construct, learning level is independent of the conceptions of learning phases described previously. Rather than focus on the phases and abilities involved in cognitive learning, learning level focuses on the increasing complexity of learning that may be required in moving trainees from cognitive to behavioral realms.

Note that trainees need to progress through all phases of cognitive

## Table 1

**Level of Learning**

| Level of Learning | Description |
|---|---|
| | Cognitive |
| Recall | Capacity to remember what has been taught (terminology, data, stated principles) at a later date; typically implies *rote retention*, and requires rehearsal for encoding into long-term memory |
| Comprehension | Requires recall, but goes beyond rote retention to *understanding the material in a context similar to that provided in training*; comprehension may reflect some degree of knowledge compilation |
| Synthesis | Involves making cognitive connections between material presented during training and other relevant knowledge, material, or common situational stimuli (i.e., understanding across contexts); goes beyond comprehension by cognitively *applying learned principles to different contexts*; may reflect advanced knowledge compilation or the beginning of procedural phase learning |
| | Behavioral |
| Practice | Requires *behavioral demonstration of appropriate knowledge in a simulated context* (typically one designed for "trying out or testing" learned skills); whereas consequences or reinforcers may be part of the practice environment, trainees know the situation is not entirely real |
| Performance | Demands *behavioral demonstration in the natural setting for which the trained skills are to be used*; typically, this is the most challenging environment because it imposes competing priorities, it may involve less support for using the skills, and it often is richer in distracting or unexpected stimuli when skills are being tested |

learning (e.g., declarative, knowledge compilation, proceduralization) to fully master each specific cognitive learning level. In the case of cognitive recall, consider the learning process for basic arithmetic material (e.g., multiplication tables). Declarative knowledge alone yields slow progress and numerous mistakes; only when learning has become proceduralized are individuals able to produce correct responses automatically.

Next, incomplete mastery of one learning level should constrain performance at higher levels. Because comprehension is a more complex level of learning than recall, inadequate recall should reduce performance on tests of comprehension.

Further, different levels of learning may be required in order for performance to be satisfactory across different situations. With cognitive learning, comprehension may be sufficient for some performance settings, and synthesis may be needed for others. Consider the example of training managers in the legal issues surrounding selection. If the goal is merely to have managers who are able to explain the law and what it means, then comprehension would be sufficient. However, if the purpose of training is to ensure that managers understand how these principles apply to a variety of situations as they face them, synthesis may be required (and needs to become automated or procedural). Finally, if the ultimate desire is that the managers actually follow these principles in their selection decisions, cognitive learning may need to be augmented with behavioral learning (i.e., interpersonal skill development); again, this learning should progress through the procedural stage).

## Task Type

In work situations, most learning needs to be demonstrated behaviorally in performance contexts. The exhibit distinguishes between cognitive and behavioral levels of learning to clarify that knowing is not the same as doing. However, an important distinction for training can be drawn between tasks that primarily require mental operations (e.g., conducting financial analyses following training in the appropriate cognitive concepts) and tasks that require motor or interpersonal skills. For tasks that are primarily cognitive, the procedural mastery of cognitive learning should be the focal concern. Although proceduralization of knowledge can occur through mental rehearsal, behavioral practice (as shown in the exhibit) is typically valuable for ensuring mastery. However, it should typically consist of written assignments that induce trainees to proceduralize *cognitive* learning.

A more complex situation applies to learning motor or interpersonal tasks because the focal concern involves *behavioral* learning. Because these tasks involve operations beyond information processing (e.g., physical performance, emotion management), the behavioral practice level is essential for simulating elements of performance that are less readily rehearsed mentally by the novice. Even though the cognitive principles of a motor task may be understood, elements of physical strength, stamina, and coordination may be mentally represented incorrectly in the absence of actual practice. In the same way, with interpersonal skills, estimates of emotional coping or of the range of variance in behavioral situations to be managed may be constrained by trainees' past exposure in the absence of practice.

Two implications of this merit attention. First, greater declarative knowledge and more extensive knowledge compilation may be required with these tasks, lengthening the training time and complexity. The learner must develop a capacity to relate cognitive learning to motor and behavioral performance. As Ackerman (1988) noted, psychomotor coordination appears important in the third stage of learning, particularly for motor tasks. This imposes requirements for self-monitoring and behavioral coordination as trainees operationalize cognitively based principles into effective performance.

Second, as interpersonal tasks become increasingly important to organizations, training designers will need to understand the levels of learning that must be involved as well as the phases of learning through which the learner must progress to master each level. To be specific, interpersonal tasks require greater learning at the level of synthesis, because they involve variable and unpredictable stimuli (dynamic complexity; see Wood, 1986). Synthesis is the level that stresses connecting the learned material with external, situational applications. It is not the motor requirements of interpersonal skills that make behavioral demonstration so challenging; rather, it is cognitive understanding of a multitude of situational demands and the effects on the situation of one's own potential responses. Because this understanding extends outward beyond the principles taught and into a wide array of applications, synthesis is required for effective interpersonal performance.

## Nonability Determinants of Learning and Performance

Thus far in this chapter, learning has been discussed as a function of mastering the cognitive knowledge and motor or interpersonal reproduction skills required to perform. Successful performance still may depend on what have been termed *nonability factors,* such as attitude, emotion-focused coping, and motivation (i.e., self-regulation). These variables can be viewed in one of two ways (both of which are evident in the literature reviewed in the next section). First, because they affect performance, if they are malleable, they may be suitable subjects for training. Then, if organizations are interested in these variables as outcomes of training, the same levels of learning would apply. For example, emotion-focused coping (e.g., dealing with an irate customer) can be learned through the introduction of principles that are subsequently recalled, comprehended, synthesized, and behaviorally demonstrated.

Second, these variables (or others) may be viewed as individual difference factors that will affect training outcomes. For example, emotion-focused coping may not be trained directly, but the organization may attend to this as part of personality or general psychological functioning in making its selection decisions, its job assignments, or its decisions about whom to train. When viewed this way, these variables are no different from ability variables such as intelligence or aptitude that apply to any learned skill (although the relevant variables will differ across tasks).

To summarize the foregoing perspectives on learning, three factors should be considered when designing training. The first of these is the specific task to be learned (e.g., the domains involved in performing the task—factual knowledge, attitude, motor or interpersonal skill). Second, attention must be given to the levels of learning required for effectiveness in typical performance situations (e.g., comprehension, synthesis, demonstrated behavioral skill). Third, more attention should be given to the phase of learning that trainees should achieve. Procedural knowledge typically is assumed, whereas actual designs may support little more than declarative knowledge or the beginnings of knowledge compilation. What is hoped (but does not always occur) is that trainees will progress through knowledge compilation and proceduralization on their own when they return to their jobs.

## Advances in Training Design

McGehee and Thayer (1961) suggested that training design could be improved by following several learning principles. These were (a) identical elements that referred to using identical stimulus–response elements in the learning and application environment; (b) teaching general principles—the rules that were involved in the learning content; (c) using stimulus variability, which involves presenting stimuli in multiple ways; and (d) attending to conditions of practice—particularly distributed sessions, overlearning, and feedback. Although much of this thinking remains valid, advances in training design have provided additional insights for improving training outcomes. Training scholars have studied effects of training design on initial skill acquisition, the maintenance or retention of learning over time, and the generalization or transfer of learned skills to different tasks or to the job context. No comprehensive methodology has been developed for any of these training outcomes, but the following discussion is organized in those terms to clarify existing knowledge for future researchers interested in them.

## Initial Skill Acquisition

Studies that compare pretest measures of performance with measures taken relatively immediately after training on a similar task are assessing short-term learning or initial skill acquisition. According to McGehee and Thayer (1961), teaching general principles is a tenet of training for initial skill acquisition. However, the content of training and level of learning need to be considered when selecting a training method.

With cognitive judgment tasks, in addition to teaching general principles, the provision of frame-of-reference (FOR) training has received considerable attention because it offers a more explicit clarification of principles related to judgment. In the performance appraisal context, FOR training defines the multiple dimensions involved in task performance, provides descriptions of behavioral incidents pertinent to each dimension, and includes practice and feedback during training. FOR training has been shown to improve recall of performance information and rating accuracy measured immediately following training (cf. Bernardin & Buckley, 1981; Sulsky & Day, 1994; Woehr, 1994).

For other cognitive tasks, mental practice may be valuable. Because *mental practice* refers to the cognitive rehearsal of the task without overt physical movement, it may also be useful for strengthening the cognitive learning required as an underpinning for some behavioral tasks. In a meta-analysis of mental practice, Driskell, Cooper, and Moran (1994) found that mental practice had a positive and significant effect on performance, although the effect was moderated by task type, the length of the mental practice intervention, and the interval between practice and performance. To be specific, the more a cognitive task required mental operations (i.e., processing), the greater the effect of mental practice. Practice times of 20 minutes were suggested as a guideline for obtaining the mean effect size results, and effects were markedly stronger when performance was measured immediately following mental practice (i.e., for initial learning vs. delayed retention of learning).

Another area in which cognitive learning is central involves the use of computers, especially computer software training. A number of studies in this area suggest the importance of self-efficacy in technology training (perhaps because some trainees feel particularly inadequate when faced with complex technology for the first time). As mentioned earlier, a study by Gist and colleagues (1989) showed that self-efficacy mediated the training–performance relationship, so that video-based modeling instruction was superior to a diskette tutorial method in providing software instruction (controlling for the content and sequencing of instruction). A series of studies by Martocchio and his colleagues has shown that the context in which the training itself is framed (i.e., context incorporated into training method) improves self-efficacy and performance. To be specific, software skill acquisition is enhanced when trainees: (a) are led to see training as an opportunity (Martocchio, 1992), (b) are encouraged to view software usage as an acquirable skill as opposed to a fixed entity (meaning that skill level is relatively static; Martocchio, 1994), and (c) are given feedback that attributes their performance to factors within their control (Martocchio & Dulebohn, 1994). Additional evidence of how self-efficacy develops during training is provided by a model containing both individual and situational antecedents (Mathieu, Martineau, & Tannenbaum, 1993).

With respect to behavioral learning, numerous studies have found behavioral modeling to be an effective means of training for behavioral skills. Decker (1980, 1982, 1984) showed that modeling works by illustrating behaviors that are symbolically encoded as rule and descriptive codes, and that modeling is aided by articulation of the codes themselves (i.e., what to do and how to do it). In a meta-analysis conducted by Burke and Day (1986), behavioral modeling was found to be superior to lecture or lecture with role play alone for improving initial skill acquisition.

Baldwin (1992) found that *display variability* (the use of positive and negative modeling as opposed to positive modeling alone) had a significant negative effect on *initial skill acquisition* (i.e., performance on a similar task when measured the same day as training). This is consistent with McGehee and Thayer's (1961) indication that stimulus similarity and repetition foster behavioral reproduction (i.e., immediate skill acquisition). However, as will be noted later, stimulus similarity may not be a strong method for skill maintenance or generalization.

Finally, Harrison (1992) showed that the combined effect of behavioral modeling and a cross-cultural simulator was superior for cross-cultural management training as compared to either approach alone. This study paved the way for the design and testing of other package approaches in which multiple techniques (that are known to be effective for specific training tasks) are combined into a stronger training approach for improving skill acquisition.

## Maintenance of Learning

In the area of learning retention for cognitive tasks, Driskell and colleagues (1994) found that the effects of mental rehearsal declined by about half when the retention period was 14 days; after about 21 days, effects fell below the .10 level that is conventionally considered to be a small effect. Thus, although mental rehearsal may enhance initial learning, it holds only limited promise for retention. By contrast, Driskell, Willis, and Cooper (1992) conducted a meta-analysis on the effectiveness of *overlearning* (the deliberate overtraining of a task beyond a set criterion of performance). Results indicated that overlearning had a significant effect on retention of moderate magnitude across both cognitive and physical tasks. Although overlearning appears more beneficial initially for cognitive tasks when compared to physical tasks, longer retention intervals did weaken its effects.

A different approach to learning retention (skill maintenance with behavioral tasks), involves the use of posttraining sessions. This can be viewed as a form of distributed sessions in which separate training sessions are held for initial skill acquisition training and for skill maintenance or generalization. Marx (1982) originally suggested the potential of behavioral self-management training in work contexts, following its successful application for preventing relapse in studies of smoking cessation and drug and alcohol rehabilitation. Building on this work and an earlier study of self-management training as a stand-alone intervention (Frayne & Latham, 1987), Gist and colleagues (1991) tested self-management as a posttraining intervention and found it superior to goal-setting training for improving maintenance of learned interpersonal skills. The self-management approach: (a) encouraged but did not require that trainees set goals, (b) asked them to identify obstacles to success, (c) had them plan how to overcome those obstacles, (d) encouraged self-monitoring with respect to progress, and (e) suggested that trainees use self-reinforcement methods to motivate interim accomplishments. The study also found that posttraining method interacted with self-efficacy so that self-management training led to superior maintenance performance among low self-efficacy individuals, whereas goal setting appeared better for high self-efficacy trainees.

In testing a more comprehensive posttraining package approach (Stevens & Gist, 1996), self-management was combined with positive and negative modeling, group-level feedback about *process norms* (i.e., skills used and neglected), and a training orientation that encouraged trainees to view the practice sessions as a chance to improve their skills. This process approach (i.e., mastery-oriented) was contrasted with an outcome approach (i.e., performance-oriented) that encouraged goals, used positive modeling only, provided group-level feedback about outcome norms (i.e., performance attainments), and supported a view that the practice sessions were an opportunity for trainees to achieve their best outcomes. The authors replicated the self-efficacy by training interaction on a more complex interpersonal task, and found that the mechanism by which mastery-oriented training worked pertained to task avoidance during the knowledge compilation stage. In particular, low self-efficacy trainees in the mastery-training condition spent more time on interim activities and more time engaging in actual task performance (i.e., both preparation and on-task activity), whereas higher self-efficacy individuals (who underperformed their counterparts in the performance-oriented condition) reported fewer interim activities and greater on-task avoidance.

Although not directly related to posttraining methods, a study by Bavetta (1992) offers some insight into the interactions noted previously. Although it involved behavioral modeling training, the focus of the study was on the effects of feedback about initial performance on posttest performance. Under conditions of emotional supportiveness, an interaction between feedback directiveness and self-efficacy influenced behavioral performance. In particular, low self-efficacy trainees performed better under directive conditions, whereas high self-efficacy trainees did better with a less directive approach. When considered along with the posttraining method by self-efficacy interaction described previously, a pattern emerges suggesting that self-management training may be superior for low self-efficacy trainees because it provides greater direction as well as sufficient encouragement to engage in the processes required for skill mastery. By contrast, goal setting training may prematurely engage self-regulatory assessments that detract from early phase learning (Kanfer & Ackerman, 1989). The findings suggest that a mastery-oriented approach facilitates knowledge compilation. However, the effect of mastery designs may be moderated by self-efficacy level, because high self-efficacy individuals may more readily achieve the procedural stage for which goal setting and self-regulatory engagement are appropriate (Kanfer & Ackerman, 1989).

## Skill Generalization and Transfer

Studies of both training and posttraining methods that pertain to the generalization of learning to different tasks or to job contexts have focused often on the behavioral domain. For example, in Baldwin's (1992) study of stimulus variability, results for skill generalization were opposite of those found for initial skill acquisition. The combination of positive and negative modeling, although leading to weaker initial skill demonstration, had a significant and positive effect on trainee generalization of skill to a different task. It should be noted that the timing of this measure occurred 1 month following training, so that this result may apply to skill retention as well.

Eden and Aviram (1993) used behavioral modeling to explore its effectiveness for boosting general self-efficacy and job-search performance for 66 individuals who were unemployed for as long as 18 weeks. They found that the treatment increased reemployment among those who were low in initial general self-efficacy but not among those for whom general self-efficacy was initially high. Again, this finding is similar to Gist and colleagues' work indicating that high self-efficacy individuals may not benefit from training methods that are known particularly to enhance self-efficacy. In terms of posttraining methods, Gist, Bavetta, and Stevens (1990) showed the superiority of self-management when compared to goal-setting training for improving skill generalization to a different task. In a subsequent study (Gist & Stevens, 1996), the finding was largely replicated using the package approach of mastery versus performance interventions. This latter study also manipulated stress conditions (high versus low stress practice conditions). Stress appeared to overwhelm training method so that no main effect resulted for either training package; however, a consistent stress-by-training interaction effect was found for skill generalization. To be specific, high stress practice combined with mastery training led to the greatest skill generalization as assessed by multiple cognitive and behavioral measures. Further, these results were related to greater learning at the level of synthesis, showing that synthesis may be necessary for skill generalization tasks. Because synthesis and skill generalization involve different applications than those originally trained, similar results may apply to transfer of learning back to organizational contexts.

## Conclusion

As with most lines of inquiry, advances in training design have raised additional questions. Further development is still needed to integrate the multiple perspectives from motivation and learning theories into a comprehensive whole. The field would also benefit from a comprehensive typology of tasks that relates specifically to organizational training. In addition, it appears that some training methods yield differential benefits depending on whether the outcomes of interest are initial skill acquisition, maintenance, or generalization; however, our understanding of the learning theory behind these findings is incomplete.

Nonetheless, it is evident that much theoretical and evidential progress has been made in the past decade in the area of training design. Advances in both motivation and learning theories have led to greater articulation of the cognitive mechanisms by which training designs improve performance. Most of these conceptual advances have been supported by convergent findings from independent training scholars. The field of training research is now positioned to address the newer challenges outlined, and practitioners can design training programs with greater confidence in achieving desired results.

## References

Ackerman, P. L. (1988). Determinants of individual differences during skill acquisition: Cognitive abilities and information processing. *Journal of Experimental Psychology: General, 117,* 288–318.

Ackerman, P. L. (1992). Predicting individual differences in complex skill acquisition: Dynamics of ability determinants. *Journal of Applied Psychology, 77,* 598–614.

Ackerman, P. L., Kanfer, R., & Goff, M. (1995). Cognitive and non-cognitive determinants and consequences of complex skill acquisition. *Journal of Experimental Psychology: Applied, 1,* 270–304.

Adams, J. S. (1963). Toward an understanding of inequity. *Journal of Abnormal Social Psychology, 67,* 422–436.

Alderfer, C. P. (1969). An empirical test of a new theory of human needs. *Organizational Behavior and Human Performance, 4,* 142–175.

Alliger, G. M., & Janak, E. A. (1989). Kirkpatrick's levels of training criteria: Thirty years later. *Personnel Psychology, 42,* 331–342.

Anderson, J. R. (1982). Acquisition of cognitive skill. *Psychological Review, 89,* 369–406.

Baldwin, T. T. (1992). Effects of alternative modeling strategies on outcomes of interpersonal-skills training. *Journal of Applied Psychology, 77,* 147–154.

Bandura, A. (1977). *Social learning theory.* Englewood Cliffs, NJ: Prentice-Hall.

Bandura, A. (1986). *Social foundations of thought and action.* Englewood Cliffs, NJ: Prentice-Hall.

Bandura, A., & Adams, N. E. (1977). Analysis of self-efficacy theory of behavioral change. *Cognitive Therapy and Research, 1,* 287–310.

Bavetta, A. G. (1992). *Effects of communicator supportiveness and directiveness on recipient performance and satisfaction.* Unpublished doctoral dissertation, University of Washington.

Beach, L. R. (1993). Broadening the definition of decision making: The role of pre-choice screening of options. *Psychological Science, 4,* 215–220.

Beach, L. R., & Mitchell, T. R. (1987). Image theory: Principles, goals, and plans in decision making. *Acta Psychologica, 66,* 201–220.

Bernardin, H. J., & Buckley, M. R. (1981). Strategies in rater training. *Academy of Management Review, 6,* 205–212.

Burke, M. J., & Day, R. R. (1986). A cumulative study of the effectiveness of managerial training. *Journal of Applied Psychology, 71,* 232–245.

Decker, P. J. (1980). Effects of symbolic coding and rehearsal in behavior-modeling training. *Journal of Applied Psychology, 65,* 627–634.

Decker, P. J. (1982). The enhancement of behavior modeling training of supervisory skills by the inclusion of retention processes. *Personnel Psychology, 35,* 323–332.

Decker, P. J. (1984). Effects of different symbolic coding stimuli in behavior modeling training. *Personnel Psychology, 37,* 711–720.

Driskell, J. E., Cooper, C., & Moran, A. (1994). Does mental practice enhance performance. *Journal of Applied Psychology, 79,* 481–492.

Driskell, J. E., Willis, R. P., & Copper, C. (1992). Effect of overlearning on retention. *Journal of Applied Psychology, 77,* 615–692.

Eden, D., & Aviram, A. (1993). Self-efficacy training to speed reemployment: Helping people to help themselves. *Journal of Applied Psychology, 78,* 352–360.

Eden, D., & Ravid, G. (1982). Pygmalion vs. self-expectancy: Effects of instructor- and self-expectancy on trainee performance. *Organizational Behavior and Human Performance, 30,* 351–364.

Eden, D., & Shani, A. B. (1982). Pygmalion goes to boot camp: Expectancy, leadership, and trainee performance. *Journal of Applied Psychology, 67,* 194–199.

Feltz, D. L. (1982). Path analysis of the causal elements in Bandura's theory of self-efficacy and an anxiety-based model of avoidance behavior. *Journal of Personality and Social Psychology, 42,* 764–781.

Frayne, C., & Latham, G. P. (1987). Application of social learning theory to employee self-management of attendance. *Journal of Applied Psychology, 72,* 387–392.

Gist, M. E. (1987). Self-efficacy: Implications for organizational behavior and human resource management. *Academy of Management Review, 12,* 472–485.

Gist, M. E. (1989). The influence of training method on self-efficacy and idea generation among managers. *Personnel Psychology, 42,* 787–805.

Gist, M. E., Bavetta, A. G., & Stevens, C. K. (1990). Transfer training methods: Its influence on skill generalization, skill repetition, and performance level. *Personnel Psychology, 43,* 501–523.

Gist, M. E., & Mitchell, T. R. (1992). Self-efficacy: A theoretical analysis of its determinants and malleability. *Academy of Management Review, 17,* 183–211.

Gist, M. E., Schwoerer, C., & Rosen, B. (1989). Effects of alternative training methods on self-efficacy and performance in computer software training. *Journal of Applied Psychology, 74,* 884–891.

Gist, M. E., & Stevens, C. K. (1996). *Effects of stress and posttraining method on cognitive learning and behavioral skill generalization.* Working paper, University of Washington, Seattle.

Gist, M. E., Stevens, C. K., & Bavetta, A. G. (1991). Effects of self-efficacy and post-training intervention on the acquisition and maintenance of complex interpersonal skills. *Personnel Psychology, 44,* 837–861.

Goldstein, I. L. (1980). Training in work organizations. *Annual Review of Psychology, 31,* 229–272.

Harrison, K. (1992). Individual and combined effects of behavior modeling and the cultural assimilator in cross-cultural management training. *Journal of Applied Psychology, 77,* 952–962.

Hull, C. L. (1943). *Principles of behavior.* New York: Appleton-Century-Crofts.

Hull, C. L. (1952). *A behavior system: An introduction to behavior theory concerning the individual organism.* New Haven, CT: Yale University Press.

Kanfer, R., & Ackerman, P. L. (1989). Motivation and cognitive abilities: An integrative/aptitude treatment interaction approach to skill acquisition. *Journal of Applied Psychology, 74,* 657–689.

Kirkpatrick, D. L. (1967). Evaluation of training. In R. L. Craig & L. R. Bittel (Eds.), *Training and development handbook* (pp. 87–112). New York: McGraw-Hill.

Korman, A. K. (1970). Toward a hypothesis of work behavior. *Journal of Applied Psychology, 54,* 31–41.

Korman, A. K. (1971). Expectancies as determinants of performance. *Journal of Applied Psychology, 55,* 218–222.

Latham, G. P., & Saari, L. M. (1979). The application of social learning theory to training supervisors through behavioral modeling. *Journal of Applied Psychology, 64,* 239–246.

Locke, E. A., Frederick, E., Lee, C., & Bobko, P. (1984). The effect of self-efficacy, goals, and task strategies on task performance. *Journal of Applied Psychology, 69,* 241–251.

Locke, E. A., & Latham, G. L. (1990). *A theory of goal setting and task performance.* Englewood Cliffs, NJ: Prentice-Hall.

Martocchio, J. J. (1992). Microcomputer usage as an opportunity: The influence of context in employee training. *Personnel Psychology, 45,* 529–552.

Martocchio, J. J. (1994). Effects of conceptions of ability on anxiety, self-efficacy, and learning in training. *Journal of Applied Psychology, 79,* 819–825.

Martocchio, J. J., & Dulebohn, J. (1994). Performance feedback effects in training: The role of perceived controllability. *Personnel Psychology, 47,* 357–373.

Marx, R. D. (1982). Relapse prevention for managerial training: A model for maintenance of behavior change. *Academy of Management Review, 7,* 433–441.

Maslow, A. H. (1943). A theory of human motivation. *Psychological Review, 50,* 370–396.

Mathieu, J. E., Martineau, J. W., & Tannenbaum, S. I. (1993). Individual and situational influences on the development of self-efficacy: Implications for training effectiveness. *Personnel Psychology, 46,* 125–147.

McClelland, D. C. (1965). Toward a theory of motive acquisition. *American Psychologist, 20,* 321–333.

McGehee, W., & Thayer, P. W. (1961). *Training in business and industry.* New York: Wiley.

Mitchell, T. R., Hopper, H., Daniels, D., George-Falvy, J., & James, L. R. (1994). Predicting self-efficacy and performance during skill acquisition. *Journal of Applied Psychology, 79,* 506–517.

Oz, S., & Eden, D. (1994). Restraining the Golem: Boosting performance by changing interpretation of low scores. *Journal of Applied Psychology, 79,* 744–754.

Silver, W. S., Mitchell, T. R., & Gist, M. E. (1995). Responses to successful and unsuccessful performance: The moderating effect of self-efficacy on the relationship between performance and attributions. *Organizational Behavior and Human Decision Processes, 62,* 286–299.

Skinner, B. F. (1971). *Beyond freedom and dignity.* New York: Alfred Knopf.

Stevens, C. K., & Gist, M. E. (1996). *Effects of self-efficacy and goal-orientation training on interpersonal skill maintenance: What are the mechanisms?* Working paper, University of Maryland, College Park.

Sulsky, L. M., & Day, D. V. (1994). Effects of Frame-of-Reference training on rater accuracy under alternative time delays. *Journal of Applied Psychology, 79,* 535–543.

Taylor, M. S., Locke, E. A., Lee, C., & Gist, M. E. (1984). Type A behavior and faculty research productivity: What are the mechanisms? *Organizational Behavior and Human Performance, 34,* 402–418.

Vroom, V. H. (1964). *Work and motivation.* New York: Wiley.

Wexley, K. N. (1984). Personnel training. *Annual Review of Psychology, 35,* 519–551.

Woehr, D. L. (1994). Understanding Frame-of-Reference training: The impact of training on the recall of performance information. *Journal of Applied Psychology, 79,* 525–534.

Wood, R. E. (1986). Task complexity: Definition of the construct. *Organizational Behavior and Human Decision Processes, 37,* 60–82.

Wood, R. E., & Bandura, A. (1989). Impact of conceptions of ability on self- regulatory mechanisms and complex decision making. *Journal of Personality and Social Psychology, 56,* 407–415.

# Part Four

# Integrating Training Methodologies and Workplace Technologies

The development of new technology, machinery, and ways of organizing work requires that workers adapt to changes or lose their jobs. As workplace technologies evolve, however, so do opportunities for implementing training in order to help individuals adapt to new ways of working. The chapters in this section highlight both the challenges that arise for individuals learning new ways of working and for researchers seeking to develop new methods for training.

The common theme in this part of the book is that there must be a link between technology and the user of the technology. What should be stressed is what we can discover in information about individual learning strategies by observing the interactions of user and technology. By implementing training in the tools used in work, we have the opportunity of observing user behavior in a much richer environment than that of the laboratory. Rather than viewing new technologies as an obstacle to be overcome in training job requirements, the technologies can be viewed as presenting exciting opportunities for implementing and improving training.

In chapter 9, Johnson and Hyde discuss two relatively new tools for training, intelligent tutoring, and virtual reality systems. The authors describe initial investigations of the promise and challenge for using virtual reality and they consider whether and why the immersion possible with virtual reality may result in improved learning and performance. They describe the capabilities of intelligent tutoring systems to recognize human error and to diagnose specific areas in need of remediation in relation to the promise they offer for more efficient refresher training and practice of infrequently used but important procedures, and, perhaps most important, the implementation of remote learning via network connections. These systems also allow for the exciting possibility of using the rich data obtained from points of trainee difficulty to update and optimize the training program itself.

In chapter 10, Salas and Cannon-Bowers describe the challenges of training team performance and the tools and methods for meeting these challenges. In this chapter, some concepts from basic research in cognitive psychology are applied to the team training context. The focus in the chapter is on keeping basic principles of learning in mind while recognizing that teamwork poses new challenges for the design of training programs.

The most obvious change in the workplace in recent years has been the increase in the frequency with which computers are used. Chapter 11 by Atlas, Cornett, Lane, and Napier and chapter 12 by Carroll address training people to use computers through the use of computers. Atlas and colleagues highlight how developments in software make new training methods (e.g., the use of animated instructions) not only possible but potentially necessary. While emphasizing the need to develop training materials that lead to long-term retention and positive transfer to the task environment, they also address the issue of the implementation of training opportunities through the design of training procedures that will actually be used. Designing training materials with the goal of making them easy and attractive to use is especially important because people are often left to their own devices in determining how much of a software package to learn and how to accomplish the learning.

Carroll also deals with the issue of maximizing the benefit derivable from training materials. He describes the results of an extensive research program in which the characteristics of people learning to use software have been studied, identified, and catered to in the development of training materials.

# Advanced Technologies in Training: Intelligent Tutoring Systems and Virtual Reality

## Debra Steele-Johnson and Belinda Gaye Hyde

**R**apidly improving and increasingly sophisticated computer-based technologies are creating a vast range of new opportunities to use computers as training tools. As the cost of these technological advances declines, the potential of advanced computer-based technologies for training must be examined. To date, the cost of sophisticated computer-based technologies has constrained their use primarily to situations in which the current training is extremely costly (e.g., current training requires a high fidelity physical simulation or expensive actual equipment) or in which student errors during training have severe consequences (e.g., where a mistake could result in serious injury or extensive damage to equipment). In this chapter we will focus on two such technologies, intelligent tutoring systems and virtual reality systems, and discuss their potential as training tools. Other related topics, such as the use of high fidelity physical and nonimmersive computer-based simulations (e.g., flight simulators) in training, computer-based or computer-assisted instruction systems, and human factors issues associated with the design of user interfaces (e.g., display design) have been addressed by others (e.g., Baudhuin, 1987; Flexman & Stark, 1987; Hays, Jacobs, Prince, & Salas, 1992; Howell, 1991; Prince, Oser, Salas, & Woodruff, 1993) and thus will be discussed only in terms of their implications for intelligent tutoring systems and virtual reality systems.

This chapter was written while the first author was at the Department of Psychology, University of Houston. The ITS evaluations completed by D. S. Johnson and associates were supported by NASA/Johnson Space Center Grant Nos. NAG 9-555, NGT 44-005-803, and NGT 44-001-800. We thank Bowen Loftin and Robert Savely of the NASA/JSC Software Technology Lab for their assistance and support.

New opportunities in training are emerging from advanced technologies such as intelligent tutoring systems and virtual reality systems. Important next steps are to better understand the nature of these technologies, examine how these technologies have been applied to date, evaluate their potential for training based on theory and current applications, and provide a research agenda for addressing unanswered questions. Some unanswered questions include (a) for what kinds of training tasks are intelligent tutoring systems or virtual reality systems particularly appropriate? (b) For what kinds of training content is immersion beneficial or necessary? And (c) what are some of the unique features of intelligent tutoring systems and virtual reality systems that are most likely to contribute to their effectiveness? This chapter is divided into two major sections, describing first the nature of intelligent tutoring systems and then virtual reality systems, particularly as the latter relates to training. In each major section, we will discuss basic components, examples of uses, and potential for training.

## Intelligent Tutoring Systems in Training

Intelligent tutoring systems reflect a relatively young and rapidly maturing technology that has the potential to greatly benefit education and training. We are already shifting the focus from proving that intelligent systems *can* be developed to demonstrating their effectiveness.

### The Concept of Intelligent Tutoring Systems

Intelligent tutoring systems (ITS) came into existence in large part to more efficiently address training needs. Education and training in educational settings, military settings, and industry can be time consuming and expensive. For example, as tools and equipment used in work settings become more sophisticated, training costs (time, money, equipment, and personnel) increase. Tools are needed to reduce the time requirements associated with learning complex tasks, to facilitate training in situations requiring sophisticated simulation equipment, and to aid in settings in which too few personnel are available to conduct the training. Indeed, ITSs have already been developed to teach a variety of topics and task activities in educational settings (e.g., Algebra Tutor, Geometry Tutor), industry (e.g., Recovery Boiler Tutor), military settings (e.g., Equipment Maintenance Tutor), and university settings (e.g.,

Pascal Tutor, LISP Tutor) (descriptions of all examples cited can be found in Seidel & Park, 1994, or Wenger, 1987). Moreover, there is evidence that ITSs are becoming easier and less costly (in terms of time and money) to develop. For example, researchers at NASA have developed a general architecture to facilitate building ITSs for various task domains (Loftin, Wang, Baffes, & Hua, 1988).

ITSs are composed of some form of intelligent instruction overlaid on a content domain. Much of the initial research on ITSs was conducted under the label *intelligent computer-aided instruction* (ICAI) or *intelligent computer-aided training* (ICAT). Computer-aided instruction (CAI) referred to the use of computers in education. The label *intelligent computer-aided instruction* indicated the addition of artificial intelligence to computer-aided instruction systems (Wenger, 1987). However, Sleeman and Brown (1982) suggested that the term *intelligent computer-aided instruction* be replaced by *intelligent tutoring systems* to indicate that instructional systems involving artificial intelligence reflect a significant shift in research methodology and not simply a refinement of computer-aided instruction.

Many researchers attribute the initial ITS research to Carbonell (1970) for his development of a system called SCHOLAR, which provided training on the geography of South America (Wenger, 1987). In the 1960s computer-aided instruction systems typically presented students with frames of information, small units of curriculum. Carbonell extended previous research by proposing an alternative method of representing information, an information structure-oriented method, which focused on representing information in terms of a *semantic network*. A semantic network is a general structure for knowledge representation proposed by Quillian (1968). Carbonell's system was also distinct from prior computer-aided instruction systems because it included a mixed-initiative dialog. That is, his system not only asked students questions but also responded to questions asked by students. Carbonell's work has been followed by the development of many other ITSs (e.g., GUIDON, Clancey, 1979, 1983; SOPHIE, Brown, Burton, & Bell, 1975; WEST, Burton & Brown, 1979; WHY, Stevens & Collins, 1977) and additional research focused on improving ITSs, for example, examining other forms of knowledge representation such as production systems (Wenger, 1987).

Although the concept of ITSs was introduced in the early 1970s, there was little research and development activity relating to ITSs until the 1980s. Sleeman and Brown (1982) offered the first book on ITSs and indicated that until the early 1980s ITS development was restricted to a small number of computer or cognitive scientists (Seidel & Park, 1994). However, interest in ITSs grew greatly in the 1980s as researchers in psychology and education began to explore practical applications of ITSs to education and training. As Siedel and Park (1994) showed, whereas approximately 50 articles on ITSs were published in the 10 years between 1970 and 1980, more than 50 articles were published in the following 5 years (i.e., between 1981 and 1985), and more than 350 articles were published between 1986 and 1991.

Until the mid-1980s, research and development continued to be limited primarily to computer or heavily computer-oriented cognitive scientists. The focus was on developing functioning systems rather than on the instructional effectiveness of the system. In addition, ITS designers selected well-structured content domains with which they were already familiar, such as math or computer programming, thus eliminating the need for other subject matter experts. Further, the focus of evaluation was on whether a functioning system could be developed, reflecting an engineering model approach to evaluation in which development of the tool was accepted as proof of the concept.

ITSs became an important issue for researchers in psychology and education only in the mid- to late 1980s. Attention shifted from developing functioning systems to practical applications of such systems in education and training. Instructional effectiveness became an issue and instructional psychologists became part of the ITS development team. The focus of evaluation also shifted to a more traditional psychology or education model, emphasizing assessment of learning outcomes using experimental designs, although few formal, experimental evaluations were actually conducted.

Another significant event in the mid- to late 1980s was reflected in the research conducted by John Anderson and his research group at Carnegie-Mellon University. Anderson and colleagues saw ITSs as effective tests for their theories of cognition. Anderson's work is particularly important for its recognition of the mutual dependence among knowledge communication systems (e.g., ITSs) and cognitive science (Wenger, 1987). He proposed a theory of cognition called ACT (Adaptive Control of Thought) and a more recent version called ACT* (ACT-star; Anderson, 1990). Two important assumptions of his ACT theory were that (a) knowledge can be represented as a set of production rules—in other words, rules describing relationships between pieces of knowledge, and (b) knowledge is acquired declaratively through instruction and then organized into productions through task experience. Using ITSs as test beds, researchers have determined that ACT* can be used successfully to model human skill acquisition in various domains (Wenger, 1987).

ITSs can be categorized in terms of three applications: tutoring, coaching, and empowering environments (Dede, 1987). Tutoring is instructor-centered and attempts to increase student comprehension in a content domain in a very structured way. Coaching is student-centered and gives learners some flexibility in practicing skills in simulated environments. Empowering environments are task-centered and allow students to freely explore a microworld; this has also been called *discovery learning*. An ITS can be built to provide simulation-based training [e.g., the Remote Maneuvering System (the robotic arm) on the space shuttle] or cognitive tutoring (e.g., physics problems, computer programming problems). ITSs historically used two-dimensional computerized task simulations, although with the advent of virtual reality, it becomes possible to discuss overlaying intelligent tutoring on three-dimensional immersive displays.

ITSs can be described as having five components: a domain expert (i.e., an expert model), a student model, a training session manager, a scenario generator, and a user interface (e.g., Loftin, 1987; Seidel, Park, & Perez, 1988). The *domain expert*, or expert model, contains information about how to perform the task. It is sometimes called the *expert knowledge base* (Biegel et al., 1988). The *student model*, sometimes called the *trainee model*, contains information about the student's knowledge. One of the more common models is the overlay model with a bug library (VanLehn, 1988). This model assumes the student is similar to the expert but with some procedures missing and uses a bug library to detect incorrect procedures (VanLehn, 1988). The student model updates the level of student performance, provides information to the tutor, and provides a permanent record of student performance and background data (Biegel et al., 1988). The third component of the ITS is the *training session manager*. This component interprets the student's actions and reports the results in system messages (i.e., statements of actions taken displayed on the computer screen) or provides coaching in tutor messages (i.e., error, hint, or help messages). The training session manager also determines when and how to remediate the student and incorporates information into the student model. A variety of remediation strategies are available (Biegel et al., 1988), depending on the desired instructional strategy. For example, the training session manager might act as a reference source (allowing students to look up needed information), a coach (suggesting appropriate responses) or a monitor (simply waiting for student responses and evaluating their appropriateness), or the training session manager might provide a demonstration. The fourth component is the *training scenario generator,* which determines the difficulty and order in which problems are administered to students. The fifth component, the *user interface,* enables the student to interact with the system to obtain, enter, and manipulate information and complete actions. Commonly used interface devices include the computer keyboard, mouse, touch panels, track balls, or joysticks.

Furthermore, Seidel and colleagues (1988) discussed six intelligent features of ITSs that distinguish them from other training technologies such as computer-aided instruction. First, ITSs have the capability to generate instructional processes matched to individual students. Second, as mentioned previously, ITSs have the capability to engage in a mixed-initiative dialog. That is, the ITS can communicate information to the student and respond to queries from the student. Third, ITSs have the capability to model the student's learning processes. Because of the domain expert and the student model, ITSs have the potential to provide a wealth of performance data for each individual, including information about the student's specific problem-solving processes. Fourth, ITSs can engage in qualitative decision making, determining on the basis of previous performance what information to provide next to the student. Fifth, ITSs are capable of making inferences. That is, based on students' inputs, the ITS makes inferences regarding students' understanding. Sixth, ITSs have the capability of being self-improving. In other words, an ITS can be designed to observe its own teaching processes and modify them based on those observations. Although these capabilities are reflected to varying degrees in existing ITSs, the intelligence that characterizes ITSs makes them distinct from other training systems in that ITSs are intended to change and improve with use, adapting to students' needs.

## ITS Applications

We will describe three ITS applications developed at NASA to illustrate several unique features that have the potential to benefit training. These will help demonstrate how ITSs can address very different types of training content and purposes and illustrate some of the features described previously. These are systems we have had the opportunity to evaluate informally to facilitate system development (Johnson, 1989, 1990; Johnson & Pieper, 1992).

The Payload Assist Module Deployment/Intelligent Computer-Aided Training system (PD/ICAT) was an ITS designed to train flight dynamics officers to deploy a Payload Assist Module satellite (Johnson, 1989). The ITS provided training on a complex procedural task in which performing the correct sequence of activities was essential. Flight dynamics experts were used to develop the domain expert. The task sequence involved 57 actions, of which 38 were required and 19 were optional. In addition, students were asked to monitor 83 display fields on eight different displays, some of which were viewed twice. The displays were duplicates of displays observed by flight dynamics officers during real task activities. In this ITS, the scenario generator only administered one "problem"—a nominal Payload Assist Module satellite deploy. Error messages were displayed providing various information depending on the nature of the error made, thus generating instructional processes matched to individual students. Second, students could engage in a mixed-initiative dialog by observing system messages describing the action step completed and by querying the system using help messages. Third, the ITS recorded data on a variety of dimensions in the form of a student model and, fourth, made inferences regarding students' understanding to determine the feedback to provide.

The Remote Maneuvering System ITS also provided training on a complex procedural task (Johnson & Pieper, 1992). However, rather than training a complete task sequence, this ITS broke the task into smaller part tasks and only provided integrated task training on the successful completion of the part task training. The Remote Maneuvering System ITS was designed to train astronauts in how to use the robotic arm on the space shuttle. The usual training is completed on high physical fidelity simulations, and the ITS was designed as a lower cost alternative to provide preliminary training. Astronauts had to complete part tasks relating to four coordinate systems and procedures such as grappling a payload and berthing the arm. The two whole tasks were deploying and retrieving a satellite. The ITS generated instructional processes matched to individual students—in other words, feedback was matched to their patterns of successes and failures in learning the part tasks. A mixed dialog was operationalized in the form of feedback, hints, and a help query system. In addition, the system used a student model to guide the recording of performance data on a variety of dimensions on a trial-by-trial basis for each student, made inferences regarding a student's understanding, and then used those inferences in decisions regarding what form of feedback to provide.

The Manual Select Keyboard ITS was designed to provide automaticity training on simple tasks; in particular, this ITS provided training on the Manual Select Keyboard tasks performed on a propulsion console (Johnson, 1990). Whereas the Payload Assist Module Deployment and Remote Maneuvering System ITSs were designed to provide training on complex procedural tasks, also referred to as *knowledge-rich tasks*, the Manual Select Keyboard ITS was designed to provide training to automaticity on simple tasks, also known as *high-performance tasks*. High-performance tasks are tasks that are simple but must be performed with great speed and accuracy. In this ITS, flight controllers learned to perform 12 simple tasks, typically involving a series of four to five steps. Flight controllers received three stages of training based on Anderson's (1990) model of skill acquisition: declarative training, speed training, and automaticity training. Flight controllers had to successfully complete training in each stage before they were advanced to the next stage. As in the previous two examples, the ITS generated instructional processes matched to individual students by individualizing the feedback provided. A mixed dialog was operationalized through a system of feedback and help messages. The system recorded data within the student model on a variety of performance dimensions on a trial by trial basis for each student. The ITS then made inferences regarding students' understanding and engaged in qualitative decisions to determine the feedback to provide and the sequence of problems to present.

These three ITSs demonstrate five of the six unique features of ITS described by Seidel and colleagues (1988). In each example, the ITS: (a) generated instructional processes matched to individual students, (b) engaged in a mixed-initiative dialog, (c) modeled students' learning processes, (d) engaged in qualitative decision making, and (e) made inferences. As a result each student experienced a somewhat different training session. Such individually tailored instruction and remediation has the potential to result in more effective learning. However, more rigorous, empirical research is needed that examines directly the effects of ITSs on learning.

## The Potential of ITSs for Training

Education and psychology offer many tools for examining the potential of ITSs for training—in other words, the tools for designing instruction and systematically examining its effects on learning. We can draw from a number of theoretical models of training systems (e.g., Dede, 1995; Duffy & Jonassen, 1992; Foreman & Pufall, 1988; Gagné, Briggs, & Wager, 1992; Goldstein, 1986, 1991; Perkins, 1991) and training effectiveness or evaluation (e.g., Baldwin & Ford, 1988; Flagg, 1990; Kraiger, Ford, & Salas, 1993; Nickerson, 1989; Noe, 1986; Reeves, 1992; Shute & Regian, 1993; Tannenbaum, Mathieu, Salas, & Cannon-Bowers, 1991). Moreover, these models share many of the same basic components. Thus, a generic model of training design can be described, composed of needs assessment, development of instructional objectives, selection of training media, design of the training program, and training evaluation. This model can then be used as an organizing framework for discussing the training potential of ITSs in order to examine how effectively ITS designers accomplish steps in training or instructional design.

Training design begins with needs assessment, including organizational analysis, person analysis, and task analysis (Goldstein, 1986). Needs assessment is a crucial step in designing training. However, many ITSs have been developed primarily as research tools intended to demonstrate the feasibility of the concept (Wenger, 1987) rather than as training tools. Indeed, in ITS development, needs assessment primarily has focused on a detailed form of task analysis, called *knowledge acquisition*, and less attention has been devoted to person or organizational analyses. Some ITSs with more complete needs assessments have been developed for use in academic settings. Where the researcher (e.g., Anderson, Boyle, & Reiser, 1985; Frye, Littman, & Soloway, 1987) is also the course instructor, the needs assessment process is relatively simple; the instructor identifies the organizational goals (i.e., the course objectives) and completes the person analysis (i.e., inventory of individuals' existing skills, knowledge, and abilities) and task analysis (i.e., knowledge, skills, and abilities required for task performance). However, the researcher–ITS designer may have to seek out the information needed to complete the organization, person, and task analyses in work settings.

Next is the development of instructional objectives, which in one sense is extensively addressed in the design of ITSs. Indeed, instructional objectives determine the decision rules used to assess student performance and determine the sequence of training tasks to be performed. However, if the instructional objectives have not been well documented or have been revised during the development of an ITS, it might be difficult to reconstruct the instructional objectives from the decision rules and difficult in turn to build them into the evaluation criteria.

The next steps are the selection of training media and the design of the program. This raises an important issue: What task domains are best suited for training using an ITS? Little is known about the relative effectiveness of the ITS as a training medium versus more traditional training media (e.g., classroom lecture, computer-aided instruction), and that effectiveness might depend on the task domain. Another important issue is when and how to provide remediation. It is unfortunate that we know little about the relative effectiveness of different types of remediation (e.g., feedback, cues, hints, or help messages), about how human tutors provide remediation, or about factors influencing the effectiveness of human tutors. On a positive note, ITSs have the ability to provide multimedia training environments—with the potential to offer a mixture of text, sounds, graphics, video, and other media (Seidel & Park, 1994).

The final step is program evaluation. However, because of the newness of the technology, little attention has been devoted to this phase. Evaluation can be time consuming and costly (Frye, Littman, & Soloway, 1987), and historically, there have been few clear guidelines for how to assess a system's effectiveness (Burns & Capps, 1988). Traditional training evaluation tools and procedures (e.g., Goldstein, 1986) offer a starting point but may not be sufficient to evaluate ITSs (Goldstein, 1989). Moreover, ITS team members might disagree about what constitutes evaluation. Indeed, computer scientists often draw from the engineering model in which the development of a functioning system basically is viewed as proof in support of the theory. However, psychologists draw from the natural science paradigm, advocating the use of experimental designs to evaluate systems.

Some basic definitions will aid in understanding issues in evaluation. For example, internal evaluation focuses on the system's architecture (which is beyond the scope of this chapter), whereas external evaluation focuses on how the system affects students' problem-solving processes (Littman & Soloway, 1988). *Formative evaluation* investigates whether the program is operating as planned, and *summative evaluation* examines the effectiveness of the final product (Scriven, 1967). Finally, laboratory experiments focus on internal validity, enabling the researcher to draw causal conclusions regarding the specific effects of variables but may have limited external validity because of their limited generalizability to the field. In contrast, field studies generally have greater external validity, providing more confidence regarding generalizability of the results but might have limited internal validity because of the inability to attribute results to specific variables. Given the newness and exploratory nature of many ITSs, most evaluations have been formative (e.g., Johnson & Pieper, 1992), relatively informal (Littman & Soloway, 1988), primarily descriptive in nature (see Wenger, 1987, pp. 59 and 133, for examples), or have used weak experimental designs such as pretests and posttests groups with no control groups (see Wenger, 1987, p. 96).

Some systematic, controlled evaluations have been completed—for example, the LISP Tutor, teaching Lisp programming (e.g., Anderson et al., 1985; Anderson, Farrell, & Sauers, 1984); Smithtown, a discovery world involving microeconomics (Shute & Glaser, 1990); Sherlock, a tutor for electronics troubleshooting (Lesgold, Lajoie, Bunzo, & Eggan, 1992); Bridge, teaching Pascal programming (Shute, 1991); a graphics design tutor (Grabinger & Pollock, 1989); and another tutor focused on Lisp programming (Schmalhofer, Kuhn, Charron, & Messamer, 1990). However, the inconsistent results even from controlled studies suggest that what influences training effectiveness is not the general approach (e.g., ITS versus computer-aided instruction) but the specific instructional strategies used (Seidel & Park, 1994). Thus, research is focusing now on what kinds of variables influence training effectiveness and to what extent ITSs can beneficially influence those variables (Seidel & Park, 1994).

Also, researchers (Seidel & Park, 1994; Shute & Regian, 1993) have suggested that a range of studies varying from carefully controlled experiments that manipulate a single or a few variables to field studies involving complex combinations of variables are needed to evaluate ITSs. For example, Seidel and Park (1994; based on Seidel & Perez, 1994) evaluate effectiveness in terms of integration of an innovative technology (e.g., ITSs) into the organization. Their model devotes relatively less attention to other evaluation criteria such as reactions, learning, and performance (Kirkpatrick, 1977). Seidel and Perez described three major stages of technology: (a) *adoption*, the initial use of the technology; (b) *implementation*, the spread of the innovation in the organization; and (c) *institutionalization*, when the innovation becomes integrated into the larger organizational system. The model also describes two major processes. *Assimilation* refers to the use of the innovation to solve a particular problem or make an existing task easier. In contrast, *accommodation* refers to being guided by the unique features of the technology to take new and different approaches to a problem or task. According to Seidel and Park (1994), the real value of a technology innovation occurs when it has become integrated into the organization and users are able to adapt to and use the uniqueness and flexibility of the system.

In a very different approach, Shute and Regian (1993) proposed a model of ITS evaluation based on seven principles. Their model is derived from the basic premises that there are tradeoffs between internal validity and external validity that determine when to use laboratory experiments versus field studies, that evaluation is a cyclical process, and that a comprehensive evaluation of an ITS requires both types of studies. Their seven principles are (a) defining the goals of the tutor, (b) defining the goals of the evaluation study, (c) selecting the appropriate design, (d) correctly operationalizing the chosen design, (e) planning the logistics of the study, (f) pilot testing the tutor and the study, and (g) determining the appropriate data analyses. By focusing explicit attention on defining the goals of the tutor and the evaluation study, their model helps integrate diverse approaches to evaluation. Moreover, their model implies that a number of studies involving a variety of evaluation designs are needed to effectively assess an ITS.

## Summary of ITSs

ITSs have been developed to provide training for diverse content and task activities. However, little is known about what task or knowledge domains are best suited for training on ITSs. Research is also needed to examine the instructional processes underlying ITSs, including what human tutors do and what influences their effectiveness. Finally, we need to take a broader approach to evaluation to answer these and other questions, conducting a range of studies to learn more about what specific variables influence ITS effectiveness, examine a given ITS, and assess its integration into the organization.

## Virtual Reality in Training

Popular media portrayal of virtual reality (VR, also known as *virtual environments, virtual worlds,* or *cyberspace*) typically depicts a well-developed technology for use in games and other entertainment purposes (Stone, 1991). Indeed, some researchers predict a wide and rapid diffusion of VR technology into the entertainment industry before its entrance into other industries such as training (Biocca, 1992a). Yet the reality of VR is that the current instantiations still leave one with the impression of a prototype technology (Biocca, 1992b).

### The Concept of VR

The origins of VR can be traced back to the late 1960s with the invention of visually coupled teleoperated systems (Kalawsky, 1993). These systems allowed an individual at a distal location to operate equipment while viewing the scene through a head-mounted display. The display relayed signals from a camera at the equipment site, the movements of which were coupled to the movements of the operator's head. Such a system might be used to handle dangerous materials from a safe distance. Today, VR is typically used to couple the individual to an artificial, computer-generated environment instead of a real, but remote, environment. The important similarity between the early systems and the VR systems of today is the feeling of immersion in the environment of the system.

VR can be defined in two ways: by the technology involved or by the psychological effects created by that technology (Biocca, 1992a). The technology is used to create a multisensory message for the user (Biocca, 1992a). Output devices relay environmental information (about the artificial environment) from the computer to one or more human sensory systems. For example, a head-mounted, three-dimensional visual display offers a slightly different view of a particular scene to each eye on either cathode ray tubes or liquid crystal displays (and retinal scanners that project light directly onto the retina are under development). Three-dimensional audio interfaces, haptic interfaces (i.e., using devices such as gloves to relay a sense of touch), olfactory interfaces, as well as treadmills, motion platforms, or specially designed chairs also might be used to create the feeling of being there (Biocca, 1992b). Input devices communicate information about the participant's movements and position to the computer. Input devices include position or orientation trackers, exoskeletons (a device that may be worn to detect the movement and flexing of the limbs), and data gloves (exoskeletons designed exclusively for the hand; Biocca, 1992b; Schlager, Boman, Piantanida, & Stephenson, 1993; Stone, 1991). Psotka (1995) maintained that the coupling of visual information in the virtual world to head movements in the real world creates the essential immersive experience.

Presence is the defining psychological component of a VR system. In an ideal situation, the end result of using VR technology is the feeling of immersion or presence in the individual user (Biocca, 1992a; Biocca, 1992b; Knerr, Lampton, Bliss, Moshell, & Blau, 1993; Kozak, Hancock, Arthur, & Chrysler, 1993; Psotka, 1995; Regian, Shebilske, & Monk, 1992; Schlager et al., 1993; Steuer, 1992). *Presence* is defined as the perception of actually being in a particular environment. When that psychological feeling of presence is mediated by a communications technology, it has been referred to also as *telepresence*. The sensation of presence has been described by Biocca (1992b) as falling on a continuum of realistic experience. Factors affecting the intensity of the sense of presence include the amount of sensory information made available to the individual, the control of sensors (such as the eyes and hands) within the environment, and the extent of the user's ability to modify the environment (Sheridan, 1992, as cited in Biocca, 1992b). Increased realism should contribute to increased feelings of presence (Biocca, 1992a).

## Examples of VR Applications

VR applications have been designed for different age groups, different purposes, and different tasks. Although most VR systems have been designed for use with adults, a few have been designed for use with children or young adults. For example, Bricken and Byrne (1992) conducted a study examining how children between the ages of 10 and 15 learned to create virtual worlds. Loftin, Engleberg, and Benedetti (1993) used VR to simulate scientific concepts and involved students in becoming part of those simulations. Finally, Merickel (1992) used VR to enhance spatially related problem-solving abilities in children through the use of two-dimensional and VR interfaces in problem-solving practice.

Two major purposes have been reflected in VR applications. One has been to learn more about how different features of VR systems affect individuals' use of and performance on those systems. For example, Knerr and colleagues (1993) created the Virtual Environment Assessment Battery to examine the effects of immersion on individuals' performance on different types of tasks. The assessment battery included visual tasks (e.g., acuity, color, and distance estimation), locomotion tasks (e.g., back-ups and turns), manipulation tasks (e.g., grasping and moving), reaction time tasks, and tracking tasks (e.g., head and device control). Knerr and colleagues (1993) then examined individuals' performance of these tasks using two different control devices to investigate potential differential effects on performance. In general, completion times were significantly different depending on the device used for all locomotion tasks and manipulation tasks but not for tracking tasks. Finally, Knerr and colleagues (1993) examined potential adverse physical symptoms resulting from using the VR system. They found that individuals suffered from simulator sickness symptoms such as fatigue, headache, and eye strain. Moreover, symptoms were worse after the second session than the first, possibly because the second session involved tasks with more movement.

A second approach to learning more about the features of VR systems has been reflected in research examining the antecedents and effects of immersion in VR. Immersion might constitute one of VR's major contributions to training, but more research is needed examining this feature. Psotka (1995) stated that the immersive experience of VR constitutes a definite qualitative shift in computer–human interaction; VR is a fundamentally different mode of communication because the individual is no longer manipulating the computer but forming a symbiotic relationship with it instead. Psotka (1995) and Regian and colleagues (1992) proposed that immersion leads to a reduction in cognitive load for the learner that is normally taken up by converting two-dimensional surfaces into three-dimensional representations. Psotka and Lewis (1994, as cited in Psotka, 1995) have suggested that individuals use cognitive resources to create a "virtual self" in which an individual relates his or her own position to that of a two-dimensional representation, such as a painting or a photograph. Indeed, they observed that there was substantial variance in individuals' judgments regarding their position in a room when the room was represented in a two-dimensional drawing, indicating that even such a simple task requires cognitive judgments and effort. In addition, Psotka and Lewis (1994) reported that the sense of immersion increased with the individual's field of view, although judgments of distance were related (nonlinearly) to actual distance even when the field of view was reduced to less than 70 degrees.

A second major purpose has been to examine the efficacy of VR systems for providing training on different types of tasks. For example, although not yet available, the military has plans to develop VR systems for individual combat training (Knerr et al., 1993) and for training dismounted soldiers (Levinson & Pew, 1993). Furthermore, Knerr and colleagues (1993) suggested that VR might be most useful for training complex skills, such as the acquisition of spatial knowledge, terrain appreciation, situational awareness (i.e., the application of particular rules in particular environments), and team combat performance.

Some researchers have examined the efficacy of VR systems for providing training on navigation tasks (Regian et al., 1992; Witmer, Bailey, Knerr, & Abel, 1994). For example, Witmer and colleagues (1994) examined individuals' performance on a VR navigation task and also assessed transfer of training to an identical physical office building. Individuals received training either in a virtual environment (VR group), in the actual building (building group), or with photographs (symbolic group). They found that the VR group performed significantly better than the symbolic group but significantly worse (although small in magnitude) than the building group, suggesting that VR may offer an attractive alternative for navigation tasks when training in the actual building is not feasible. Regian and colleagues (1992) also examined the efficacy of VR for training on a navigation task. Individuals received navigational training in a three-level, twelve-room VR maze. For the learning test, individuals navigated three new tours (given a starting point and a destination point), visiting the fewest number of rooms possible. Regian and colleagues (1992) found that individuals passed through fewer rooms than would be expected by chance, indicating that learning of the physical layout had occurred. Moreover, individuals given a two-dimensional representation showed poorer and more variable test performance. Researchers also have examined the efficacy of VR for training on a console task (Regian et al., 1992), flight in inertial space (Beckman, 1993), remote operation of robotic devices (Miner & Stansfield, 1993; Stansfield, 1993), and a simple psychomotor task (Kozak et al., 1993). Regian and colleagues (1992) designed a simulation of a control console, requiring individuals to learn a complex 17-step procedure. All research participants learned the procedure and were able to perform perfectly in the testing phase of the experiment, indicating that they did learn in the virtual world.

Beckman (1993) described a VR developed for simulating flight in inertial space, in which the pilot is flying out of the earth's atmosphere, lacking a horizon or any other visual cues to alert the pilot to his or her orientation. This type of flight is not well represented in traditional flight simulators and thus difficult to train. Miner and Stansfield (1993; Stansfield, 1993) developed a VR to train individuals to operate robotic devices remotely for cleaning up underground storage tanks containing hazardous waste. The operator can navigate through an environment, program the robots through voice commands and hand gestures, receive feedback on the operations, and modify instructions to the robot.

By contrast, Kozak and colleagues' (1993) research highlighted the importance of selecting tasks appropriate for VR training. Research participants were trained to pick up small cylindrical objects and place them in target positions in a real environment. Results revealed that participants who received training on the real task performed better initially compared to participants who had received VR training or no training. (These performance differences decreased in later blocks of trials on the transfer task, but this was because of practice effects on the real task.) Kozak and colleagues (1993) suggested that VR is ineffective in training simple motor tasks. Indeed, one can infer from Kozak's and other research that VR is likely to have the greatest potential impact on complex, procedural tasks or visualization tasks and little or no impact on simple psychomotor tasks.

## The Potential of VR for Training

Now that the technology is available for creating environments with intense telepresence, the psychological and industrial communities have become interested in the possible applications of VR as a training technology. The major proposed advantage of using VR in training is the potential beneficial effects of immersion available in VR systems (Knerr et al., 1993; Kozak et al., 1993; Schlager et al., 1993). Many virtual worlds are designed to aid the user in building accurate mental models of different situations or environments (Biocca, 1992b). Researchers (Psotka, 1995; Regian et al., 1992) have suggested that using VR in training may reduce cognitive load by eliminating the need for a trainee to convert two-dimensional training materials into three-dimensional representations. Thus, using VR might enable users to focus more cognitive resources on learning the task rather than creating three-dimensional representations. In addition, immersion might increase the user's motivation (enhanced by the excitement typically associated with new technology) and lead to greater transfer of learned skills to the real world (Psotka, 1995; Regian et al., 1992).

Other proposed advantages of using VR in training include the capability of modeling more complete task environments, providing multi-user, interactive training for users in different locations, and facilitating the development of new training scenarios at a lower cost. For example, Regian and colleagues (1992) posited that training quality would be enhanced because characteristics of the real world and the interaction between a student and his or her environment can be modeled in a VR environment. In addition, through long-distance computer communication, VR offers the possibility of training multiple users at different locations on the same simulation at the same time in an interactive manner (Schlager et al., 1993). Finally, similar to traditional simulators, VR systems enable one to provide training on otherwise dangerous, risky, or expensive tasks (Schlager et al., 1993) and to provide real-time performance monitoring and feedback (Miner & Stansfield, 1993). However, in comparison to modifying or creating simulator equipment, one has the potential using VR to create new training scenarios more easily (Miner & Stansfield, 1993; Schlager et al., 1993) and at a lower cost (Kozak et al., 1993).

Several obstacles must be overcome and research issues addressed before we can use VR effectively for training. Stone (1991) and Kozak and colleagues (1993) have pointed to limitations of the equipment that might result in a decreased sense of presence, such as heavy and cumbersome headsets, low spatial resolution, the narrow field of view presently available in the headsets, primitive methods of force and tactile feedback, and inappropriate time lags in tracking performance. Moreover, some of these limitations might result in simulator sickness.

These technological constraints raise important research questions, including whether and why immersion results in improved learning and performance. It is unclear to what extent VR facilitates the building of mental models or the accuracy of models thus created. If immersion has beneficial effects, it could be explained by the increased realism of the situation (in which case, physical fidelity would probably be a very important component of the system), the constrained focus of attention of trainees submersed in the VR or the heightened motivation in trainees excited about working with this new technology.

Another important research question relates to the influence visual, auditory, and haptic fidelity has on learning and performance (Levinson & Pew, 1993). This issue has been discussed extensively in the context of physical simulators such as flight simulators (e.g., Lintern, Roscoe, & Sivier, 1990), although no resolution to the problem has been reached. Moreover, different types of tasks or different task elements might have different fidelity requirements. For example, lower visual fidelity might be required for objects in the distance or lower auditory fidelity might be required for a primarily visual task.

Furthermore, important research questions arise from the occurrence of simulator sickness. Simulation sickness might result from sensory distortions (possibly resulting from limitations in the current technology) or sensory cue conflict (i.e., conflicting messages from the different sensory modalities; Levinson & Pew, 1993; Schlager et al., 1993). However, research is needed to examine directly the posited causes. Biocca (1992a) stated that concerns about simulator sickness are well founded and well documented and may inhibit diffusion of the technology. Although only a few individuals seemed to experience dramatic sickness in VR training studies (e.g., Knerr et al., 1993), the potential for injury to the individual and lack of understanding of the processes resulting in simulator sickness highlight the importance of this issue. It is unfortunate that although normative information on sickness in flight simulators is available, norms for VR applications are not available because of the newness of the technology. Therefore, it is difficult to judge the general effects of VR on simulator sickness or compare the effects of one VR system relative to others.

Finally, if VR is going to compete with other training methods, it is important to evaluate the learning that occurs in VR for specific applications, determine tasks and task elements best suited for training in VR, and examine the relative expense of developing VR training systems. Training or instructional design principles from education and psychology should be applied to help ensure training effectiveness, and the effectiveness of VR training systems should be directly examined. VR offers a three-dimensional immersive display with multisensory inputs. The training potential is enormous but has yet to be realized. Indeed, as the technology evolves, we might expect to see more ITSs overlaid on this sophisticated simulation technology. However, the potential benefits of VR, as well as ITSs, will be realized only to the extent that the training provided on such systems is based on sound training design and evaluation.

## Conclusion

In summary, ITSs and VR offer powerful new technologies that have the potential to facilitate training in many areas of industry and the military. However, limitations in our understanding of the processes involved in human tutoring constrain the use of ITSs as training tools and limitations involved in designing and implementing VR training worlds hinder their immediate use on a large scale. Both ITSs and VR systems take extensive time and expense to develop, and the equipment necessary for implementation is currently quite expensive as well. Schlager and colleagues (1993) predicted that commercial companies will begin to produce low cost VR equipment designed for the general public, and particularly for entertainment applications, that the high volume produced will not produce sufficient fidelity for complex training applications, and that much of the high fidelity equipment will continue to be developed at a high cost (with improvements in fidelity) by government agencies such as NASA and the U.S. Air Force. Moreover, unresolved fidelity and simulator sickness problems may slow down efforts to implement VR training (Kozak et al., 1993; Schlager et al., 1993; Stone, 1991). However, the potential as yet largely unexamined benefits of ITS and VR technologies seem great. ITSs have the potential to individualize training and map students' learning of problem-solving processes. VR systems have the potential to offer training simulations and environments with high psychological fidelity, high flexibility, and a strong sense of presence. Both technologies are becoming a reality, and as they enter the world of work, ITSs and VR systems hold the promise of increased training effectiveness.

## References

Anderson, J. R. (1990). *Cognitive psychology and its implications.* New York: W. H. Freeman.

Anderson, J. R., Boyle, C. F., & Reiser, B. J. (1985). Intelligent tutoring systems. *Science, 228,* 1–7.

Anderson, J. R., Farrell, R., & Sauers, R. (1984). Learning to program in LISP. *Cognitive Science, 8,* 87–129.

Baldwin, T. T., & Ford, J. K. (1988). Transfer of training: A review and directions for future research. *Personnel Psychology, 41,* 63–105.

Baudhuin, E. S. (1987). The design of industrial and flight simulators. In S. M. Cormier & J. D. Hagman (Eds.), *Transfer of learning: Contemporary research and applications* (pp. 217–237). New York: Academic Press.

Beckman, B. C. (1993). *VR flight control display with six-degree-of-freedom controller and spherical orientation overlay.* Pasadena, CA: NASA. (NTIS No. N93-30416/0/HDM)

Biegel, J. E., Interrante, L. D., Sargeant, J. M., Bagshaw, C. E., Dixon, C. M., Brooks, G. H., Sepulveda, J. A., & Lee, C. H. (1988). Input and instruction paradigms for an intelligent simulation training system. *Proceedings of the First Florida Artificial Intelligence Research Symposium* (pp. 250–253). Orlando, FL: AI Research Symposium.

Biocca, F. (1992a). Communicating within VR: Creating a space for research. *Journal of Communication, 42,* 5–22.

Biocca, F. (1992b). VR technology: A tutorial. *Journal of Communication, 42,* 23–72.

Bricken, M., & Byrne, C. M. (1992). *Summer students in VR: A pilot study on educational applications of VR technology* (Report No. HITL-TP-R-92-1). Seattle: Washington Technology Center, Washington University. (ERIC Document Reproduction Service No. ED 358 853)

Brown, J. S., Burton, R. R., & Bell, A. G. (1975). SOPHIE: A step towards a reactive learning environment. *International Journal of Man-Machine Studies, 7,* 675–696.

Burns, J. L., & Capps, C. G. (1988). Foundations of intelligent tutoring systems: An introduction. In M. C. Polson & J. J. Richardson, (Eds.), *Foundations of intelligent tutoring systems* (pp. 1–19). Hillsdale, NJ: Erlbaum.

Burton, R. R., & Brown, J. S. (1979). An investigation of computer coaching for informal learning activities. *International Journal of Man-Machine Studies, 11,* 5–24.

Carbonell, J. R. (1970). AI in CAI: An artificial intelligence approach to computer-assisted instruction. *IEEE Transactions on Man-Machine Systems, 11,* 190–202.

Clancey, W. J. (1979). Tutoring rules for guiding a case method dialogue. *International Journal of Man-Machine Studies, 11,* 25–49.

Clancey, W. J. (1983). GUIDON. *Journal of Computer-Based Instruction, 10,* 8–14.

Dede, C. (1987). Artificial intelligence applications to high-technology training. *Educational Communication and Technology Journal, 35,* 163–181.

Dede, C. (1995). The evolution of constructivist learning environments: Immersion in distributed, virtual worlds. *Educational Technology, 35,* 46–52.

Duffy, T. M., & Jonassen, D. H. (1992). *Constructivism and the technology of instruction: A conversation.* Hillsdale, NJ: Erlbaum.

Flagg, B. N. (1990). *Formative evaluation for educational technologies.* Hillsdale, NJ: Erlbaum.

Flexman, R. E., & Stark, E. A. (1987). Training simulators. In G. Salvendy (Ed.), *Handbook of human factors* (pp. 1012–1038). New York: Wiley.

Foreman, G., & Pufall, P. D. (1988). *Constructivism in the computer age.* Hillsdale, NJ: Erlbaum.

Frye, D., Littman, D. C., & Soloway, E. (1987). The next wave of problems in ITS: Confronting the "user issues" of interface design and system evaluation. In J. Psotka, L. D. Massey, & S. A. Mutter (Eds.), *Intelligent tutoring systems: Lessons learned* (pp. 451–478). Hillsdale, NJ: Erlbaum.

Gagné, R. M., Briggs, L. J., & Wager, W. W. (1992). *Principles of instructional design.* Ft. Worth, TX: Harcourt Brace.

Goldstein, I. L. (1986). *Training in organizations: Needs assessment, development, and evaluation.* (3rd ed.). Monterey, CA: Brooks/Cole.

Goldstein, I. L. (1989). *Training and development in organizations.* San Francisco: Jossey-Bass.

Goldstein, I. L. (1991). Training in work organizations. In M. D. Dunnette & L. M. Hough (Eds.), *Handbook of industrial and organizational psychology* (Vol. 2, pp. 507–619). Palo Alto, CA: Consulting Psychologists Press.

Grabinger, R. S., & Pollock, J. (1989). The effectiveness of internally-generated feedback with an instructional expert system. *Journal of Educational Computing Research, 5*, 299–309.

Hays, R. T., Jacobs, J. W., Prince, C., & Salas, E. (1992). Requirements for future research in flight simulation training: Guidance based on a meta-analytic review. *International Journal of Aviation Psychology, 2*, 143–158.

Howell, W. C. (1991). Human factors in the workplace. In M. D. Dunnette & L. M. Hough (Eds.), *Handbook of industrial and organizational psychology* (Vol. 2, pp. 209–269). Palo Alto, CA: Consulting Psychologists Press.

Johnson, D. S. (1989). The development of expertise on an intelligent tutoring system. In W. B. Jones & S. H. Goldstein (Eds.), *National Aeronautics & Space Administration/American Society for Engineering Education Summer Faculty Fellowship Program 1989* (NASA/Johnson Space Center Grant No. NGT 44-001-800). Houston, TX: NASA/JSC. (Report No. NASA-CR-185601)

Johnson, D. S. (1990). Training effectiveness of an intelligent tutoring system for a propulsion console trainer. In R. B. Bannerot & S. H. Goldstein (Eds.), *National Aeronautics & Space Administration/American Society for Engineering Education Summer Faculty Fellowship Program 1990* (NASA/Johnson Space Center Grant No. NGT 44-005-803). Houston, TX: NASA/JSC. (Report No. NASA-CR-185637)

Johnson, D. S., & Pieper, K. F. (1992). *An evaluation of training effectiveness of an intelligent tutoring system* (NASA/Johnson Space Center Grant No. NAG 9-555) Houston, TX: NASA/JSC. (Report No. NASA-CR-190916)

Kalawsky, R. S. (1993). *The science of VR.* Workingham, England: Addison-Wesley.

Kirkpatrick, D. L. (1977). Evaluating training programs: Evidence vs. proof. *Training and Development Journal, 31*, 9–12.

Knerr, B. W., Lampton, D. R., Bliss, J. P., Moshell, J. M., & Blau, B. S. (1993, May). *Assessing human performance in virtual environments.* Paper presented at the 1993 Intelligent Computer-Aided Training and Virtual Environment Technology Conference, Houston, TX.

Kozak, J. J., Hancock, P. A., Arthur, E. J., & Chrysler, S. T. (1993). Transfer of training from VR. *Ergonomics, 36*, 777–784.

Kraiger, K., Ford, J. L., & Salas, E. (1993). Application of cognitive, skill-based, and affective theories of learning outcomes to new methods of training evaluation. *Journal of Applied Psychology, 78*, 311–328.

Lesgold, A., Lajoie, S. P., Bunzo, M., & Eggan, G. (1992). A coached practice environment for an electronics troubleshooting job. In J. Larkin, R. Chabay, & C. Sheftic (Eds.), *Computer-assisted instruction and intelligent tutoring systems: Establishing communication and collaboration* (pp. 201–238). Hillsdale, NJ: Erlbaum.

Levinson, W. H., & Pew, R. W. (1993). *Use of virtual environment training for individual combat simulation.* Alexandria, VA: Army Research Institute for the Behavioral and Social Sciences. (NTIS No. AD-A263 546/4/HDM)

Lintern, G., Roscoe, S. N., & Sivier, J. E. (1990). Display principles, control dynamics, and environmental factors in pilot training and transfer. *Human Factors, 32*, 299–317.

Littman, D., & Soloway, E. (1988). Evaluating ITSs: The cognitive science perspective. In M. C. Polson & J. J. Richardson (Eds.), *Foundations of intelligent tutoring systems* (pp. 209–242). Hillsdale, NJ: Erlbaum.

Loftin, R. B. (1987). *A general architecture for intelligent training systems.* Final Report, NASA/ASEE Summer Faculty Fellowship Program, Johnson Space Center. (Contract No. 44-001-800)

Loftin, R. B., Engleberg, M., & Benedetti, R. (1993). Virtual environments for science education: A virtual physics laboratory. In P. R. Hyde & R. B. Loftin (Eds.), *Pro-*

*ceedings of the contributed sessions of the 1993 intelligent computer-aided training and virtual environment technology conference* (p. 190). Houston, TX: NASA, Johnson Space Center.

Loftin, R. B., Wang, L., Baffes, P., & Hua, G. (1988). An intelligent training system for space shuttle flight controllers. *Telematics and Informatics, 5*, 151–161.

Merickel, M. L. (1992, April). *A study of the relationship between VR (perceived realism) and the ability of children to create, manipulate, and utilize mental images for spatially related problem solving.* Paper presented at the Annual Convention of the National School Boards Association, Orlando, FL. (ERIC Document Reproduction Service No. ED 352 942)

Miner, N. E., & Stansfield, S. A. (1993). *An interactive VR simulation system for robot control and operator training.* Albuquerque, NM: Sandia National Labs. (NTIS No. DE94002040/HDM)

Nickerson, R. S. (1989). New directions in educational assessment. *Educational Researcher, 18*, 3–8.

Noe, R. A. (1986). Trainees' attributes and attitudes: Neglected influences on training effectiveness. *Academy of Management Review, 11,* 736–749.

Perkins, D. (1991). Technology meets constructivism: Do they make a marriage? *Educational Technology, 31,* 18–23.

Prince, C., Oser, R., Salas, E., & Woodruff, W. (1993). Increasing hits and reducing misses in CRM/LOS scenarios: Guidelines for simulator scenario development. *International Journal of Aviation Psychology, 3,* 69–82.

Psotka, J. (1995). Immersive Tutoring Systems: VR and Education and Training [On-line, 27 pp.]. Available Internet: http://alex-immersion.army.mil/vr.html.

Psotka, J., & Lewis, S. A. (1994). *Effects of field of view on judgments of self-locations.* Unpublished manuscript.

Quillian, M. R. (1968). Semantic memory. In M. Minsky (Ed.), *Semantic information processing* (pp. 227–270). Cambridge, MA: MIT Press.

Reeves, T. C. (1992). Evaluating interactive multimedia. *Educational Technology, 32,* 47–53.

Regian, J. W., Shebilske, W. L., & Monk, J. M. (1992). VR: An instructional medium for visual spatial tasks. *Journal of Communication, 42,* 136–149.

Schlager, M. S., Boman, D., Piantanida, T., & Stephenson, R. (1993). *Forecasting the impact of virtual environment technology on maintenance training.* Menlo Park, CA: SRI International. (NTIS No. N94-11570/6/HDM)

Schmalhofer, F., Kuhn, O., Charron, R., & Messamer, P. (1990). An implementation and empirical evaluation of an exploration environment with different tutoring strategies. *Behavior Research Methods, Instruments, & Computers, 22,* 179–183.

Scriven, M. (1967). The methodology of evaluation. In *Perspectives of Curriculum Evaluation.* (American Educational Research Association Monograph, No. 1). Chicago: Rand McNally.

Seidel, R. J., & Park, O. C. (1994). An historical perspective and a model for evaluation of intelligent tutoring systems. *Journal of Educational Computing Research, 10,* 103–128.

Seidel, R. J., Park, O. C., & Perez, R. S. (1988). Expertise of ICAI: Development Requirements. *Computers in Human Behavior, 4,* 235–256.

Seidel, R. J., & Perez, R. S. (1994). An evaluation model for investigating the impact of innovative educational technology. *Technology Assessment in Education and Training, 1,* 177–212.

Sheridan, T. (1992). Musings on telepresence and virtual presence. *Presence, 1,* 120–126.

Shute, V. J. (1991). Who is likely to acquire programming skills? *Journal of Educational Computing Research, 7,* 1–24.

Shute, V. J., & Glaser, R. (1990). A large-scale evaluation of an intelligent discovery world: Smithtown. *Interactive Learning Environments, 1,* 51–77.

Shute, V. J., & Regian, J. W. (1993). Principles for evaluating intelligent tutoring systems. *Journal of Artificial Intelligence in Education, 4,* 245–272.

Sleeman, D., & Brown, J. S. (1982). *Intelligent tutoring systems.* New York: Academic Press.

Stansfield, S. A. (1993). *A computer-based training system combining VR and multimedia.* Albuquerque, NM: Sandia National Laboratories. (NTIS No. DE93013678/HDM)

Steuer, J. (1992). Defining VR: Dimensions determining telepresence. *Journal of Communication, 42,* 73–93.

Stevens, A. L., & Collins, A. (1977). The goal structure of a Socratic tutor. *Proceedings of the National ACM Conference* (pp. 256–263). New York: Association for Computing Machinery.

Stone, R. J. (1991). VR and cyberspace: From science fiction to science fact. *Information Services & Use, 11,* 283–300.

Tannenbaum, S. I., Mathieu, J. E., Salas, E., & Cannon-Bowers, J. B. (1991). Meeting trainees' expectations: The influence of training fulfillment on the development of commitment, self-efficacy, and motivation. *Journal of Applied Psychology, 76,* 759–769.

VanLehn, K. (1988). Student modeling. In M. C. Polson & J. J. Richardson (Eds.), *Foundations of intelligent tutoring systems* (pp. 55–78). Hillsdale, NJ: Erlbaum.

Wenger, E. (1987). *Artificial intelligence and tutoring systems.* Los Altos, CA: Morgan Kaufmann.

Witmer, B. G., Bailey, J. H., Knerr, B. W., & Abel, K. (1994). Training dismounted soldiers in virtual environments: Route learning and transfer. *Proceedings of the 16th Annual Interservice/Industry Training Systems and Education Conference* (pp. 2–11). Orlando, FL: Interservice/Industry Training Systems.

# 10

# Methods, Tools, and Strategies for Team Training

## Eduardo Salas and Janis A. Cannon-Bowers

The advent of team-based organizational systems has generated an immense interest in how to manage, compose, and train teams. Today, modern industrial and public organizations rely on teams to perform many complex, critical, and dangerous tasks. In fact, teams have become a way of life in many organizations. Therefore, it is not surprising that a number of recent publications have focused on understanding the nature of teams, the dynamics of teamwork, and the variables that affect team performance (Guzzo & Salas, 1995; Hackman, 1990; Levine & Moreland, 1990; Sundstrom, DeMeuse, & Futrell, 1990).

Although this body of knowledge has generated a wealth of information about what constitutes effective (and ineffective) team performance, theoretically based and empirically proven methods and tools for optimizing and maintaining effective team functioning are still lacking. To be specific, few have addressed which training strategies are needed to ensure team effectiveness (Salas, Cannon-Bowers, & Johnston, in press; Tannenbaum, Salas, Cannon-Bowers, 1996), or what the available methods and tools are for team training. Although some progress has been made in this regard (see Salas, Bowers, & Cannon-Bowers, 1995), there is a need to determine systematically what makes up team training.

At the core of this problem is the lack of agreement on what constitutes team training. For example, to some, team training is a single

We would like to thank Scott I. Tannenbaum, Miguel Quiñones, and Addie Ehrenstein for their comments on earlier drafts. The views expressed in this chapter are those of the authors and do not reflect the official position of the organization with which we are affiliated.

program or intervention (Alkov, 1994). To others, it is a set of methods and tools that focuses on team skills (Tannenbaum et al., 1996). Still others argue that team training is similar to a team-building exercise (Woodman & Sherwood, 1980), and a few believe that it is simply training individuals together toward a common goal (Briggs & Naylor, 1965; Hall & Rizzo, 1975).

So what is team training? Is it different from individual training? Which theoretical bases guide the design of team training systems? What are the targeted knowledge, skills, and attitudes for effective teamwork? What are the instructional methods needed for training teams? What instructional support or tools are needed to design and deliver team training? In this chapter we will try to answer these questions.

In particular, we briefly discuss the advancements in team training research. We do this in three parts. First, we discuss the nature of team performance in order to set the stage for what comprises team training. Second, we outline a number of tools and methods needed for the design, delivery, and evaluation of team training. Third, we discuss how these tools and methods define and shape team training strategies. We end with a short discussion of the needs and implications of team training research in the twenty-first century.

## The Nature of Team Performance

For team training to be effective, one must first understand the nature of team performance. That is, we need to understand which knowledge, skills, and attitudes the team must possess in order to be effective and as a basis on which to design training. This is important because we argue that for team training to be effective, it must have a clear content, with specific objectives that focus on turning a collection of individuals into a team. Therefore, the content of team training comes from having a clear understanding of the phenomenon—that is, teamwork—that we want to improve.

Team performance is dynamic, multifaceted, complex, and often elusive. Many variables impinge on and affect team performance (Salas, Dickinson, Converse, & Tannenbaum, 1992). Variables that influence team performance include the team leader, team members, characteristics of the task, and work structure (see Salas et al., 1992; Tannenbaum, Beard, & Salas, 1992, for further discussion). Effective teamwork requires team members to balance a number of factors (e.g., individual

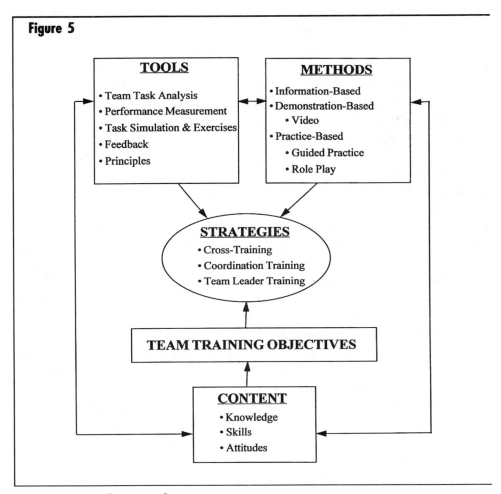

Components of team performance.

abilities, motivation, experience, personalities, and different roles), syn-
chronize events and resources, coordinate actions, and pool information from many sources in order to succeed. For those who are concerned about training teams, these complexities offer formidable
challenges. Therefore, understanding team performance is a must for
specifying the content of team training.

In recent years a number of researchers have investigated team
performance in complex environments (see Hackman, 1990; McIntyre
& Salas, 1995; Orasanu & Salas, 1993; Wiener, Kanki, & Helmreich,
1993) and have begun to shed light on what constitutes an effective
team and how team performance can best be defined. These research-

ers have been driven to answer questions such as: What are the essential characteristics and indicators of effective team functioning? Which competencies are required? Some answers have emerged. Figure 5 illustrates the three main components that make up team performance.

To begin with, there is a behavioral requirement in team performance. That is, team members perform actions that allow them to communicate, coordinate, adapt, and complete complex interdependent tasks to accomplish an overall goal, mission, or objective. In fact, research has shown that teamwork consists of a series of related behaviors that include back-up behaviors, mutual performance monitoring (i.e., self-correction), closed-loop communication, motivational reinforcement, adaptation to novel situations, and predictions of other member's behaviors (Hackman, 1990; McIntyre & Salas, 1995). In turn, these behaviors have been linked to effective team performance (Oser, Mc-Callum, Salas, & Morgan, 1989; Kleinman & Serfaty, 1989; McIntyre & Salas, 1995; Prince & Salas, 1993).

There is also a cognitive component (i.e., knowledge requirement) in team performance. For example, Cannon-Bowers, Salas, and Converse (1993) have suggested that team members must process shared mental models (or knowledge structures) about the task, their teammates' roles, and the situation in order to maintain performance, especially under stressful conditions. To be more specific, these authors maintained that when sudden or novel events are encountered, teams must rely on preexisting knowledge and expectations about how to perform in order to function effectively. Others have suggested similar notions (Klimoski & Mohammed, 1995; Orasanu, 1990; Stout, Cannon-Bowers, & Salas, in press). In fact, some evidence suggests that effective teams under high stress communicate less because they employ *implicit coordinating mechanisms*—that is, team members of effective teams learn to anticipate each other's needs and task requirements, as well as to generate expectations that allow them to perform without overt strategizing (Kleinman & Serfaty, 1989; Orasanu, 1990).

Finally, attitudes play a significant role in team performance. Team members' beliefs about the task and how they feel about each other make a difference. This is an area in which considerable research has been conducted at the individual level but in which there has been little focus on the team context. However, we know that the degree of cohesion, morale, and motivation of team members affects team functioning (Cooper, White, & Lauber, 1980; Ruffell-Smith, 1979). We also know that beliefs about the importance of teamwork affect team processes and performance outcomes (Driskell & Salas, 1992; Gregorich, Helmreich, & Wilhelm, 1990). More recently, Guzzo and colleagues, borrowing from Bandura (1986), have argued that *potency*—the belief that the group can perform the task—improves team performance (Guzzo, Yost, Campbell, & Shea, 1994). Although it is difficult to draw definite conclusions, it is clear that attitudes serve to strengthen team effectiveness and, therefore, are critical in team functioning.

In sum, individuals in teams "think, do, and feel" to function; they must have a set of competencies that are behavioral, cognitive, and affective in nature. Cannon-Bowers, Tannenbaum, Salas, and Volpe (1995) summarized the teamwork literature and offered a set of competencies required for effective team performance. Consistent with what has been presented in this chapter, these authors categorized team competencies as either being knowledge-, skill-, or attitude-related. In addition, they maintained that team competencies could vary on two other bases—they could be task-specific or generic or team-specific or generic. They then used these competencies as a basis to hypothesize about the focus of team training content and choice of training method. However, one of the shortcomings of Cannon-Bowers, Tannenbaum, and colleagues' (1995) framework, as well as other frameworks in the team training area, is that it does not provide a systematic definition of what makes up a team training strategy. Our aim is to make more systematic the discussion of training strategies for teams.

## Team Training

We begin this section by addressing two issues that influence our thinking. First, our definition of a team and boundaries for generalization of the team training concepts presented are as follows. We define a *team* as a set of two or more individuals acting independently to achieve shared, common objectives (Morgan, Glickman, Woodard, Blaiwes, & Salas, 1986). Further, we are most interested in teams that are hierarchically structured, teams in which there is high task interdependence, intense communication among team members, pooled information from multiple sources, and a need for constant coordination among members. Moreover, this classification is particularly relevant to teams that perform in hostile, dangerous, or stressful environments, in which members are required to make complex, multicomponent decisions under severe time pressures and have specialized roles, responsibilities, and task-specific knowledge (Dyer, 1984; Orasanu & Salas, 1993; Salas et al., 1992). For the purpose of this chapter these characteristics most closely describe the kinds of teams for which team training is important, although concepts presented may have applicability to other types of teams and training as well.

The second issue we now outline is what we exclude from our characterization of team training. We do this because it is often the case that assumptions are made about team training that are not representative of the kind of teams or situations just described. The assumptions and components underlying these programs (e.g., labels, approaches, format) are not theoretically rooted or principled with regard to methods and tools needed to enhance team performance. In fact, these assumptions are simplistic and do not take into account complex situations that may require a team-specific (i.e., intact team) or task-specific (i.e., context driven) strategy of team training. Therefore, we argue that team training is not simply a place or a location in which a group of individuals go to engage in non–task-related exercises and goals (e.g., rock climbing). Although these exercises may have merit, they are not consistent with our conceptualization of team training. In addition, team training is not necessarily a single program or intervention. That is, it is not necessarily an off-the-shelf set of curricula, exercises, charts, or videos that can be applied to any team situation.

It is unfortunate that there is a tendency in the military and other environments to equate team training with placing trainees in a high-fidelity simulator to practice complex skills or by networking trainees across distributed locations to participate in a human-in-the-loop military scenario. We contend that this is not team training either. These environments offer opportunities for effective team training, but without supporting instructional tools we do not know what has been learned or how we can improve performance (Salas et al., 1995).

By contrast, we believe that team training is a set of theoretically based strategies or instructional processes. It is based on the science and practice of designing and delivering instruction to enhance and maintain team performance under different conditions. It involves creating a learning environment whereby team members can receive facts, concepts, and knowledge about team missions, objectives, tasks, and role expectations. It allows team members to understand and observe the knowledge, skills, and attitudes and performance required, to practice them, and to receive feedback on them. Team training strategies are made up of tools for diagnosing, assessing, and remediating team performance and methods that are based on solid theoretical notions about team performance and create the opportunity for learning. Together, these tools, methods, and content yield a set of strategies (or approaches). Before launching a more detailed presentation of the structure of team training, we first summarize some of the major theoretical work that has driven much of the team training research in recent years.

## Theoretical Bases for Team Training

In a general sense, team training is a way of addressing team performance problems. It is concerned with designing and developing instructional strategies for influencing teamwork in complex environments. The design of these instructional strategies has been guided by a set of theoretical underpinnings.

### Models of Team Performance

General conceptual frameworks of team performance have guided team training research for a number of years. For example, Salas and colleagues (1992) and Tannenbaum and colleagues (1992) have developed a team effectiveness model that describes, in general, the factors that influence team performance. This framework includes four types of input variables. First, *individual characteristics* refer to the aspects that individuals bring to the team, such as attitudes, abilities, and motivations. Second, the framework specifies *team characteristics* as variables that affect the composition of the team. These include factors such as the process structure and member homogeneity. Third, *task characteristics* are variables that are related to the nature of the team task that needs to be accomplished. These variables include the task complexity, workload, and task type. Fourth, the set of input variables are referred to as *work characteristics*. These are variables that affect how the team organizes itself for the purpose of accomplishing the task. Illustrations of these variables include team norms and communication structures.

Together, input variables influence the team processes (e.g., coordination, cooperation, and communication) needed to execute the task and are moderated to some extent by organizational (e.g., resources available) and environmental characteristics (e.g., stress). In turn, these processes determine different types of team outcomes (e.g., quality, quantities, latency, error, satisfaction). It is worth noting that this framework includes training variables as influencing the team processes. To be specific, the framework argues that principles of team learning, training design, and task analysis results are critical for team training. However, despite the fact that this model is a comprehensive guide for team performance research, it does not specify how to design training for teams.

Similar models have been used in the aviation context to guide cockpit resource management training design (Helmreich & Foushee, 1995). These researchers used McGrath's (1984) general group performance model as a conceptual framework to guide what should be important in team training.

Although there is not a one-to-one correspondence between this model and training design, the conceptual framework has been useful as a general guide for hypothesis testing and to uncover specific knowledge, skills, and attitudes required for effective team performance.

## Shared Mental Models

The mental model construct has also been used as an explanatory mechanism by those concerned with how teams perform under adverse conditions (Cannon-Bowers et al., 1993; Johnson-Laird, 1983; Rouse & Morris, 1986). Building on the mental models literature at the individual level, Cannon-Bowers and colleagues extended this notion to team performance. To be specific, Cannon-Bowers and colleagues hypothesized that members of an effective team possess a number of accurate mental models (or knowledge structures) and share these with their teammates so that they can generate predictions and expectations about their teammates' roles, the task demands, and the equipment used (also see Rentsch, Heffner, & Duffy, in press; Zaccaro, Gualtieri, & Minionis, 1995). Therefore, teams with shared mental models are more likely to have accurate expectations regarding the team's needs and demands; this allows the team to make adjustments in order to maintain effective team performance. This is critical because team members can then predict the needs and information requirements of their teammates, as well as anticipate their actions in order to adjust behaviors. Often adjustments can be accomplished without overt communications or strategizing (Kleinman & Serfaty, 1989), which is costly under high-workload or emergency conditions.

This theory provides a basis for hypothesizing about how teams can

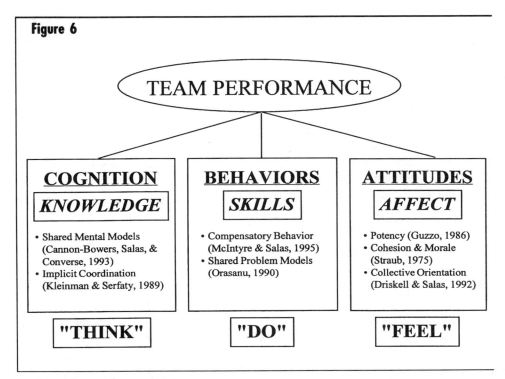

**Figure 6**

The structure of team training.

be trained. The objectives of training then become to foster in team members knowledge structures of the task, their teammates' roles, and the process by which the two interact. These knowledge structures are prerequisites to effective teamwork, communication, and performance.

## The Structure of Team Training Design

Although a suitable theoretical basis exists to establish team training needs, there is still a question of how team training should be structured and what makes up effective team training. As noted, team training can be depicted as the process by which we create a set of instructional strategies aimed at enhancing knowledge, skills, attitudes, processes, and outcomes of individuals performing in highly interdependent tasks. Yet it is still reasonable to ask, How do we define this set of instructional strategies? How do we design or create team instructional strategies? What is the structure of team training? We believe that the structure of team training revolves around four main elements. These are portrayed in Figure 6, and we discuss them in more detail in subsequent sections.

As an overview, the model in Figure 6 shows that there are basic tools that help design team training. These tools serve as the bases for defining and organizing the delivery as well as the implementation of team training. More important, these tools provide the instructional support (e.g., feedback, performance, monitoring) needed to convert simple practice into training. Products and information from these tools, in combination with appropriate methods (i.e., how information is delivered in training) and guided by learning objectives help create team-focused instructional strategies. The strategies are a set of plans or mechanisms that should be used to facilitate the acquisition of the specified team training objectives. These strategies are not only designed from the tools and methods but also from the content required (i.e., targeted knowledge, skills, and attitudes). Therefore, instructional strategies for team training are the combination of methods, tools, and content required to accomplish specific team performance objectives. We contend that these four elements are necessary for effective team training.

There are also other factors (e.g., organizational issues, situational constraints) that influence the design of team training. For example, one cannot ignore the fact that cost may shape how the training is delivered—in some cases high fidelity simulations are not cost-effective to accomplish team training objectives, whereas in others the potential cost savings warrants their use.

We now turn attention to describing in more detail the elements of team training depicted in Figure 6. To do this, the following sections focus attention on each of the four elements of team training. Our purpose is to focus on the tools, methods, and objectives that make up team training strategies and not on team training content. As noted, there has been a considerable amount of research that discusses and integrates the body of knowledge on the content of team training (see Stevens & Campion, 1994; Cannon-Bowers, Tannenbaum, Salas, & Volpe, 1995; Prince & Salas, 1993); for this reason, we feel there is no need to discuss further this element of team training.

## Tools for Team Training

For any training to be effective, its design must take into account the trainee, the learning environment, and the task or context (Cannon-

Bowers, Salas, Tannenbaum, & Mathieu, 1995; Goldstein, 1993). The design of training depends on having available mechanisms that enable instructional designers to decompose the tasks to be learned, develop learning objectives, establish performance criteria, create opportunities to practice the targeted knowledge, skills, and attitudes, and receive appropriate feedback. Those mechanisms are made possible by instructional support tools. Tools are also needed for team training, so we briefly review research aimed at optimizing the use of these tools. We focus on five tools: (a) team task analysis; (b) performance measurement; (c) task simulations and exercises; (d) feedback; and (e) principles of learning, team training, and diagnosis. We discuss these because of their implications to team training and the recent theoretical advances as well as empirical and practical studies.

## Team Task Analysis

Task analysis is imperative for designing and conducting effective training. Although there is considerable research on this topic (Harvey, 1991), little is focused at the team level. However, a few researchers have attempted to apply task analysis to the context of teams. For example, Bowers, Baker, and colleagues have developed an approach to uncover the coordination demands of complex team tasks (Bowers, Baker, & Salas, 1994; Bowers, Morgan, Salas, & Prince, 1993). Their approach extends traditional task analysis by specifying tasks requiring coordination. That is, experts are asked to provide information (e.g., difficulty, importance) on each task in which there is interdependency. The information obtained is then used to specify team training objectives and to guide the development of realistic scenarios for practice. Bowers and colleagues have applied this approach to an aviation environment and demonstrated its utility (Bowers et al., 1994).

Levine and Baker (1991) tested a methodology aimed at creating a job analysis taxonomy for team training. The Multi-Phase Analysis of Performance system (MAP; Levine, Brannick, Coovert, & Llobet, 1988) was used to design team training for a PC-based flight simulator. They found that the MAP system was useful for team training design and further, they outlined a set of procedural steps for conducting a team task analysis. To be more specific, the MAP system employs a number of methods to collect information about the interdependent nature of the tasks. It systematically creates a task inventory that is used to focus team training objectives. Although this system needs further testing and

validation, it is one of the few efforts to examine teamwork requirements using task analytic methods. Recent work by Campion and colleagues (Campion, 1994; Campion, Medsker, & Higgs, 1993) has also
begun to suggest that job analytic tools are needed to examine teamwork knowledge, skills, and attitudes.

In sum, team task analysis sets the stage for team training. This
tool provides the basis on which the team training development process evolves and matures. Perhaps most important, this process gener-
ates the team learning objectives and specifies the importance of
cues, conditions, events, actions, and communication flows needed
for effective performance. However, more research is needed to refine
and validate this tool; this issue will be addressed in a later section.

## Performance Measurement

Measurement is paramount to training. Without some sort of performance measurement, there is little opportunity for learning to occur
during training. Measurement is the basis for assessing, diagnosing, and
remediating performance during training (Cannon-Bowers & Salas, in
press). Considerable research has gone into developing this tool for
team training and a great deal of progress has occurred (Salas et al.,
1995). Several approaches have emerged in recent years (see Baker &
Salas, 1992). These approaches range from using critical incidents
(Morgan et al., 1986), applying skill-based techniques (Prince & Salas,
1993), modeling procedures (Coovert & McNelis, 1992), to event-based
scales (Fowlkes, Lane, Salas, Franz, & Oser, 1994; Johnston, Cannon-
Bowers, & Jentsch, 1995). Most of the emphasis has been on uncovering
behaviors that lead to effective or ineffective team performance. Taken
together, these approaches serve to describe and evaluate team performance and can be used in team training to guide instructional activities
(e.g., debriefing the team).

In order for performance measures to be complete and useful, they
must help integrate the different pieces of information needed to understand the complexity of team performance. Therefore, a number of
features are needed in this tool. First, it should capture the moment-
to-moment processes that make up teamwork (Cannon-Bowers & Salas,
in press). That is, the performance measures should collect information
about the activities, responses, behaviors, and strategies that are used
by team members in task accomplishment. This feature is the basis for

feedback on how the team accomplished the various tasks and, therefore, a must for team training. Second, related to this is the need for the measurement system to capture the team's outcomes as they perform the task (Cannon-Bowers & Salas, in press). Third, the focus of the measurement should not only be at the team level but also at the individual level (see Cannon-Bowers & Salas, in press) because many times during feedback one has to diagnose whether individuals are proficient at their tasks. This dictates the kind of remediation to provide the team. Fourth, performance measures should capture the multifaceted nature of team performance. That is, they should not only assess behaviors but also decision making (cognitive processes), communication, and attitudes. This may require multiple methods of capturing data.

Cannon-Bowers and Salas (in press) argued that the purpose of training—and therefore team training—is to assess, diagnose, and remediate skill deficiency, thus the performance measurement tool must gather information that supports this. Without these features, team training is ad hoc, informal, unsystematic, and without a metric to determine the trainees' learning and progress (Salas et al., 1995).

## Task Simulations and Exercises

Opportunities to practice required team knowledge, skills, and attitudes are imperative. Very little research has been done to better understand the nature of practice in teams. We maintain that practice cannot be a set of random events—and practice alone does not equate to training. Although we will discuss this issue further in the following sections, it is important to recognize that in team training, practice must be structured and guided by creating realistic task simulations and exercises that enhance learning opportunities.

Task simulations and exercises are tools that are designed to provide cues (i.e., stimuli) to the trainee. These cues are triggers for actions and can be embedded in a context-specific situation. These tools can be simulation-based and vary in their degree of physical and cognitive fidelity. A key element in task simulations and exercises is the scenario or exercise—one way to guide practice in team training is through the scenario or a script that outlines a series of carefully crafted events (that is, based on learning objectives and targeted knowledge, skills, and attitudes).

Hall and colleagues developed a methodology for creating scenarios to enhance opportunities to practice (Hall, Dwyer, Cannon-Bowers, Salas, & Volpe, 1993). The methodology takes into consideration the required knowledge, skills, and attitudes, the workload needed or desired, and the learning objectives of the team. The scenarios have built-in events and cues (or triggers) throughout the exercises, so that team members can practice and receive feedback on actions, activities, or strategies performed.

In the same way, Prince and colleagues, in an aviation context, derived a set of guidelines for designing simulations and exercises aimed at allowing cockpit crews to practice together (Prince, Oser, Salas, & Woodruff, 1993; Shrestha, Prince, Baker, & Salas, 1995). It is beyond the scope of the current discussion to treat these guidelines in detail (see Prince et al., 1993; Shrestha et al., 1995, for complete detail); however, the following guidelines are of particular interest to this discussion: (a) design exercises or simulators or role plays with cognizance of the specific types of behaviors required, (b) develop clear objectives for specific team member behavior expected in each exercise and build in opportunities for the behaviors of interest to be demonstrated, (c) build in the opportunity for the team members to demonstrate the behavior of interest more than one time, (d) design exercises as part of the total training program (i.e., as a means to allow practice on previously discussed or demonstrated knowledge, skills, and attitudes), (e) consider all the matters that may be important to creating the illusion of reality in simulated exercises, and (f) include all team members in the exercise either by their actual participation or by role play of the facilitator.

Technological advances have also generated a number of useful tools for team training. These include high fidelity simulators (Andrews, Waag, & Bell, 1992) and networking capabilities (Alluisi, 1991). For example, in the military, Distributed Interactive Simulation (DIS) is a widely used tool for training collectives. DIS is a networking architecture that allows dispersed simulators and operational equipment to be interconnected for military exercises. Although these are potentially useful tools, these kind of task simulations and exercises are expensive practice devices for use in instances in which appropriate learning may or may not occur if carefully crafted scenarios, augmented by performance measurements and feedback tools, are not used to create an instructional strategy.

# Feedback

Closely related to performance measurement is feedback. Trainers use the information provided in assessing performance as a means to deliver accurate, timely, and detailed feedback. Considerable research has been conducted on the nature of feedback during training. However, this body of knowledge has not been specifically addressed at the team level.

We contend that although there must be similarities between feedback for individual and team training, in terms of timing and sequencing, there are also differences in feedback focus and delivery at the team level. Team feedback must provide meaningful information to trainees at both the individual and team levels (Cannon-Bowers & Salas, in press). That is, the feedback must indicate whether arguments in individual functioning, team functioning, or both must occur in order to improve subsequent performance. This may seem obvious, but it is often difficult to tease out the individual or team contribution to a particular task. Moreover, although some behavior is considered to be "team level" behavior, it may be that the particular competency underlying the behavior exists at the individual level. For example, communication quality can be assessed at the team level, but in order to improve it, feedback may be needed at the individual level (i.e., indicating how a teammate can communicate better).

Cannon-Bowers, Tannenbaum, and Volpe (1995) provided a framework for conceptualizing team competencies that included a consideration of whether the competency was held at the team or individual level. They suggested that feedback (as well as performance measures) must be directed at the appropriate level in order to be effective. In addition, the delivery mechanisms of feedback must also be geared toward either individual, team, or both levels. This implies that, at least part of the time, the team receives feedback *as a team*. In cases in which team members are geographically dispersed (as is the case in the military and in many modern organizations), better mechanisms to deliver team-level feedback are needed. Advancing technology—including video teleconferencing and distributed interactive simulation—provide promising tools to solve this problem.

Furthermore, individual team members are an important source of feedback for one another. Blickensderfer, Cannon-Bowers, and Salas (1994) developed a team self-correction strategy designed to train team members to provide feedback to one another. This strategy requires empirical validation so that it can be applied in work settings.

## Principles

No training tool box can be complete without instructional principles. To be specific, principles of learning, training, team training, and diagnosis are essential to effective team training. These principles serve as the underpinning of effective team training design and delivery. If appropriately applied to team training, designers can use learning principles as a basis to develop effective, efficient training systems in applied situations.

There are a number of theoretically based and empirically proven instructional principles in the literature that are relevant for team training. For example, in terms of principles of learning, a number of authors have summarized the basic and applied learning literature well (e.g., Fisk, Lee, & Rogers, 1991; Glaser, 1987; Kyllonen & Alluisi, 1987; Schneider, 1985). These principles provide the foundation for creating conditions during training that foster the acquisition of knowledge and skill. In the same way, principles of training have been offered by Baldwin and Ford, 1988; Cannon-Bowers, Salas, Tannenbaum, and Mathieu, 1995; Cream, Eggemeier, and Klein, 1978; Kirkpatrick, 1976; and Noe and Schmitt, 1986; just to name a few. These researchers have been concerned with gaining an understanding of the components that encompass training effectiveness. The issues have ranged from motivation to learn, to typologies for evaluation, to transfer of training. There are more macro issues that influence training delivery as well (see Tannenbaum, Cannon-Bowers, Salas, & Mathieu, 1993).

A set of team training principles have also emerged in recent years. These are summarized in the exhibit. These principles have helped the design and delivery of a number of team training approaches (see Kozlowski, Gully, Salas, & Cannon-Bowers, 1996; Salas, Cannon-Bowers, & Blickensderfer, in press; Volpe, Cannon-Bowers, Salas, & Spector, in press) and therefore can be useful tools in future applications. *Guidelines*—that is, prescriptive statements that translate these principles into practice—have also been generated (see Salas et al., 1996; Swezey & Salas, 1992).

For example, Cannon-Bowers and Salas (in press) have argued that diagnosis is a critical function performed during training. Diagnosis is the basis for remediation, linking skill deficiencies to training objectives and strategies. It is unfortunate that the literature has not produced solid principles of diagnosis for team training. However, we should note that advances in intelligent tutoring systems and in modeling expertise should begin to delineate principles of diagnosis and enhance this tool.

## Exhibit

### Principles of Team Training

Individual proficiency must precede team training.
Team training must evaluate, diagnose and remediate team performance.
Team training systems must allow for:
   information presentation, demonstration of teamwork competencies (i.e., knowledge, skills, and attitudes), practice, and feedback.
Team training must emphasize the nature of task interdependency.
Team training must emphasize teamwork competencies.
Team training must create systematic opportunities to practice the required team competencies.
Team members who belong to multiple teams require at the minimum, transportable team competencies.
When transportable competencies are required, some training can be focused at the individual level.
Teams that require competencies that are specific to that team should benefit from training as intact teams and should incorporate feedback that leads to shared or common expectations for task performance.
Teams that require competencies that are specific to a team task should be allowed to practice and receive feedback in the actual task environment (or in one as close as possible).
Guided practice (e.g., task simulation and feedback) may be an effective training strategy for teams that require task-specific competencies.
Cross-training is an effective team strategy for teams that require exposure to the task.
Positional knowledge training may be useful for teams that require task-specific information.
Guided practice that exposes the actual team members to the variety of situations they may confront on the job is an effective team strategy.

*Note.* Adapted from Salas, Cannon-Bowers, and Blickensderfer (1993); Cannon-Bowers, Tannenbaum, Salas, and Volpe (1995).

In sum, these tools—team task analysis, performance measures, feedback, task simulations, and principles of learning—provide an important function in team training. They help in the analysis of complex team performance before, during, and after team performance. More important, these tools (especially performance measurement) build powerful accounts of team knowledge, skills, and abilities acquisition, thereby making team training an effective approach to enhancing team performance. Therefore, the investment in researching and developing these tools has high potential payoff.

## Methods of Team Training

The products of the tools we just described shape the methods used for team training. We define the methods of team training as how one delivers the training (i.e., the media). Although the methods described in the next section are not unique to team training, a number of methods have been used for team training purposes over the past few years. We describe areas in which research has emerged in applying training methods to enhance team training. For discussion purposes, we classify these according to whether training primarily facilitates the delivery of concepts, facts, knowledge, or theories—*information-based methods*; or illustrates by visual behaviors, actions or strategies to be learned—*demonstration-based methods*; or whether training allows the trainee hands-on practice and provides feedback on progress—*practice-based methods*.

### Information-Based Methods

These are the most widely used methods in training and include lectures, slide presentations, and computer-based instruction or other methods for which the goal of training is to present information (as opposed to providing practice or building skills). These methods are easy to implement, they are cost-effective, and they are used for training large numbers of people. In general, they are a passive method for conveying information about team goals, individual responsibilities, and task interdependencies. They also provide a means for clarifying teammate roles, expectations and, more important, to impart knowledge. Information-based methods provide the opportunity for trainees to understand required team knowledge such as cue–strategies associations and shared task models.

There are also more cognitively oriented methods such as advanced organizers. *Advanced organizers* are a type of cue or framework that provide the trainee with a mechanism that facilitates the organization and retention of information (Mayer, 1979). Kraiger, Salas, and Cannon-Bowers (1995) conducted a study to determine the efficacy of advanced organizers to facilitate skill acquisition. Kraiger and colleagues (1995) found that advanced organizers moderated the relationship between learning and performance, such that those who received advanced organizers learned more and performed better than those who did not.

## Demonstration-Based Methods

These methods implement the learning objectives in a medium in which the trainees can observe the required behaviors, actions, or strategies. The trainee is a passive observer of a situation, scenario, or exercise in which a number of learning points are embedded. These sets of methods are effective for allowing the presentation of a complex, dynamic, and multifaceted performance (such as teamwork). Furthermore, they serve as a builder of shared mental models or expectations of how to coordinate and communicate (Salas, Cannon-Bowers, & Johnston, in press); as such they are an important team training method.

These methods have been applied in a number of team training situations. For example, in the aviation context, team training includes a video presentation of effective (or ineffective) crew coordination behavior on a number of skills (Fowlkes et al., 1994; Prince & Salas, 1993). This method has also been extended to team-based, knowledge-rich environments. A multimedia (e.g., animation, simulation) delivery system for tactical team decision-making situations has been suggested (Cannon-Bowers, Salas, Duncan, & Halley, 1994; Salas, Cannon-Bowers, & Johnston, in press). This method allows team members to observe situations in which there are no real opportunities to practice (because of cost or safety considerations).

## Practice-Based Methods

These methods are critical to team training. Consistent with our philosophy of training, we include the feedback tools as an integral part of practice-based methods. However, before understanding how and when to use these methods, we must first address the structure of practice.

We have noted that practice does not equal training. Practice is a necessary, but not sufficient, condition for learning. To be effective, practice needs to be guided by cuing, feedback, coaching, or any other mechanism that helps the trainee to understand, organize, and assimilate the learning objectives. However, practice, especially for team training, is not well understood and is often misused (Salas et al., 1995). There are a number of questions that need to be answered before applying this method to team training. For example, team training designers should have guidelines about how to sequence the practice (i.e., easy to hard) or the timing of practice (i.e., individual skills or team skills first?). Guidelines need to be made available about massed versus distributed team learning, requirements for practice with intact or ad hoc teams, and practice with or without cuing. Although some of these guidelines are not available, some have recently emerged (see Cannon-Bowers, Tannebaum, Salas, & Volpe, 1995; Salas, Cannon-Bowers, & Blickensderfer, 1993; Swezey & Salas, 1992) and are being applied to a number of team training situations.

The methods commonly used in team training include role-playing and behavior modeling techniques, computer-based simulations, and guided practice. Role-playing and behavior modeling techniques allow individuals the opportunity to practice the targeted learning objectives and to receive feedback. These methods are widely used in aviation (see Prince et al., 1993; Weiner et al., 1993), in which trainees observe situations where crews have successfully dealt with an emergency. The trainees then participate (role play) in realistic situations that they have learned by observing. In some cases, this role-playing is in the classroom, and in other cases PC-based simulation or high fidelity simulators are used to practice and get feedback. In the same way, behavioral modeling techniques have been used to train assertiveness in copilots (Smith & Salas, 1991).

In sum, the methods of team training are information, demonstration, or practice-based. These are the media in which we deliver the learning objectives. We should note at this point that team training methods rely on the products and information from the tools. The methods serve as an instructional medium; they are content free. The tools make the methods useful for learning. Also, tools by themselves are not effective for training; they too are content free. So what orchestrates the tools and methods? What takes the tools and methods and creates a learning environment for teams?

## Strategies in Team Training

We have argued that training tools are the instructional support for effective team training. These tools are an integral part of the training process, and without them we are just exposing trainees to a task—providing practice but not necessarily training. We have also argued that methods provide the instructional medium on which we deliver the training. These two interdependent elements combine with content to create training strategies for teams (see Figure 6). Some of these team training strategies are general, and some are very specific. They take many forms and foci. In fact, it is possible to have two training strategies made up of the same tools and methods but with different content (and objectives) so that they appear to be distinct. Therefore, effective team training is a process of designing instructional strategies from tools and methods to enhance identified team knowledge, skill, process, and performance deficiencies.

Table 2 illustrates a number of team training strategies with associated tools, methods, and content. This table reveals that similar content (e.g., team leader skills) may be trained with distinct sets of methods and tools (sometimes being information-based and sometimes being practice-based). In the following sections, we describe in more detail several popular team training strategies and research associated with their effectiveness. We do this to highlight the interaction of tools, methods, and content in shaping team training strategies.

## Illustrations of Team Training Strategies

There are a number of strategies that have emerged in the literature that are worth discussing. They have different objectives, format, and focus, but they all incorporate the properties discussed previously to some degree.

## Cross-Training

Many teams experience frequent turnover. Therefore, there is an on-going need to train inexperienced personnel to perform well within an experienced team. Cross-training can help to mitigate teamwork decline as a result of constant personnel changes. The rationale behind cross-training is that exposure to, and practice on, other teammates' tasks should result in better team member knowledge with respect to teammates' task responsibilities and coordination requirements (Cannon-Bowers & Salas, 1990).

Cross-training is based on shared mental model theory (Cannon-Bowers et al., 1993). As noted, Cannon-Bowers and colleagues hypothesized that members of effective teams need a number of mental models or knowledge structures to generate predictions and expectations about the team task and teamwork without the need to employ overt communication. Volpe and colleagues (in press) further hypothesized that the objective of training is to foster in team members sufficient mental representation of the task interdependency, team role structure, and

## Table 2

### Sample Team Training Strategies With Corresponding Tools and Methods

| Strategy | Tools | Methods | Content |
|---|---|---|---|
| Cross-Training | • Performance measures<br>• Learning principles<br>• Team task analysis (TTA) | • Information-based lecture<br>• Information-based multi-media | • Interpostional knowledge (IPK)<br>• Shared mental models |
| Cross-Training | • Performance measures<br>• TTA<br>• Learning principles<br>• Simulations<br>• Feedback | • Practice-based: guided practice<br>• Demonstration-based: Role modeling | • Shared knowledge<br>• Task-specific roles and responsibilities |
| Team training coordination | • Performance measures<br>• Feedback<br>• Simulations<br>• Learning principles | • Information-based lecture<br>• Information-based video<br>• Practice-based: Guided practice | • Compensatory behavior<br>• Team situational awareness<br>• Communication flow<br>• Mutual performance monitoring |
| Team leader training | • TTA<br>• Performance measures | • Information-based lecture<br>• Information-based seminar/workshop | • Setting goals<br>• Team leader behavior |
| Team leader training | • TTA<br>• Performance measures<br>• Feedback<br>• Simulations | • Practice-based: Guided practice, behavior modeling | • Observing performance<br>• Giving feedback<br>• Debriefing skills |
| Team building | • TTA<br>• Learning principles<br>• Feedback | • Information-based video<br>• Practice-based: role play | • Interpersonal skills<br>• Collective orientation<br>• Cohesion |

how the two interact. Therefore, cross-training becomes an available instructional strategy for enhancing and maintaining teamwork.

This strategy has been tested in both the laboratory and in the field. For example, Volpe and colleagues (in press) tested the effects of cross-training on team functioning of 40 two-person teams operating a PC-based simulator. The cross-training condition included information about each person's position and the opportunity to practice operationally relevant tasks pertaining to both parties' functional responsibilities. The findings suggested that cross-training a new member on each member's task responsibility and role may mitigate performance degradation associated with turnover.

In the same way, Duncan and colleagues (in press) tested a PC-based training system aimed at cross-training team members of a complex military command and control task. The training system was also designed based on shared mental model theory (Rouse, Cannon-Bowers, & Salas, 1992). It consisted of allowing team members to observe (via demonstration) and practice the different positions in a five-person team. The results showed that the trained team (using the PC-based team training system called the team model trainer) significantly improved the members' interpositional knowledge and their communication strategy.

We argue that cross-training is a plausible and effective set of team training strategies that can enhance the team's anticipatory behavior and foster communication and coordination strategies. It is the combination of tools and methods with content that creates a mechanism for teams to learn complex taskwork behavior, cognition, and attitude. Training is accomplished by (a) providing relevant and meaningful information about other team members, the task, the equipment, and the situation; (b) demonstrating effective and ineffective teamwork; (c) allowing for practice in realistic context or with the relevant characteristic of the task; and (d) providing feedback.

## Team Coordination Training

This is a team training strategy that has been applied in aviation settings (Prince & Salas, 1993), medical environments (Gaba, Howard, & Small, 1995), and in complex team decision-making situations (Salas, Cannon-Bowers, & Johnston, in press). Although they have many common features, the content in these various settings is different.

These training strategies have in common the team training objectives (i.e., to foster teamwork in the cockpit, the surgical room, or in the combat information center.) All draw their theoretical underpinnings from a general framework of team performance, but in the case of the team decision-making situations also borrow from shared mental model theory. All the situations here combine tools (e.g., task simulator, feedback) and methods (e.g., demonstration- and practice-based) to derive team training.

The delivery of team training is different because of the requirements dictated by each environment. For example, in commercial aviation, team coordination training is primarily a seminar (information-based) approach lasting several hours, which culminates in the simulation for practice with feedback. The corresponding strategy on the military side is much more integrated throughout the training pipeline in which lectures and demonstrations of effective (and ineffective) teamwork are conducted in the classroom (although some role-playing might occur). This culminates with practice in a simulator, in which feedback is also given. In the command and control team situation, trainees receive instruction in adaptive strategies and the team leader also gets instruction on transmitting situation assessment updates to all team members (in order to elicit anticipatory information). Also, the teams are allowed to practice in a simulator while performing on these training scenarios. These strategies have been tested empirically and have shown team performance improvements (e.g., see Fowlkes et al., 1994; Leedom & Simon, 1995; Salas, Cannon-Bowers, & Johnston, in press).

## Toward the Twenty-First Century

We will now discuss team training in the next century. We structure the discussion around the elements of team training.

### Team Training Tools

In terms of principles, we expect that team training research will continue to be influenced by cognitive psychology. Shared mental models theory, shared cognition, and knowledge structures are areas that need further study and refinement. To be more specific, these theories must be better integrated with training and team performance theories to be of value to team training design. Related to this, the study of cognition will also have a positive impact on the design of team task analysis techniques. Progress in this area is being made at the individual level; similar development is needed at the team level.

Another influence on team training tools will be technology. Advances in technology have already influenced training in general and also team training. For example, the computer networking capabilities available now present challenges for team training, particularly for task simulations (Alluisi, 1991). The capability to link individuals across the world to create virtual teams will be exploited more in the future (Salas, Cannon-Bowers, & Johnston, in press). Therefore, we need research that incorporates or facilitates the use of validated techniques for developing effective simulations for use in distributed team training.

Advanced technology is also having an impact on our ability to collect performance measurement data. Systems are currently under development that will allow fine-grained collection and automated analysis of team performance during an exercise (Cannon-Bowers & Salas, in press). This capability will improve vastly our ability to assess complex team performance, particularly in tasks in which moment-to-moment changes are important to performance. It will also aid in our ability to provide meaningful feedback as a means to improve team performance. In terms of delivery mechanisms for feedback, a promising technology is video teleconferencing (or distance learning). This technology would allow team members who are physically dispersed to receive team member feedback. This is a crucial capability as the tendency for organizations to imply *virtual teams* (teams that communicate electronically) continues to rise.

## Team Training Methods

The advent of intelligent tutoring systems will also revolutionize team training in the future. These systems will provide an alternative method for team training. The challenges in developing intelligent tutoring are still at the individual level but have a high payoff if solved and applied to the team level. Moreover, to be most effective, we need theoretically rooted guidelines for implementing particular team training into an intelligent tutoring format.

Multimedia technology also offers a tremendous opportunity as a team training method (Cannon-Bowers, Salas, Duncan, & Halley, 1994). In fact, multimedia technology may be appropriate as a means to implement information-based, demonstration-based, or practice-based team training. To apply multimedia effectively, therefore, we need to know more about the underlying principles of when to use animation, simulation, or video in training. We need theoretically rooted and empirically proven guidelines to design multimedia systems for team training.

## Team Training Strategies

We have maintained in this chapter that team training strategies are made up of tools, methods, and content. Therefore, advances of the sort listed previously that will improve the methods and tools of team training will also improve team training strategies. Beyond this, team training strategies in the future should be empirically tested more often than has been typical. Increased attention needs to be paid to validating team training strategies, particularly in field settings. Also, research needs to be directed at understanding the impact of the organizational context as these team training strategies are tested and implemented (Kozlowski & Salas, in press; McIntyre & Salas, 1995).

## Conclusion

This chapter was motivated by the need to integrate the science and practice of team training. We have defined team training as a set of strategies that create a context in which team skills can be practiced, assessed, and learned. Team training design is based on both team and task knowledge, skills, and abilities requirements as elicited through team task analysis. Further, we contend that team training is theoretically rooted and practically useful. Team training strategies are comprised of a set of tested tools and methods that in combination offer a learning environment for teams. We also believe that team training is more than a "feel-good" intervention or a simulation or a networking capability—it is, to reiterate, an instructional process supported by tools, methods, and content. We also mention that team training is ongoing, not a one-time event. It is the continuous assessment of requirements, needs, and deficiencies with strategies for enhancing team performance. Finally, we hope this chapter motivates and encourages those involved in the science and practice of team training to seek newer and better strategies to improve team performance.

# References

Alkov, R. A. (1994). Enhancing safety with aircrew coordination training. *Ergonomics in Design*, 13–18.

Alluisi, E. A. (1991). The development of technology for collective training: SIMNET, a case history. *Human Factors, 33*, 343–362.

Andrews, D. H., Waag, W. L., & Bell, H. H. (1992). Training technologies applied to team training: Military examples. In R. W. Swezey & E. Salas (Eds.), *Teams: Their training and performance* (pp. 283–327). Norwood, NJ: Ablex.

Baker, D. P., & Salas, E. (1992). Principles for measuring teamwork skills. *Human Factors, 34*, 469–475.

Baldwin, T. T., & Ford, J. K. (1988). Transfer of training: A review and directions for future research. *Personnel Psychology, 41*, 63–105.

Bandura, A. (1986). *Social foundations of thought and action.* Englewood Cliffs, NJ: Prentice-Hall.

Blickensderfer, E. L., Cannon-Bowers, J. A., & Salas, E. (1994). Feedback and team training: Team self-correction. *Proceedings of the Second Annual Mid-Atlantic Human Factors Conference* (pp. 81–85). Washington, DC: Human Factors Society.

Bowers, C. A., Baker, D. P., & Salas, E. (1994). Measuring the importance of teamwork: The reliability and validity of job/task analysis indices for team-training designs. *Military Psychology, 6*, 205–214.

Bowers, C. A., Morgan, B. B., Jr., Salas, E., & Prince, C. (1993). Assessment of coordination demand for aircrew coordination training. *Military Psychology, 5*, 95–112.

Briggs, G. E., & Naylor, J. C. (1965). Team versus individual training, training task fidelity, and task organization effects on transfer performance by three-man teams. *Journal of Applied Psychology, 49*, 387–392.

Campion, M. A. (1994). Job analysis for the future. In M. G. Rumsey, C. B. Walker, & J. H. Harris (Eds.), *Personnel selection and classification* (pp. 1–13). Hillsdale, NJ: Erlbaum.

Campion, M. A., Medsker, G. J., & Higgs, A. C. (1993). Relations between work group characteristics and effectiveness: Implications for designing effective work groups. *Personnel Psychology, 46*, 823–850.

Cannon-Bowers, J. A., & Salas, E. (1990, April). *Cognitive psychology and team training: Shared mental models in complex systems.* Symposium presented at the Fifth Annual Conference of the Society for Industrial and Organizational Psychology, Miami, FL.

Cannon-Bowers, J. A., & Salas, E. (in press). A framework for developing team performance measures in training. In M. T. Brannick, E. Salas, & C. Prince (Eds.), *Assessment of measurement of team performance: Theories, methods and applications.* Hillsdale, NJ: Erlbaum.

Cannon-Bowers, J. A., Salas, E., & Converse, S. A. (1993). Shared mental models in expert team decision making. In N. J. Castellan, Jr. (Ed.), *Current issues in individual and group decision making* (pp. 221–246). Hillsdale, NJ: Erlbaum.

Cannon-Bowers, J. A., Salas, E., Duncan, P. C., & Halley, E. J. (1994). Application of multimedia technology to training for knowledge-rich systems. *Proceedings of the 16th Annual Interservice/Industry Training Systems Conference.* Washington, DC: IITS.

Cannon-Bowers, J. A., Salas, E., Tannenbaum, S. I., & Mathieu, J. E. (1995). Toward theoretically based principles of training effectiveness: A model and initial empirical investigation. *Military Psychology, 7*, 141–164.

Cannon-Bowers, J. A., Tannenbaum, S. I., Salas, E., & Volpe, C. E. (1995). Defining team competencies and establishing team training requirements. In R. Guzzo and E. Salas (Eds.), *Team effectiveness and decision making in organizations* (pp. 333–380). San Francisco: Jossey Bass.

Cooper, G. E., White, M. D., & Lauber, J. K. (Eds.). (1980). Resource management on the flight deck. *Proceedings of a NASA industry workshop* (NASA Technical Report No. CP-2120). Moffet Field, CA: NASA Ames Research Center.

Coovert, M. D., & McNelis, K. (1992). Team decision making and performance: A review and proposed modeling approach employing petri nets. In R. W. Swezey & E. Salas (Eds.), *Teams: Their training and performance* (pp. 247–280). Norwood, NJ: Ablex.

Cream, B. W., Eggemeier, F. T., & Klein, G. A. (1978). A strategy for the development of training devices. *Human Factors, 20,* 145–158.

Driskell, J. E., & Salas, E. (1992). Collective behavior and team performance. *Human Factors, 34,* 277–288.

Duncan, P. C., Rouse, W. B., Johnston, J. H., Cannon-Bowers, J. A., Salas, E., & Burns, J. J. (in press). Training teams working in complex systems: A mental model based approach. In W. B. Rouse (Ed.), *Human/technology interaction in complex systems* (Vol. 8). Greenwich, CT: JAI Press.

Dyer, J. L. (1984). Team research and training: A state-of-the-art review. In F. A. Muckler (Ed.), *Human factors review: 1984.* Santa Monica, CA: Human Factors Society.

Fisk, A. D., Lee, M. D., & Rogers, W. A. (1991). Recombination of automatic processing components: The effects of transfer, reversal, and conflict situations. *Human Factors, 33,* 267–280.

Fowlkes, J. E., Lane, N. E., Salas, E., Franz, T., & Oser, R. (1994). Improving the measurement of team performance: The TARGETS methodology. *Military Psychology, 6,* 47–63.

Gaba, D. M., Howard, S. K., & Small, S. D. (1995). Situation awareness in anesthesiology. *Human Factors, 37,* 20–31.

Glaser, R. (1987). Expertise and learning: How do we think about instructional processes now that we have discovered knowledge structures? In D. Klahr and K. Kotovsky (Eds.), *Complex information processing* (pp. 269–282). Hillsdale, NJ: Erlbaum.

Goldstein, I. L. (1993). *Training in organizations.* (3rd. ed.). Belmont, CA: Wadsworth.

Gregorich, S. E., Helmreich, R. L., & Wilhelm, J. A. (1990). The structure of cockpit management attitudes. *Journal of Applied Psychology, 75,* 682–690.

Guzzo, R. A., & Salas, E. (Eds.). (1995). *Team effectiveness and decision making in organizations.* San Francisco: Jossey-Bass.

Guzzo, R. A., Yost, P. R., Campbell, R. J., & Shea, G. P. (1994). Potency in groups: Articulating the construct. *British Journal of Social Psychology, 32,* 87–106.

Hackman, J. R. (Ed.). (1990). *Groups that work: (And those that don't): Creating conditions for effective teamwork.* San Francisco: Jossey-Bass.

Hall, J. K., Dwyer, D. J., Cannon-Bowers, J. A., Salas, E., & Volpe, C. E. (1993). Toward assessing team tactical decision making under stress: The development of a methodology for structuring team training scenarios. *Proceedings of the 15th Annual Interservice/Industry Training Systems and Education Conference* (pp. 87–98). Washington, DC: National Security Industrial Association.

Hall, E. R., & Rizzo, W. A. (1975). *An assessment of U.S. Navy tactical team training* (TAEG Report No. 18). Orlando, FL: Training Analysis and Evaluation Group.

Harvey, R. J. (1991). Job analysis. In M. D. Dunnette & L. M. Hough (Eds.), *Handbook of industrial and organizational psychology* (2nd ed., Vol. 2, pp. 71–164). Palo Alto, CA: Consulting Psychologists Press.

Helmreich, R. L., & Foushee, H. C. (1995). Why crew resource management? Empirical and theoretical bases of human factors training in aviation. In E. L. Wiener, B. G. Kanki, & R. L. Helmreich (Eds.), *Cockpit resource management* (pp. 3–45). San Diego, CA: Academic Press.

Johnson-Laird, P. (1983). *Mental models.* Cambridge, MA: Harvard University Press.

Johnston, J. H., Cannon-Bowers, J. A., & Jentsch, K. A. (1995). Event-based performance measurement system for shipboard command teams. *Proceedings of the First International Symposium on Command and Control Research and Technology* (pp. 268–276). Washington, DC: Center for Advanced Command Concepts and Technology of the National Defense University.

Kirkpatrick, D. L. (1976). Evaluation of training. In R. L. Craig (Ed.), *Training and development handbook* (2nd ed.). New York: McGraw-Hill.

Kleinman, D. L., & Serfaty, D. (1989). Team performance assessment in distributed decision making. *Proceedings of the Symposium on Interactive Networked Simulation for Training* (pp. 22–27). Orlando: University of Central Florida.

Klimoski, R., & Mohammed, S. (1995). Team mental model: Construct or metaphor? *Journal of Management, 20,* 403–437.

Kozlowski, S. W., Gully, S. M., Salas, E., & Cannon-Bowers, J. A. (1996). Team leadership and development: Theory, principles, and guidelines for training leaders and teams. In M. Beyerlein, S. Beyerlein, & D. Johnson (Eds.), *Advances in interdisciplinary studies of work teams: Team leadership* (pp. 253–291). Greenwich, CT: JAI Press.

Kozlowski, S. W. J., & Salas, E. (in press). A multilevel organizational systems approach for the implementation and transfer of training. In J. K. Ford, S. W. J. Kozlowski, K. Kraiger, E. Salas, & M. Tannenbaum (Eds.), *Improving training effectiveness in work organizations.* Hillsdale, NJ: Erlbaum.

Kraiger, K., Salas, E., & Cannon-Bowers, J. A. (1995). Measuring knowledge organization as a method for assessing learning during training. *Human Factors, 37,* 804–816.

Kyllonen, P. C., & Alluisi, E. A. (1987). Learning and forgetting facts and skills. In G. Salvendy (Ed.), *Handbook of human factors* (pp. 124–153). New York: Wiley.

Leedom, D. K., & Simon, R. (1995). Improving team coordination: A case for behavioral-based training. *Military Psychology, 7,* 109–122.

Levine, E. L., & Baker, C. V. (1991). Team task analysis: A procedural guide and test of the methodology. In E. Salas (Chair), *Methods and tools for understanding teamwork: Research with practical implications.* Symposium presented at the Sixth Annual Conference of the Society for Industrial and Organizational Psychology, St. Louis, MO.

Levine, E. L., Brannick, M. T., Coovert, M. D., & Llobet, J. M. (1988). *Job/task analysis methodologies for teams: A review and implications for team training.* (Technical Report No. 88-019). Orlando, FL: Naval Training Systems Center. (Contract No. DAAL03-86-D-0001).

Levine, J. M., & Moreland, R. L. (1990). Progress in small group research. *Annual Review of Psychology, 41,* 585–634.

Mayer, R. E. (1979). Twenty years of research on advance organizers: Assimilation theory is still the best predictor of results. *Instructional Science, 8,* 133–167.

McGrath, J. E. (1984). *Groups: Interaction and performance.* Englewood Cliffs, NJ: Prentice-Hall.

McIntyre, R. M., & Salas, E. (1995). Measuring and managing for team performance: Emerging principles from complex environments. In R. Guzzo and E. Salas (Eds.), *Team effectiveness and decision making in organizations* (pp. 149–203). San Francisco: Jossey-Bass:

Morgan, B. B., Jr., Glickman, A. S., Woodard, E. A., Blaiwes, A. S., & Salas, E. (1986). *Measurement of team behaviors in a Navy environment* (NTSC Technical Report No. 86-014). Orlando, FL: Naval Training Systems Center.

Noe, R. A., & Schmitt, N. (1986). The influence of trainees' attitudes on training effectiveness: Test of a model. *Personnel Psychology, 39,* 497–523.

Orasanu, J. (1990, October). *Shared mental models and crew performance.* Paper presented at the 34th Annual meeting of the Human Factors Society, Orlando, Florida.

Orasanu, J., & Salas, E. (1993). Team decision making in complex environments. In G. Klein, J. Orasanu, R. Calderwood, & C. E. Zsambok (Eds.), *Decision making in action: Models and methods* (pp. 327–345). Norwood, NJ: Ablex.

Oser, R. L., McCallum, G. A., Salas, E., & Morgan, B. B., Jr. (1989). *Toward a definition of teamwork: An analysis of critical team behavior* (NTSC Technical Report Number 89-004). Orlando, FL: Naval Training Systems Center.

Prince, C., Oser, R., Salas, E., & Woodruff, W. (1993). Increasing hits and reducing misses in CRM/LOS scenarios: Guidelines for simulator scenario development. *International Journal of Aviation Psychology, 3,* 69–82.

Prince, C., & Salas, E. (1993). Training and research for teamwork in the military aircrew. In E. L. Wiener, B. J. Kanki, & R. L. Helmreich (Eds.), *Cockpit resource management* (pp. 337–366). San Diego, CA: Academic Press.

Rentsch, J. R., Heffner, T. S., & Duffy, L. T. (in press). What you know is what you get from experience: Team experience related to teamwork schemas. *Group and Organization Management.*

Rouse, W. B., Cannon-Bowers, J. A., & Salas, E. (1992). The role of mental models in team performance in complex systems. *IEEE Transactions on Systems, Man, and Cybernetics, 22,* 1296–1308.

Rouse, W. B., & Morris, N. M. (1986). On looking into the black box: Prospects and limits in the search for mental models. *Psychological Bulletin, 100,* 349–363.

Ruffell-Smith, H. P. (1979). *A simulator study of the interaction of pilot workload with errors, vigilance, and decisions.* (NASA Technical Report No. TM-78482). Moffet Field, CA: NASA-Ames Research Center.

Salas, E., Bowers, C. A., & Cannon-Bowers, J. A. (1995). Military team research: Ten years of progress. *Military Psychology, 7,* 55–76.

Salas, E., Cannon-Bowers, J. A., & Blickensderfer, E. L. (1993). Team performance and training research: Emerging principles. *Journal of the Washington Academy of Sciences, 83,* 81–106.

Salas, E., Cannon-Bowers, J. A., & Blickensderfer, E. L. (in press). Enhancing reciprocity between training theory and practice: Principles, guidelines, and specifications. In J. K. Ford, S. W. J. Kozlowski, K. Kraiger, E. Salas, & M. Tannenbaum (Eds.), *Improving training effectiveness in work organizations.* Hillsdale, NJ: Erlbaum.

Salas, E., Cannon-Bowers, J. A., & Johnston, J. H. (in press). How can you turn a team of experts into an expert team?: Emerging training strategies. In C. Zsambok & G. Klein (Eds.), *Naturalistic decision making.* Hillsdale, NJ: Erlbaum.

Salas, E., Dickinson, T. L., Converse, S. A., & Tannenbaum, S. I. (1992). Toward an understanding of team performance and training. In R. W. Swezey & E. Salas (Eds.), *Teams: Their training and performance* (pp. 3–29). Norwood, NJ: Ablex.

Schneider, W. (1985). Training high-performance skills: Fallacies and guidelines. *Human Factors, 2,* 285–300.

Shrestha, L. B., Prince, C., Baker, D. P., & Salas, E. (1995). Understanding situation awareness: Concepts, methods, and training. In W. B. Rouse (Ed.), *Human technology interaction in complex systems* (Vol. 7, pp. 45–84). Greenwich, CT: JAI Press.

Smith, K. A., & Salas, E. (1991, March). *Training assertiveness: The importance of active participation.* Paper presented at the 37th Annual Meeting of the Southeastern Psychological Association, New Orleans, LA.

Stevens, M. J., & Campion, M. A. (1994). The knowledge, skill and ability requirements for teamwork: Implications for human resource management. *Journal of Management, 20,* 503–530.

Stout, R. J., Cannon-Bowers, J. A., & Salas, E. (in press). The role of shared mental models in developing team situational awareness: Implications for training. *Training Research Journal.*

Sundstrom, E., DeMeuse, K. P., & Futrell, D. (1990). Work teams: Applications and effectiveness. *American Psychologist, 45,* 120–133.

Swezey, R. W., & Salas, E. (1992). Guidelines for use in team-training development. In R. W. Swezey & E. Salas (Eds.), *Teams: Their training and performance* (pp. 219–245). Norwood, NJ: Ablex.

Tannenbaum, S. I., Beard, R. L., & Salas, E. (1992). Team building and its influence on team effectiveness: An examination of conceptual and empirical developments. In K. Kelley (Ed.), *Issue, theory and research in industrial organizational psychology* (pp. 117–153). Amsterdam: Elsevier.

Tannenbaum, S. I., Cannon-Bowers, J. A., Salas, E., & Mathieu, J. E. (1993). *Factors that influence training effectiveness: A conceptual model and longitudinal analysis* (NAWCTSD Tech. Rep. No. 93-011). Orlando, FL: Naval Air Warfare Center.

Tannenbaum, S. I., Salas, E., & Cannon-Bowers, J. A. (1996). Promoting team effectiveness. In M. West (Ed.), *Handbook of work group psychology* (pp. 503–529). Sussex, England: John Wiley and Sons.

Volpe, C. E., Cannon-Bowers, J. A., Salas, E., & Spector, P. (1996). The impact of cross-training on team functioning. *Human Factors, 38,* 87–100.

Weiner, E. L., Kanki, B. J., & Helmreich, R. L. (Eds.). (1993). *Cockpit resource management.* San Diego, CA: Academic Press.

Woodman, R. W., & Sherwood, J. J. (1980). Effects of team development intervention: A field experiment. *Journal of Applied Behavioral Science, 16,* 211–227.

Zaccaro, S. J., Gualtieri, J., & Minionis, D. (1995). Task cohesion as a facilitator of group decision making under temporal urgency. *Military Psychology, 7,* 77–93.

# The Use of Animation in Software Training: Pitfalls and Benefits

**Robert Atlas, Larry Cornett, David M. Lane, and H. Albert Napier**

**T**oday there are millions of computers available for use at work or at home, ranging from personal computers to much more powerful super computers. The power of computers has increased so much over the past few years that even personal computers are now practical platforms for training methods using graphics, sound, and animation. The use of multimedia in training has widespread applicability. However, in this chapter we focus on the use of multimedia to train people how to use software.

Changes in available hardware have made multi–media-based training practical at a time when changes in software have made it appear necessary. Graphical user interfaces (GUIs; e.g., the Macintosh operating system, Microsoft Windows, and related software) are typically easier for new users to learn than command-based systems (Temple, Barker, & Sloane, 1990). However, their widespread adoption places new demands on the traditional process of using text-based instructions to train people to use software applications. Command-based software can be taught well with simple text instructions because the user interacts with the software simply by entering a defined sequence of commands for each operation performed. However, GUIs require multiple operations at different locations on the screen as well as choices from specific menus. Because users interact with graphical objects, it is helpful to demonstrate what the different objects look like, where they are located, and so forth. Thus, presenting training information visually seems more appropriate for teaching the use of these systems. Users can see how to perform procedures and can immediately observe the results. The present concern is with the use of *animated demonstrations*—on-screen playback of correct interface procedures—as training tools for software.

It would seem that there are several possible advantages to using animation for training, particularly for training users of GUI-based software. Animated training more closely resembles the method by which people usually learn procedures in areas other than human–computer interaction: visual observation of another person performing the procedure, listening to the accompanying verbal explanations, and attempting to imitate the demonstrated procedure. Animated demonstrations, unlike written instructions, can also incorporate spoken material, which can be used to describe and explain the visual images in more detail (Baggett, 1984).

Software products that incorporate animation-based training in their tutorials and help systems have been available for some time. The animated tutorials used in Microsoft Office teach new users step-by-step procedures using both text and animation. As another example, Lotus Development Corporation's 1-2-3 spreadsheet (1993) program includes a narrated *animated tour of features*—interactive animations that teach new users how to use the software—and a multimedia tool called *ScreenCam* that allows people to record screen activity and sound. This last feature can be used to create presentations, tutorials, and specifically tailored help sessions for other users. A final example of the increasing use of animation is the *Apple Guide* employed in version 7.5 of the Apple Macintosh operating system. The *Guide* provides help on a variety of topics and leads users through procedures step-by-step. It circles areas of the screen and highlights text in red to show users where to perform the next step of the procedure and will even complete a step for users if they are uncertain about how to continue.

It is clear that the use of animation and related methods in training and tutorials will continue to increase over the next several years. What is not as clear is the best way to use animation to train people how to use computers. Duffy, Palmer, and Mehlenbacher (1992) suggested that animation may be most useful for introducing an application to a new user, for helping to explain particularly confusing procedural steps, and for providing an overview of long procedural tasks. However, they doubted whether animation alone would be appropriate for demonstrating long tasks because users would have difficulty remembering all of the information without some text or outline as a reference.

Another issue relates to factors influencing the likelihood that an individual will use the various training methods available. Designing training methods that people enjoy is extremely important because it is often difficult to motivate users to learn more about their software. We begin our review by summarizing research showing that most users never learn more than the minimal amount they need to get their job done even if other, more efficient methods are available. We also consider whether animation can be used successfully as a motivational as well as an instructional tool.

The training methods that people enjoy are not always the methods that result in the best learning (Schmidt & Bjork, 1992). We will review evidence regarding the effectiveness of animated training and conclude that animation training, if not designed carefully, can lead to very shallow processing and less long-term retention than text-based training.

Because designing for active learning is evidently important for the success of animated training, we summarize the more general evidence for and against exploration and problem solving, two methods that require that the trainee be an active learner, as opposed to more passive reception of examples. We consider some evidence indicating that the study of examples is not necessarily entirely passive.

We conclude by discussing how the principles of training considered in this chapter can be used to maximize the efficiency of animation-based training. We briefly discuss our own research in which we attempted to overcome the disadvantages of animation training first described by Palmiter and Elkerton (1991a, 1991b, 1991c). Finally, we offer our recommendations on the design of animation-based instructions.

## Motivational Aspects of Animation Training

Computer systems change in function and design so rapidly that training in a formal setting (e.g., college) is not sufficient for a lifelong career that requires computer use (Landauer, 1987). Users may have to engage in continuing learning activities. These activities may take the form of training initiated by an employer and provided through formal training programs either within the company or through outside organizations. However, often people are left to their own devices when determining their training needs and the methods to use (i.e., manuals, tutorials, training tapes, etc.).

## User Preferences and the Trouble With Training

Most people dislike learning how to use a new computer system or software because they feel temporarily incompetent until they master the system (Carroll, 1987). They resent the intrusion of forced learning that is typical of traditional training programs into their controlled focus on tasks and getting the job done. As such, traditional learning is often frustrating, difficult, time-consuming, and disappointing. One contributing factor is that training and reference manuals are often designed with the assumption that if users want to learn something, they will sit down and patiently read the manual, practice the skills, and finally integrate everything into a complete and concise understanding (Carroll & Rosson, 1987). The problem with this approach is that users do not passively absorb information; they are active learners. They prefer to jump in and try things out as they learn by performing meaningful tasks and making sense out of how the system works and reacts (Carroll, 1987). They integrate their previous knowledge of the real world and other systems with what they are actively learning and frequently rely on quick and incomplete hypotheses to complete their goals (chapter 12, this volume; Mack, Lewis, & Carroll, 1990; Shneiderman, 1987).

This dislike for forced and formal learning is probably one reason why most users have a small repertoire of commands and functions that they use on a daily basis (Ashworth, 1992) and only use a fraction of a system's features (Napier, Batsell, Lane, & Guadagno, 1992; Sutcliffe & Old, 1987). These findings are related to the *production paradox*. Carroll and Rosson (1987) found that even experienced users rarely take the time to learn new methods that would increase their efficiency. Instead, they tend to rely on a few well-learned procedures to accomplish most of their tasks, even though those procedures may be inefficient. They want to accomplish the most that they can with a minimal learning investment and feel that they need only know the features that help them accomplish the tasks that they commonly perform. However, this avoidance of the error-prone learning process and the effort of learning and remembering new procedures may result in the use of inefficient, time-consuming methods and difficulty in adopting new methods later.

This reluctance to learn new methods could be reduced if information is easy to find and understand and practice is more task-oriented, especially if it results in users being more likely to pause and learn new information in the midst of performing their tasks. These considerations have contributed to the increasing popularity of online documentation, which is now included with almost all computer software. Designers are realizing that in addition to benefiting the user, online help has made their systems more usable. Kearsley also noted that "improvements in the usability are translated into financial benefits in the form of reduced product support and marketing costs" (1988, p. 71). Krauss, Middendorf, and Willits (1991) noted that the advantages of online help are that it is always available, it is less bulky than hard copy, keyword searching is possible, and it is easy to distribute and update. However, there are large individual differences in how people seek information when they are learning new software. Some people may prefer to use online help and tutorials, but others may find it just as tedious as traditional manuals.

## A Role for Animated Demonstrations?

How should computer-based training be designed in order to optimize the acquisition and retention of knowledge, while at the same time providing the learning environment that users prefer? Using animated demonstrations to provide show-me-how help is one approach that may avoid some of the problems associated with other methods. Animated instructions are a full-motion recording of the computer screen as the task is being performed correctly (i.e., as if by an expert) and can incorporate sound as well. For example, the user can watch the cursor moving on the screen demonstrating the correct sequence of object and menu selections for a particular task and listen to a human voice describing what is being done and why.

Woolf (1992) noted that one significant effect of the increasing use of multimedia teaching systems is that people are often eager to interact with the system. She mentioned one case in which recovery boiler operators willingly spent up to 76 hours in 3 months using a graphical computer tutor simply because they enjoyed interacting with the system. Cornett (1993) also found that learners typically enjoy using animated instructions. Individuals who were presented with animated demonstrations for learning the multimedia authoring system HyperCard skills reported that they liked the animations, found them helpful, and if given the opportunity would choose animated instructions over text-based instructions.

It seems obvious that training systems people enjoy using have a tremendous advantage, because the best system in the world is virtually useless unless people are willing to use it frequently. Thus, the use of animation for training would have an inherent motivational advantage over text-based instructions (e.g., user manuals), which often gather dust on a shelf. However, we must also determine whether the time spent studying animated instructions would ultimately be useful.

## Efficacy of Animation-Based Instruction

Although the focus of this review is on the use of computer-based animation displayed directly on the user's computer screen, research using videotaped animations of computer tasks is of obvious relevance.

### Previous Research

Gist, Rosen, and Schwoerer (1988, 1989) compared an interactive tutorial method with an animation condition that displayed a human instructor on videotape performing the tasks. They found animation to be superior to the tutorial and suggested that modeling enhances learning through the vicarious experience of observing the model because individuals can observe each task being performed correctly and be shown the feedback and end states. It would seem that an animated training method would incorporate many of these advantages, because it displays the task being performed in real time by an expert user while a human voice explains the procedures more fully, even though the actual human expert is not visible.

Animations sometimes encourage users to explore the computer interface actively, and this exploration leads to more learning than would occur through more traditional learning methods (Payne, Chesworth, & Hill, 1990). Waterson and O'Malley (1992) argued that motivational factors are the reason that the animated demonstrations used in their study were superior to traditional text-based instructions for teaching novices how to use a computer graphics application. They noted that animation may be most effective for highly visual interfaces that encourage learning by exploration.

However, in a series of studies Palmiter & Elkerton (1991a, 1991b, 1991c, 1993; Palmiter, Elkerton, & Baggett, 1991) provided an extremely important caution about the possible disadvantages in using animation in computer-based training. These authors carefully considered both the long- and short-term effectiveness of animation for training in the use of an authoring system (HyperCard).

The basic comparisons in these studies were between research participants trained using text instructions and those trained with animated demonstrations. Performance during training was better for participants in the animation condition: They were faster and more accurate than participants trained using text instructions. However, performance a week later showed the opposite effect: The animation group was slower and less accurate than the text group.

The subjective responses to the training favored the animation condition: Individuals in the text condition indicated that they would have liked to see animated demonstrations whereas individuals in the animation condition showed little inclination to view text-based instructions. Moreover, individuals in the animation condition reported that they enjoyed the instructions more than did their counterparts in the text condition.

## Palmiter and Elkerton's Passive Learning Hypothesis

Palmiter and Elkerton hypothesized that the animations in their studies encouraged individuals to engage in rote memorization of procedures, mimicking the animations without encoding the information as thoroughly as users who were presented with only written instructions. This hypothesis implies that a problem with animation training is that it encourages passive learning, a method that is not effective for long-term retention (Avner, Moore, & Smith, 1980). This argument and the results of Palmiter and Elkerton's experiments are consistent with other research showing that, generally speaking, training procedures that require more of the learner lead to poor immediate performance but good long-term performance, whereas procedures that require less of the learner lead to good immediate performance but poor long-term performance (Schmidt & Bjork, 1992).

The implications of Palmiter and Elkerton's findings, taken together with the other research reviewed on motivational aspects of software training programs, are not encouraging for the success of software training in general. With standard non–animation-based instructions, users typically spend so little time learning about their software that they use it inefficiently (Carroll, 1987). However, users enjoy and learn from animated instructions but are poor at remembering what they have learned. Are there ways to design training methods that incorporate animation but do not result in overly passive reception of information and poor retention? With this question in mind we review the evidence regarding the pros and cons of active learning.

## Active Versus Passive Learning

"It's better to figure it out for yourself" has a plausible ring, and related ideas under such names as *discovery learning* and *exploratory learning* have a long history in psychological and educational theory and research.

### General Advantages of Active, Discovery Learning

Bruner (1961) advocated long-term programs of discovery learning, but two of his suggested benefits of discovery—learning the heuristics of discovery and aid to memory processing—are as likely to apply to learning in more restricted or temporary contexts. Illustrating this point, McDaniel and Schlager (1990) found that discovery learning did not enhance transfer of a previously learned strategy but enhanced performance when a transfer task required discovery of a new strategy. This finding is consistent with Bruner's assertion that discovery learning promotes learning of the heuristics of discovery.

Recently, particularly in the domain of human–computer interaction, much research has defined discovery learning in terms of exploration, which is largely initiated by the student (Carroll, Mack, Lewis, Grischkowsky, and Robertson, 1985; Charney, Reder, & Kusbit, 1990; Kamouri, Kamouri, & Smith, 1986). Carroll (e.g., chapter 12; Carroll, 1984) has found large advantages of guided exploration over traditional training methods. Carroll and colleagues (1985) found that a guided exploration condition led to both faster training on a word processor and better transfer than did use of a traditional manual.

Despite these examples, empirical evidence regarding the value of discovery learning is mixed. A number of variables can interact with mode of instruction, including time since learning, difficulty of learning task, difficulty of transfer task, age of individuals, materials and task, prior relevant knowledge, requirement to verbalize learned principles, presentation of rules or principles to discovery groups, amount of guidance, and intelligence of participants (Hermann, 1969).

Though the empirical evidence is mixed, there is some support for the idea that there are advantages to discovery learning. Hermann (1969) reviewed a variety of discovery learning experiments. He concluded that, overall, the discovery method resulted in better transfer but that providing examples of rules that can be used to solve the problems resulted in better retention. He also concluded that, overall, discovery learning is relatively more effective at longer delays between learning and transfer. There is some more recent evidence that active learning leads to very good long-term retention (Conway, Cohen, & Stanhope, 1991, 1992; Semb & Ellis, 1994; Specht & Sandlin, 1991). For example, Conway and colleagues (1991) found that memory for research methods taught in the context of experiments designed and conducted by students did not decline over a period of 12 years.

## General Disadvantages of Discovery Learning

In spite of these advantages, many possible drawbacks to discovery or exploratory learning have been suggested. Friedlander (1965) argued that skill in performing operations, presumably acquired through rote and drill, may often be the key to understanding concepts. He also emphasized the potential problem of frequent failures in discovery. Consistent with the memory facilitation associated with self-generation in other research (e.g., Slamecka & Graf, 1978), the student's errors may be more memorable to the student than a teacher's corrections.

Williams and Farkas (1992) posed three challenges to exploratory learning of computer tasks:

1. It may be inefficient and ineffective in anything but simple applications.
2. It unnecessarily dictates to learners the depth of learning to achieve.
3. It focuses on the learner's acquisition of declarative knowledge at the expense of procedural knowledge.

In general, Williams and Farkas felt that in many cases a user is better served by being given efficient procedural instruction than by being forced to attempt to induce declarative knowledge.

Bruner (1961) discussed the potential benefits of discovery learning largely in terms of problem solving. Perhaps those benefits can largely be realized by carefully assigning selected problems, thus avoiding some of the drawbacks of learner control.

## Relative Merits of Problems and Examples in Training

In basic research, problem solving has been found to benefit both retention (Adams et al., 1988; Auble & Franks, 1978; Jacoby, 1978; Lockhart, Lamon, & Gick, 1988) and transfer (Adams et al., 1988; Lockhart et al., 1988; Needham & Begg, 1991). Results on the benefits of problem solving are also mixed: Perfetto, Bransford, and Franks (1983) and Perfetto, Yearwood, Franks, and Bransford (1987) found that incorrect solution attempts interfered with access to relevant information acquired earlier.

Sweller's cognitive load theory suggests that problem solving can even interfere with learning. This is because novices' typical strategy of reducing differences between the current state and the goal state distracts attention from the conceptually important aspects of the problem yet does not provide the practice for rule automation. Alternative training exercises such as worked examples or so-called reduced-goal problems often lead to better transfer than does problem solving (Owen & Sweller, 1985; Paas, 1992; Paas & Merrienboer, 1994; Pierce, Duncan, Gholson, Ray, & Kamhi, 1993; Sweller, Chandler, Tierney, & Cooper, 1990; Sweller & Cooper, 1985; Ward & Sweller, 1990).

There are studies in which problem solving has led to better performance than worked examples, however. Charney and Reder (1986) and Charney and colleagues (1990) compared problem solving with directed execution of procedures (worked examples) as methods of learning to operate a spreadsheet program. Problem solving was the more difficult form of training, but it produced the best performance on a later test.

One possible explanation for this inconsistency in the literature lies in the nature of the tasks studied. Problem solving seems most likely to lead to excessive cognitive load and interference with learning for difficult problems and domains. As Paas and Merrienboer noted,

> The fact that most studies dealt with rather complex cognitive domains, such as mathematics, physics, and computer programming, seems to be no coincidence. . . . It is exactly these domains that are characterized by high processing load, in which the largest effects of worked examples could be expected. (1994, p. 131)

Another possibility is that the delay of 2 days until test in Charney and Reder (1986), Charney and colleagues (1990), and Kamouri and colleagues (1986) favored the more difficult form of study, just as individuals given text instructions performed best on the delayed test in the studies of Palmiter and Elkerton (1991a, 1991b, 1991c, 1993).

There is nonetheless hope of overcoming any disadvantage for retention resulting from the relative ease of studying examples or, more specifically, animated instructions. Variability of training has been found to increase difficulty during acquisition but ultimately enhance transfer (Bassok & Holyoak, 1987; Gick & Holyoak, 1987; Schmidt & Bjork, 1992). Study of more varied examples also leads to relatively better performance (Gick & Holyoak, 1983; Paas & Merrienboer, 1994; Reed & Bolstad, 1991).

There is ample evidence that students attend to examples in instructional settings (Chi, Bassok, Lewis, Reimann, & Glaser, 1989; LeFevre & Dixon, 1986; VanLehn, 1986) and often refer to examples when solving problems (Anderson, Farrell, & Sauers, 1984; Chi, Bassok, Lewis, Reimann, and Glaser, 1989; Pirolli & Anderson, 1985). Students using examples attempt to explain the examples to themselves (Chi et al., 1989; Ferguson-Hessler & de Jong, 1990; Pirolli & Anderson, 1985; Pirolli & Bielaczyk, 1989), and good learners self-explain to a greater extent than do poor learners. Teaching students effective self-explanation leads to improved learning (Bielaczyk & Recker, 1991). It also appears that how much students learn during problem solving can depend on how well they understand previously studied examples (Pirolli, 1991; Pirolli & Anderson, 1885; VanLehn, Jones, & Chi, 1992).

In summary, training methods that require the learner to take a more active role in the learning process are ultimately more effective than those methods that allow the learner to receive information passively. But the self-explanation effect and the benefits associated with varied examples give hope of devising training regimes and materials that people will be motivated to use and that will nonetheless produce the good retention associated with active learning.

## Designing for Enjoyment and Retention

In our laboratory, we sought to develop a method for using animation in training that results in better long-term retention than simply demonstrating how to perform the tasks. An important difference between animation and text is that animation can provide auditory information in parallel with the visual presentation of the animation. Palmiter, Elkerton, and Baggett (1991) tried supplementing animated instructions with an auditory version of procedural instructions and found no difference between animations alone and animations presented simultaneously with auditory information. Thus, the presentation of the information using two modalities does not improve performance.

### Experiment 1

We hypothesized that using the auditory modality to provide conceptual rather than procedural information would encourage trainees to think about what they are doing, thus discouraging the passive mimicking of an animation. Therefore, our first experiment examined use of auditory information as a supplement to the visually based demonstrations. We presented auditory information that provided users with conceptual information connecting the performance of the task to more general principles. For example, one problem called for creating a *field*, an area in which text can be typed. When the procedures for doing so were illustrated using an animation, the conceptual information discussed the task more generally in terms of *objects*, noting that a *field* is one type of *object*. We felt providing conceptual information would be helpful because it can help users build a mental framework on which to base the related procedural information (Bayman & Mayer, 1988; Halasz & Moran, 1983).

Three training conditions—text, animation, and animation-plus conceptual verbal information—were used to train individuals on HyperCard authoring tasks much like those used by Palmiter and Elkerton. The participants were 39 undergraduate students from Rice University who participated to fulfill course requirements. Participants reported having a minimum of 2 months experience with a computer using software with a GUI but had no experience using HyperCard as an authoring tool. Individuals participated on 2 separate days. The first day, encompassing training and the immediate test, required about 90 minutes. The second day of the experiment, 7 days after the first, required about 1 hour. Participants were tested on tasks identical to, similar to, and distinctly different from the tasks used in training.

On the identical tasks, the essential elements of the findings of Palmiter and Elkerton were replicated: Participants in the animation condition performed much better on an immediate test but much poorer on a delayed test than did participants in the text condition. The performance of the animation-plus-conceptual verbal information condition was similar to that of the animation group in the training session and similar (and not significantly different from) the text group on the delayed test. We are not certain why, but we were unable to replicate on the similar or the different tasks Palmiter and Elkerton's finding of lower performance on a delayed test following animation training. No significant effects were found on either of these tasks.

The results of this experiment are generally consistent with Palmiter and Elkerton's suggestion that participants trained by animated instructions use mimicry, whereas those trained by text instructions use richer encoding schemes. A related explanation is that tasks for which greater effort is required result in better recall (Catrambone, 1989; Charney & Reder, 1986; Kamouri et al., 1986; Schmidt & Bjork, 1992). Participants in the text condition may have been forced beyond mimicry to interpret and apply their instructions and to explore when they were unable to interpret those instructions, resulting in more elaborate encoding and better long-term recall.

This experiment provides at least some support for the notion that supplementing animated instructions with conceptual auditory information provides the early performance advantage of animation without paying a penalty in long-term retention. As a follow-up to this experiment, we sought to design the method of presenting animation we thought would be best and to determine whether it produces long-term retention that is even better than that produced by text instructions.

## Experiment 2

To attempt to improve long-term retention in the animation condition, we made the animations slightly different from the tasks that the participants were asked to perform in training. For example, the animated instruction for one task demonstrated how to create a new button, name it "Read Book," and place it above a picture of some books, whereas the actual task goal required the button to be named "Open Book" and placed below the books. Thus, the training tasks were problems that could be solved by applying what was shown in a similar but not identical example. We hypothesized that this modification would reduce mimicry and promote long-term retention of skills. The animated instructions used the auditory channel to present conceptual information relating to the tasks as in the animation-plus-conceptual verbal information condition in Experiment 1.

The participants were 22 undergraduate students from Rice University who took part in order to fulfill course requirements. As in Experiment 1, participants reported having a minimum of 2 months experience with a computer using software with a GUI but had no experience using the HyperCard authoring tools. The participants were randomly assigned to the two groups with an equal number of participants in each group.

Experiment 2 used HyperCard stacks functionally equivalent to those of Experiment 1, as well as the same number of HyperCard tasks plus two practice tasks based on Microsoft Word (Microsoft, 1994) and

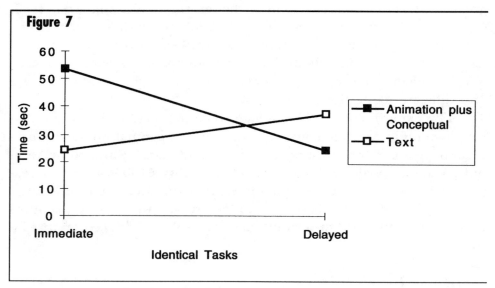

Figure 7

Response time on the identical tasks in Experiment 2.

Microsoft Excel. The task instructions were prepared in the same manner as for Experiment 1.

Two between-subjects training conditions were used: (a) text and (b) animation-plus-conceptual verbal information. The animation-plus-conceptual verbal information condition in Experiment 2 differed from the animation-plus-conceptual verbal information condition in Experiment 1 in that the animations in Experiment 2 showed slightly different tasks than the ones the trainees were to perform. As in Experiment 1, participants were tested on tasks identical to, similar to, and different from those used in training.

The combination of conceptual information and using animations slightly different from the training tasks had a profound effect on the retention of the skills learned and performance on the delayed test for the animation-plus-conceptual verbal information group. Unlike the findings of Palmiter and Elkerton (1991a, 1991b, 1991c, 1993) and those for the identical tasks in Experiment 1, training in the animation-plus-conceptual verbal information condition led to greater improvement after a delay than did training with text. As can be seen in Figure 7 the group trained with animation-plus-conceptual verbal information decreased their times on the identical tasks from the immediate to the delayed test, whereas the text group increased their times. The training

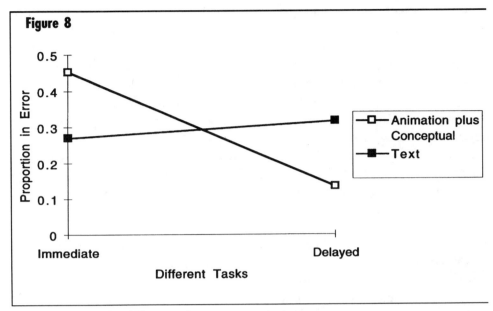

**Figure 8**

Error rates on the different tasks in Experiment 2.

condition by the session interaction was significant. Note that although the text group performed better on the immediate test and the animation-plus-conceptual verbal information group performed better in the delayed test, neither of these differences was significant. Because individual differences in performance on tasks of these sorts are generally so large, between-subjects effects such as these are tested with very low power. The change in performance from the immediate to the delayed condition is a within-subjects effect and therefore tested with more power.

Although there were no significant differences on the similar tasks, the pattern found with the identical tasks was also found for errors made on the different tasks (see Figure 8). Error rate is the more relevant variable for the different tasks because the main issue was whether or not a participant could solve a novel task. Moreover, because of the high error rate on the different tasks, the data on response time are difficult to interpret. The interaction was significant for errors but was not significant for response time. Therefore, the effect of delay was more deleterious for participants in the text condition than participants in the animation-plus-conceptual verbal information condition. However, the performance of the animation-plus-conceptual verbal information group was not significantly better than the text group in the delayed condition. As discussed before, the design of this experiment is not well suited to the detection of between-subject differences. Therefore, we cannot claim that the animation-plus-conceptual information leads to better performance, but we can say that it leads to better retention. Further experiments using more participants or an effective covariate to determine if the animation-plus-conceptual verbal information condition of Experiment 2 actually leads to better performance may help resolve this issue.

The results of Experiment 2 provide a contrast to the findings of Experiment 1 and to those of Palmiter and Elkerton. The text group was faster during the training session and actually practiced the tasks twice as many times as the animation-plus-conceptual verbal information group, the members of which spent more of their time using the animated instructions. Whereas the animation-plus-conceptual verbal information group's performance times and accuracy improved steadily across sessions, the text group's performance often remained stable or became worse. The animation-plus-conceptual verbal information group actually performed slightly faster and more accurately than the text group on the delayed test.

Learning with the improved animated demonstrations resulted in better long-term retention of skill knowledge and better transfer (e.g., the different tasks) than learning from reading written text. However, it is difficult to determine whether the effectiveness of this form of training was a result of the design of the animation, the spoken conceptual information, or the combination of both. The addition of the conceptual information may have made the procedures more meaningful, and meaningful information is more easily remembered (Kieras & Bovair, 1984; Rose, 1989), which in turn promotes transfer (Catrambone, 1989; Halasz & Moran, 1983). But the conceptual material seems to have been of more limited value in Experiment 1 than in Experiment 2. It is possible that the participants in Experiment 2, who were unable to directly mimic the modified animated instructions were more likely to make use of the conceptual information than the participants in Experiment 1, who could have performed tasks correctly simply by mimicking what they had observed in the animated demonstrations. Overall, these findings indicate that animation can be an effective method of training procedural skills in a graphical environment like HyperCard, as long as they are designed to reduce mimicry and provide a meaningful conceptual framework for learners.

## Suggested Guidelines

At this point we can suggest some guidelines for the design and implementation of animated instructions. If the task to be learned is relatively simple, then it may be worthwhile to have learners try to perform the tasks without instructions, forcing them to engage in problem solving, an approach that Charney and Reder (1986) found effective. If the task is too complex for this to be practical or if a learner fails to complete a task in a short time, instructions should be presented with an animated demonstration of the correct procedures supplemented by spoken conceptual information. However, the animation should demonstrate the general procedures for the tasks, without direct reference to the actual objects that the learners will be using to practice the tasks. This approach will discourage simple mimicry of the instructions and possibly promote deeper cognitive processing of the information. The learners should also be presented with the procedural steps in written form for quick reference, because many users feel that animation seems too slow for quickly reviewing procedures. However, each written procedural step should be linked to a short animated segment to provide the users with an opportunity to see how the task is performed. This instructional design is likely to be very effective for training for long-term retention of computer skills.

## Conclusion

The goal of training in computer applications should be to support posttraining performance (Schmidt & Bjork, 1992). How well users can perform their skills in the long term is much more important than how well they perform immediately following training, and there are several factors that seem to support long-term retention of skill. Conditions that provide added difficulty for learners usually result in poor initial performance but better delayed performance (Catrambone, 1989; Charney & Reder, 1986; Kamouri et al., 1986; Schmidt & Bjork, 1992). These more difficult conditions require a deeper level of cognitive processing, which results in better learning. Also, making the procedural information more meaningful by providing a conceptual framework may aid skill retention and help learners transfer their skills to novel situations (Bayman & Mayer, 1988; Kieras & Bovair, 1984; Rose, 1989). Baggett (1987) also found that the best retention of skill resulted when the learners first practiced a task hands-on before watching a narrated film of the procedures. In many organizations, personal computer software training is accomplished using instructors. Usually, the instructor's computer is connected to a projector that the class participants can observe. Each student has access to a personal computer during the training class. After the instructor demonstrates a procedure, the students then attempt the same process on their computer. The instructor often discusses concepts as the procedure is explained and demonstrated. This approach is similar to the animation-plus-conceptual verbal information condition of our experiments. To improve long-term retention, the instructor might demonstrate a procedure and direct the students to complete the procedure for a task in a similar but slightly different manner. For example, the instructor might change the font size for a document to 12 points and direct the students to make the font size 14 points.

In summary, animation promises to be an effective tool in training the use of computer software. It is enjoyable and therefore can motivate users to learn more about their software. Unlike text-based instruction, animation is easy to integrate visual and auditory information in animation training. The auditory information should not provide information completely redundant with the information displayed visually but instead should supplement the procedural information shown visually with conceptual information. The disadvantage is that animation has the potential to result in mimicry and very superficial learning. However, it appears that introducing slight differences in the task being shown in the animation and the task the user is asked to perform helps to reduce mimicry and rote learning and therefore improve long-term retention.

## References

Adams, L. T., Kasserman, J. E., Yearwood, A. A., Perfetto, G. A., Bransford, J. D., & Franks, J. J. (1988). Memory access: The effects of fact-oriented versus problem-oriented acquisition. *Memory and Cognition, 16*(2), 167–175.

Anderson, J. R., Farrell, R., & Sauers, R. (1984). Learning to program in LISP. *Cognitive Science, 8*, 87–129.

Ashworth, C. A. (1992). Skill as the fit between performer resources and tasks demands: A perspective from software use and learning. *Proceedings of the Fourteenth Annual Conference of the Cognitive Science Society* (pp. 444–449). Hillsdale, NJ: Erlbaum.

Auble, P. A., & Franks, J. J. (1978). The effects of effort toward comprehension on recall. *Memory and Cognition, 6*(1), 20–25.

Avner, A., Moore, C., & Smith, S. (1980). Active external control: A basis for superiority of CBI. *Journal of Computer-Based Instruction, 6*(4), 115–118.

Baggett, P. (1984). Role of temporal overlap of visual and auditory material in forming dual media associations. *Journal of Educational Psychology, 76*(3), 408–416.

Baggett, P. (1987). Learning a procedure from multimedia instructions: The effects of film and practice. *Applied Cognitive Psychology, 1,* 183–195.

Bassok, M., & Holyoak, K. J. (1987). Interdomain transfer between isomorphic topics in algebra and physics. *Journal of Experimental Psychology: Learning, Memory, and Cognition, 15,* 153–166.

Bayman, P., & Mayer, R. E. (1988). Using conceptual models to teach BASIC computer programming. *Journal of Educational Psychology, 80*(3), 291–298.

Bielaczyc, K., & Recker, M. M. (1991). Learning to learn: The implications of strategy instruction in computer programming. In L. Birnbaum (Ed.), *The International Conference on the Learning Sciences* (pp. 39–44). Charlottesville, VA: Association for the Advancement of Computing in Education.

Bruner, J. S. (1961). The act of discovery. *Harvard Educational Review, 31,* 21–32.

Carroll, J. M. (1984). Minimalist training. *Datamation, 30*(19), 125–136.

Carroll, J. M. (1987). Preface. In J. Carroll (Ed.), *Interfacing thought: Cognitive aspects of human-computer interaction.* Cambridge, MA: Bradley Books.

Carroll, J. M., Mack, R. L., Lewis, Grischkowsky, N. L., & Robertson, S. R. (1985). Exploring exploring a word processor. *Human-Computer Interaction, 1,* 283–307.

Carroll, J. M., & Rosson, M. B. (1987). Paradox of the active user. In J. Carroll (Ed.), *Interfacing thought: Cognitive aspects of human-computer interaction* (pp. 80–111). Cambridge, MA: Bradley Books.

Catrambone, R. (1989). Specific versus general instructions: Initial performance and later transfer. *Proceedings of the Human Factors Society 33rd Annual Meeting* (pp. 1320–1323). Santa Monica, CA: Human Factors Society.

Charney, D. H., & Reder, L. M. (1986). Designing interactive tutorials for computer users. *Human-Computer Interaction, 2,* 297–317.

Charney, D. H., Reder, L. M., & Kusbit, G. W. (1990). Goal setting and procedure selection in acquiring computer skills: A comparison of tutorials, problem solving, and learner exploration. *Cognition and Instruction, 7,* 323–342.

Chi, M. T. H., Bassok, M., Lewis, M. W., Reimann, P., & Glaser, R. (1989). Self-explanations: How students study and use examples in learning to solve problems. *Cognitive Science, 13,* 145–182.

Conway, M. A., Cohen, G., & Stanhope, N. (1991). On the very long-term retention of knowledge acquired through formal education: Twelve years of cognitive psychology. *Journal of Experimental Psychology: General, 120*(4), 395–409.

Conway, M. A., Cohen, G., & Stanhope, N. (1992). Very long-term memory for knowledge acquired at school and university. *Applied Cognitive Psychology, 6,* 467–482.

Cornett, L. L. (1993). *Animated demonstrations versus text: A comparison of training methods.* Unpublished master's thesis, Rice University, Houston, TX.

Duffy, T. M., Palmer, J. E., & Mehlenbacher, B. (1992). *Online help: Design and evaluation.* Norwood, NJ: Ablex.

Ferguson-Hessler, M. G. M., & de Jong, T. (1990). Studying physics texts: Differences in study processes between good and poor performers. *Cognition and Instruction, 7,* 41–54.

Friedlander, B. Z. (1965). A psychologist's second thoughts on concepts, curiosity, and discovery in teaching and learning. *Harvard Educational Review, 35,* 18–38.

Gick, M. L., & Holyoak, K. J. (1983). Schema induction and analogical transfer. *Cognitive Psychology, 14,* 1–38.

Gick, M. L., & Holyoak, K. J. (1987). The cognitive basis of knowledge transfer. In

S. M. Cormier & J. D. Hagman (Eds.), *Transfer of learning* (pp. 9–46). New York: Academic Press.

Gist, M., Rosen, B., & Schwoerer, C. (1988). The influence of training method and trainee age on the acquisition of computer skills. *Personnel Psychology, 41,* 255–265.

Gist, M., Rosen, B., & Schwoerer, C. (1989). Effects of alternative training methods on self-efficacy and performance in computer software training. *Journal of Applied Psychology, 74*(6), 884–891.

Halasz, F. G., & Moran, T. P. (1983). Mental models and problem solving in using a calculator. In *Proceedings of CHI '83. Human Factors in Computing Systems* (pp. 212–221). New York: Association of Computing Machinery.

Hermann, G. (1969). Learning by discovery: A critical review of studies. *Journal of Experimental Education, 38*(1), 59–72.

Jacoby, L. I. (1978). On interpreting the effects of repetition: Solving a problem versus remembering a solution. *Journal of Verbal Learning and Verbal Behavior, 17,* 649–667.

Kamouri, A. L., Kamouri, J., & Smith, K. H. (1986). Training by exploration: Facilitating the transfer of procedural knowledge through analogical reasoning. *International Journal of Man-Machine Studies, 24,* 171–192.

Kearsley, G. (1988). *Online help systems—Design and implementation.* Norwood, NJ: Ablex.

Kieras, D. E., & Bovair, S. (1984). The role of a mental model in learning to operate a device. *Cognitive Science, 8,* 255–273.

Krauss, F. S., Middendorf, K. A., & Willits, L. S. (1991). A comparative investigation of hard copy vs. online documentation. *Proceedings of the Human Factors Society 35th Annual Meeting* (pp. 350–353). Santa Monica, CA: Human Factors Society.

Landauer, T. K. (1987). Relations between cognitive psychology and computer system design. In J. Carroll (Ed.), *Interfacing thought: Cognitive aspects of human-computer interaction* (pp. 1–25). Cambridge, MA: Bradley Books.

LeFevre, J., & Dixon, P. (1986). Do written instructions need examples? *Cognition and Instruction, 3,* 1–30.

Lockhart, R. S., Lamon, M., & Gick, M. L. (1988). Conceptual transfer in simple insight problems. *Memory and Cognition, 16*(1), 36–44.

Lotus Development Corporation. (1993). Lotus 1-2-3 [Computer software]. Cambridge, MA: Author.

Mack, R. L., Lewis, C. H., & Carroll, J. M. (1990). Learning to use word processors: Problems and prospects. In J. Preece & L. Keller (Eds.), *Human-computer interaction* (pp. 185–204). Englewood, NJ: Prentice-Hall.

McDaniel, M. A., & Schlager, M. S. (1990). Discovery learning and transfer of problem-solving skills. *Cognition and Instruction, 7*(2), 129–159.

Microsoft Corporation. (1994). Word [Computer software]. Redmond, WA: Author.

Napier, H. A., Batsell, R. R., Lane, D. L., & Guadagno, N. S. (1992, Winter). Knowledge of command usage in a spreadsheet program. *Database,* 13–21.

Needham, D. R., & Begg, I. M. (1991). Problem-oriented training promotes spontaneous analogical transfer: Memory-oriented training promotes memory for training. *Memory and Cognition, 19*(6), 543–557.

Owen, E., & Sweller, J. (1985). What do students learn while solving mathematics problems? *Journal of Educational Psychology, 77*(3), 272–284.

Paas, F. G. W. C. (1992). Training strategies for attaining transfer of problem-solving skill in statistics: A cognitive load approach. *Journal of Educational Psychology, 84*(4), 429–434.

Paas, F. G. W. C., & Merrienboer, J. J. G. V. (1994). Variability of worked examples and transfer of geometrical problem-solving skills: A cognitive load approach. *Journal of Educational Psychology, 86*(1), 122–133.

Palmiter, S., & Elkerton, J. (1991a). Animated demonstrations vs. written instructions for learning procedural tasks: A preliminary investigation. *International Journal of Man-Machine Studies, 34*, 687–701.

Palmiter, S., & Elkerton, J. (1991b). *An evaluation of animated demonstrations for learning computer-based tasks.* (Technical Report C4E-ONR-4). Ann Arbor: University of Michigan.

Palmiter, S., & Elkerton, J. (1991c). An evaluation of animated demonstrations for learning computer-based tasks. *Proceedings of CHI '91 Human Factors in Computing Systems* (pp. 257–263). New York: Association of Computing Machinery.

Palmiter, S., & Elkerton, J. (1993). Animated demonstrations for learning procedural computer-based tasks. *Human-Computer Interaction, 8*, 193–216.

Palmiter, S., Elkerton, J., & Baggett, P. (1991). Animated demonstrations versus written instructions for learning procedural tasks: A preliminary investigation. *International Journal of Man-Machine Studies, 34*, 687–701.

Payne, S. J., Chesworth, L., & Hill, E. (1990). *Animated demonstrations for exploratory learners* (IMB Research Report No. 15714). New York: T. J. Watson Research Center.

Perfetto, G. A., Bransford, J. D., & Franks, J. J. (1983). Constraints on access in a problem-solving context. *Memory & Cognition, 11*, 24–31.

Perfetto, G. A., Yearwood, A. A., Franks, J. J., & Bransford, J. D. (1987). Effects of generation on memory access. *Bulletin of the Psychonomic Society, 25*, 151–154.

Pierce, K. A., Duncan, M. K., Gholson, B., Ray, G. E., & Kamhi, A. G. (1993) Cognitive load, schema acquisition, and procedural adaptation in nonisomorphic analogical transfer. *Journal of Educational Psychology, 85*, 66–74.

Pirolli, P. (1991). Effects of examples and their explanations in a lesson on recursion: A production system analysis. *Cognition and Instruction, 8*, 207–259.

Pirolli, P., & Anderson, J. R. (1985). The role of learning from examples in acquisition of recursive programming skills. *Canadian Journal of Psychology, 39*, 240–272.

Pirolli, P., & Bielaczyk, K. (1989). Empirical analyses of self-explanation and transfer in learning to program. In G. M. Olson & E. E. Smith (Eds.), *Proceedings of the 11th Annual Conference of the Cognitive Science Society* (pp. 450–457). Hillsdale, NJ: Erlbaum.

Reed, S. K., & Bolstad, C. A. (1991). Use of examples and procedures in problem solving. *Journal of Experimental Psychology: Learning, Memory, and Cognition, 17*, 753–766.

Rose, A. M. (1989). Acquisition and retention of skills. In G. MacMillan (Ed.), *Applications of human performance models to system design.* New York: Plenum Press.

Schmidt, R. A., & Bjork, R. A. (1992). New conceptualizations of practice: Common principles in three paradigms suggest new concepts for training. *Psychological Science, 3*(4), 207–217.

Semb, G. B., & Ellis, J. A. (1994). Knowledge taught in school: What is remembered? *Review of Educational Research, 64*(2), 253–286.

Shneiderman, B. (1987). *Designing the user interface.* Reading, MA: Addison-Wesley.

Slamecka, N. J., & Graf, P. (1978). The generation effect: Delineation of a phenomenon. *Journal of Experimental Psychology: Human Learning and Memory, 4*, 592–604.

Specht, L. B., & Sandlin, P. K. (1991). The differential effects of experiential learning activities and traditional lecture classes in accounting. *Simulation & Gaming, 22*(2), 196–210.

Sutcliffe, A. G., & Old, A. C. (1987). Do users know they have user models? Some experiences in the practice of user modelling. In H. Bullinger & B. Shackel (Eds.), *Human Computer Interaction - Interact '87* (pp. 35–41), Amsterdam: North Holland.

Sweller, J., Chandler, P., Tierney, P., & Cooper, M. (1990). Cognitive load as a factor in the structuring of technical material. *Journal of Experimental Psychology: General, 119*(2), 176–192.

Sweller, J., & Cooper, G. A. (1985). The use of worked examples as a substitute for problem solving in learning algebra. *Cognition and Instruction, 2*(1) 59–85.

Temple, Barker, & Sloane, Inc. (1990). *The benefits of the graphical user interface: A report on new primary research.* Lexington, MA: Author.

VanLehn, K. (1986). Arithmetic procedures are induced from examples. In J. Hiebert (Ed.), *Conceptual and procedural knowledge: The case of mathematics* (pp. 130–180). Hillsdale, NJ: Erlbaum.

VanLehn, K., Jones, R. M., & Chi, M. T. H. (1992). A model of the self-explanation effect. *The Journal of the Learning Sciences, 2*, 1–59.

Ward, M., & Sweller, J. (1990). Structuring effective worked examples. *Cognition and Instruction, 7*(1), 1–39.

Waterson, P., & O'Malley, C. (1992). Using animated demonstrations to teach graphics skills. In A. Monk, D. Diaper, & M. D. Harrison (Eds.), *Proceedings of HCI 92: People and Computers VII* (pp. 463–474). Cambridge: Cambridge University Press.

Williams, T. R., & Farkas, D. K. (1992). Minimalism reconsidered: Should we design documentation for exploratory learning? *Special Interest Group Computer Human Interaction Bulletin, 24*, 41–50.

Woolf, B. (1992). Hypermedia in education and training. In D. Kopec & R. B. Thompson (Eds.), *Artificial intelligence and intelligent tutoring systems: Knowledge-based systems for teaching and learning* (pp. 97–109). New York: Ellis Horwood.

# Toward Minimalist Training: Supporting the Sense-Making Activities of Computer Users

**John M. Carroll**

The minimalist approach to computer software training was developed to respond to a class of typical and serious user errors that are not dealt with successfully by *step-by-step instruction*. The minimalist approach demonstrates how taking user errors seriously provides design requirements for training and documentation. The minimalist approach has guided the design of a variety of experimental materials, which have proved to be more effective than systems-style alternatives.

During the 1980s, a group at the IBM Watson Research Center developed the minimalist approach to training design. In essence, this approach took seriously what people appeared to be trying to do when they were getting started with new computer systems and applications by means of conventional, self-instruction materials. It sought to support more effectively the goals and activities of the users, rather than trying to convince them that they needed to do other things. This approach succeeded at speeding up performance improvement and has proven to generalize to many types of systems and applications.

In this overview I first sketch the typical and troublesome predicaments that plague new computer users—suggesting that these are not an accidental assortment but are understandable as direct consequences of a general and powerful problem-solving strategy. Taking these predicaments seriously as principled consequences of organized user effort encouraged a focus on reducing the obstacles to self-directed discovery and achievement that can inhere in modern systems and documentation. I review a variety of minimalist materials that in various ways try to support the learner's problem-solving strategies and thereby to facilitate faster and more successful training.

## The Active Learner

In general, people at all levels of skill make an impressive variety of errors. To a great extent, the problems people have depend on idiosyncratic details of the particular system they use. However, problems can also be usefully classified into types. The section that follows inventories and summarizes several critical and typical usability problems people have in getting started with computer interfaces, ranging from traditional character-box, menu-based styles to high-resolution graphics, direct manipulation styles (Carroll, 1990; Carroll & Mazur, 1986; Mack, Lewis, & Carroll, 1983; Rosson & Carroll, 1990; Singley, Carroll, & Alpert, 1991). The description is couched at a granularity appropriate to provide guidance for interface and documentation designers.

1. *People tend to jump the gun.* When using a system for the first time, people often try to engage in activity before becoming familiar with even the basics of using the system. This can work well if a person has appropriate background knowledge or access to a more experienced user. But it can also be problematic. In studies of the Apple Lisa system (Carroll & Mazur, 1986), users sometimes switched the system on before inserting the tutorial LisaGuide diskette. Switching the system on seems like a good place to start, but in this case it was jumping the gun: To use the tutorial, the system must be booted from that diskette and not from its hard disk.

2. *People are not always careful planners.* New users often become intrigued by functions irrelevant to their actual concerns or take actions without analyzing even their immediate consequences. For example, in studies of the IBM Displaywriter (Carroll & Carrithers, 1984), people sometimes selected *program diskette tasks* from the *initial menu*, instead of the more appropriate *typing tasks*, which is the gateway to editing and printing functions. *Program diskette tasks* entrains a variety of system maintenance functions that new users do not need to use and typically cannot understand. In the Lisa system, people placed system applications in the *wastebasket* in order to experiment with deletion; some of them were motivated to confirm that a given applica-

tion had in fact been deleted by throwing away several more. This is sound reasoning, but poor planning. One individual we observed discarded more than half the functionality of the system.

3. *People are not good at systematically following procedures.* New users often very rapidly skip among several sections of a manual, or among several volumes in a training library, following what in essence is an ersatz procedure that was never intended or designed. They attempt to execute section previews (jumping the gun) and reviews—even though previews and reviews are meant only to be read. At a more fundamental level, people have trouble following instructions that are ordered *extrinsically*—that is, sequenced in the sense of labeled and numbered steps but without clearly motivated prerequisite relationships. For example, the instruction set in Figure 9 was problematic for new users of the Lisa system: It was not clear to users which steps were to be read before doing anything (the two immediately below it, which is odd in a sense because these are two drawn from a series of five, or the two labeled with arrows). People rarely follow extrinsic injunctions to "read everything before doing anything." In the situation of Figure 9, users were unable to see the point of the exercise. They were able to put everything aside, but then, staring at an empty screen, they wondered what to do next.

4. *People's reasoning about situations is often subject to interference from what they know about other, superficially similar situations.* Users may spontaneously refer to prior knowledge about typewriters, and erroneously deduce the operation of keys like *spacebar* and *return* (which typically alter text as well as moving the input pointer). Prior knowledge can override an interpretation that the designer intends. The Lisa system used a *tear off* command to generate new objects from templates. Users were able to apply this with some difficulty to stationery pads; some had trouble stemming from their prior experiences of writing on a pad before tearing off the current sheet. However, applying the *tear off* command to folder objects caused serious confusion: people had never encountered a folder pad before, nor the idea that one obtains a folder by tearing it off from something. Under such uncertainty, users can reach in-

**Figure 9**

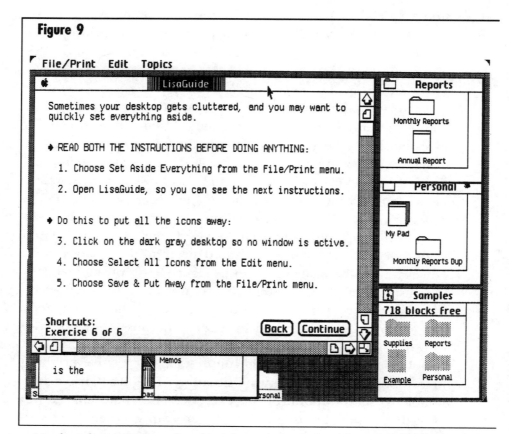

Numbered steps in an on-line tutorial: Executing Step 1, closes the tutorial—including the display of Steps 2 through 5. The "remedy" is to implore the learner to read everything before doing anything, though it is not immediately clear to what "both the instructions" refers.

correct conclusions about cause and effect relationships in an interface.

5. *People are often poor at recognizing, diagnosing, and recovering from errors they make.* It is not always clear when an error has been made; even when the user suspects something has gone wrong, it may be difficult to understand just *what* went wrong and to determine how to address it. New users may queue multiple print jobs or alter the print queue itself without recognizing the consequence until much later when they try to operate the printer and are surprised by the number, sequence, and appearance of their output. In the Displaywriter, mistyping a diskette name in an edit or print command had the

consequence that the system would prompt for the erroneously named diskette to be inserted. It was unlikely that the user would have already formatted and named a diskette with that particular typo as its name, hence the whole command had to be canceled. The problem was that the command to cancel that command was itself quite advanced and not even presented in the instruction manual. Hence the only remedy they could avail themselves of was to switch off the system and reboot. This error recovery entailed some side effects of its own (any open file would be saved incompletely and with errors necessitating a subsequent diskette recovery procedure).

These problems raise serious questions about the well-established systems approach to the design of instructional documentation (e.g., see Gagné & Briggs, 1979). This approach assumes that a functional decomposition of a skill domain dictates an appropriate instructional treatment: Instructional events (previews, practice exercises, tests, reviews) are orchestrated to address individual training objectives in a rational sequence—for example, an exercise on pointing and clicking, followed by one on dragging. The systems approach assumes that learners will patiently ensure prerequisites, accurately follow procedures, engage prior knowledge only as directed, and make no mistakes. The patterns just described repudiate these assumptions, and indeed raise the question of whether the systems approach in part causes these problematic situations.

## Sense-Making

Users of computer equipment and other tools are fundamentally motivated to accomplish real tasks. Both the organizational context for using new software and the internalized standards that people have for determining what is worth spending time on bias users against a "practice for the sake of practice" attitude. New users want to get started fast, do things on their own, engage what they already know, and accomplish goals they understand and value. People want to take initiative and reason things out instead of merely reading about concepts and procedures. They resent rigidly structured exercises that compel them to essentially copy text character for character and then subject them to fatuous praise for these trivial accomplishments: "Excellent!'' They like to test hypotheses they generate in the course of problem-solving.

People want to make sense of their learning activities. But this active orientation to learning is not served well by the step-by-step sequence of preview, practice, test, and review, typical of systematic instruction (Gagné & Briggs, 1979). Indeed, sense-making provides a psychological explanation of the five general user problems listed previously. Instead of merely reflecting deficiencies in systems-style documentation, these problems can be seen as indicators of specific human propensities in reasoning and performance, as principled guides to the development of more effective approaches to the design of systems and documentation. The five general user problems correspond to five components of a powerful problem-solving strategy, one that covers most cases of human performance quite well.

1. *People learn by doing; they try to act in order to understand.* Learning involves more than merely acquiring information. A person starting to use a complex tool like a computer will not succeed by "writing to disk" myriad previews and exercise steps. The person must integrate knowing with doing, and this can only occur through meaningful action.

2. *People learn by thinking and reasoning; they generate and test hypotheses in order to understand.* The level and kind of activity required to effectively develop skill necessarily involves self-directed thinking and reasoning. Following a numbered set of exercise steps is neither active nor challenging enough. Indeed, it places people in a double-bind: Try to understand, to think about what you are doing and you will get off the track, but try to stay on the track and you will mentally go to sleep and learn nothing. Even when users attentively followed their practice exercises, they sometimes were uncertain about what they had achieved or why—as one individual put it, "What did we do?''

3. *People seek to work in a meaningful context and toward meaningful goals.* A desire to get something done is what makes people want to use a computer tool in the first place. It orients effort to practical progress. Perhaps the worst thing instruction can do is to place an obstacle of numbered steps and well-decomposed training objectives in the way of practical progress. People starting to use an office application system want to do real work—immediately. One user of an on-line tutoring facility

complained, "I want to do something, not learn how to do everything."

4. *People rely on their prior knowledge when they try to manage and assimilate new experience.* Relating what someone already knows to new things makes it vastly easier for them to remember and be able to use new knowledge in appropriate contexts. This enables the rapid extraction of meaning from new situations that is perhaps the most potent aspect of human reasoning. However, when situations conflict with prior understanding, when they are difficult to interpret given what is already known, then reasoning and performance are impaired, and this powerful, adverse effect is not significantly mitigated by providing a purely structural organization, like the "training hierarchies" of systems-style instruction.

5. *People use error diagnosis and recovery episodes as a means of exploring the boundaries of what they know.* Errors play a far more varied role in skill development than merely one of distracting and frustrating performance. An error can be the touchstone for an intellectual exploration, a vehicle for discovering what is known and what is not currently known. In a serious sense, errors are prerequisite conditions for developing skill at all. But in order to use errors to improve understanding and performance, people need to be able to recognize when they have made an error, they need to be able to reason about what caused the error and how it can be dealt with. Systems-style training material typically assumes that people will follow instructions errorlessly. It provides little or no support to users who have made an error and must diagnose and correct it in order to recover. But perhaps worse, systems-style material fails to use error recovery as an opportunity for making instructional points and improving performance.

There is a simple, albeit paradoxical way to summarize these points: *Just the things that make people good learners (the desire to make sense and to accomplish meaningful work) also create the problems that ruin systems-style documentation.* People need to make sense in order to perform, but they need to perform in order to make sense (Carroll & Rosson, 1987). The challenge of designing usable systems and documentation is to allow people to make sense of their own skill development activity and thereby to refine what they already know and discover new things as well.

## Minimalist Instruction

This analysis suggests an alternate direction for instructional design, one that seriously seeks to support what learners are trying to do in the way they are trying to do it. Consider two contrasting views of learner error. In the systems approach, one merely tries to control error, printing steps in boldface and imploring users to be careful. From an active user perspective, the view is completely different: Errors are expected; they are unavoidable; they are concomitants of genuine engagement and creative activity; they are opportunities for learning. If users take initiative in directing their own activity, they will make errors. The problem for designers of systems and documentation is to manage the consequences of errors so that the least complications and the greatest possible benefits obtain.

An instruction model appropriate for active users cannot demand that people sit at the interface and read. People do not want to do this, and they in fact do *not* do it. The minimalist model takes this hard reality as a starting point. The sheer volume of training material must be minimal. The ever-present sales pitch should be cut (the user has already bought the system); section overviews, previews, and reviews should be drastically cut (users often try to execute them); far less how-it-works information should be presented (new users do not have to know details of magnetic recording to use diskettes). Installation should be simple (for example, loading a single diskette). System and tutorial screens should differ as little as possible (tutorial screens often get confusingly cluttered). The overhead of jargon in the documentation itself should be minimized (for example, eliminating fine distinctions between *topics* and *chapters* or between *message lines* and *information lines*).

The minimalist approach has several themes in common with the lean programming approach of the 1960s (e.g., Rummler, 1965). *Lean programming* stressed minimizing the number of frames in a training package by making the individual steps as large as possible. The design of a lean programming package is to be guided by a task analysis of the user's actual training needs and propensities. However, lean programming contrasts with the minimalist approach in its reliance on step-by-step exercises (in contrast to real work activities) and its ambition to preclude user error (in contrast to seeing error as a learning opportunity and inevitable in either case).

The five general user problems and five aspects of powerful, general problem-solving strategies can be recast as five minimalist principles (Carroll, 1990):

1. *Allow learners to get started fast.* Reduce overhead and repetition; eliminate nonessential verbiage; reject the notion that every function must be covered, because people never master every function even when every function is covered. Offer the user meaningful activities as soon as possible.
2. *Rely on people to think and to improvise.* Encourage but guide user inference; leave out material that can be inferred. Do not try to *give* the user an understanding when you can allow the user to *create* an understanding.
3. *Embed information in real tasks.* Introduce real work immediately. Instruction, no matter how well-organized, will fail if it fails to support the goals people bring to the situation.
4. *Take advantage of what people already know.* Even if it is possible to understand without analogy, it is too abstract and cumbersome.
5. *Support error recognition and recovery.* Errors cannot be avoided, but they can confuse and frustrate people. If they are properly managed they may play useful roles.

The process of creating minimalist instruction involves detailed task analysis to understand specifically what users wish to accomplish and how they are likely to proceed and to err. The design builds a sequence of realistic tasks with absolutely minimized expository and rote support. As in the case of lean programming, minimalist documentation is elaborated as empirically required through the course of user try-outs (Carroll & Rosson, 1985).

## Allow Learners to Get Started Fast

Training designers may want to build instructional monuments; learners want to get past the instruction to do something real. A minimalist's first-line response to this is to offer learners less to read and more to do: brief manuals and lots of realistic activity. Guided exploration cards were designed to scrutinize fundamental assumptions about how much information and structure was required by office workers learning to use word-processing equipment (Carroll, Mack, Lewis, Grischkowsky, & Robertson, 1985). Each card briefly addressed a particular functional goal that could be understood on the basis of specific prior knowledge of office tasks (irrespective of computers, for example, the goal of "typing something" in Figure 10). The cards were deliberately incomplete, often providing only hints, so that users would stay focused on the task. The cards were unstructured: Each card addressed its functional goal without reference to material covered on other cards; the set of cards was delivered as an unbound deck. Finally, each card included specific checkpoint information (to help users detect and diagnose errors) and error recovery information (to help them get back on track).

Experimental evaluations showed that people using the guided exploration cards spent substantially less time yet still performed better on a transfer of skill posttest than people using a commercially developed self-study manual. Taking skill efficiency to be achievement per unit time, the cards were nearly three times as efficient as the manual. Moreover, qualitative analysis of activity protocols showed that the guided exploration cards worked as they were designed to work: They increased attention to the task, they encouraged users to explore (and to do so successfully), they helped people recognize and recover from errors, and they provided a better understanding of task goals. Bell Northern Research subsequently developed a single guided exploration card as the principal training and reference documentation for their Norstar telephone system (see Carroll, 1990).

Particularly at the outset of instruction, it is important to guarantee progress. It can be stimulating to veer off the prescribed path—to explore or to recover from an error—but only if one has some confidence that the prescribed path is still there. In getting users started fast, we often try to scale down the problem space in which they will be acting. One technique we have used is *training wheels* function blocking—that is, simply making advanced functions nonexecutable for learners in the early stages of a tutorial (Carroll & Carrithers, 1984). Learners "see" where the functions are (i.e., in which menus), but they cannot get tangled in those functions at the start and thereby pulled off-path and slowed down with respect to their task-oriented goals.

The Training Wheels interface was designed to block the consequences of major new-user errors. Thus, if a user prematurely selected an advanced function the keystroke would be intercepted and thrown away. Instead of suffering the tangling consequences of such an error, the user was merely informed by a special system message that the function or choice had been disabled in the training system. The Training Wheels design simultaneously reduced the sheer amount of training

**Figure 10**

TYPING SOMETHING

In the terminology of the computer, you will be "creating a document". Use the Task Selection Menu to tell the computer that you want to create a document.

You can give your document <u>any</u> <u>name</u> you want, but you <u>cannot</u> use the same name for two different documents.

You can begin to type when you see a typing page on the screen:

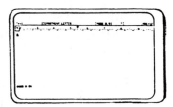

(Think of this display as a blank piece of paper but remember that you do not need to worry about margins or tabs)

Press the big RET (carriage return) key to start a new line (or to skip lines).

When you are <u>done</u> <u>typing</u> or want to leave the typing page to do something else, you want (in the terminology of the computer) to "<u>end</u> use" of your document: Press REQST, type the word "end", and press ENTER.

As you are typing, what you type will appear on the screen.

If you cannot get the Create menu, try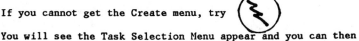

You will see the Task Selection Menu appear and you can then try again.

Is the name of the new document unique?

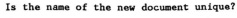

Guided Exploration card: Typing Something is a familiar goal, even to word-processing novices. The card presents a series of procedural hints, a checkpointing hint, and suggestions for error recovery. The different types of information on the card are indicated by iconic labels.

material (that is, error consequences that cannot occur need not be explained) and increased support for error recovery (by attenuating the consequences of certain serious errors). Most important, it accomplished this by making learning by doing more attractive and more feasible (Carroll, Kellogg, & Rosson, 1991).

The approach was to modify the user interface of a commercial word processor, the Displaywriter, to make these error states unreachable. Thus, to continue with earlier examples, it was common for people to misspecify a diskette name. But the error of misspecifying a diskette name is not trivial; it often led to extended periods of frustrating error recovery. The Training Wheels interface blocked the diskette name problem by accepting only the correct diskette name (and continuing to prompt until it was entered correctly), instead of allowing the system to hang itself up waiting for a nonexistent diskette to be mounted. This is shown in Figure 11. Users frequently queued multiple print jobs only to lose track of them before they could be printed. When an unexpected document emerged from the printer, they sometimes engaged in spurious error recovery, in the course of which they might commit real errors. The print queue problem was blocked by limiting the queue to one print job at a time. Instead of suffering the consequences of these errors, the person was merely informed by a special system message that the function or choice had been disabled in the training system.

This design facilitated the minimalist design principles enumerated earlier. It simultaneously allowed the designer to slash training verbiage and better support error recovery: Less verbiage needs to be directed at errors with blocked consequences. It also helped to force a coordination of the system and training by focusing early on real tasks and activities: Error blocking is intended to promote learning by doing. The Training Wheels system looked exactly like the complete commercial system. All of the menus and other displays, as well as the hardware, were exactly the same. If the user followed an error-free course of behavior in creating and printing a simple document, no difference would indeed ever become apparent. However, if a user committed one of the errors that had been blocked, the Training Wheels system would allow the user to get back on course by shielding the person from the tangling consequences of these errors.

In several experimental studies, new users were asked to type and print out a simple document with either the Training Wheels interface or the complete Displaywriter system software. The results of these stud-

**Figure 11**

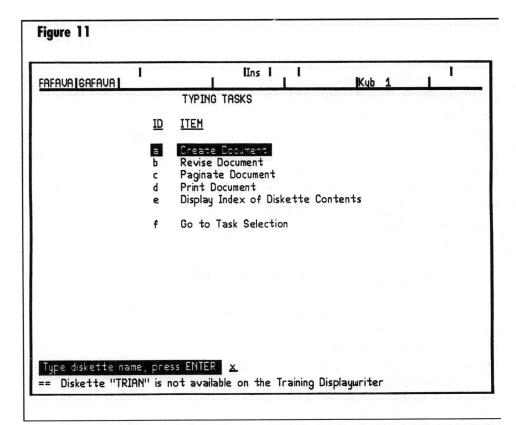

Training Wheels: The interface "blocked" the diskette name error, continuing to prompt for the correct diskette until it was loaded, regardless of what name the user typed (or mistyped). Below the prompt, an error blocking message appeared, informing the user that the immediately prior request (in this case, the specification of TRIAN as the diskette name, instead of TRAIN) was "not available."

ies were quite encouraging: People using the Training Wheels system got started faster, produced better work, and spent less time not only on the errors that our design blocked but on the errors we did not block—indicating a generalized facilitation of skill. Moreover, the magnitude of these advantages increased over the course of the experiment (Carroll & Carrithers, 1984). Finally, those using the Training Wheels system were able to continue developing advanced Displaywriter skills more efficiently after switching to the full function interface (Catrambone & Carroll, 1987).

More recent work has continued to develop the case for getting learners started rapidly using brief and action-oriented materials. The Minimalist Tutorial and Tools for Smalltalk (MiTTS; Rosson, Carroll, &

Bellamy, 1990) introduced procedural programmers (experts in languages like PASCAL and C) to the object-oriented programming language Smalltalk. A 35-page manual is used in conjunction with an instructional environment that presents a graphical animation of a blackjack card game. After 15 minutes the programmer is exercising real code in the blackjack application; in 2 hours the programmer is making changes to the application design and implementation; after 4 to 6 hours the programmer is working on open-ended programming projects enhancing other applications and their graphical user interfaces in novel ways (Carroll & Rosson, 1995). This is a skill domain in which professional programmers often take days or weeks to get started using systems-style tutorials (Rosson & Carroll, 1990).

## Rely on People to Think and Improvise

It is always sad to see a learner trying to cooperatively use typical instructional material and worrying that it might be a mistake to think! Making inferences is engaging to people and very effective in promoting comprehension and memory. A key goal of the *Minimal Manual* (Carroll, Smith-Kerker, Ford, & Mazur-Rimetz, 1987–1988) is to help users edit and print their own documents as quickly as possible. Procedural details are specified to require learners to reason on their own, to become more exploratory, and therefore more involved in their activity (for example, in Figure 12 the cursor key function is identified by a reference to one of the arrow keys; it is left to the user to work out the navigational details). Once a function had been discussed, users were expected to be able to recall, reconstruct, or retrieve it (thus, after printing was introduced, they were told merely to print). Stress was placed on foregrounding tasks that the learners might recognize and were already prepared to think about; chapters had titles like "Printing Something on Paper" instead of "Menus, Messages, and Helps" (the latter a real and notorious example). Users created their first document only seven pages into the *Minimal Manual.* In the commercial manual the creation of a first document was delayed until page 70. Many skills were practiced and refined through open-ended "on your own" exercises, as illustrated in Figure 12. We wanted to get the learners thinking about word-processing skill and activity as soon as possible.

Our results were extremely encouraging. In one experiment, people used one of five training methods (including two variations of the

**Figure 12**

Topic 6: 2

DELETING BLANK LINES

The Displaywriter stores blank lines as carrier return **CHARACTERS.**

USE ↑ TO POSITION THE CURSOR AT THE BEGINNING OF THE SECOND LINE OF THE FIRST PARAGRAPH OF Smith Letter.

PRESS CARRIER RETURN ONCE.

You have inserted a blank line in the paragraph.

USE ↑ TO POSITION THE CURSOR AT THE BEGINNING OF THE BLANK LINE -- ALL THE WAY AT THE LEFT.

As you can see, a special highlighted carrier return character appears. This is the special character that was inserted when you originally pressed CARRIER RETURN.

PRESS THE DEL KEY.

WHEN THE DISPLAYWRITER PROMPTS YOU: Delete What?, PRESS ENTER.

The blank line disappears. You have deleted the special CARRIER RETURN character.

ON YOUR OWN

You can use these techniques to insert and then delete underlined and centered material. Experiment with deletion. When you are finished, END the Smith Letter document, and then print it out.

*Minimal Manual:* The specification of cursor movement is incomplete, relying on the user to experiment and discover procedural details. The "blank line" metaphor is employed as a minimal explanation of line-end formatting characters. An "on your own" exercise is included to practice and refine skills in a more realistically open-ended task context.

*Minimal Manual*) for up to 7 full working days. The *Minimal Manual* proved to be substantially faster than the other manuals for the basic topic areas it covered—and it produced achievement at least as good as the other methods. The *Minimal Manual* only covered basic topics, whereas the commercial manuals covered advanced topics as well. In a later phase of the experiment, *Minimal Manual* users were transferred to the advanced topics sections of a commercial manual. They still were substantially faster, but in this comparison their performance on achievement tests was better by a factor of eight. In sum, this experiment provided evidence that the final *Minimal Manual* was an order of magnitude more effective than systems-style commercial manual designs (Carroll et al., 1987–1988). A follow-up experiment showed that encouraging inference was specifically effective in creating the advantages of the *Minimal Manual* (Black, Carroll, & McGuigan, 1987).

In more recent work, my colleagues and I have tried to support particular kinds of inference, appropriate to particular training domains. In the *view matcher* environment for learning Smalltalk (Carroll, Singer, Bellamy, & Alpert, 1990) we provided a set of coordinated views of a running application. Programmers could run a graphics application, like a gomoku game (a generalization of tic-tac-toe), and explore the execution stack of Smalltalk methods at various points in the game flow. Such a real and open-ended task can be introduced succinctly in the instruction (it took one manual page), but it can provide the learner with a substantial opportunity to create an understanding through genuine work activity. Instead of telling programmers how interactive Smalltalk applications are designed and implemented, we made it convenient and interesting for the programmers to find out on their own.

My colleagues and I have also tried to support and encourage learner reflection. In the MoleHill intelligent tutoring system for Smalltalk programming (Singley & Carroll, 1995; Singley et al., 1991), we provided a *goalposter* window that displayed our best guess about the learner's current goal hierarchy (presented as an indented list). Our hope was that this visualization would promote more reflection on the part of the learner about how various goals are related and about which goals should be pursued. MoleHill also included a *guru* tool, an animated bitmap of a wizened Smalltalk programmer, which could be called up at the end of a tutorial project to provide situated critique on ways the programmer could improve his or her strategy. We hoped that immediately after completing a project, the learner would be especially receptive to suggestions about new ways to think about working on the project (Alpert, Singley, & Carroll, 1995).

## Embed Information in Real Tasks

Adult learners want to create a work product. To such learners, learning a word processor "for learning's sake" seems ridiculous. In our early work on office systems, my colleagues and I always gave prominence to typing, printing, and revising real documents. In the Bell Northern Research (BNR) guided exploration card, the user is invited to adjust ring volume and set a personal ring—a task that has immediate and concrete consequences in the work environment—but that also provides a context for learning about system components and feature codes more generally. In field trials, the BNR group found that 78% of their users read the card through; the comparison figure for standard materials is no higher than 30%. Moreover, 90% of the users claimed that the cards were as good or better than standard materials and as complete. Even in cases for which there were back-up manuals, half of the users relied only on the card. During the development process, they found it was easier to get useful feedback in field trials, because people really were reading and using the materials. Their cards cost about a fifth as much to produce as standard materials (see Carroll, 1990).

In the Smalltalk programming domain, we rejected syntax exercises in favor of creating and enhancing concrete software objects and applications. For example, in the *view matcher* (Figure 13), we presented a graphical gomoku game with a special *stealmove* method that permitted the game to occasionally take two moves at once; our objective was to evoke motivation in the learner directed at understanding and correcting this behavior (Carroll et al., 1990). In our MiTTS package, we guided learners in enhancing a blackjack game, redefining one of its methods to streamline the flow of the game (Rosson et al., 1990). In the MoleHill intelligent tutoring system, we guided learners to create a new kind of textpane that displays input characters in uppercase—it is comprehensible, concrete, and empowering for a new Smalltalk programmer to be able to make a fundamental change in the system's functionality in the first instructional project (Singley et al., 1991).

Another aspect of embedding information in real tasks is to provide commentary and help information without interrupting the learner's activity. This is a tricky balancing problem: Often it can be distract-

**Figure 13**

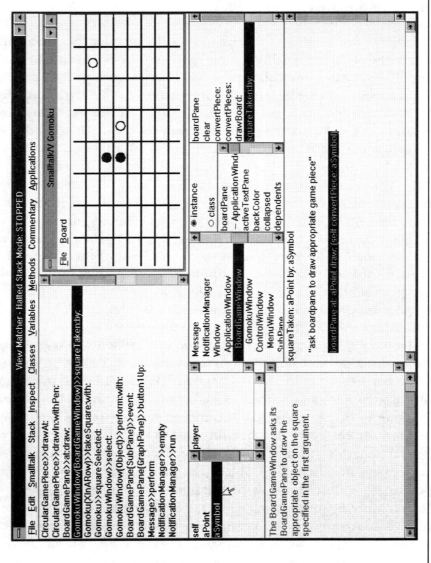

View Matcher: The View Matcher coordinates multiple views of a running Smalltalk program. The Application View (a gomoku game board) is in the upper right; the Stack View in the upper left displays the methods currently executing, the Inspector View (the two panes below the Stack View) displays objects involved in the currently selected method computation, the Commentary View in the lower left displays an application-level description of the currently-executing code, the Hierarchy View (the grouping of four panes in the lower right) is a filtered code browser providing access to the classes and methods that constitute the application.

ing to provide help that is not under the user's control (Carroll & McKendree, 1991). But often this is because system-initiated help interrupts the learners saying, in effect, "Wait! You made a mistake!" My colleagues and I have developed a number of techniques for passively providing commentary as a side-effect of the user's activity, but the commentary merely provides concomitant information. For example, Mole-Hill includes a *commentator* tool that provides problem-specific documentation for chunks of selected code (code the user has selected in the course of editing the program). The View Matcher includes a *commentary* pane in which a task-oriented description of the currently displayed program state is documented; it is intended to help guide the learner's analysis of the current execution stack (see Figure 12). Both of these documentation tools are editable—that is, the learner can add or edit the displayed text to make it more personally useful in the future.

## Take Advantage of What People Already Know

Figure 12 illustrates how the *Minimal Manual* sought to engage the user's prior knowledge. In describing procedures for removing unwanted line-end characters from the data stream, the manual specifically introduced the "blank line" metaphor as a way of identifying the problem. (Calling something a *blank line* emphasizes that it is a thing, not just nothing, and that it needs to be addressed.) It is important to note, however, that it then went on to identify the difference between the metaphoric reference (a physical blank line) and the word processing problem (the presence of a line-end character). In an ideal situation, pointing to such a divergence would serve not only to aid users in correcting this specific problem but also to initiate processing, leading to more general insights about the control of page layout via special formatting characters (Carroll & Mack, 1985).

One of the main things my colleagues and I try to do with the commentary tools in learning environments like MoleHill and the View Matcher is to create a bridge between the concepts our learners already have (e.g., the procedural programming concept of a "call stack" of procedures that call other procedures in order to execute) and the concepts we are trying to help them construct (e.g., again in the View Matcher, the "method execution stack" of methods currently in communication with other methods—in our case, trying to finish processing a user request made through the interface controls). People rely on what they already know when they try to learn about something novel anyway; we try to put that meta-strategy to productive use. In the case of View Matcher, this led us to immediately present our Smalltalk learners with a code visualization that typically is not encountered until a later stage of use (see Figure 13).

Some of the prior knowledge users have is of course attained in the current learning context, just at a slightly earlier point in time. In our MiTTS package we tried to explicitly leverage this kind of prior knowledge by using a *scaffolded design* (Bruner, 1960). In the first part of the tutorial, the programmer works with a purely functional view of the blackjack game—only the application classes and methods are presented; no code is shown. The programmer creates blackjack objects in a workspace and sends messages to them to study how the game makes computations. In the second part of the tutorial, the programmer is provided with the user interface classes and methods and with the View Matcher environment for tracing message sends in conjunction with running the application. At this point, no Smalltalk code is displayed. In the third part, the programmer again works with only the blackjack classes and methods in a workspace, but now the code is shown and the programmer analyzes the code-level details and makes code enhancements. In the fourth part, the game and its user interface are presented via the View Matcher environment with all the relevant codes; the programmer works on a user interface enhancement. This presentation allows simpler, initial experiences to directly support subsequent, more complex activity; it reinforces the software architecture of separating application code from user interface code; it even helps the learner sort out the difference between the basic Smalltalk environment and system tools and the special View Matcher environment we created (Carroll & Rosson, 1995; Rosson et al., 1990).

My colleagues and I have also experimented with adapting typical real-world helping situations to an electronic venue. In our Specialist Help demonstration system (Kirson, Carroll, Eckhoff, Kelley, & Canetti, 1988), we created video clips in which "typical users" described episodes from their use of the system as a means of conveying rules-of-thumb to new users. This kind of helping occurs naturally in user communities; we were interested in whether it could be packaged as random-access video information. The demonstration seemed intriguing, but the system was never built.

## Support Error Recognition and Recovery

People do not want to make errors or to spend time recovering from errors. Many features in our instructional systems seek to reduce the number and severity of learner errors by simplifying the problem domain (e.g., hiding task-irrelevant complexity, as the View Matcher does in displaying only the Smalltalk classes and methods that are relevant to the current application project; Carroll et al., 1990), by protecting learners from error consequences (as Training Wheels function blocking does; Carroll & Carrithers, 1984), and by explicitly coordinating different information sources (as the View Matcher does by presenting a set of coordinated, alternative views of a running application; Carroll et al., 1990), and as the minimal manuals do by incorporating many checkpoints—for example, "Can you find this prompt on the display: Type ID letter to choose ITEM; press ENTER" (Carroll et al., 1987–1988).

Errors are, however, compelling opportunities to learn. In our manuals, my colleagues and I worked hard to develop error recovery information: When people realize they have made an error, they can become acutely focused on the problem of recovering. They become more interested in how the system or tutorial software works. All this can be quite productive in the end if the manual or other tutorial material provides adequate guidance and support. The *Minimal Manual* was less than a quarter the length of the standard Displaywriter manual (it included no repetition, summaries, reviews, practice exercises, or material not related to doing office work); however, relative to the commercial, systems-style manual, it significantly increased error recovery material. For example, new Displaywriter users often had trouble with the diskette name concept and misspecified a diskette when prompted, which had the effect of leaving the system hung up. The system recovery procedure for this problem, perhaps because it involved a compound keypress, was not presented in the introductory documentation. Based on the fact that beginning users actually made the error and could not recover from it, the *Minimal Manual* included the specific error recovery procedure.

As mentioned earlier, my colleagues and I provided a GoalPoster tool in the MoleHill tutor that displayed a best-guess analysis of the learner's current goal tree. When a goal was recognized that was not part of the correct project solution, it was displayed in the GoalPoster in red. Of course, the system's analysis of the learner's goals was not presented as foolproof, but these red goals were at least suggestions about where the learner might look in his or her own planning for a possible error. The learner could request help on any goal listed in the GoalPoster, but help for the red goals guided error recovery (Anderson, Boyle, Farrell, & Reiser, 1989; Singley & Carroll, 1996).

## The Challenge of a Better Design Practice

Minimalism has shown itself to be a broadly applicable, technical approach to the paradox of sense-making. Many techniques have been developed; many more remain to be developed. Certainly, in the past decade no other approach to instructional design has produced such consistently strong and positive results in such a variety of application domains, learner populations, and research–development contexts (van der Meij & Carroll, 1995). However, minimalist design for active users is not necessarily easy design.

The minimalist approach requires that one take a tough-minded position. One must put a higher premium on what can be eliminated than on what can be included. One must rely on the user to be a competent manager of the situation. One must deliberately not explain everything, but rather explain only what is necessary. One must incorporate testing with real users to determine what tasks are initially important, interesting, and attractive, and one must use that information to direct the development of the system and training. Perhaps most important, when there is a user problem, one must not automatically add functions or build additional training modules but must consider removing the function or documentation material associated with the problem. This is a radical alternative.

The minimalist approach is not easily implemented from an organizational standpoint, because it fundamentally conflicts with the standard practice of providing overly thorough systems and documentation and of remedying observed user problems with the addition of further enhancements. Professionals often prefer methods that are well-specified, even if plodding, and are satisfied with results that are mediocre. This is just the right strategy for someone who suspects he or she may actually be incompetent. Minimalism is not for these people. It is wide open methodologically; it requires that the instructional designer seriously understand the application domain, seriously understand the learner's prior knowledge and understanding of the task. It urges the designer to create new techniques, new kinds of opportunities for learners—to take the chance of creating excellent instruction. Rummler (1965) encountered a similar problem with lean programming: Managers worried that without the minute, rote steps, the program could not be complete. As Rummler put it, they confused buying training frames with buying change in behavior.

Learners too have been socialized to systematic design. I have been asked many times by learners for drill-and-practice, for a thicker manual—even though they were performing significantly better than their control-group colleagues. Derivative research is now beginning to appear that suggests minimalist approaches are suitable for "courageous" learners but not for "timid" learners. Clearly, the issue must be settled by further research, but my guess is that this is indeed simply a matter of learners being socialized by systematic instructional design that is fundamentally unsuitable for them but still familiar and therefore (perversely) preferable.

Because change is always difficult, it is important to focus on the well-documented examples of pioneering change. The Learning Products Group of Hewlett-Packard's Electronic Design Division applied the minimalist model to the development of training materials for the HP Printed Circuit Design System, a computer-aided design (CAD) system (Vanderlinden, Cocklin, & McKita, 1988; Vanderlinden, McKita, & Cocklin, 1988). The group was motivated to try a different approach to training design by the poor performance of step-by-step materials, particularly with regard to learner retention.

Initially, they were concerned that the complexity of the CAD system would limit the applicability of a minimalist approach: The command and menu sequences required for basic CAD operations are more deeply nested than those in the text systems. And they confessed the fear they experienced in giving up a more established design approach: "As technical writers, we were trained to write specific, clear, and complete procedures for end-users. The GE [guided exploration] approach ran contrary to our training in that it required us to write truncated 'hints' that were often left purposefully incomplete. We simply had to learn to take risks in the hopes that we would create tutorials that would provide users a more active learning situation" (Vanderlinden, McKita, & Cocklin, 1988).

Their evaluation studies showed that the minimalist materials were superior to standard self-study materials across CAD tasks. The minimalist users incurred fewer problems in carrying out tutorial exercises and required fewer experimenter interventions. After training, the minimalist users completed a posttest in half the time taken by their self-study counterparts. During the posttest, the minimalist users were more likely to solve their problems by trying things out with the system, whereas the self-study people were more likely to reread the tutorial. On the basis of these tests, the Hewlett-Packard group decided to use the minimalist model for the final product. Their minimalist materials were iteratively refined by addressing specific problems identified in the initial testing and were extended into a complete tutorial for the entire CAD system. Subsequent user testing has shown even greater performance advantages for the complete minimalist curriculum (Vanderlinden, McKita, & Cocklin, 1988).

## Conclusion

Things are changing in the right direction. Every time an instructional designer takes the chance to address the paradox of sense-making and succeeds, there is a little more pressure on the plodders hiding behind merely systematic methods and mediocre results. Once we know we can do better, why should we settle for that? In the same way, when a person who might have been classified as a "timid" learner takes the chance to seek meaning in instructional activity, perhaps engaging in opportunistic exploration after an error the manual designer overlooked, the tyranny of systematic expectations eases. Once we know that learning by doing, by thinking, by engaging in genuine activities, by using what we already know, and by recovering from error can be effective and efficient, why should we settle for drill-and-practice that barely works? People can learn to design better instructional materials, and they can also learn to prefer better instructional materials.

## References

Alpert, S. R., Singley, M. K., & Carroll, J. M. (1995). Multiple multimodal mentors: Delivering computer-based instruction via specialized anthropomorphic advisors. *Behaviour and Information Technology, 14,* 69–79.

Anderson, J. R., Boyle, C. F., Farrell, R., & Reiser, B. J. (1989). Cognitive principles in the design of computer tutors. In F. Morris (Ed.), *Modeling cognition* (pp. 93–134). New York: Wiley.

Black, J. B., Carroll, J. M., & McGuigan, S. M. (1987). What kind of minimal instruction manual is most effective. In J. M. Carroll & P. P. Tanner (Eds.), *Proceedings of*

*CHI+GI'87 Human Factors in Computing Systems and Graphics Interface* (pp. 5–9). New York: Association for Computing Machinery.

Bruner, J. (1960). *The process of education.* Cambridge, MA: MIT Press.

Carroll, J. M. (1990). *The Nurnberg Funnel: Designing Minimalist instruction for practical computer skill.* Cambridge, MA: MIT Press.

Carroll, J. M., & Carrithers, C. (1984). Blocking learner errors in a training wheels system. *Human Factors, 26*(4), 377–389.

Carroll, J. M., Kellogg, W. A., & Rosson, M. B. (1991). The task-artifact cycle. In J. M. Carroll (Ed.), *Designing Interaction: Psychology at the human-computer interface* (pp. 74–102). New York: Cambridge University Press.

Carroll, J. M., & Mack, R. L. (1985). Metaphor, computing systems, and active learning. *International Journal of Man-Machine Studies, 22,* 39–57.

Carroll, J. M., Mack, R. L., Lewis, C. H., Grischkowsky, N. L., & Robertson, S. R. (1985). Exploring exploring a word processor. *Human Computer Interaction, 1,* 283–307.

Carroll, J. M., & Mazur, S. A. (1986). LisaLearning. IEEE *Computer, 19*(11), 35–49.

Carroll, J. M., & McKendree, J. E. (1991). Interface design issues for intelligent advisory systems. In A. Kent & J. G. Williams (Eds.), *Encyclopedia of computer science and technology* (pp. 111–142). New York: Marcel Dekker.

Carroll, J. M., & Rosson, M. B. (1985). Usability specifications as a tool in iterative development. In H. R. Hartson (Ed.), *Advances in human-computer interaction* (pp. 1–28). Norwood, NJ: Ablex.

Carroll, J. M., & Rosson, M. B. (1987). Paradox of the active user. In J. M. Carroll (Ed.), *Interfacing thought: Cognitive aspects of human-computer interaction* (pp. 80–111). Cambridge, MA: MIT Press.

Carroll, J. M., & Rosson, M. B. (1995). Managing evaluation goals for training. *Communications of the Association of Computing Machinery, 38*(7), 40–48.

Carroll, J. M., Smith-Kerker, P. A., Ford, J. R., & Mazur-Rimetz, S. A. (1987–1988). The minimal manual. *Human Computer Interaction, 3,* 123–153.

Carroll, J. M., Singer, J. A., Bellamy, R. K. E., & Alpert, S. R. (1990). A view matcher for learning Smalltalk. In J. C. Chew & J. Whiteside (Eds.), *Proceedings of CHI'90: Human Factors in Computing Systems* (pp. 431–437). New York: Association of Computing Machinery.

Catrambone, R., & Carroll, J. M. (1987). Learning a word processing system with training wheels and guided exploration. In J. M. Carroll & P. P. Tanner (Eds.), *Proceedings of CHI+GI'87 Human Factors in Computing Systems and Graphics Interface* (pp. 169–174). New York: Association of Computing Machinery.

Gagné, R. M., & Briggs, L. J. (1979). *Principles of instructional design.* (2nd ed.). New York: Holt, Rinehart, & Winston.

Kirson, D. S., Carroll, J. M., Eckhoff, R., Kelley, J. F., & Canetti, S. (1988, May). Specialist help with multiple media. In *CHI'88 Conference on Human Factors in Computing Systems,* SIGGRAPH Video Review, 30.

Mack, R. L., Lewis, C. H., & Carroll, J. M. (1983). Learning to use word processors: Problems and prospects. *Association of Computing Machinery Transactions on Office Information Systems, 1*(3), 254–271.

Rosson, M. B., & Carroll, J. M. (1990, January). Climbing the Smalltalk mountain. *Special Interest Group on Computer–Human Interaction Bulletin, 21*(3), 76–79.

Rosson, M. B., Carroll, J. M., & Bellamy, R. K. E. (1990). Smalltalk Scaffolding: A minimalist curriculum. In J. C. Chew & J. Whiteside (Eds.), *Proceedings of CHI'90: Human Factors in Computing Systems* (pp. 423–429). New York: Association of Computing Machinery.

Rummler, G. A. (1965, December). The economics of lean programming. *NSPI Journal.* Reprinted in *Improving Human Performance, 3,* 1973, 211–216.

Singley, M. K., & Carroll, J. M. (1996). Synthesis by analysis: Five modes of reasoning that guide design. In T. P. Moran & J. M. Carroll (Eds.), *Design rationale: Concepts, techniques and use* (pp. 241–255). Hillsdale, NJ: Erlbaum.

Singley, M. K., Carroll, J. M., & Alpert, S. A. (1991). Psychological design rationale for an intelligent tutoring system for Smalltalk. In J. Koenemann-Belliveau, T. Moher, & S. Robertson (Eds.), *Empirical studies of programmers, Fourth Workshop* (pp. 196–209). Norwood, NJ: Ablex.

Van der Meij, H., & Carroll, J. M. (1995). Principles and heuristics for designing minimalist instruction. *Technical Communication, 42*(2), 243–261.

Vanderlinden, G., Cocklin, T. G., & McKita, M. (1988). Designing tutorials that help users learn through exploration. *Proceedings of the International Professional Communications Conference* (pp. 295–299). New York, NY: IEEE Professional Communication Society.

Vanderlinden, G., McKita, M., & Cocklin, T. G. (1988). Testing and developing minimalist tutorials: A case history. *Proceedings of the 35th International Technical Communications Conference* (pp. 196–199). Arlington, VA: Society for Technical Communication.

# Index

Abel, K., 240
Abilities, 156
Abrahamson, E., 50
Abstracted knowledge, 102
Abstraction, 93
Accommodation, 236
Ackerman, P. L., 143, 182, 208–209, 212, 217–218
ACT (Adaptive Control of Thought) theory, 92, 97, 228
Active learner, 304–307
Adams, J. S., 203–204
Adams, L. T., 289
Adaptability
   defining and investigating, 109–110
   importance of transfer environment in building, 111–112
Adaptive expertise, 91
   and learning outcomes, 93–96
   research gap on, 110
   versus routine expertise, 92–93
   training design strategies to build, 99–108
Ad hoc category node hypothesis, 129–130
Adler, P. S., 177
Adoption stage in technology, 235
Advanced manufacturing techniques (AMT), 21
Advanced organizers, 99, 101–102, 266
Aging workforce
   training implications of, 16–18
   as trend, 16

Albert, S., 42
Albrecht, K., 103–104
Alderfer, C. P., 46, 202
Alderman, R., 66
Alexander, G. P., 42
Alkov, R. A., 250
Allen, G. A., 80
Alliger, G. M., 153, 179
Alluisi, E. A., 262, 264, 273
Alpert, S. A., 304, 317–318, 324
Altmann, A., 103–105
Alutto, J. A., 50–51
Ames, C., 107, 182
Anderson, J. R., 3, 68, 71, 92, 98, 121, 165, 208, 228, 232–233, 235, 291, 324
Anderson, M. C., 80
Andrews, D. H., 262
Animation
   in demonstrations, 282, 285–286
   efficacy of, in instruction based on, 286–287
   motivational aspects of, in training, 283–286
   in software training, 281–298
Apprenticeship model, 161–162
Archer, J., 107
Argyris, C., 40
Arthur, E. J., 238, 240–242, 244
Ash, R. A., 32
Ashe, D. K., 190
Ashford, S. J., 49
Ashworth, C. A., 284

Assimilation, 236
Attitudinal measures, 154
Auble, P. A., 289
Ausubel, D. P., 99
Automaticity, 119–120, 154
Automatic performance, development
    of, 135
Automatic processing, 98, 160
Aviram, A., 218
Avner, A., 287

Baddeley, A. D., 67, 71, 73–74
Baffes, P., 227
Baggett, P., 282, 286, 291, 297
Bagshaw, C. E., 229
Bahrick, H. P., 66–67, 71
Bailey, J. H., 240
Baker, D. P., 259–260, 262
Baldwin, T. T., 3, 34, 46, 89, 91, 152,
    178–179, 181, 187, 215, 218, 233,
    264
Bandura, A., 183, 203–204, 206–207,
    253
Bassok, M., 101, 161, 290–291
Batsell, R. R., 284
Baudhuin, E. S., 225
Bavetta, A. G., 205, 216–218
Baylis, G., 120, 128–131, 143
Bayman, P., 292, 297
Beach, L. R., 37, 204
Beard, R. L., 250, 255
Beckman, B. C., 240–241
Beckschi, P. F., 33
Beer, M., 32, 39, 41, 55
Begg, I. M., 289
Behavioral learning, 211–212
Behavioral modeling, 217–218, 268
Behavior paradigm, 159–160
Beissner, K., 166, 169
Belasco, J., 50–51
Bell, A. G., 227
Bell, E. L., 46
Bell, H. H., 262
Bellamy, R. K. E., 315, 317–318, 322
Benedetti, R., 238
Benjamin, A. S., 61, 63, 76
Bereiter, C., 95, 106
Bernardin, H. J., 214
Beyer, J. M., 49
Biasiotto, J., 66
Biegel, J. E., 229

Bielaczyk, K., 291
Bierhoff, H. W., 43–44
Biersner, R. J., 46, 182–183, 186
Biocca, F., 237–238, 241, 243
Bird, A. M., 71
Birren, J. E., 17
Bjork, E. L., 80
Bjork, R. A., 4, 34, 36, 38, 61, 63–64,
    67, 69, 71, 73–76, 78–81, 83–84,
    91, 97, 283, 287, 290, 293, 297
Black, J. B., 317
Blaiwes, A. S., 253, 260
Blau, B. S., 238–241, 243
Bless, H., 79
Blickensderfer, E. L., 263–264, 268
Bliss, J. P., 238–241, 243
Blocked conditions, 69
Bloom, B. S., 156
Bobko, P., 205
Bolman, L. G., 32, 51
Bolstad, C. A., 291
Boman, D., 238, 241–244
Booth, B., 69, 71
Borman, W. C., 41
Bosman, E. A., 16–18
Bovair, S., 296–297
Bower, G. H., 72
Bowers, C. A., 254, 259, 261, 267
Boyle, C. F., 233, 235, 325
Brannick, M. T., 259
Bransford, J. D., 81, 289
Brebner, J., 121–124
Bretz, R. D., Jr., 38, 40
Bricken, M., 238
Briggs, G. E., 250
Briggs, L. J., 110, 178, 233, 307–308
Broach, D., 45, 184
Brodbeck, F., 104
Brooks, G. H., 229
Brown, J. S., 75, 161, 163, 227
Brown, K. G., 107
Bruner, J. S., 289
Buckley, J., 133, 135
Buckley, M. R., 214
Bunzo, M., 235
Burke, M. J., 35, 215
Burns, J. L., 234
Burton, R. R., 227
Busato, V. V., 103, 106
Butterfield, E. C., 93, 97, 105, 109
Byrne, C. M., 238

Cairney, P., 121, 124
Calderwood, R., 133
Campbell, D. T., 34, 44–45, 170
Campbell, J. P., 31, 38, 170
Campbell, R. J., 253
Campion, M. A., 258, 260
Canetti, S., 321
Cannon-Bowers, J. A., 101, 112, 188–189, 233, 249–250, 252–254, 256, 258, 260–264, 266–269, 271, 273
Capps, C. G., 234
Carbonell, J. R., 227
Cardy, R. L., 39
Career ladders, 26
Carey, L., 155, 158
Carlo, M. S., 94, 153, 170
Carlson, R. A., 71, 103
Carnevale, A. P., 35
Carrithers, C., 304, 312, 315, 324
Carroll, J. M., 284, 287–288, 304, 309, 311–313, 315, 317–318, 322, 323–324
Carron, A. V., 66
Carson, C. E., 132–133, 139
Carson, K., 39
Carter, R. C., 135
Cascio, W. F., 34, 151
Catalano, J. F., 68
Catrambone, R., 293, 296–297, 315
Cavazos, R., 70–71
Chamberlin, C., 66
Chandler, P., 290
Chao, G. T., 24
Charness, N., 16–18
Charney, D. H., 288, 290, 293, 297
Charron, R., 235
Chesworth, L., 286
Chi, M. T. H., 92, 94, 167, 291
Choice-reaction tasks, skill at responding in, 120–131
Christina, R. W., 63, 83
Chrysler, S. T., 238, 240–242, 244
Cisero, C. A., 94, 153, 170
Clancey, W. J., 227
Clark, C. S., 183, 192
Clark, R. E., 99, 101
Classical conditioning, 202
Clinton-Cirocco, A., 133
Cocklin, T. G., 326–327
Cognitive apprenticeship, 163
Cognitive learning, 4, 97, 179, 208–211

Cognitive load theory, 290
Cognitive maps, 94
Cohen, G., 289
Cohen, M. D., 37
Cohen, R. L., 43–44
Cole, P., 107
Collins, A., 161, 163, 227
Compatibility effects, 121–127
Complexity of jobs, 21–23
Computer-aided instruction (CAI), 227
Computer-assisted instruction systems, 225
Computer-based simulations, 225
Computer-based training (CBT), 168
Computer software training, 215
Computer users, sense-making activities of, in minimalist training, 303–326
Conditioning
    classical, 202
    operant, 202–203
Configural stimuli, problem of unequal training and search for, 137–142
Connor, S., 44
Construct validation, 170
Contemporary learning theory, 209
Contextual influences, in training effectiveness, 177–194
Continuous learning, 1
Converse, S. A., 250, 252, 254–256, 269
Conway, M. A., 289
Cook, T. D., 34, 44–45, 48
Cooke, N. J., 21, 89, 167
Cooper, C., 214, 216
Cooper, G. E., 252
Cooper, M., 290
Coovert, M. D., 259–260
Cordray, D. S., 27
Cormier, S. M., 97
Cornett, L. L., 285
Correct responding, 72
Cotten, D. J., 66
Cotton, J. L., 185
Crandall, S. R., 178
Cream, B. W., 264
Creative staffing, 26
Criterion problem, 170
Cronbach, L. J., 111, 170, 182, 189
Cross-cultural management training, 215–216
Cross-training, 269, 271

Cutrell, E., 138–142, 144
Czerwinski, M. P., 62, 138–144

Daft, R., 52
Dandridge, T. C., 49
Daniels, D., 208
Dansereau, F., 181
Davis, D. D., 25
Day, D. V., 214
Day, J. D., 96
Day, N. E., 38
Day, R. R., 35, 215
Deal, T. E., 32, 51
Decatur, M., 44
Decker, P. J., 159–160, 215
Declarative knowledge, 165, 208, 210
Decontextualized knowledge, 101
Dede, C., 229, 233
Deductive approach, 102
DeJong, R., 128
Demaree, R. G., 190
DeMeuse, K. P., 249
Demonstration-based methods of team
    training, 267
Dempster, F. N., 36, 71, 84
Design, 110
Deutsch, M., 44
Development paradigm, 160–161
Diagonal transfer task, 141
Dick, W., 155, 158, 166
Dickinson, T. L., 250, 254–255
Dimick, D. E., 32, 35, 53
Dipboye, R. L., 12
Discovery learning, 229
    distinction between error-training
        and, 104–105
    general advantages of active, 288–
        289
    general disadvantages of, 289
    research on, 102–103, 105
    studies, 102–103
Display variability, 215
Distributed Interactive Simulation
    (DIS), 262
Diversity
    changes in definition of, 19–20
    training implications of, 19–21
DiVesta, F. J., 101
Dixon, C. M., 229
Dixon, N. M., 37, 40
Dixon, P., 291

Dobbins, G. H., 39, 183, 192
Domain expert, 229
Domingues, D. A., 70–71
Dorner, D., 95
Downsizing, 2, 24–26
Driskell, J. E., 214, 216, 253
Drucker, P. F., 1, 22, 25
Druckman, D., 34, 36, 38
Dunnette, M. D., 38
Duffy, L. T., 256
Duffy, T. M., 233, 282
Duguid, P., 161, 163
Dulebohn, J., 215
Duncan, J., 124, 136–137
Duncan, M. K., 290
Duncan, P. C., 267, 271, 273
Dunnette, M. D., 38
Dutta, A., 6, 62, 92, 98, 121–131, 143
Dutton, J. E., 49
Dweck, C. S., 107, 159
Dwyer, D. J., 250, 262
Dyer, J. L., 254

Earles, J. A., 179, 182
Eckhoff, R., 321
Eden, D., 207, 218
Egan, D. E., 103
Egeth, H. E., 135
Eggan, G., 235
Eggemeier, F. T., 133, 135, 264
Elio, R., 98
Elkerton, J., 283, 286–287, 290–291,
    294
Elliott, E. S., 107
Ellis, H. C., 71
Ellis, J. A., 289
Elshout, J. J., 103, 106
Engleberg, M., 238
Epstein, W., 75
Equipment Maintenance Tutor, 226
Error-based learning, 104
Error-based training, 105
    distinction between discovery learn-
        ing and, 104–105
Estes, W. K., 67, 80
Etelapelto, A., 95, 105
Evaluation criteria, linking training ob-
    jectives to, 151–173
Evaluation measures, framework for de-
    veloping, 155–167
Executive-level skills, building, 105–108
Exercise, 261–262

Expectancy theory, 203
Expert knowledge base, 229

Fairness perceptions, 184
Farkas, D. K., 289
Farnham-Diggory, S., 159–161
Farr, J. L., 184, 191
Farrell, R., 235, 291, 324
Fatigue, effect of, on learning, 66
Faust, G. W., 156
Feature integration theory (FIT), 136
Feedback, 263
    frequency of, 96
        impact of, on learning, 67–68
    need for, in self-regulation, 205–206
Feldman, D. C., 47
Feldman, E. M., 62, 133, 138–142, 144
Feltovich, P. J., 92, 94
Feltz, D. L., 205
Ferris, G. R., 32, 47
Filipczak, B., 19
Fischer, R. L., 27
Fischoff, B., 77, 80
Fisher, C. D., 42
Fisher, D. L., 137–138
Fisher, L. M., 17
Fisk, A. D., 98, 133–135, 142–143, 264
Fiske, D. W., 170
Fitts, P. M., 92
Flagg, B. N., 233
Flavell, J. H., 95
Fleishman, E. A., 179–182
Flexman, R. E., 225
Flight simulators, 225
Floden, R. E., 51
Folger, R., 43, 45, 184, 187
Ford, J. K., 3–6, 20, 34, 38, 61–62, 89–
    91, 93–94, 99, 107, 109, 111, 152–
    154, 157–162, 164, 166–167, 170,
    172–173, 178–179, 181, 183, 185,
    189, 191–193, 233, 264
Ford, J. L., 233
Ford, J. R., 315, 318
Foreman, G., 233
Formative evaluation, 234
Foushee, H. C., 256
Fowlkes, J. E., 260, 267, 272
Frame-of-reference (FOR) training, 214
Francis, J. L., 19
Franks, J. J., 81, 289
Franz, T., 260, 267, 272

Frayne, C., 204, 216
Frederick, E., 205
Fredericksen, J. R., 4
Free-sort tasks, 167
Frensch, P. A., 95
Frequent feedback, 96
Frese, M., 103–105
Friedlander, B. Z., 289
Froggatt, D. A., 185
Frye, D., 233–234
Fullerton, H. N., 19
Futrell, D., 249

Gaba, D. M., 271
Gagné, R. M., 34, 110, 153, 156, 166,
    178–179, 185, 233, 307–308
Galade, G., 135
Garbart, H., 135
Garner, W. R., 132
Gelade, G., 136
George-Falvy, J., 208
Ghatala, E. S., 95
Ghiselin, B., 19
Ghodsian, Dina, 61, 63
Gholson, B., 290
Gick, M. L., 3, 71, 83, 91, 97–99, 101–
    102, 109–110, 289–291
Gilliam, P., 19–20, 23, 28, 89, 177,
    179–180
Gist, M. E., 183, 204–206, 209, 215–
    218, 286
Gitomer, D. H., 161
Glaser, R., 92, 94, 101, 161, 164, 167,
    235, 264, 291
Glenberg, A. M., 75
Glickman, A. S., 253, 260
Goal setting training, 217
Goff, M., 209
Goldsmith, T., 169
Goldstein, A. P., 160
Goldstein, I. L., 2, 4–6, 19–20, 23, 28,
    33–34, 35–36, 39, 65, 89–90, 155,
    158, 177–180, 185, 191–193, 201,
    233–234, 259
Golembiewski, R. T., 52
Gooding, R. Z., 185
Goranson, R. E., 77
Gormican, S., 136
Grabinger, R. S., 235
Graf, P., 289
Graham, S., 108

Gramopadhye, A. K., 6
Graphical user interfaces (GUIs), 281
Gray, D. B., 44
Greenberg, J., 43–45, 187
Greeno, J. G., 83, 103
Greenockle, K. M., 103, 110
Gregorich, S. E., 253
Greiner, J. M., 106
Griffin, D. W., 77
Grischkowsky, N. L., 288, 311
Groen, G. J., 94–95, 105
Guadagno, N. S., 284
Gualtieri, J., 256
Guided discovery, 104
GUIDON, 227
Gulliland, S. W., 184
Gully, S. M., 107, 111–112, 264
Guru tool, 317
Guzzo, R. A., 35, 249, 253

Hackman, J. R., 249, 251–252
Hagman, J. D., 80
Halasz, F. G., 292, 296
Hall, D. T., 18, 25, 26
Hall, J. K., 250, 262
Hall, K. G., 70–71, 84
Hall, R. J., 181
Halley, E. J., 267, 273
Hancock, P. A., 238, 240–242, 244
Hand placement, effect of, 124–125
Hansen, C. D., 39, 48
Haptic interfaces, 237
Harbison-Briggs, K., 164
Harding, F. D., 181
Harris, K. R., 108
Harrison, K., 215
Harvey, R. J., 26, 259
Hatano, G., 92–93, 104
Hayes, A., 136
Hays, R. T., 225
Hedlund, J., 24
Heffner, T. S., 256
Heinbokel, T., 104
Helmreich, R. L., 251, 253, 256, 268
Hempel, W. E., 179, 182
Hermann, G., 102, 288
Hesketh, B., 104–105
Heuristic search methods, 92
Hicks, W. D., 46, 186
Higgs, A. C., 260
Higher-order knowledge, 159

High-performance tasks, 232
Hill, E., 286
Hines, T., 38
Hinrichs, J. R., 32–33, 35–36
Hofer, S. M., 17
Hogan, R. M., 80
Hollister, L. A., 38
Holyoak, K. J., 3, 71, 83, 91–92, 97, 99,
    101–102, 109–110, 290–291
Hopper, H., 208
Horn, J. L., 17
Howard, A., 22–23, 26, 28
Howard, S. K., 271
Howell, W. C., 21, 89, 225
Hua, G., 227
Hull, C. L., 202
Hults, B. M., 191
Human Factors and Ergonomics Soci-
    ety, 4–5
Human factors psychologists, 3
Human learning, perspectives on, 207–
    213
Human motivation and learning, 202–
    207
Human resource management (HRM),
    32
Human Resources Research Organiza-
    tion (HumRRO), 33
Humphreys, G. W., 136–137
Hunt, R. R., 71
HyperCard, 286
    authoring tasks, 292
    skills, 285
Hypermedia, 168
Hypermedia training (HMT), 168–169
Hyper-text training (HMT), 168–169
Hypothesis testing, 103–104

Identical elements, theory of, 97
Implementation, stage in technology,
    235
Implicit coordinating mechanisms, 252
Inagaki, K., 92–93, 104
Individual characteristics, 255
Industrial–organizational psychologists
    focus of, 3
    on transfer of training, 4
Information-based methods of team
    training, 266
Initial skill acquisition, 215

Institutional impediments to posttraining assessment, 64–65
Institutionalization, stage in technology, 235–236
Instructional objectives, 155
  generating learning outcomes from, 157–164
Instructional strategies, identification of, 162–163
Instructional systems design (ISD), 31
  barriers to implementing, 39–52
  evaluation of, 34–35
  failure to implement, 35–39
  needs assessment in, 33
  potential inflexibility of approach, 46–47
  psychological research in design and implementation of instructional program, 34
  rational approach to training, 32–55
  timing for successful implementation of, 52–54
Instruction objectives, distinction between learning outcomes and, 155
Instructor's effectiveness, evaluating, 76–78
Intelligent computer-aided instruction (ICAI), 227
Intelligent tutoring, 168, 226, 231–232
  applications of, 230–232
  concept of, 226–230
  potential of, for training, 233–236
International competition, 23
Interpersonal skills, importance of, 89
Interrante, L. D., 229
In-training assessment
  obstacles to, 65–78
  reconsidering, 78–84
Isenberg, D. J., 37
Ivancic, K., 104–105
Izawa, C., 84

Jackson, P. R., 21–22, 177
Jackson, S. E., 19, 54
Jacobs, J. W., 225
Jacoby, L. L., 63, 67, 73–75, 77–80
James, L. A., 190
James, L. R., 190, 208
Janak, E. A., 153, 179
Jasechko, J., 75
Jennings, K. R., 185

Jentsch, K. A., 260
Jesaitis, P. T., 38
Jette, R. D., 35
Job families, creation of, 26
Jobs, increasing complexity of, 21–22
  training implications, 22–23
Johns, G., 39, 41, 47–48, 53
Johnson, D. S., 231–232, 235
Johnson, T. R., 36
Johnson-Laird, P., 256
Johnston, J. H., 249, 260, 267, 271, 273
Jonassen, D. H., 166, 169, 233
Jones, A. P., 190
Jones, J., 46
Joyce, W. F., 49, 190
Judge, T. A., 32, 47
Jung, K., 101
Just in Time Inventory Systems (JIT), 21, 23

Kahnweiler, W. M., 39, 48
Kalawsky, R. S., 237
Kamhi, A. G., 290
Kamouri, A. L., 102–103, 288, 290, 293, 297
Kamouri, J., 102–103, 288, 290, 293, 297
Kanfer, R., 182, 208–209, 217–218
Kanki, B. J., 251, 268
Kaplan, R. M., 156
Karasick, B. W., 191
Karoly, P., 106
Kasserman, J. E., 289
Katzell, R. A., 35
Kavanagh, M. J., 192
Kearsley, G., 179, 285
Kelley, C. M., 63, 73–75, 77–80
Kelley, J. F., 322
Kellogg, W. A., 313
Kelly, L., 37
Kerr, R., 69, 71
Kerr, S., 36, 48
Kieras, D. E., 296–297
Kimberly, J. R., 52
Kintsch, W., 80
Kirkpatrick, D. L., 45, 154, 172, 179, 207, 235, 264
Kirrane, D. E., 37
Kirson, D. S., 321
Klausmeier, H. J., 162–163, 166
Klein, G. A., 133, 264

Klein, H. J., 194
Klein, K. J., 181
Kleiner, B. M., 68
Kleinman, D. L., 252, 256
Klimoski, R. J., 46, 186, 252
Knerr, B. W., 238–241, 243
Knowledge, 156
    abstracted, 101
    acquisition of, 233
    compilation of, 208
    declarative, 165, 208, 210
    decontextualized, 101
    linking previous with new, 99–100
    organization of, 154
    procedural, 208
Knowledge structures, 94–95, 102–105
Koh, K., 102
Komaroff, A. L., 37
Konovsky, M. A., 184, 187
Korman, A. K., 204
Kossek, E. E., 47, 52
Kozak, J. J., 238, 240–242, 244
Kozlowski, S. W. J., 24, 61–62, 107, 112,
    184, 191, 264, 274
Kraiger, K., 3, 34, 89–91, 93–94, 99,
    101, 107, 109–111, 152–154, 157–
    162, 164, 166–167, 169–170, 172–
    173, 178–179, 233, 266
Kramer, A. F., 133, 135
Krathwohl, D. R., 156
Krauss, F. S., 285
Kraut, A. I., 160
Krebs, M. J., 120
Kübler, A., 79
Kuhn, O., 235
Kumar, K., 49
Kusbit, G. W., 288, 290
Kyllonen, P. C., 264

Laabs, J. J., 38
Ladd, R. T., 183, 192
Lado, A. A., 42
Lajoie, S. P., 235
Lamon, M., 289
Lampton, D. R., 238–241, 243
Landauer, T. K., 71, 80, 283
Lane, D. L., 284
Lane, N. E., 260, 267, 272
Lang, J., 103–104
Larkin, J. H., 95

Latham, G. P., 33, 37, 39, 178, 201,
    203–205, 216
Lauber, J. K., 252
Laumann, E. O., 177
Lawler, E. E., III, 42
Leach, J. A., 39
Lean programming, 310
Learner control, research on, 106–107
Learner's performance, 72–73
    instructor's perspective of, 72–73
Learning, 152
    continuous, 1
    error-based, 104
    levels of, 209–211
    maintenance of, 216–218
    motivation to, 182–183
    nonability determinants of, 212–213
    versus performance, 66
Learning outcomes, 153–157
    and adaptive expertise, 93–96
    distinction between instruction objec-
        tives and, 155
    generating, from instructional objec-
        tives, 157–164
    scope of, 158
Lee, A., 103, 110
Lee, C. H., 204–205, 229
Lee, M. D., 133, 142, 264
Lee, T. D., 66, 68, 71
LeFevre, J., 291
Left-right assignment, 125–126
Leggett, E. L., 107
Lengnick-Hall, M. L., 185
Lesgold, A., 235
Leung, K., 184
Leventhal, G. S., 45, 184
Levin, J. R., 95
Levine, E. L., 32, 249
Levine, J. M., 259
Levinson, H., 38
Levinson, W. H., 240, 243
Lewis, C. H., 284, 288, 304, 311
Lewis, L. K., 39
Lewis, M. W., 291
Lewis, S. A., 238–239
Li, W., 184
Lightwood, N., 140–141
Lindblom, C. E., 37
Lintern, G., 243
Lippert, R. C., 177
LISP Tutor, 227

Littman, D. C., 233–234
Llobet, J. M., 259
Locke, E. A., 185, 203–205
Lockhart, R. S., 289
Loftin, R. B., 227, 229, 238
Logan, G. D., 120–121, 136
Loher, B. T., 46, 178, 187
London, M., 152, 159
Longman, D. J. A., 67, 71, 73–74
Lundeberg, M. A., 106, 108
Lundy, D. H., 103

Mack, R. L., 284, 288, 304, 311, 320
Mager, R. F., 155, 158
Magill, R. A., 68, 70–71, 84
Magjuka, R. J., 46, 178, 187
Mahler, W. A., 80
Manual Select Keyboard ITS, 232
March, J. G., 37
Marshall, K., 27
Martineau, J. W., 183, 192, 215
Martocchio, J. J., 40, 178, 183, 188–
    189, 206, 215
Marx, R. D., 34, 216
Masia, B. B., 156
Maslow, Abraham, 202
Mastery orientation, 107
Mastery-oriented training, 107–108
Mathieu, J. E., 46, 183, 187–188, 192,
    215, 233, 250, 259–260, 264
Maurer, T. J., 191
Mayer, R. E., 83, 99, 101, 266, 292, 297
Mazur, S. A., 304
Mazur-Rimetz, S. A., 315
McCallum, G. A., 252
McClelland, D. C., 202
McDaniel, M. A., 93, 103, 110, 288
McEnery, J. M., 46
McGhee, W., 213–215
McGrath, J. E., 256
McGraw, K. L., 164
McGuigan, S. M., 317
McHugh, P. P., 112
McIntyre, R. M., 251–252, 274
McKendree, J. E., 320
McKita, M., 325–326
McLaughlin, S. D., 36–37
McNelis, K., 260
Means-end analysis, 92
Medsker, G. J., 260
Meehl, P. E., 170

Mehlenbacher, B., 282
Meloth, M. S., 106
Melton, A. W., 67
Mental models, 94, 160
Mental practice for cognitive tasks, 214
Merickel, M. L., 238
Merrienboer, J. J. G. V., 290–291
Merrill, M. D., 156
Messamer, P., 235
Messick, S., 160
Metacognition, 95–96
    promoting processing in, 107
    research on teaching individuals
        skills in, 105–106
Metacognitive instruction, role of, 106
Meyer, J. W., 50–51
Middendorf, K. A., 285
Milkovich, G. T., 47
Miller, J., 128
Mindful processing, 93
Miner, N. E., 240–242
Minimalist training, sense-making activi-
    ties of computer users, 303–326
Minimalist Tutorial and Tools for
    Smalltalk, 315
Minionis, D., 256
Mintzberg, H., 37
Mirvis, P. H., 18, 25, 26
Mitchell, T. R., 183, 204–206, 208
Mitroff, I., 49
Mohammed, S., 252
MoleHill intelligent tutoring system,
    318, 324
    for Smalltalk programming, 317
Monk, J. M., 238–242
Moore, C., 287
Mooser, C., 104
Moran, A., 214
Moran, T. P., 292, 296
Moreland, R. L., 249, 259
Morgan, B. B., Jr., 252–253, 259–260
Morgan, R. L., 70–71
Morris, C. D., 81
Morris, N. M., 256
Morrison, J. E., 33
Moshell, J. M., 238–241, 243
Motivation
    and animation training, 283–286
    effect on learning, 179, 182–183
Motivational measures, 154
Motivational theory, 202–204

Motowidlo, S. J., 41
Mulder, G., 128
Mulder, L. J. M., 128
Mullen, E. J., 36
Multimedia technology in team train-
    ing, 273–274
Multi-phase analysis of performance sys-
    tem, 259
Mumaw, R. J., 6
Mumford, M. D., 180–182
Murray, H. G., 95
Murray, V. V., 32, 35, 53
Myers, G. L., 98, 134–135

Nadler, G., 177
Napier, H. A., 284
Narens, L., 95
Nason, E. R., 107
Nathan, B. R., 159–160
Naylor, J. C., 250
Needham, D. R., 289
Needs
    assessment of, in instructional sys-
        tems design, 33, 35–36
    definition of, 202
Nelson, G. D., 93, 97, 105, 109
Nelson, T. O., 95
Newell, A., 92, 120
Newman, S. E., 161, 163
Newton, L., 76–77
Nickerson, R. S., 233
Nicoletti, R., 130
Nisbett, R. E., 179, 181
Noe, R. A., 20, 38, 46, 178–179, 181–
    183, 191, 193, 233, 264
Nonability determinants of learning
    and performance, 212–213
Noncategorizable mappings, 129
Nordhaug, O., 47, 189

Objective measures, 65
Objective performance
    interpreting, 65–72
    making more diagnostic, 81–84
O'Connor, E. J., 192
O'Farrell, B., 177
Old, A. C., 284
Olsen, J. P., 37
O'Malley, C., 286
Operant conditioning, 202–203
Orasanu, J., 251–252, 254

Organizational climate, 190–193
Organizational involvement, variations
    of, in training, 27–28
Organizational transfer climate, defini-
    tion of, 191
Oser, R. L., 225, 252, 260, 262, 267–
    268, 272
Osgood, C. E., 83
Ostroff, C., 5–6, 185
Outcomes. See also Learning outcomes
    affective, 90
    cognitive, 90
    skill-based, 90
Out-sourcing, 25
Overlearning, 89, 96, 216
Owen, E., 290
Owston, R. D., 165
Oz, S., 207

Paas, F. G. W. C., 290–291
Palmer, J. E., 282
Palmiter, S., 283, 286–287, 290–291,
    294
Papstein, P. V., 103–104
Parente, F. J., 71
Park, D., 17
Park, O. C., 227–230, 232, 234–236
Pashler, H., 120, 128–131, 143
Passive learning hypothesis, 287
Patel, V. L., 94, 105
Patrick, J., 97, 109
Payload Assist Module Deployment, 232
Payload Assist Module Deployment/In-
    telligent Computer-Aided Training
    system (PD/ICAT), 231
Payne, S. J., 286
Pease, D., 103, 110
Perez, R. S., 229–230, 232, 235
Perfetto, G. A., 289
Performance
    learning versus, 66
    nonability determinants of, 212–213
    relation between self-efficacy and,
        204–205
Performance domain, 166–167
    examination of, 163–164
Performance measurement, 260
Perkind, D., 233
Perkins, D. N., 93, 101–102, 105
Perturbation, 160
Peters, L. H., 192

Peverly, S. T., 101
Pew, R. W., 240, 243
Peyerl, R., 103–104
Pfeffer, J., 47, 52–53, 188
Phye, G. D., 4
Piantanida, T., 238, 241–244
Pieper, K. F., 231, 235
Pierce, K. A., 290
Pirolli, P., 291
Pollock, J., 235
Polson, M. C., 168
Pomerantz, J, R., 132–133, 139
Positive transfer of training, 91
Posner, M., 92
Posttraining assessment, impediments to, 64–65
Power distance, 19
Powers, M. L., 35
Practice-based methods of team training, 267–268
Pressley, M., 95
Previous knowledge, linking, with new knowledge, 99–100
Prince, C., 225, 252, 258–260, 262, 267–268, 271
Pristach, E. A., 132, 139
Pritchard, R. D., 191
Problem-solving skills, 92, 103–104
    importance of, 89
Proceduralization, 160
Procedural knowledge, 208
Process norms, 217
Proctor, R. W., 6, 92, 98, 121–128, 130–131, 143
Production paradox, 284
Prumper, J., 103–104
Psotka, J., 238–239, 241–242
Psychological research, state of, related to training, 2–5
Psychomotor coordination, 212
Pufall, P. D., 233
Pure discovery, 104
Pygmalion effects, 207

Quillan, M. R., 227
Quiñones, M. A., 2, 4, 178–184, 189, 191–192

Raisinghani, D., 37
Random conditions, 69

Random practice, effect of, on learning, 69–72
Rational approach to training. See Instructional systems design (ISD)
Ravid, G., 218
Ray, G. E., 290
Reactions, 152
Reaction tasks, 119
Real tasks, embedding information in, 318–320
Recovery Boiler Tutor, 226
Redding, R. E., 33
Reder, L. M., 75, 288, 290, 293, 297
Ree, M. J., 179, 182
Reed, S. K., 291
Reeve, T. G., 121, 124, 128
Reeves, T. C., 233
Regian, J. W., 233, 235–236, 238–242
Reigeluth, C. M., 156
Reimann, P., 291
Reinforcement schedules, 96
Reiser, B. J., 233, 235, 324
Remote Maneuvering System, 229, 231–232
Rentsch, J. R., 256
Response-selection effects, 130–131
Response-selection processes, 120
Restructuring, 2
Results, 152
Richardson, J. J., 168
Rikli, R., 71
Ritter, F. E., 75
Rizzo, W. A., 250
Robertson, S. R., 288, 311
Rogers, W. A., 133, 142, 264
Role-playing, 268
Ronen, S., 23
Roscoe, S. N., 243
Rose, A. M., 296–297
Rosen, B., 183, 215, 286
Rosenbloom, P., 120
Rosow, J. M., 177, 189
Ross, L., 77, 181
Rosson, M. B., 284, 304, 309, 311, 313, 315, 317–318, 322, 323
Roth, E. M., 6
Rouiller, J. Z., 4, 33, 178, 191–192
Rouse, W. B., 256, 271
Rousseau, D. M., 25, 181
Routine expertise versus adaptive expertise, 92–93

Rowan, B., 50
Royer, J. M., 3, 94, 109, 153, 170, 179
Ruffell-Smith, H. P., 252
Rummler, G. A., 310, 325
Russell, J. S., 35
Ryder, J. M., 33
Ryman, D. H., 46, 182–183, 186

Saari, L. M., 36–37, 201
Sackett, P. R., 36
Sacuzzo, D. P., 156
Salancik, G. R., 188
Salas, E., 3, 34, 46, 90, 93–94, 101, 112, 152–154, 157–160, 164, 167, 170, 172–173, 178–179, 183, 187–189, 192, 225, 233, 249–256, 258–264, 266–269, 271–274
Salmoni, A. W., 68, 71
Salomon, G., 93, 101–102, 105
Salthouse, T. A., 17
Sanders, A. F., 127
Sandlin, P. K., 289
Sargeant, J. M., 229
Sauers, R., 235, 291
Sawyer, R. J., 108
Scaffolded design, 321
Scardamalia, M., 95, 106
Schein, E. H., 42
Schlager, M. S., 93, 103, 110, 238, 241–244, 288
Schleiffenbaum, E., 104
Schmalhofer, F., 235
Schmidt, R. A., 4, 63, 66–68, 71, 81, 91, 97, 283, 287, 290, 293, 297
Schmitt, N., 46, 179, 264
Schneider, B., 190–191
Schneider, W., 98, 103, 121, 133–135, 137, 141, 143, 264
Schneiderman, B., 284
SCHOLAR, 227
Scholkolpf, J., 95
Schooler, J. W., 79
Schooler, L. J., 68, 71
Schuler, R. S., 19, 54
Schulte-Gocking, H., 103–104
Schumaker, J. B., 106
Schwartz, B. L., 76
Schwarz, N., 79
Schweiger, D. M., 185
Schwoerer, C., 183, 215, 286
Scott, W. R., 51

*ScreenCam*, 282
Scriven, M., 234
Seabaugh, G. O., 106
Sego, D. J., 4, 179, 181, 183, 189, 191–192
Seibold, D. R., 39
Seidel, R. J., 227–230, 232, 234–236
Self-consistency theory, 204
Self-efficacy, 183–184, 204
  effect on learning, 179
  relation between performance and, 204–205
Self-efficacy interaction, 217–218
Self-fulfilling prophecy, 207
Self-instructions, 95–96
Self-management training, 216–217
Self-monitoring, training on, 106
Self-regulation, 205–207
  components of, 106
Self-regulatory capacities, 203–204
Semantic network, 227
Semb, G. B., 289
Sense-making, 307–309
Sepulveda, J. A., 229
Serfaty, D., 252, 256
Service sector
  growth of, 23, 24
Shadish, W. R., Jr., 48
Shani, A. B., 207
Shared mental models, 256–257
Sharpe, R., 48
Shea, G. P., 253
Shea, J. B., 70–71
Shebilske, W. L., 238–242
Shephard, M., 121, 124
Sheridan, J. A., 18
Sheridan, T,, 238
Shiffrin, R. M., 98, 121, 133–134, 136–137, 140–141, 143
Shockley-Zalabak, P., 46
Shrestha, L. B., 262
Shute, V. J., 233, 235–236
Silver, W. S., 205–206
Simon, H. A., 92
Singer, J. A., 317–318
Singer, R. N., 103, 110
Singley, M. K., 304, 317–318, 324
Sistrunk, F., 32
Sivier, J. E., 243
Skill-based outcomes, 90
Skill generalization, 218

and transfer, 218
Skills, 156
    initial acquisition of, 214–216
Skinner, B. F., 104, 202
Slamecka, N. J., 289
Sleeman, D., 227
Slocum, J. W., 190
Small, S. D., 271
Smith, E. M., 24, 61–62, 103, 107, 111, 181, 189
Smith, K. A., 268
Smith, K. H., 102–103, 288, 290, 293, 297
Smith, R. G., 33
Smith, S., 287
Smith-Kerker, P. A., 315
Smolensky, M. W., 5
Snow, R. E., 111, 182, 189
Snyder, B. S., 95
Social cognitive theory, 204, 207
Software training, use of animation in, 281–298
Soloway, E., 233–234
SOPHIE, 227
Sorcher, M., 160
Sorra, J., 4, 179, 183, 191–192
Spatial choice-reaction tasks, 121–122
Spatial compatibility effects, persistence of, 123–124
Spatial compatibility practice effects, 121–127
Spatial mapping, effect of, on reaction times, 124–125
Specht, L. B., 289
Spector, B. A., 32, 39, 41, 55
Spector, P., 264, 269, 271
Spieth, W. R., 66
Staley, C. C., 46
Stanhope, N., 289
Stansfield, S. A., 240–242
Stark, E. A., 225
Stealmove method, 318
Steinbach, R., 106
Steinberg, E. R., 106–107
Steinmetz, C. S., 1
Step-by-step instruction, 303
Stephenson, R., 238, 241–244
Sternberg, R. J., 95
Sternberg, S., 134
Steuer, J., 238
Stevens, A. L., 227

Stevens, C. K., 205, 209, 216–218
Stevens, M. J., 258
Stimulus characteristics and training in visual search, 131–135
Stimulus features, searching for, 135–137
Stimulus–response compatibility effects, 121
Stimulus–response compatibility tasks, practice effects in, 125
Stone, R. J., 237–238, 242, 244
Stout, R. J., 252
Strack, F., 79
Strayer, D. L., 133, 135
Student model, 229
Study habits, research on improving, 106
Subjective experience
    interpreting, 72–78
    making more diagnostic, 79–81
Subjective measures, 65
Sulsky, L. M., 214
Summative evaluation, 234
Sundstrom, E., 249
Sutcliffe, A. G., 284
Sweller, J., 290
Swezey, R. W., 264, 268
Symbolic stimuli, skill at responding to, 128–130
Synthesis, 212
Systems perspective on training, 5–6

Tannenbaum, S. I., 39, 46, 90, 151, 178, 183, 187–189, 192, 215, 233, 249–250, 253–255, 258–260, 263–264, 268
Tanner, N. S., 137–138
Target–distractor similarity, 136
Tarulli, B. A., 191
Tasks
    characteristics, 255
    embedding information in real, 318–320
    simulations and exercises, 261–262
    statements, 156
    types of, 119, 211–212
Taylor, M. S., 204
Team characteristics, 255
Team coordination training, 271–272
Team performance
    models of, 255–256

Team performance (*Cont.*)
nature of, 250–253
Team task analysis, 259–260
Team training, 249–274
demonstration-based methods of, 267
information-based methods of, 266
multimedia technology in, 273–274
practice-based methods of, 267–268
strategies in, 268–272, 274
structure of design, 257–258
theoretical bases for, 255–257
tools for, 258–265, 272–273
Technology, influence of, on team
training, 273
Teichner, W. H., 120
Telecommute, 25–26
Telepresence, 238
Tennyson, R. D., 107
Terborg, J. R., 35
Tessmer, M., 168
Tharenou, P., 46
Thayer, P. W., 12, 15, 213–215
Theoret, A., 37
Thiemann, P., 104
Thomas, J. R., 66
Thompsett, R. E., 38, 40
Thompson, J. D., 53
Thompson, S. C., 189
Thoms, P., 194
Thorndike, E. L., 97, 179
Three-dimensional audio interfaces,
237
Tibodeaux, M. S., 49
Tierney, P., 290
Total Quality Management (TQM), 21
Townsend, J. T., 134
Trabasso, T., 72
Tracey, J. B., 192
Traditional learning approach, 102
Trainee characteristics, role of, on
training effectiveness, 181–184
Trainee model, 229
Training. *See also* Team training
definition of, 1–3
evaluation of, 152–155
framing of, 188–190
importance of, 2
levels of criteria in, 152–153
methods of, 1
participation in decisions on, 185–
188

potential of virtual reality for, 241–
243
rational approach to, 32–55
short-term versus long-term consequences of, 66–72
state of psychological research related to, 2–5
systems perspective on, 5–6
Training design, 96
advances in, 97–98, 213–218
in building adaptive expertise, 99–
108
effectiveness of, 110–111
future directions for, 108–112
implications for skill acquisition,
maintenance, and generalization,
201–219
need for creativity in, 90
review of research on, 89
traditional industrial–organizational
perspective to, 89
Training effectiveness, contextual influences on training, 177–194
Training employees, variations in organizational involvement in, 27–28
Training implications
of aging workforce, 16–18
of diversity, 19–21
Training methodologies and workplace
technologies, integrating, 223–224
Training objectives, linking to evalua-
tion criteria, 151–173
Training scenario generator, 230
Training session manager, 229
Training systems, designing effective,
149–150
Training wheels function blocking,
312–313, 323
Transfer-appropriate processing, assess-
ing, 81–82
Transfer during training, tests of, 82–
84
Transfer environment, importance of,
in building adaptability, 111–112
Transfer of training, 3–4
Transfer research, 3
Treisman, A., 135–136
Trice, H. M., 49–51
Tsui, A. S., 47
Tubbs, M. E., 122
Tuning, 160

Turnage, J. J., 21, 189
Twichell, C. M., 20
Two-choice spatial compatibility task, practice effects in, 122

Umiltà, C., 130
Uncertainty avoidance, 19
User interface, 230

Vanderlinden, G., 325–326
Van der Meij, H., 324
Van der Spiegel, J., 177
Van Duren, L., 127
VanLehn, K., 229, 291
Van Rossum, J. H., 68
Van Zandt, T., 134
Variable practice, effect of, on learning, 68–69
Veenman, M. V. J., 103, 106
Verbal knowledge, 154
Vidulich, M., 133, 135
Vieira, A., 136
View matcher, 317, 318
Virtual Environment Assessment Battery, 239
Virtual reality (VR), 237
    concept of, 237
    examples of, 238–241
    potential of, for training, 241–243
Virzi, R. A., 135
Visual search
    implications for training, 142
    stimulus characteristics and training in, 131–135
    tasks in, 119
Volet, S. E., 106, 108
Vollrath, D. A., 185
Volpe, C. E., 253, 258, 262–264, 268–269, 271
Voogel, A., 99, 101
Vroom, V. H., 203

Waag, W. L., 262
Wade-Benzoni, K. A., 25
Wager, W. W., 110, 178, 233
Wagner, J. A., 185
Wall, T. D., 21–22, 177
Wallace, S. R., Jr., 20, 170
Walter, C. B., 68, 71
Wang, L., 227
Wänke, M., 79

Wankmuller, I., 103–104
Ward, M., 290
Warr, P., 16
Waterson, P., 286
Webster, J., 40, 183
Weeks, D. J., 68
Weeks, J. L., 181
Wehrenberg, S. B., 36
Weick, K. E., 37
Weiner, E. L., 268
Weiner, S. S., 51
Weissbein, D. A., 111
Welford, A. T., 120
Wendel, R., 103–104
Wenger, E., 227–229, 233, 235
WEST, 227
Wexley, K. N., 33, 201
Wheeler, M. L., 20
White, B. Y., 4
White, M. D., 252
WHY, 227
Whyte, G., 37
Wideman, H. H., 165
Wiener, E. L., 251
Wiener, Y., 39
Wierda, M., 128
Wilensky, A. S., 39, 48
Wilhelm, J. A., 253
Wilk, S. L., 183, 191, 193
Williams, T. R., 289
Willis, R. P., 216
Willits, L. S., 285
Wilson, B., 107
Wilson, M. C., 42
Wilson, T. D., 79
Winstein, C. J., 68, 71
Witmer, B. G., 240
Witt, L. A., 45, 184
Woehr, D. L., 214
Wolf, G., 190
Wood, R. E., 206, 212
Woodard, E. A., 253, 260
Woodruff, W., 225, 262, 268
Woods, S. B., 151
Woodworth, R. S., 97, 179
Woolf, B., 285
Workforce
    aging of, 16–18
    changes in, 16
    downsizing in, 24–26
    increased diversity in, 18–21

Workplace technologies, integrating with
    training methodologies, 223–226
Wroten, S. P., 152, 178

Yacci, M., 166, 169
Yancey, G. B., 37
Yaure, R. G., 71
Yearwood, A. A., 289

Yeh, Y-Y., 133, 135
Yost, P. R., 253
Yukl, G. A., 39, 90, 178, 188–189

Zaccaro, S. J., 256
Zager, R., 177, 189
Zapf, D., 103
Zimmerle, D. M., 36–37

# About the Editors

**Miguel A. Quiñones** is currently assistant professor of psychology at Rice University. He received his BS in psychology from Texas A&M University (1987) and MA (1990) and PhD (1993) in industrial and organizational psychology from Michigan State University. He has published in *Personnel Psychology*, the *Journal of Applied Psychology*, and the *Training Research Journal* and has presented numerous papers at professional conferences. Dr. Quiñones has consulted with the U.S. Air Force on various training design, evaluation, and transfer issues, as well as with private organizations on a variety of applied psychological projects. He is an active member of the Society for Industrial and Organizational Psychology, American Psychological Association, American Psychological Society, and the Academy of Management. He also serves on the editorial boards of the *Journal of Applied Psychology* and *Personnel Psychology*.

**Addie Ehrenstein** (formerly Addie Dutta) is assistant professor of psychology at Rice University and is currently working as a guest scientist at the Institut für Arbeitsphysiologie an der Universität Dortmund. She received her PhD in cognitive psychology from Purdue University in 1993. She is co-author, with Robert W. Proctor, of *Skill Acquisition and Human Performance*, and with Kathryn C. Campbell and Robert W. Proctor, of *Workbook in Human Factors for Simple and Complex Systems*.